Wissenschaftliche Untersuchungen
zum Neuen Testament · 2. Reihe

Herausgeber/Editor
Jörg Frey

Mitherausgeber / Associate Editors
Friedrich Avemarie · Judith Gundry-Volf
Martin Hengel · Otfried Hofius · Hans-Josef Klauck

195

Terence C. Mournet

Oral Tradition and Literary Dependency

Variability and Stability in the Synoptic Tradition
and Q

Mohr Siebeck

TERENCE C. MOURNET, born 1969; 1999 M.T.S. in Biblical Studies at Eastern Baptist Theological Seminary, PA; 2003 Ph.D. Theology at University of Durham, UK; Adjunct Instructor of New Testament at North American Baptist Seminary, SD.

BS
2555.52
.M68
2005

ISBN 3-16-148454-1
ISSN 0340-9570 (Wissenschaftliche Untersuchungen zum Neuen Testament 2. Reihe)

Die Deutsche Bibliothek lists this publication in the Deutsche Nationalbibliographie; detailed bibliographic data is available in the Internet at *http://dnb.ddb.de*.

The book was printed by Druckpartner Rübelmann GmbH in Hemsbach on non-aging paper and bound by Buchbinderei Schaumann in Darmstadt.

Printed in Germany.

Preface

This book is a revised version of my Ph.D. thesis, which was submitted to the University of Durham, UK in 2003. My interest in oral tradition began during the writing of my master's thesis in 1999. During that work, which focused on the "third quest" of historical Jesus research, I soon recognized the important place that oral tradition had in the discussion. This led me to inquire further about how oral communication functioned in antiquity, with particular reference to the development of the early Jesus tradition and Q. This work is an attempt to take seriously the *Sitz im Leben* in which the Jesus tradition was first proclaimed and within which it subsequently developed.

I recall with delight the many people who have played a significant role in both my academic and personal development over these last fifteen or so years. I thank the faculty of North American Baptist Seminary, and I am, to this day, grateful for the way in which they introduced me to the difficult questions which would provide the basis for subsequent academic inquiry. In particular, I thank Prof. Michael Hagan for his personal interest in my well-being during my time in South Dakota, and for modeling the holistic approach to Christian education that I hope to emulate someday. I also thank Profs. Glenn Koch and Manfred T. Brauch of Eastern Baptist Theological Seminary for supervising my master's thesis and for their valuable contribution to my theological education.

My wife and I had the privilege of studying at the University of Durham, UK from 1999 to 2003. Upon relocating to Durham in September 1999, we immediately felt at home among the supportive faculty and staff of the Department of Theology. There is truly a collegial spirit within the department, and I am thankful for being able to experience, if even for a short time, the benefits from being in such an environment. The constant support of the faculty was a source of strength that I find difficult to put into words. I thank Prof. Loren Stuckenbruck for both his personal support and his academic expertise. On more than one occasion I benefited from our interaction about oral tradition, and Krista and I will always value the friendship we share with him and his family. This type of support made the arduous task of Ph.D. study manageable.

I especially thank my Ph.D. supervisor Prof. James D. G. Dunn and his wife Meta for the great impact that they have had on both my work and my life over the last several years. On a personal level, they welcomed Krista and me into their home as if we were family and provided us with invaluable advice and support. On a professional level, the symbiotic relationship that Prof. Dunn and I have is one which I will forever cherish. His perceptive critique of my work and his ability to get at the "heart of the matter" compelled me to reevaluate my line of argumentation on more than one occasion. I am thankful for the time he has been willing to spend interacting with my work. Our sessions together were challenging, educational, and perhaps most important of all, encouraging. Never before have I met someone who is able to formulate his thoughts with such clarity and to articulate them with such lucid language. I look forward to our continued interaction in the future.

I am particularly grateful to Prof. Jörg Frey and the other editors of WUNT for accepting this manuscript for publication. This work has, no doubt, benefited greatly from Prof. Frey's helpful comments and suggestions. In addition, I am also thankful for the personal warmth and kindness which both he and Dr. Henning Ziebritzki have extended to Krista and me over the past several years.

On a personal level, there are many people without whom this work would have never seen the light of day. In particular, I thank my mother who has provided me with abundant support during what has been a long and difficult journey. Her encouragement enabled me to pursue my vocation in a discipline that reaps far less financial reward than that for which I initially trained in university. May she be blessed in return for the countless blessings she has extended to so many others.

Last, but by no means least, I must thank my wife Krista for her patience and for her willingness to "put up with me" during the challenging time of writing a thesis and this subsequent monograph. The emotional strain was perhaps the most difficult aspect of postgraduate work, and at times that burden was more than I could manage alone. Without her love, support, and encouragement, I do not think I would have had the strength to "run the race" to its completion. This book is therefore dedicated to Krista —

Two are better than one, because they have a good reward for their toil. For if they fall, one will lift up the other; but woe to one who is alone and falls and does not have another to help (Eccl 4:9–10).

Soli Deo gloria –

Terence C. Mournet
New York, January 2005

Table of Contents

List of Tables

List of Illustrations

Abbreviations

The abbreviations used in this work are from Patrick H. Alexander et al., eds., *The SBL Handbook of Style: For Ancient Near Eastern, Biblical, and Early Christian Studies* (Peabody, Mass.: Hendrickson, 1999). For sources and periodicals not listed there, I have relied upon H. G. Liddell, R. Scott, and H. S. Jones, *A Greek-English Lexicon* (9th ed.; Oxford: Oxford University Press, 1968). Additional abbreviations are listed below:

JAF   Journal of American Folklore
OrT   Oral Tradition

Chapter 1

Introduction

Texts — it is hard to imagine what Western civilization would be like without them. Books occupy a place in society unlike that of any other item. They have become fully integrated into our daily lives and we interact with them in varied contexts on a frequent basis. We keep them in our "personal libraries" and display them prominently in our living rooms for ornamental or decorative purposes. We use them when preparing food in the kitchen or to relax in bed after a difficult or stressful day. They accompany us whilst on holiday, entertain us when we are bored, and we are quite willing to divest a significant percentage of our personal resources both to obtain them and protect them from harm.

We have even created an entire industry dedicated to producing products used in conjunction with books. One glance around my work area reveals many items that have been invented for the sole purpose of supporting our modern print culture. There is the reading lamp, a large desk cluttered with many books, a bookshelf within arm's reach, and several other items that would defy description if it were not for the existence of books. In particular, my attention is directed towards the intriguing foldable steel device which, when erected on my desk, serves no purpose other than to keep a book upright, at the proper reading angle, and open to the correct page.

While it is clear that these items are inventions designed to facilitate personal interaction with a text, how often have we considered that *writing itself is an invention*? Such a question might seem odd, but the reality is that writing has not always been a tool at our disposal — at either a societal or an individual level. At some point in our pre-history, an individual came up with a new and revolutionary idea for expressing the various phonemes of human speech in a form never before utilized. He or she picked up a sharp pointed instrument and began the process of developing a coherent, repeatable system of representing — or re-presenting human speech via inscribed symbols that could be revocalized at another time in the future. Of course, this technology developed like any technology with which we are familiar today. It required refinement, adjustment, and some attempts simply failed and were left by the wayside. Even the more successful attempts did not come to fruition overnight. The alphabet itself proved to be an incredibly complicated invention that took many centuries to develop, only achieving its full potential with the development of the Greek alphabetic script in the eighth century B.C.E.[1] Eric Havelock's work on this "technology" of literacy has had fundamental implications for how we understand our current place within what Marshall McLuhan has called the "Gutenberg Galaxy."[2] Havelock suggests that "alphabetic technology is of a kind which ceases to be recognizable as a technology. It interweaves itself into the literate consciousness of those who use it so that it does not seem to them that they could ever have done without it."[3]

Among our concerns in this study is the extent to which we are products of a thorough-going literacy culture. Literacy is so interwoven into our current collective consciousness that we find it difficult to detach ourselves to the extent necessary to analyze objectively both the texts and traditions of antiquity. As products of the "hyper-literate" twenty-first century, we need to reflect on the ways in which our immersion in the technology of writing has affected how we study ancient texts and in particular, how we understand the composition of the Synoptic Gospels.

The "problem" of oral tradition is by no means a new one in New Testament research and hardly needs a detailed introduction here. The need to incorporate a working model of oral tradition into any cogent model of early Christianity is readily evidenced by the prominence given the discussion in *introductory* texts on the subject.[4] In short, the

---

[1] Havelock argues that the Greek script was the first successful attempt to develop an alphabet, and he dates its invention to approximately 700 B.C.E. (Eric Havelock, *The Literate Revolution in Greece and Its Cultural Consequences* [Princeton: Princeton University Press, 1982], 15). For Havelock, scripts such as the many Semitic variants (e.g, Hebrew, Aramaic, etc.) were not considered to be alphabets for they lacked several features, in particular, the lack of vocalization meant that there was potential ambiguity between different words. The Greek script was the first to eliminate ambiguity and have the ability to represent any possible phoneme. For more on this see, below, chs. 2, 4.

[2] See Marshall McLuhan, *The Gutenberg Galaxy: The Making of Typographic Man* (Toronto: University of Toronto Press, 1962). McLuhan's book focused on the dramatic effect that the printing press had on the Western mind by bringing about a new era in human history that subsequently affected modes of thinking and human consciousness. For a brief summary of McLuhan's work see Eric A. Havelock, *The Muse Learns to Write: Reflections on Orality and Literacy from Antiquity to the Present* (New Haven: Yale University Press, 1986), 26–28 .

[3] Havelock, *Literate Revolution*, 29.

[4] E. P. Sanders devotes an entire chapter to "Creativity and Oral Tradition," see *Studying the Synoptic Gospels* (Philadelphia: Trinity University Press, 1989), 138–145. Also, Bart D. Ehrman, *The New Testament: A Historical Introduction to the Early Christian* (New York: Oxford, 1997), 45, and Craig L. Blomberg, *Jesus and the Gospels: an Introduction and Survey* (Nashville: Broadman & Holman, 1997), 81–86. Although

recognition that oral tradition was a vital factor in the development and transmission of early Christian material is now almost universally accepted, and has become an *a priori* assumption in the field of Synoptic Gospel research.[5] This is not surprising once one examines the development of the historical-critical method and its leading proponents of the nineteenth and twentieth centuries, as we will do in chapter three.

The study of oral tradition and its role in the development of the pre-literary traditions about Jesus, along with the ongoing effect of orality on the tradition's literary descendants has been examined extensively for more than two centuries. The academic interest in the oral Jesus tradition dates back to the late eighteenth century writings of the interdisciplinary scholar J. G. Herder (1744–1803).[6] Herder was no small figure of his time and played an influential role in the shift away from the Enlightenment era to the Romantic era that was to follow. As an interdisciplinary scholar, Herder brought to bear upon the New Testament his many insights derived from various fields of research — philosophy, linguistic theory, and the newly emerging field of folklore studies. His concern was different from that of his predecessors who were engaging the New Testament from particularly rationalistic perspectives. While his contemporaries were postulating Matthean priority by way of literary dependency, Herder's radical approach was far more "romantic" than J. J. Griesbach's highly

---

these texts are intended to be *introductory* texts on the New Testament and the Synoptic Gospels, they are important indicators of the current state of New Testament research.

[5] Both Walter Ong and Robert Culley also associate the widespread acceptance of the oral origins of the Biblical text to the work of Hermann Gunkel (1862–1932); see Walter J. Ong, *Orality and Literacy: The Technologizing of the Word* (New York: Methuen, 1982), 173, and Robert C. Culley, "An Approach to the Problem of Oral Tradition," *Vetus Testamentum* 13 (1963): 113. Schmithals is among the few who suggest that the tradition was literary from the first ("Vom Ursprung der synoptischen Tradition," *ZTK* 94 [1997]: 288–316).

[6] See Johann Gottfried Herder. "Vom Erlöser der Menschen. Nach unsern ersten drei Evangelien (1796)." Pages 137–252 in Herders Sämmtliche Werke XIX (Ed. B. Suphan. Berlin: Weidmannsche Buchhandlung, 1880). Also, Herder's work on John which contains an appendix on the problem of the interrelationship among the Gospels (Johann Gottfried Herder. "Von Gottes Sohn, der Welt Heiland. Nach Johannes Evangelium. Nebst einer Regel der Zusammenstimmung unserer Evangelien aus ihrer Entstehung und Ordnung [1797]." Pages 253–424 in Herders Sämmtliche Werke XIX [Ed. B. Suphan. Berlin: Weidmannsche Buchhandlung, 1880]). Kümmel, despite his somewhat misleading summary of Herder, provides the easiest access to some of Herder's writings; see his *Introduction to the New Testament* (The New Testament Library London: SCM Press, 1966), 38, and *The New Testament: The History of the Investigation of its Problems* (London: SCM Press, 1973), 79. Jörg Frey was kind enough allow me to read his forthcoming article to be included in a volume dedicated to the works of J. G. Herder (Arbeiten zur Kirchengeschichte; Berlin: de Gruyter, 2005). His work provides a helpful summary of the significance of Herder's work on the Gospels.

"clinical" solution to the problem of Synoptic interrelationships. Herder suggested that behind the canonical Synoptic Gospels was an alleged "oral gospel" that contained the preaching of Jesus and his disciples.

As history will testify, Herder's then radical approach did not have any significant lasting impact on the study of the Synoptic Gospels. Rather, his writings have been generally neglected or relegated to footnotes or introductions to works such as this.[7] However, this is not to suggest that oral tradition itself was forgotten about or played no part in subsequent work on the formation of the Biblical tradition. Rather, Herder's emphasis on the role of *das Volk* led to the eventual coining of the term "folklore," and it is through that field that he would have a lasting impact on subsequent Biblical scholars such as Hermann Gunkel, Rudolf Bultmann, and Martin Dibelius.

Gunkel (1862–1932) is widely recognized as the father of modern form criticism. Although the roots of the form-critical method with which Gunkel is associated date back to the Enlightenment scholar Baruch Spinoza (1632–1677)[8], it is in Gunkel's work that we have the twentieth-century model of form criticism that we have come to recognize. Gunkel was born just following the death of the great folklorist Wilhelm Grimm and one year prior to the death of his brother, Jacob Grimm. By this time the seventh edition of the Grimm's *Kinder-und Hausmärchen* was available (1857), and it had a strong impact on nineteenth and twentieth-century European academia. The Grimm Brothers had compiled their folklore collection from predominantly German sources that they had edited and "smoothed out" during the process of transcribing them into their printed forms.[9] They had a diffusionist approach to folklore, in that they believed that traditions common among different people-groups were attributable to the *diffusion* of a tradition from one culture to the other. This diffusionist approach to folklore was not surprisingly coupled with the concept of a "pure" form of a tradition. According to the Grimm Brothers, traditions originated in pure forms, and their subsequent transmission to other cultures by way of diffusion resulted in the

---

[7] There were a few scholars who interacted with Herder. J. C. L. Gieseler (1818) developed Herder's insights and proposed that the original oral gospel was transmitted in Aramaic and then gave rise to two different Greek forms upon which the Synoptic Gospels were based. See Walter Schmithals, *Einleitung in die synoptischen Evangelien* (Berlin: de Gruyter, 1985) and c.p. Kümmel, *Introduction*, 38 for his summary of the "tradition hypothesis."

[8] See David Laird Dungan, *The History of the Synoptic Problem* (ABRL; New York: Doubleday, 1999), 199–260, *passim*, for more on Spinoza and the political agenda behind his pioneering method of historical criticism.

[9] The Grimm Brothers made editorial changes to their recorded versions. They "polished" the stories and in doing so made them less useful for future folklorists.

degradation of the original pure form. All of this was facilitated by the then commonly accepted "superiority" of Western civilization, and in particular, that of Europe.[10]

The influence of the "Brothers Grimm" on Gunkel was profound. By the time Gunkel wrote his *Genesis*,[11] there were a multitude of different folkloristic models on offer, each of which provided the biblical scholar with a unique and attractive glimpse into the pre-textual traditions behind the now inscribed canonical texts. In particular, the work of folklorists such as Axel Olrik[12] and Vladimir Propp[13] who themselves were building upon the work of the Brothers Grimm, served as inspiration to Gunkel and others who were interested in tracing the development of early pre-textual oral traditions into their full canonical representations.[14] Gunkel adopted the Grimm Brothers' view of the oral/folk traditions, including the principle that traditions developed as individual disconnected units that were subsequently developed and expanded upon from what was an originally "pure" form. Gunkel envisioned the process of oral transmission as follows:

In the leisure of a winter evening the family sits about the hearth; the grown people, but more especially the children, listen intently to the beautiful old stories of the dawn of the world, which they have heard so often yet never tire of hearing repeated.[15]

This view of oral tradition which was based upon the work of the Grimm Brothers would be clearly reflected in the developing method of *Formgeschichte*, a method that would remain at the center of New Testament research for the first half of the twentieth century and which we will examine in more detail in chapters two and three.

What is surprising about the above summary of the development of the form-critical view of oral tradition is that while many of the

---

[10] Isidore Okpewho in his work on African oral tradition summarizes the Grimm Brothers diffusionist view as such: "if any similarities were found between tales told in Africa and those told in Europe, the former should be seen as offshoots of the parent Indo-European culture. The Grimm Brothers made such a statement because they were working under the prejudice that culture can only spread from a superior to an inferior people, not the other way round — and Africa was of course considered racially inferior to Europe" (Isidore Okpewho, *African Oral Literature* [Indianapolis: Indiana University Press, 1992], 7).

[11] Hermann Gunkel, *Genesis* (Macon: Mercer, 1997).

[12] Axel Olrik, "Epic Laws of Folk Narrative," in *The Study of Folklore* (ed. Alan Dundes; Englewood Cliffs: Prentice-Hall, 1965).

[13] Vladimir Propp, *Morphology of the Folktale* (Austin: University of Texas Press, 1968).

[14] See Hermann Gunkel, *The Folktale in the Old Testament* (Sheffield: Almond Press, 1987) and *The Legends of Genesis* (New York: Schocken Books, 1964).

[15] Gunkel, *Genesis*, 41.

aforementioned premises supporting the theses of Gunkel, Bultmann and Dibelius have been shown to be deficient, the overall *Sitz im Leben* that is proposed by the early form critics has remained relatively unchanged. For the most part, New Testament scholarship has accepted their proposed setting for the development and transmission of the early Jesus tradition. Oral tradition remains at the center of most scholarly constructs and despite one's possible reservations about the overall agenda of form criticism, it is difficult to envisage a setting that is *radically* different than that suggested by Bultmann, Dibelius, *et al.*[16] It is highly likely that the earliest stages of the tradition *were* entirely oral — with the exception of Jesus writing in the sand in (John 8:6, 8:8)[17], there is simply no evidence that he had written any books or texts, or that he would have had the ability to do so had he desired.[18]

Despite the shared recognition that the early Jesus tradition was *oral* in its origins, the early form-critics continued to approach the tradition from a *strictly literary* perspective. In essence, they had acknowledged that oral tradition played a significant role in the formation of the Synoptic Tradition, but they had not come to grips with the *implications* of that fundamental premise. They worked from an unrealistic view of tradition transmission and gospel formation, assuming that both oral and literary tradition developed in an essentially uniform, *linear* fashion. This linearity has traditionally been expressed in two different forms. Either, like

---

[16] After more than a century of work on the Synoptic Gospels from a form-critical perspective, scholars *still* assume that oral tradition was integral to the formation and transmission of the Jesus tradition, and unfortunately, many scholars *still* misunderstand how oral tradition functions (see ch. 3, below). Of course, as is the case with any thesis, there have been those who have questioned this elementary assumption. Recently, Alan R. Millard, *Reading and Writing in the Time of Jesus* (Sheffield: Sheffield Academic Press, 2000), 197, has written about the possibility that the earliest witnesses of the Jesus tradition (i.e., those who listened to Jesus' speech) might have taken notes during the course of the performance itself. While not disputing that the Jesus tradition was essentially oral in its origins, Millard does attempt to push the date of the inscription of the Jesus tradition back far earlier than most scholars. Also, see Barry Henaut's study on oral tradition and Mark 4, in which he has a chapter entitled "Oral Tradition Taken For Granted" (*Oral Tradition and the Gospels: the Problem of Mark 4* [JSNTSup 82; Sheffield: JSOT Press, 1993], 28–74). There, Henaut questions an approach that assumes the presence of an oral "substratum" behind the text prior to searching for evidence of literary redaction within the text. See below, ch. 3 for more on Henaut's reliance upon the literary paradigm.

[17] John 8:6 — ὁ δὲ ᾽Ιησοῦς κάτω κύψας τῷ δακτύλῳ κατέγραφεν εἰς τὴν γῆν; John 8:8 — καὶ πάλιν κατακύψας ἔγραφεν εἰς τὴν γῆν.

[18] Even if one adopts Millard's thesis regarding the early inscription of the Jesus tradition, that does not mean that oral tradition can be dismissed from the discussion. See below (chs. 4, 5).

Bultmann and Dibelius envisioned, the *Tendenz* of the tradition was towards growth and expansion,[19] or, as Vincent Taylor would later argue, contraction and the "rounding-off" of a tradition was what happened over time as a natural result of the transmission process. In either case, the tradition was marked by a linearity and predictability that allowed them to chart the course of the past development of the Jesus tradition in both its pre-inscribed and inscribed forms.

All of these factors have led to the current situation, in which oral tradition is often given "lip service" but is not dealt with as a serious phenomenon in the development of the early Jesus tradition. Oral tradition has at times been expressed in "either/or" terms. That is, arguments against the role of oral tradition in the formation of the Synoptic Tradition have often been formulated against what is best described as a caricature of the "oral argument." This has led to a position where oral "advocates" such as Herder have been presented as somehow representative of all those who approach the question of Synoptic interrelationships from a non-literary perspective. By arguing against a caricature of the "oral argument" and framing the question in an either "oral or literary" matter, it seems reasonable that one would choose the literary hypothesis over its oral alternative.[20] W. C. Allen, despite his affirmation of the role of orality in Synoptic formation, wrote in 1899 that the oral theory "hopelessly breaks down" when argued from an exclusive perspective.[21] He was correct to note that the association of oral tradition with these extreme positions has made it more difficult for subsequent scholars to incorporate a more nuanced view of oral tradition in their models of Synoptic relationships.

This misunderstanding has understandably contributed to the current state of New Testament scholarship where the role of oral tradition in the

---

[19] Such a view can be seen clearly in the work of the Jesus Seminar; see Robert W. Funk and Roy W. Hoover, *The Five Gospels: the Search for the Authentic Words of Jesus. New Translation and Commentary* (New York: Macmillan, 1993). For a critique of such a view see Terence C. Mournet, "A Critique of the Presuppositions, Sources, and Methodology of Contemporary Historical Jesus Research" (M.T.S. Thesis, Eastern Baptist Theological Seminary, 1999).

[20] This was recognized as far back as 1899 by W. C. Allen who noted that the "extravagances" of the "oral tradition" theory have caused negative reaction against any solution to the Synoptic problem that incorporates oral tradition into its model; see his "Did St. Matthew and St. Luke use the Logia?," *Expository Times* 11 (1899): 425.

[21] Allen, "Logia," 425. F. G. Downing notes that this type of reasoning continues today. In addressing the work of John Kloppenborg, Downing correctly emphasizes that Kloppenborg has worked with a model of dichotomy between the oral and written media: "The dichotomy between 'oral' and 'textual' remains central — and remains unsubstantiated," F. G. Downing, "Word-Processing in the Ancient World: The Social Production and Performance of Q [evidence for Oral Composition of Gospel Tradition]," *Journal for the Study of the New Testament* 64 (1996): 41.

formation of the Synoptic Gospels often has been relegated to a subordinate position in preference for what is, at times, an unrealistic setting for the composition of the Gospels. Here we have an example of the extent to which a valuable and insightful thesis (i.e., inter-gospel literary dependency) can be pushed too hard and too far. The *textual critic* David Parker summarizes this highly "literary" approach to the Synoptic Gospels in a chapter devoted to examining the Synoptic Problem:

We examined Koester's suggestion that Matthew and Luke can be used as primary manuscript evidence for the recovery of the text of Mark, and were not convinced. We studied Streeter's solution to the problem of the Minor Agreements and, while defending his right to emend, found his solution to be unsatisfactory. We could also have studied writers who conduct their source criticism from printed editions with no reference whatever to the manuscript evidence. The basic problem in all these hypotheses is the use of a model which separates the process of creating Gospels and the process of copying them. In the study of the Synoptic Problem, the production of each Synoptic Gospel is often treated as though it were identical with the publishing of a printed book today: the author prepares the text, the printer prints it, the publisher publishes it, the booksellers sell it, and we have in our hands Matthew, Mark or Luke. All that we have to do is to buy all three, take them home, lay them out on our desk and compare them. Then we can come up with our solutions.[22]

Given our familiarity with texts and the ease with which we interact with them, it is quite understandable to assume that the ancients worked with texts as we do.[23] Parker is correct in suggesting that this approach to the Synoptic Tradition is problematic, and his assessment of the situation is perceptive. To rephrase his statement in terms applicable to the current inquiry, we suggest that many hypotheses based upon an underlying early form-critical model have, at times, worked with the Synoptic Tradition from a thoroughly post-Gutenberg perspective. Approaches that adopt

---

[22] David C. Parker, *The Living Text of the Gospels* (Cambridge: Cambridge University Press, 1997), 117–118. Also, Kim Haines-Eitzen, *Guardians of Letters: Literacy, Power, and the Transmitters of Early Christian Literature* (Oxford: Oxford University Press, 2000), 69: "the assumption that a scribe would have at hand several copies of different texts and be able to compare similar passages, or even collate manuscripts, is an assumption based in part on evidence from a later period and in part on exceptional cases such as Tatian."

[23] In critiquing Michael Goulder's view of Luke's compositional technique, Robert A. Derrenbacker, "Greco-Roman Writing Practices and Luke's Gospel," in *The Gospels According to Michael Goulder: a North American Response* (ed. Christopher A. Rollston; Harrisburg: Trinity Press International, 2002), 64, writes, "Modern writers are very familiar with desks as writing and working surfaces, usually standing thirty inches or so off the ground. The picture of this working environment is one where a writer spreads his/her work out on desks or writing tables and works in an environment of controlled chaos as letters, essays, and articles are composed on paper or computer, surrounded by stacks of books, notes, and journals. However, ancient writers and scribes, of course, did not work in this fashion."

concepts of a "fixed" text, or assume that a solution to the Synoptic Problem is a matter of fitting together the various pieces of the Synoptic "puzzle" have approached the question of Synoptic interrelationships from an *exclusively literary* perspective. This leads us to question whether such a view of Synoptic interrelationship is a historically viable option given what we now know about ancient compositional techniques and the relationship between oral communication and written texts.

It is only relatively recently that scholars have begun to inquire as to the relationship between oral communication and written texts. At one time the consensus was that ancient Israel was a highly literate society: Torah training was mandatory, young men were given a "proper" education and were taught to read and write, people had access to texts, and scholars assumed that the Hebrew Bible reflected the widespread literacy of Israel in general. Much was the same as far as most Greco-Roman scholars were concerned. Prior to 1960, classical scholars worked under the premise that the works of Homer were "high" works of literature produced by a proficient, highly educated author. All of these views have now been questioned, and it is now commonplace to read detailed treatments of the question of oral tradition in studies on ancient *literacy*.[24]

It is therefore important to re-examine a highly literary approach to questions concerning the formation of the Synoptic Tradition. Many factors must be considered when asking how a gospel author might have interacted with a source text and/or an ongoing oral tradition. It will not suffice to *assume*, as illustrated above, that the gospel authors would have necessarily preferred texts *over* oral tradition. An exploration of the complex relationship between oral communication and written texts is necessary and will provide a means by which one can further evaluate previous approaches to the Synoptic Tradition.[25]

This leads us in turn to reflect in more detail upon the implications of a highly "literary" approach to the question of Synoptic interrelationships. The most direct entry point into the discussion is by way of "Q". It is unnecessary at this stage to address in detail all of the arguments both for and against the existence of the hypothetical source. It is fair to suggest that most gospel scholars now accept Q as a working hypothesis, despite the vocal protest of a minority. While we will refrain from engaging in the rigorous debate over the various aspects of Q such as its genre, theology, etc., there are other areas of investigation that are worthy of further attention.

Much of the recent work undertaken on Q has been directed toward the reconstruction of its original form. The *International Q Project (IQP)* has

---

[24] See below, ch. 4.

[25] See below, ch. 4.

been instrumental in this area and has provided the critical tools necessary to interact with the two-source hypothesis in a way not previously possible. A fundamental premise behind the work of the *IQP* is that Q was a *text* — not simply a collection of oral tradition with which the gospel authors interacted while composing their respective Gospels. Such an assumption is in many respects a reasonable one. Of the many arguments put forth in support of such a thesis, the argument from order and the high level of verbatim agreement between Matthew and Luke traditionally have been the two strongest indicators that there was a textual *Vorlage* behind the Matthean and Lukan double tradition. Indeed, the high level of verbatim agreement between Matthew and Luke in passages where they "overlap" in content was the primary reason for positing a Q source to begin with. Subsequently, this high level of verbatim agreement has been a necessary focal point of any discussion on the existence of Q. Once again these fundamental premises have been supported by a great weight of scholarship, and it is not our desire to question either of these tenets, although a few fundamental questions remain.

First, there is widespread disagreement over the scope of Q. There are those who maintain that that the siglum "Q" should be reserved only for the non-Markan, Matthean and Lukan double tradition passages which have a high enough level of verbatim agreement to definitively indicate that they are from the same source document. Others use the term as a more loosely defined category to describe all of the non-Markan shared passages in Matthew and Luke. This list could be expanded to include several other theses regarding Q, but space does not permit us to do so here. What is significant to note is that there is a fundamental disagreement over the definition of Q and the scope, or boundaries of the source itself. It is a profound disagreement, and the issue goes far beyond a dispute over nomenclature.

The fundamental crux of the issue of verbatim agreement and the scope of Q is in regard to the observed differences in verbatim agreement in those passages assigned to the hypothetical source. Scholars have addressed this question and have asked whether it is a methodologically sound practice to attribute passages of such varying levels of verbatim agreement to the same source *text* of Q. In this case, it has been mentioned that the levels of verbatim agreement in passages attributed to Q range from approximately 8% to 100%.[26] Following such an observation, some suggest that a "Q" comprised of pericopes with such low levels of agreement no longer resembles the source which was originally posited to account for the *high levels of agreement* between the Matthean and Lukan double tradition. Within the context of our discussion of *oral tradition*, we

---

[26] See below, ch. 6.

must ask whether the significant disparity in the level of agreement in passages often attributed to Q can be, at least to a certain extent, accounted for by the presence of an oral tradition that most scholars suggest was in active circulation in and among the early Christian communities until at least the second or third century C.E.

One of our principal aims of this thesis shall be to inquire as to whether an interdisciplinary approach to the double tradition pericopes might illuminate our understanding of the formation of the early Jesus tradition and in particular the Synoptic Gospels. We shall pay particular attention to the recent advances in the area of oral tradition and folklore studies, and proceed to examine further some recent theses that have suggested that oral tradition can account for some of the so-called "Q passages" that exhibit a low level of verbatim agreement.[27]

The aforementioned questions, regarding oral tradition, literary dependency, and Q, have played an extensive role in the ongoing discussions within New Testament research. Therefore, it is only appropriate that we set out to investigate some of these important questions and we will do so by means of an interdisciplinary approach informed by recent studies on oral tradition. As we reflect upon the complex interrelationship between oral communication and written texts, we hope to reach a position where we can evaluate better previous approaches to the Synoptic Tradition. In particular, we hope to examine how a more thoroughly thought-through model of oral communication might inform the way in which we approach the Matthean and Lukan double tradition.

Before proceeding, it will be helpful to describe in brief summary how the following argument will unfold. Although the importance of oral tradition has been recognized in *principle*, we shall note, in chapter 2, that the literary paradigm has in fact dominated recent approaches to the Synoptic Gospels. This will lead us to take time, in chapter 3, to examine in greater detail some previous attempts to take serious account of oral tradition and to determine its proper role in the discussion of Christian origins. During our survey of previous scholarship, we shall observe that although progress has been made toward counteracting a strictly literary approach to the Gospel tradition, the need remains for a much more careful analysis of the relationship between orality and literacy in antiquity. This will lead us to examine further, in chapter 4, the historical setting in which

---

[27] Henry Wansbrough posed this question back in 1991: "[g]iven that so much of our material reflects substantial literary interdependence, can the presence of only a few fixed points of verbal agreement between some of these traditions count as evidence of oral transmission?" (introduction to *Jesus and the Oral Gospel Tradition*, edited by Henry Wansbrough [JSNTSup 64; Sheffield: JSOT Press, 1991], 14).

the Jesus tradition was initially performed and subsequently transmitted. We shall then develop a more thoroughly thought-through model of oral communication (chapter 5). During the development of our model of oral communication, we will highlight several characteristics of oral communication which have recently been studied by both folklorists and New Testament scholars alike. In particular, we will explore variability and stability, and examine recent scholarship that has suggested that these characteristics play a prominent role within the Synoptic Tradition itself. In the final chapter of this study (chapter 6), we will seek to accomplish two major objectives. First, we will develop a methodology which can be used to study the significance of variability and stability within the Synoptic Tradition. Second, we will utilize our methodology in an examination of a selection of double tradition pericopes, and see to what extent it can help address the questions posed above.

Chapter 2

Textual Dependency and the Synoptic Gospels

2.1 Introduction

As we will see in the discussion that follows, much of the work on the Synoptic Gospels has been negatively impacted by the *a priori* assumption that the relationship between them is one of *exclusive inter-Gospel textual dependency*. This bias towards a strictly literary model of Synoptic interrelationships has influenced greatly how we understand the complex process of Gospel development. By exposing this bias inherent in much New Testament research, we will be in a position to re-evaluate how we approach and interpret the Jesus tradition in both its pre-textual and inscribed forms.

2.2 The Problem of Language

2.2.1 *"Oral Literature"- a non sequitur*

If we are to unravel the often-unexposed bias towards inter-Gospel textual dependency as the exclusive model of Gospel interrelationships, we must begin at the foundation of the problem; that is, the difficulty in describing an oral performance with terms that derive from the visually based world of texts. When orality is described with textual terms, or is defined as a mere variant of textuality, the subsequent studies' methods and conclusions will have been unconsciously influenced towards an understanding of the tradition as the exclusive product of textual redaction and copying. At first this might seem to be a minor semantic issue[1] and therefore one which does not have a great impact on the study of oral cultures and the traditions that they transmit. However, upon further inspection it will become clear that describing orality with terms from the nomenclature of textuality only obfuscates the study of the tradition.

---

[1] Ruth Finnegan, *Oral Poetry: Its Nature, Significance, and Social Context* (Cambridge: Cambridge University Press, 1977), 16, argues that the issue is a minor one indeed.

One does not have to read very extensively in the field of folklore or New Testament studies to come across terms such as "oral text" or "oral literature." As early as 1955, William Bascom in his work on African folklore recognized the difficulty in using terms such as "unwritten literature," "popular literature," "folk literature," "primitive literature," and "oral literature."[2] He recognized correctly that the use of these terms was a "contradiction in unmistakable opposition"[3] and therefore proposed the term "verbal art" in an attempt to describe the fluid character of oral performance. "Verbal art" is a descriptive term that Bascom felt was well suited to deal with traditions that exist only in performance.[4] Much of the research on folklore and oral tradition including that of Bascom, had, at the time, taken place outside the realm of New Testament scholarship;[5] therefore it is not surprising that the implications of Bascom's work did not have a discernable impact on New Testament scholarship, as evidenced in Charles Lohr's article "Oral Techniques in the Gospel of Matthew" written six years later in 1961.[6] Needless to say, Bascom's proposal was not widely embraced within his own discipline either. Sixteen years after Bascom's "Verbal Art," Bennison Gray wrote "Repetition in Oral Literature"[7] which appeared in the same Journal (Journal of American Folklore) but did not appropriate any of Bascom's suggestions, for he continued to use the term "oral literature" when describing the processes of oral communication and aural reception.[8]

---

[2] William R. Bascom, "Verbal Art," *Journal of American Folklore* 68 (1955): 246.

[3] Bascom, "Verbal Art," 246.

[4] Bascom, "Verbal Art," 246. Bascom did not use the actual term "performance." He used "verbal art" to describe a "folktale" which cannot be captured and "exhibited in museums" but rather resembles "unwritten music and the dance" ("Verbal Art," 246). Walter Ong also uses "self-explanatory circumlocutions — 'purely oral art forms', 'verbal art forms' . . . and the like" (*Orality and Literacy*, 14). Ong does not seem to be aware of Bascom's work although he uses similar terms.

[5] Bultmann's appeal to *Kleinliteratur* was not based upon a *detailed* study of folklore itself, but was based upon what he felt were "obvious" characteristics therein. E. P. Sanders notes this problem with Bultmann's work, see E. P. Sanders, *The Tendencies of the Synoptic Tradition* (SNTSMS 9; Cambridge: Cambridge University Press, 1969), 26.

[6] Charles H. Lohr, "Oral Techniques in the Gospel of Matthew," *Catholic Biblical Quarterly* 23 (1961): 403–435. For Lohr's use of "textual" terminology see "Oral Techniques," 408–409, 411–412, 414, 425. Lohr is not to be unfairly singled out for his use of terms from the realm of literacy, but his work is illustrative for it comes from the pivotal time immediately following the publication of Lord's highly influential and revolutionary *Singer*.

[7] Bennison Gray, "Repetition in Oral Literature," *Journal of American Folklore* 84 (1971): 289–303.

[8] Gray like Bascom, highlighted the need for "terminological consistency" for he felt that the term "folk literature" is not distinct from "oral features of oral literature." For

Although Bascom's "Verbal Art" was published in 1955, it was not until the early 1980's that several major works on orality and literacy began to take seriously the difficulty in using textual terms to describe orality. It was primarily through the work of Walter Ong, Eric Havelock, and Werner Kelber that New Testament scholars began to seek what insight might be gained into the Jesus tradition via an appeal to contemporary sociological studies on orality, and in particular the difficulty in using textual terms to describe orality.[9] Ong's work in particular has been embraced by New Testament scholars; his extended illustration regarding the inappropriate use of "textual language" to describe orality is illuminating:

Thinking of oral tradition or a heritage of oral performance, genres and styles as "oral literature" is rather like thinking of horses as automobiles without wheels. You can, of course, undertake to do this. Imagine writing a treatise on horses (for people who have never seen a horse) which starts with the concept not of horse, but of "automobile," built on the readers' direct experience of automobiles. It proceeds to discourse on horses by always referring to them as "wheelless automobiles," explaining to highly automobilized readers who have never seen a horse all the points of difference in an effort to excise all idea of "automobile" out of the concept "wheelless automobile" so as to invest the term with a purely equine meaning. Instead of wheels, the wheelless automobiles have enlarged toenails called hooves; instead of headlights or perhaps rear-vision mirrors, eyes; instead of a coat of lacquer, something called hair; instead of gasoline for fuel, hay, and so on. In the end, horses are only what they are not. No matter how accurate and

Gray the oral characteristics of oral literature are also descriptive of the "folk," and therefore "folk literature" = "oral literature"; unfortunately however, his subsequent use of the term "oral literature" was not much of an improvement. He attempted to address potential ambiguity with regard to understanding that "folk literatures" are highly oral, and therefore should not be described with different terms, but rather should be incorporated under the umbrella of "oral features of oral literature." Although this line of argumentation can be helpful, it still does not address the difficulties in the use of the term itself; see Gray, "Repetition," 290. Gray continued to use the phrases such as "oral literature," "oral literary work," "oral narrative," "oral narrative prose," without recognizing the difficulty inherent with the use of such terms when dealing with oral performance. The terms occur too frequently to list them all. In addition, there were many other examples of the use/misuse of the term "oral literature" during the same time as Gray. In particular, Ruth Finnegan, *Oral Literature in Africa* (Oxford: Oxford University Press, 1970), and "How Oral is Oral Literature?," *BSOAS* 37 (1974): 52–64. Also, it is rather striking that the collection at Harvard University in honor of Milman Parry is entitled, "The Milman Parry Collection of Oral Literature."

[9] All three scholars' most influential works were published during the two year-span of 1982–1983. For the difficulty of using "textual terms," see Ong, *Orality and Literacy*, 12–13; also, Havelock's comments on the existence of a "textual bias" (*Muse*, 123). Kelber also describes the "disproportionately print-oriented hermeneutic" often used in the study of the Bible (*The Oral and the Written Gospel: The Hermeneutics of Speaking and Writing in the Synoptic Tradition, Mark, Paul, and Q* [Philadelphia: Fortress Press, 1983], xv).

thorough such apophatic description, automobile-driving readers who have never seen a horse and who hear only of "wheelless automobiles" would be sure to come away with a strange concept of a horse. The same is true of those who deal in terms of "oral literature," that is, "oral writing." You cannot without serious and disabling distortion describe a primary phenomenon by starting with a subsequent secondary phenomenon and paring away the differences. Indeed, starting backwards in this way — putting the car before the horse — you can never become aware of the real differences at all.[10]

Ong's vivid illustration brings us to the point at hand; the use of "textual" terms to describe orality reveals through their use a fundamental misunderstanding of the very concept of oral tradition, and thrusts a specifically *text-centered approach* onto any subsequent analysis of the Jesus tradition. Ong has noted that "[t]exts have clamored for attention so peremptorily that oral creations have tended to be regarded generally as variants of written productions"[11], and Havelock asks whether it is possible to describe adequately an oral culture via textual terminology.[12] It is this view of oral tradition that can lead to a text-centered approach to the Jesus tradition. For example, describing an oral performance as a "text" can conjure up images of fixity and stability often associated with a fixed manuscript tradition, when in fact the vast majority of oral performances are more flexible than fixed, and using terms such as "literature" can imply that one is describing a conscious attempt to form a well organized and logically presented narrative, when once again, this is perhaps not the best way in which to envision the oral traditioning process.[13] More directly to the point, the exclusive use of terms from the domain of texts to describe a process such as oral communication does nothing but disservice to the tradents of such oral traditions and subsequently the traditions they handed down which were eventually incorporated into a text.

---

[10] Ong, *Orality and Literacy*, 12–13.

[11] Ong, *Orality and Literacy*, 8. Foley echoes this as well: ". . . the word *literature* describes words composed in letters by a lettered person. To prefix the adjective 'oral' to this core idea may be an admirable and well-intentioned attempt to cancel out that etymology, but the result is nosensical. What 'oral literature' really boils down to is a name for 'letterless verbal art in letters' or 'letterless verbal art composed by a lettered person.' You can see how even our terminology reveals its bias. Down deep, we've been scrambling rather desperately to carve out a place for nonwritten forms within the conventional world of literature. What we haven't been doing is recognizing that our familiar world is actually only one part of an immensely larger and — for many of us — largely unexplored universe of verbal art" (Foley, *How to Read*, 27) .

[12] Havelock, *Muse*, 44.

[13] See below, ch. 3, for more on the idea that high levels of organization and structure are by-products of textuality, not orality. On a lighter note, Bascom writes that the term "oral literature," "has associations with dental hygiene on the one hand and with Freudianism on the other" ("Verbal Art," 246).

In sum, the use of literary terms to *write* about *orality* indicates a deep misunderstanding of the character of oral tradition and the way in which it is transmitted. Sometimes it is difficult to avoid using textual terminology or editorial language to describe the processes of tradition transmission or textual Gospel production. Therefore, we will adopt an approach of full-disclosure as modeled by Havelock, and attempt to note instances when linguistic terminology itself has become a possible hindrance in the discussion.[14]

2.2.2 Editorial Language and the Jesus Tradition

The use of "textual" terminology to describe orality is only the first of many difficulties encountered when studying the Synoptic Gospels from our place within the "Gutenberg Galaxy." Beyond the difficulty in choosing appropriate terms to describe oral performance, there is the common and often quite unconscious use of textual editorial *methods* to describe the work of the evangelists, which eventually culminated in the Gospel texts. This practice is not problematic in itself once the tradition history behind any particular passage has been determined with complete confidence. For example, once it has been demonstrated that any one Gospel pericope is *textually dependent* upon another parallel passage, it would then be appropriate to liken the work of an evangelist to that of an editor, using textual methods such as copying, deleting, appending, inserting, etc. What is problematic however, is that these editorial terms are often used *before* an attempt has been made to uncover the nature of the relationship between two or more parallel passages. It is not possible to engage here in a comprehensive survey of this difficulty, but we will highlight several examples of this tendency in Synoptic Gospel research.

It should come as no surprise that commonly used terms such as "redaction" and "copying" are derived from the visually oriented world of textuality. These terms, among many others, are meaningful only when one is working with physical texts from within a manuscript tradition. "Redaction" and "copying" are both methods that require the use of pre-existing physical source material (texts), apart from which the terms are devoid of any significance. Texts are physical, tangible objects that can be manipulated and treated like pieces in a puzzle — each piece can be moved around and test-fitted in an almost limitless number of permutations

---

[14] Havelock continually notes when he is using "textual" terms to describe orality: "[f]rom the first question it was possible to deduce, though the deduction was avoided, that an "oral literature," if the paradox be allowed, would be qualitatively different from a "literate" literature . . ." (*Muse*, 27); also, "[w]e tend to think of the oral storyteller as concerned with his overall 'subject' (a literate term) for which he creates a narrative 'structure' (again a literate term)" (*Muse*, 76).

until the puzzle has been completed.[15] This is in stark contrast to oral tradition, which only exists within the context of performance, and unlike the pieces of the aforementioned puzzle, cannot be arranged nor edited in the same manner as can a physical text.[16] Is it possible to "edit" an oral performance? Can an oral performer "conflate" several earlier versions of no longer extant performances to create a new, original performance? Unfortunately, the implicit answer given previously by some New Testament scholars has been "yes." Perhaps this is illustrated most vividly via the no longer acceptable view of the Gospel authors as simply "scissors and paste" editors and not authors/composers in their own right.[17] Literary imagery abounds in this now abandoned concept of Synoptic Gospel production. Although this misconception has been corrected, the inappropriate use of literary terms to describe the formation of the Synoptic Gospels continues to reveal the extent to which Gospel scholarship is either unaware of or perhaps unwilling to deal with the implications of contemporary oral theory on the study of the extant Synoptic texts.

The misuse of these editorial terms can be found across a wide spectrum of New Testament scholarship, crossing all boundaries within the discipline. Adherents to the so-called "orthodox" two-source hypothesis as well as advocates of other less widespread theories (i.e., Griesbach, Goulder, and Farrer, etc.), all engage in the inappropriate use of editorial terms under the *a priori* assumption that all parallel Synoptic traditions are literary descendants of one another. We shall now examine several examples of the extent to which a thoroughgoing literary paradigm has affected the study of the Synoptic Gospels. The order in which we address the following two categories of Synoptic solutions might initially appear awkward. However, for reasons which will become apparent as the discussion unfolds, it is more convenient for the development of the subsequent analysis that we begin with "alternative" approaches, and then move into recent discussions of the two-source hypothesis and Q.

---

[15] As we will note below, this is analogous how Farmer views the Synoptic Problem.

[16] Much emphasis has been placed on this particular aspect of oral performance, see below, ch. 4.

[17] Here, redaction criticism has been the primary agent of change in terms of how we view the authorial contribution to the writing process; e.g., Hans Conzelmann, *The Theology of St. Luke* (New York: Harper & Row, 1960), *et al.*

2.3   Alternative Source Hypotheses

The widespread use of editorial language is so prevalent in Gospel studies that it would difficult to interact with all of the secondary literature in a comprehensive manner. Therefore, in this section, we will focus on a limited, but nevertheless significant cross-section of scholarship. In what follows, it will become evident how deeply indebted New Testament scholarship is to the literary paradigm. We will interact primarily with the work of Farmer and Sanders. The choice of these two scholars is intentional, for they represent two important voices of dissent against the almost *de facto* "two-source" solution to the Synoptic Problem.[18] Farmer has argued throughout his career for a Griesbachian solution to the Synoptic Problem (i.e., Matthean priority with Luke having access to Matthew, and Mark conflating both Matthew and Luke), and Sanders is willing to accept a modified version of Goulder's hypothesis (i.e., that Matthew used Mark and Luke used them both);[19] a position currently

---

[18] Also noteworthy is Hengel's recent contribution to the debate on the Synoptic Problem (Martin Hengel, *The Four Gospels and the One Gospel of Jesus Christ* [London: SCM Press, 2000]). Hengel suggests, in contrast to Goulder/Sanders, that Matthew had used both Mark and Luke as sources for his own gospel. In contrast to the highly "literary" approaches to the problem, Hengel's approach is not based on a comprehensive literary-critical investigation of the tradition. Rather, he approaches the problem from a primarily historical perspective and suggests that only these methods "will take us further" in the debate (*Four Gospels*, 207). In his summary to ch. VII, Hengel outlines eight points which result from his investigation. They are, in brief summary: 1) Matthew used both Mark and Luke in the writing of his Gospel. 2) Matthew also used one or more Logia collections which were available to him at the time, including that mentioned by Papias. Matthew also had access to "special material which in part could also derive from oral tradition and frequently had legendary character." 3) Matthew had access to "similar, indeed possibly almost identical, traditions from the logia tradition and at the same time from Luke." 4) The question of the "minor agreements" is solved. At times Matthew is influenced by Luke's "rewording of Mark," and thus the MA's are explicable on this basis. 5) "all attempts to reconstruct a single contained logia source, along with the conjectures about the strata of its redaction, its different theologies and communities seem questionable." 6) the focus of historical investigation shifts to the two earliest gospels (i.e., Mark and Luke) and the question of their sources and subsequent composition. 7) "if the logia tradition nevertheless shows some corresponding tendencies, this is connected with the preaching of Jesus and of the earliest Palestinian primitive community." 8) "[a]nyone who wants to maintain the existence of 'Q' in the form hat has been conjectured hitherto must produce stringent proof that in principle Matthew cannot be dependent on Luke." For all these points see *Four Gospels*, 205–207.

[19] The modification that Sanders requires to Goulder's hypothesis is the addition of external sources for some of the sayings material, and other "undefined" sources (*Studying*, 117). Although Sanders does not state it specifically, presumably he could follow the Farrer Hypothesis upon which Goulder's thesis is based. See, Austin M.

advocated with force in the UK by Mark Goodacre.[20] Our goal in what follows is not to suggest that a literary solution is in anyway inadequate, but rather to elucidate the extent to which an assumption of exclusive literary dependency can affect how we approach and analyze the Synoptic Tradition.

2.3.1   William Farmer

As a preface to our discussion on Farmer, it is necessary to point out in more detail the reason for paying close attention to his work. We will examine Farmer as an example, not because he is unusual in his assumption that Synoptic variants can (and therefore should) be explained in terms of literary dependency. On the contrary, a literary solution to the Synoptic Problem has been the prevailing "orthodoxy" for more than a century. But Farmer's analysis of the problem and his own solution is so explicit and so heavily dependent on literary dependency that he provides a classic example of a solution to the Synoptic Problem and an explanation of the Synoptic variants in *de facto* exclusively literary terms.

In order to evaluate Farmer's work in relation to our current discussion regarding textual dependency, it is necessary to examine in some detail the way in which his argument for a Griesbachian solution to the Synoptic Problem develops.[21] Farmer details his approach to the Synoptic Problem through listing a sequential series of sixteen "steps" which he suggests lead to his proposed conclusion. He begins his section "A New Introduction to the Problem" (i.e., the Synoptic Problem) with what he labels as "Step I." Here his thesis is that, "The similarity between Matthew, Mark, and Luke is such as to justify the assertion that they stand in some kind of literary relationship to one another."[22] Farmer offers the following passages as evidence for his assertion regarding textual dependency: (1) the feeding of the four thousand (Matt 15:32–39//Mark

---

Farrer, "On Dispensing With Q," in *Studies in the Gospels: Essays in Memory of R. H. Lightfoot* (ed. D. E. Nineham; Oxford: Blackwell, 1955).

[20] See Mark Goodacre, "A Monopoly on Marcan Priority? Fallacies at the Heart of Q," in *SBL 2000 Seminar Papers* (SBLSP 39; Atlanta: Society of Biblical Literature, 2000), *The Case Against Q: Studies in Markan Priority and the Synoptic Problem* (Harrisburg: Trinity Press International, 2002), and *The Synoptic Problem: A Way Through the Maze* (London: Sheffield Academic Press, 2001), 122–161. Also, see Goodacre's "The Case Against Q" website for a clear and concise summary of his position (http://www.ntgateway.com/Q).

[21] Farmer argues for the "reopening" of the question of the Synoptic Problem (*The Synoptic Problem* [New York: Macmillan, 1964], vii-xi), in which he strongly critiques B. H. Streeter's work; see Farmer's appendix B for his harsh critique of Streeter (*Synoptic Problem*, 287–293).

[22] Farmer, *Synoptic Problem*, 202.

8:1–10), (2) Jesus in the Synagogue at Capernaum (Mark 1:21–28//Luke
4:31–37), (3) The Centurion's Servant (Matt 8:7–10//Luke 7:6–9), and (4)
The Healing of a Leper (Matt 8:2–4//Mark 1:40–45//Luke 5:12–16).[23]

After suggesting that the Synoptic Gospels are in some form of literary
relationship with one another, Farmer proceeds to establish the foundation
upon which he will build his hypothesis. In "Step II," he presents in a
rather "scientific-like" manner all possible combinations of ways in which
any three documents can be textually interrelated to one another.[24] To this
end, he presents eighteen possible solutions to the Synoptic Problem which
are based solely on the textual interrelationship of the three Synoptic
Gospels without an appeal to any external sources.[25] For Farmer, the way
forward in the debate is to examine these eighteen solutions and then to
choose the one that best explains the extant data.[26]

Farmer then makes a critical move in "Step III" of his argument. He
suggests that "these eighteen [possibilities] should be given first
consideration."[27] Without so indicating, Farmer has invoked what is often
labeled "Occam's Razor", a maxim which in principle accords more
credibility to the hypothesis that provides the simplest explanation for the
similarities and differences between the Synoptic Gospels.[28] He

---

[23] As will be addressed in a later chapter, one of Farmer's "proof texts" (The
Centurion's Servant) is not necessarily a clear candidate for textual dependency. See
below, chapter 6; also James D. G. Dunn, "Jesus in Oral Memory: The Initial Stages of
the Jesus Tradition," in *SBL 2000 Seminar Papers* (SBLSP 39; Atlanta: Society of
Biblical Literature, 2000), 298–301.

[24] Farmer uses the term "direct literary dependency" to describe the way in which any
three documents may be related to one another (*Synoptic Problem*, 208).

[25] Farmer, *Synoptic Problem*, 208–209. Robert H. Stein, *The Synoptic Problem: an
Introduction* (Grand Rapids: Baker Book House, 1987), 46–47, also adopts Farmer's
eighteen possible combinations. He goes on to suggest that of the eighteen possible
combinations, only three have "commended themselves over the years," see Stein,
Synoptic Problem, 46. According to Stein these are the Augustine Hypothesis
(Matt→Mark→Luke), the Griesbach Hypothesis (Matt→Luke, Mark uses both Matt and
Luke), and the Holtzmann/Streeter hypothesis (Mark→Matt; Mark→Luke). Interestingly,
Stein associates this third possibility with the "orthodox" two-source hypothesis, despite
the obvious fact that such a hypothesis requires an external source. Stein therefore uses
these possibilities differently than does Farmer. Farmer's methodology does not allow for
the inclusion of hypothetical sources; therefore, he does not see this as a viable option.

[26] Farmer goes on to later suggest that he will indeed argue for one of the eighteen:
". . . as long as one seeks to solve the Synoptic Problem without having recourse to such
conjectural sources, he is led to posit direct literary dependence between Luke and
Matthew" (*Synoptic Problem*, 221).

[27] Farmer, *Synoptic Problem*, 209.

[28] Although Farmer does not label his argument as such, "Occam's Razor" is based
upon the writings of William of Occam (alt. "Ockham," ca. 1280–1349 C.E.). The maxim
is based upon the premise — *pluralitas non est ponenda sine neccesitate* (Entities should

acknowledges that the degree of verbatim agreement *could* be accounted for by positing another external source apart from the canonical Gospels (i.e., Q),[29] but he argues that this approach "should not be utilized until after an attempt has been made to explain it [i.e., the verbatim agreements] on the simplest terms, namely on the hypothesis that one Evangelist copied the work of the other . . . The reason for this is that it is wrong to multiply hypothetical possibilities unnecessarily."[30]

Farmer then proceeds to briefly outline the reasons why he feels that of the eighteen solutions which should be considered, only six of them are "viable."[31] In summarizing the possible reasons behind the agreements between two or more Synoptic Gospels, he writes:

Thus, for example, agreement between the first and the second against the third would result from circumstances where the second *copied* something from the first which the third did not *copy* exactly or at all, either from the first or the second. And agreements between the second and the third against the first would result from circumstances where the third *copied* something from the second which was not in the first. And finally, agreements between the first and the third against the second would result from circumstances where the third *copied* something from the first which the second had *copied* less exactly or not at all [italics mine].[32]

---

not be multiplied unnecessarily). Farmer's method privileges the simplest explanation, and therefore goes beyond what is attainable via the application of "Occam's Razor," which should not be used heavy-handedly as a tool to eliminate alternative explanations from the start. See Christopher M. Tuckett, "Response to the Two Gospel Hypothesis" (ed. David L. Dungan; BETL 95; Leuven: Leuven University Press, 1990), 47–62 and his "The Existence of Q," in *The Gospel Behind the Gospels: Current Studies on Q* (ed. Ronald A. Piper; SNTSSup 75; Leiden: Brill, 1995), 11–16; also see A.D. Jacobson, "The Literary Unity of Q," *JBL* 101 (1982): 365–389 for a critique of this aspect of Farmer's argument.

[29] It is important to note that Farmer envisions the medium of these sources to be *textual* — "[t]he same degree of verbatim agreement [i.e., between the Synoptic Gospels] could be accounted for on the hypothesis that each Evangelist independently *copied* one or more common or genetically related sources [italics mine]" (Farmer, *Synoptic Problem*, 203).

[30] Farmer, *Synoptic Problem*, 203. Farmer's key difficulty lies in his use of the term "unnecessarily." Although he argues that a "Q" source text is "unnecessary" for his basic model of Synoptic Gospel interrelationships, he is at times willing to posit a source external to the canonical gospels (William Farmer, "A Fresh Approach to Q," in *Christianity, Judaism and Other Greco-Roman Cults: Studies for Morton Smith at Sixty* [ed. Jacob Neusner; Studies in Judaism in Late Antiquity; Leiden: E. J. Brill, 1975], 46–48). Goulder also argues that his hypothesis is to be preferred over others that postulate additional source documents ("Luke's Compositional Origins," *NTS* 39 [1993]). See F. G. Downing, "A Paradigm Perplex: Luke, Matthew and Mark," *New Testament Studies* 38 (1992): 34 for a critique of this aspect of Goulder's hypothesis.

[31] Farmer, *Synoptic Problem*, 209.

[32] Farmer, *Synoptic Problem*, 210.

As is evident in the above excerpt, Farmer uses the editorial term "copying" several times while describing the six possible solutions to the Synoptic Problem — "where the second writer *copied* the first, and the third had *direct access* to both the first and the second [italics mine]."[33] Note how his use of editorial language is descriptive of his understanding of the process of Gospel formation. This language used by Farmer to describe the process of Gospel composition is reflective of his foundational steps 1–4 as described above. In arguing for simplicity, and by choosing from among the six possible solutions, Farmer has framed the discussion in almost exclusively literary terms.[34] That is, he has not only built his argument upon the supposition that the three Synoptic Gospels are in "some kind of *direct* literary dependency [italics mine]" with one another (which is surely correct),[35] but he has pressed forward to assert that the Synoptics are *exclusively* related to one another in linear terms.[36] While the basic supposition regarding some sort of literary relationship between the Synoptics is accepted almost unanimously by Synoptic scholars, Farmer has moved beyond that basic supposition in an attempt to explain all of the *common content* in terms of literary redaction of a prior source *text*.[37]

It is true that the Griesbach Hypothesis could allow room for oral tradition — most obviously in the gospel of Matthew (as a whole), the special "L" material, and the material unique to Mark. However, an examination of Farmer's writings suggests that even this most basic possibility is either dismissed or conceived of in terms of literary

---

[33] Farmer, *Synoptic Problem*, 210.

[34] Sherman Johnson states that "Farmer has studied the literary phenomena almost exclusively in trying to show that Mark could have used Matthew and Luke alternately" (*The Griesbach Hypothesis and Redaction Criticism* [SBLMS Atlanta: Society of Biblical Literature, 1990], 3).

[35] Farmer, *Synoptic Problem*, 208.

[36] "linear" is used here to describe how each of the eighteen possibilities presented by Farmer have one and only one "connection" with one another. For example, A→B→C, A→C→B, B→A→C, B→C→A, C→A→B, C→B→A, etc. For Farmer's list of all eighteen solutions see *Synoptic Problem*, 208–209.

[37] This critique goes beyond Farmer, and can be applied to a greater or lesser extent to all variants of the Griesbach hypothesis. Both Griesbach and Henry Owen shared much in common. Both scholars held to Matt→Luke→Mark progression by way of literary dependency. Their work was derived from the desire to justify the differences among the Gospels; see Dungan, *History*, 314–318. Also, along similar lines, Rist writes "Those scholars who have wanted to argue the Augustinian position that Matthew (or an Aramaic Matthew) is the earliest Gospel, and that Mark depends on Matthew, have accepted the orthodox view that the problem is one of *direct literary dependence* [italics mine]" (John M. Rist, *On the Independence of Matthew and Mark* [SNTSMS 32; Cambridge: Cambridge University Press, 1978], 2).

redaction. Over ten years after writing *The Synoptic Problem*, Farmer suggests that Matthew composed his gospel, not from an earlier apostolic Gospel, but rather "out of a great variety of pre-existing materials including several important collections of logia material . . . [s]ome of these collections of sayings material may have been known to the evangelist Matthew combined in one or more large composite sources from which he has made selections."[38] He continues to suggest in the same paragraph that "[o]n the Griesbach hypothesis, there is no redactional evidence to suggest that the author of Matthew has composed any of the tradition in these collections. On the contrary they all seem to have been *edited* into his work largely unaltered from *pre-existing texts written in Greek* [italics mine]."[39] Here it is envisioned that the material that Matthew used in composing his gospel was *written tradition*, not oral tradition.

Likewise, Farmer suggests that in addition to Matthew, Luke "had access to other source material — not *another* 'source' — be it noted, but a plurality of other written Greek texts."[40] Once again, the process envisioned is the *literary redaction* of a prior source *text*, not the possible incorporation of oral tradition into the written Gospels of Matthew and Luke.

Farmer is also willing to accept the existence of additional source material in places where Luke appears to be more original or "primitive" than Matthew. For the apocalyptic material in Luke 17 and Matt 24, Farmer acknowledges the difficulty in attributing Luke's version to his redaction of Matthew. Therefore, he is willing to accept that Luke had obtained his version from another source. Instead of being open to the possible influence of oral tradition, the source envisioned by Farmer is "an apocalyptical source, that Luke has *copied* [italics mine]."[41] Once again, when Farmer is led to look beyond the Synoptic texts to explain the canonical form of a tradition, what is envisioned is the Gospel writer's appropriation of a *written* source. The possibility that the Matthean and Lukan versions are derivative from a living oral tradition is not given any serious attention.

---

[38] Farmer, "Fresh Approach," 45.

[39] Farmer, "Fresh Approach," 45.

[40] Farmer, "Fresh Approach," 45. In this context, Farmer is concerned about the special "L" material that is not paralleled in Matthew — ". . . it is necessary to postulate collections of Jesus tradition . . . This is clearly the case with Lucan parables. Many of these parables are not in Matthew. Where did the author of Luke get them? He must have gotten them from some source other than Matthew" (Farmer, "Fresh Approach," 46).

[41] Farmer, "Fresh Approach," 47. Farmer continues by acknowledging the "possibility that in this one instance I may have a source common to Luke and to Matthew" (Farmer, "Fresh Approach," 47).

In *theory*, oral tradition can play a role in Farmer's thesis regarding the formation of the Synoptic Tradition. However, in practice, oral tradition is forced into the periphery and plays no appreciable role in the formulation of Farmer's theory on Synoptic interrelationships. The model that Farmer has established predisposes one towards a view of the tradition as the exclusive product of redactional literary activity, and all of the *common material* is subsequently examined from such a view.

Our survey of Farmer's work has shown how his presuppositions and methodology not surprisingly had a significant impact upon his conclusions.[42] His appeal to "Occam's Razor" along with the formulation of the eighteen possible solutions seems rather reasonable at first, but upon further analysis proves less than convincing. He used "Occam's Razor" to eliminate *from the start* the possibility that one of the more complex, alternative theories might account best for the observable phenomena within the Synoptic Tradition. However, the aim should be to reconstruct the most reasonable hypothesis that best accounts for the evidence, not simply to conform the evidence to fit into the simplest model possible.

Unfortunately, the rigid, mechanistic approach adopted by Farmer does not account seriously for the dynamism that almost certainly was at work during the formation of the Synoptic Gospels. It is unlikely that the three Synoptics were related in a manner as straightforward as that envisaged by Farmer. On the contrary, it is highly likely, despite the fact that it is ultimately impossible to prove beyond doubt, that the Gospel writers had access not only to multiple written sources, but also to a body of "living" oral tradition that functioned in the early Jesus communities for at least the first several centuries of the Christian movement.[43] Although beginning

---

[42] A variant of L. T. Johnson's term "creeping certitude" seems fitting in this instance. Johnson uses the following to illustrate the use of the term: "if it can be demonstrated with a high degree of probability that sometime in the past I baked a pumpkin pie, it cannot be inferred from this fact that I baked other pumpkin pies. Still less can it be inferred that I cooked other things, or loved cooking, or was a professional cook and baker" (*The Real Jesus: The Misguided Quest for the Historical Jesus and the Truth of the Traditional Gospels* [San Francisco: HarperSanFrancisco, 1996], 130). Farmer engages in a similar method by linking several seemingly logical statements together to conclude as he does. He begins with 1) an appeal to the simplest solution, then 2) presents the eighteen possible solutions to the Synoptic Problem, and finally 3) demonstrates how his solution best accounts for the observable phenomena. Farmer builds logical statement upon logical statement to give the reader, by inference, the misleading sense that his thesis must be correct.

[43] In this case, the criss-cross copying of various editions of the Gospels as envisioned by M. E. Boismard, despite his thoroughly *literary* approach to the problem, might reflect more closely the complex *Sitz im Leben* of the early Christian movement than do the more "simple" theories proposed by scholars like Farmer, and other

with an approach similar to that of Farmer may give one a sense of security in thinking that the problem can be solved via a formal, "scientific-like" approach to the tradition, the problem of inter-Gospel relationships is most probably much more intricate and complicated than that envisioned by Farmer. The historical realities behind the composition of the Synoptic Gospels require that we question any overly reductionist, rigid solution to the problem of Synoptic interrelationships.

The argument of this current investigation is that it makes sense to follow through with the *a priori* highly plausible hypothesis that the earliest Christians of the first generation (and beyond) knew a "living" oral tradition (as well as literary, written sources) and that Matthew and Luke knew of and drew on at least some of these oral traditions in composing their respective gospels. The argument is *not* that the variant gospel traditions can *only* be explained on an "oral hypothesis," or that it can be demonstrated in any particular case that an oral hypothesis provides a better explanation of the Synoptic variants than a literary hypothesis. The argument is simply a "protest" against the prevailing exclusive dependence on the literary hypothesis, and to demonstrate that an explanation in terms of the Evangelists' knowledge of variant oral performances has a degree of plausibility which has been far too much ignored.

2.3.2 E. P. Sanders

Sanders has accomplished much in his career as a New Testament scholar. He almost single-handedly ushered in a new era in Pauline studies with his "new perspective" on Paul,[44] and has written several highly influential works on Jesus including *Jesus and Judaism*, *The Historical Figure of Jesus*, and *Studying the Synoptic Gospels*.[45] His influence in the field makes Sanders an appropriate object of inquiry for our present discussion.

Sanders' book, *The Tendencies of the Synoptic Tradition*, was the fruit of his doctoral dissertation in which he sought to determine if earlier form-critical assumptions regarding the tendencies of the Synoptic Tradition were justified. Specifically, what Sanders had hoped to determine through a detailed study of the Jesus tradition was the validity of the "laws of transmission" as posited by the early form critics. This was of utmost importance for Sanders, who argued that Bultmann and Dibelius did not test their hypothesis of growth and expansion to the whole of the Synoptic Tradition, but rather presupposed "laws," and then provided examples

---

advocates of exclusive inter-Gospel textual dependency. For an apt summary of Boismard's theory, see Sanders and Davies, *Studying*, 105.

[44] E. P. Sanders, *Paul and Palestinian Judaism* (Philadelphia: Fortress Press, 1977).

[45] E. P. Sanders, *Jesus and Judaism* (Philadelphia: Fortress Press, 1985); *The Historical Figure of Jesus* (London: Penguin Books, 1993); *Studying*.

from the Synoptic Gospels, rabbinic parallels, Apocryphal Gospels, etc., which supported their pre-existing view of the material. In his summary of the form-critical "laws of transmission" he concluded that "the form critics did not derive the laws from or apply the laws to the Gospels systematically, nor did they carry out a systematic investigation of changes in the post-canonical literature."[46] On several occasions, Sanders provided examples of this tendency to present external evidence only if it happened to concur with their preconceived "laws."[47] Not only did Sanders test the claims of the early form-critics such as Bultmann and Dibelius, but he also interacted with more recent studies by scholars such as Gerhardsson and Taylor, who both held a radically different view of the character and development of the tradition than did both Bultmann and Dibelius.[48]

In the main body of *Tendencies*, Sanders sets out to test the validity of posited form-critical "laws" such as, "Increasing Length as a Tendency"

---

[46] Sanders, *Tendencies*, 26.

[47] In addressing the question of whether or not names tended to be added to the tradition over time, Sanders noted that in the case of Bultmann, "[t]he laws were derived from a partial examination of the evidence, and partially used in the study of the Synoptics. Whether one wishes to derive the laws from the Synoptics and apply them elsewhere or derive them from elsewhere and apply them to the Synoptics, the same criticism holds: the Synoptic evidence has not been completely and systematically presented" (*Tendencies*, 25). Sanders noted that Bultmann "mentions four instances in which an Apocryphal Gospel has added a name to the Synoptic Tradition . . . but what of instances in the Apocryphal Gospels in which names drop out?" (*Tendencies*, 25). This critique was against not only Bultmann and Dibelius, but also Taylor, despite his fundamentally opposite view regarding the "tendency" of the tradition, see Sanders, *Tendencies*, 25. Also, see *Tendencies*, 19–20 for Sanders' critique of Bultmann's use of rabbinic sources.

[48] Although Sanders did deal with the work of Gerhardsson, it was done in more of a summary fashion as compared to the detailed manner in which he critiqued the work of Bultmann and Dibelius. Sanders correctly noted that Gerhardsson did not deal directly with the Synoptic Tradition, but rather was concerned about the technical process behind early Christian tradition-transmission. Gerhardsson described his own work as follows: "It seems therefore to be highly necessary to determine what was the technical procedure followed when the early Church *transmitted,* both Gospel material and other material. This investigation will be devoted to an attempt in this direction" (*Memory and Manuscript: Oral Tradition and Written Transmission in Rabbinic Judaism and Early Christianity* [Uppsala: C. W. K. Gleerup, 1961], 14–15). As for Taylor, Sanders notes that in contrast to Bultmann and Dibelius, Taylor maintains a "consistent position" for his thesis regarding the tendency for details to *drop out* over time, and his affirmation of Markan priority. Taylor is consistent, for Mark is the most detailed Gospel (when describing events of the "triple-tradition") and therefore the first. Sanders also labels Bussmann as "consistent," although for his opposite view of details=late, therefore, Mark is the last Gospel. On this topic of "consistency," see Sanders, *Tendencies*, 146–147.

(ch. 2), "Detail and the Tendency of the Tradition" (ch. 3), and others.[49] Following his detailed study of the Synoptic Tradition, Sanders concludes that there are very few, if any, significant tendencies therein.[50] From this perspective, Sanders' *Tendencies* is to be commended, for it provided a well-needed corrective to the often assumed but not supported claims that expansion, growth, elaboration, and linear development, were descriptive of what occurred to the Jesus tradition over time, and specifically to the Synoptic Tradition itself. Due to the influence that *Tendencies* has had on New Testament scholarship,[51] it is necessary to elucidate the extent to which Sanders' methods and subsequent conclusions are negatively impacted due to his immersion in the world of texts and textual methods.

Sanders' further, and more significant critique of Bultmann is with regard to the methodological assumptions he makes concerning textual dependency. According to Sanders, Bultmann gives examples of addition and/or change that occurs within the rabbinic sources, and then uses this to illustrate that a similar tendency occurs within the Synoptic Tradition. Sanders correctly makes the point that:

(1) It *is* only an example . . . [Bultmann] does not undertake to show, nor does he refer to anyone else as having shown, that expansion is a general characteristic of Rabbinic passages . . . there may be many more cases of abbreviation than of expansion. Thus it is clear that the law of expansion has not been proved in Rabbinic literature and then applied to the Synoptic material. It seems more likely that the reverse process has taken place. (2) *Bultmann does not find it necessary to show that the passage from the Mekilta*

---

[49] Some other "tendencies" tested by Sanders include, "Diminishing Semitism and the Tradition" (*Tendencies*, 190–255), "Direct Discourse and Conflation (*Tendencies*, 256–271).

[50] Sanders concludes that, "[t]here are no hard and fast laws of the development of the Synoptic Tradition. On all counts the tradition developed in opposite directions. It became both longer and shorter, both more and less detailed, and both more and less Semitic. Even the tendency to use direct discourse for indirect, which was uniform in the post-canonical material which we studied, was not uniform in the Synoptics themselves. For this reason, *dogmatic statements that a certain characteristic proves a certain passage to be earlier than another are never justified*" (*Tendencies*, 272). Also, see Stein who uses Sanders' work as evidence that "[o]ften they [laws] are not even tendencies! How can we make a tendency out of the fact that sometimes the tradition tends to become shorter and sometimes longer, that sometimes names tend to be added and sometimes dropped?" (*Synoptic Problem*, 182).

[51] Many scholars have presented Sanders' conclusions as definitive evidence against a singular "tendency." For but a few examples, see Stein, *Synoptic Problem*, 49, 182, John P. Meier, *A Marginal Jew* [New York: Doubleday, 1991], 182, and W. D. Davies and Dale C. Allison, *A Critical and Exegetical Commentary on the Gospel According to St. Matthew* [International Critical Commentary Edinburgh: T & T Clark, 1988], 1:104. Also, see Christopher M. Tuckett, *The Revival of the Griesbach Hypothesis: An Analysis and Appraisal* [Cambridge: Cambridge University Press, 1993], 10 for his description of how Farmer's argument changed as a result of Sanders' *Tendencies*.

is a lineal descendent of the passage from the Mishnah. For all we are told, the two passages could have altered a common ancestor in different ways and actually provide examples of diverse tendencies. (3) Bultmann . . . really claims to show by a few references to Rabbinic literature on the point of expansion is 'that Rabbinic stories did occasionally undergo supplementary expansion' [italics mine].[52]

Sanders' point (2) (above italics) is of greatest interest in the context of our current discussion. Here it is apparent that Sanders is aware of the danger in assuming that the rabbinic material from the Mekilta is a "lineal descendent" of that in the Mishnah. As Sanders notes correctly, if the two passages are *not* lineal descendants of one another, then we are *not* able to legitimately speak of any sort of "tendency" within the rabbinic material under consideration.[53] This is a valid critique of Bultmann's work; but as we will observe, it is also a valid critique of Sanders' own work.

The warning that Sanders raises regarding Bultmann's use of rabbinic sources also extends to the Synoptic Gospel tradition. When dealing with any parallel Synoptic passages, before we try to discern "tendencies," or other possible redactional activity by one or more authors, we must ask the same question as did Sanders regarding "lineal descendents." If we accept the possibility that the similarities and differences between parallel Gospel traditions could be accounted for by non-editorial processes, then we must reflect on the implications of such a view. Such a view requires an openness to other external influences on the final form of the gospel texts, one of which is the ongoing influence of oral tradition.

Sanders himself recognizes that the possible influence of oral tradition on the early non-canonical Jesus tradition requires careful attention. If the ongoing influence of oral tradition can account for some of the parallels between the Synoptic Gospels and other extra-canonical traditions, then we are faced with the same situation as was Bultmann with regard to the rabbinic source material; that is, non-textually dependent parallel traditions *cannot* form the basis for determining "laws of transmission" nor can they be used to demonstrate, or question, tendencies within the Synoptic Tradition.

It is at this point that Sanders appeals to the work of Helmut Koester. Koester's work represents a potentially fundamental shift in how we understand the process by which the extra-canonical Gospels and the writings of the Apostolic Fathers were created.[54] According to Koester, the

---

[52] Sanders, *Tendencies*, 19–20. Sanders cites Rudolf K. Bultmann, *The History of the Synoptic Tradition* (New York: Harper and Row, 1963), 63.

[53] The aforementioned hypothetical "common ancestor" to the Mishnah and Mekilta (according to Sanders) could be either a text or perhaps oral traditional material, although it is not important at this time to determine which of the two possibilities is more likely.

[54] Helmut Koester, *Synoptische Überlieferung bei den apostolischen Vätern* (Texte und Untersuchungen zur Geschichte der altchristlichen Literatur 65; Berlin: Akademie-

Jesus tradition as evidenced in the Apostolic Fathers is not derivative from the Synoptic Gospels, but rather is testimony to various "streams" of oral tradition that were circulating in parallel alongside the canonical Gospel tradition. This acknowledgement of Koester's work is welcomed, for it takes seriously the cultural setting in which the Jesus tradition was inscribed in textual form.[55] Sanders appropriates Koester's thesis and uses it to develop criteria by which he will choose material worthy for inclusion in his study. His following summary of Koester's work is illuminating:

Koester's view is that there existed a free oral tradition which, until about the year 150, could be drawn upon. This oral tradition paralleled the Synoptics, and was, in part at least, the very *Vorstufe* of the Synoptics themselves. Thus, most of the Apostolic Fathers actually stand on the same level as the Synoptic Gospels with regard to the early Christian tradition. Both the early Fathers and the canonical Gospels drew from the same resources. The only clear exceptions are II Clement and Did. 1.3–2.1, which Koester

---

Verlag, 1957), 3. Sanders cites two other scholars who hold a view similar to that of Koester, see Jean-Paul Audet, *La Didachè: Instructions des apôtres* (Paris: Gabalda, 1958), 166–186. Sanders incorrectly attributes the same view to Richard Glover, "The Didache's Quotations and the Synoptic Gospels," *New Testament Studies* 5 (1958): 12–29. Glover does *not* argue for oral tradition behind the Didache, rather he attributes the similarities between the Didache and Matthew to another source *text* behind both documents — "the Didache does not bear witness to our Gospels, but quotes directly from sources used by Luke and Matthew . . ." ("Didache's Quotations," 13). Regarding the possibility of oral tradition to account for some of the agreements shared by the Didache and Luke, he states that "oral tradition can hardly explain all the Didachist's, he suggests that oral tradition is not "in any case, a very promising theory." (Glover, "Didache's Quotations," 22). In a footnote to the above quotation, Glover reveals his particular view of oral tradition: "[i]f Jewish scholars made a fetish of burdening their memories in preference to using paper and ink, Gentiles did not" (Glover, "Didache's Quotations," 22). The incorrect assumption is that the Gentiles transmitted tradition in a distinctely different manner than did the Jews. See below, ch. 4 for more on how oral tradition was an integral part of tradition transmission for all people in antiquity. Glover later concludes that the Didache is, for the most part, based upon "Q" ("Didache's Quotations," 25–29).

[55] It is necessary to recognize that Koester's thesis regarding oral tradition is intertwined with his view that orthodoxy and heresy remain unseparated from one another until the time of Irenaeus. If the Apostolic Fathers cited fixed, authoritative texts, then this would potentially set the stage for an earlier distinction between orthodoxy and heresy. Other scholars have argued for a stronger use of the Gospels prior to Irenaeus; see Köhler's work on the early reception of Matthew's gospel (Wolf-Dietrich Köhler, *Die Rezeption des Matthäusevangeliums in der Zeit vor Irenäus* [WUNT II 24; Tübingen: Mohr, 1987]). Hengel also emphasizes the early use of the Gospels in Christian worship, and suggests that Justin's *Apology* is a "witness to this essentially earlier respect for the collection of the four Gospels in the church in Rome and probably also in Asia Minor," and that Justin's writings indicate that the Gospels were already read aloud in worship for a significant period of time, see Hengel, *Four Gospels*, 19–20.

regards as having used our Synoptic Gospels, or at least as having used sources which were themselves dependent upon our Gospels.[56]

To rephrase Koester's thesis in terms of our discussion, the Apostolic Fathers are not textually dependent upon the Synoptic Gospel tradition nor do they appropriate the Synoptic Tradition by means of conscious editorial methods. Rather, the Apostolic Fathers are witnesses to a living oral tradition that thrived in the early Jesus communities for at least the first several centuries C.E. It is quite clear that Sanders considers this possible influence of oral tradition upon a manuscript tradition to be a very important factor to consider when choosing source material for his study. Therefore, due to this possible influence of oral tradition, Sanders *will not* include in his study *any* writings of the Apostolic Fathers except for the aforementioned II Clement and Did. 1:3–2:1, which according to Koester, are clearly textually dependent upon the Synoptic Gospels. Sanders recognizes that for any source to be useful in his study, it *must be textually dependent* upon another source that is demonstrably derivative of the same "stream" of tradition. Not only does he apply this criterion to the Apostolic Fathers, but he also applies this criterion to the extra-canonical, or Apocryphal gospel tradition.

Through his use of the same "criterion of dependency," Sanders feels that the uncertainty regarding the possible dependence of the Gospel of Thomas upon the Synoptic Gospels "renders the Gospel of Thomas unusable for our purposes."[57] Sanders bases his conclusion on the work of several scholars, both advocates for the independence of Thomas as well as those who argue for Thomas' dependence on the Synoptics.[58] This reinforces once again the fact that, for Sanders, the issue of direct literary dependency is of utmost importance for his study.

It is now necessary to evaluate Sanders' *Tendencies* by means of his own "criterion of dependency." Although Sanders faulted Bultmann for assuming that the Mekilta is a "lineal descendent" of the Mishnah, he

---

[56] Sanders, *Tendencies*, 37.

[57] Sanders, *Tendencies*, 43.

[58] Sanders interacts with several scholars' work on Thomas. In particular, those who argue for some sort of independence between Thomas and the Synoptics — 1) an independent Aramaic tradition behind Thomas (Quispel, Montefiore, Guillaumont), 2) an independent and perhaps quite early tradition (Jeremias, Hunzinger); and also those who argue for some form of dependence of Thomas on the Synoptic Tradition (Gärtner, Schrage). For Sanders' summary of the Thomas/Synoptics debate (as of 1969), see Sanders, *Tendencies*, 40–45. No consensus has been reached since 1969. For a recent argument for independence see, John Dominic Crossan, *Four Other Gospels: Shadows on the Contours of Canon* (Minneapolis: Winston, 1985), 35, and Helmut Koester, *Ancient Christian Gospels* (Philadelphia: Trinity University Press, 1990), 85–86; for dependence upon the Synoptic Gospels see, Meier, *Marginal Jew*, 1:131–139.

makes the same methodological error when dealing with the Synoptic Tradition. When studying the Synoptic Gospel tradition, Sanders operates under the assumption that *every* Synoptic parallel is the product of *textual* redaction of another parallel Synoptic text. Throughout *Tendencies* Sanders engages in a comparison of the Synoptic Tradition without recognizing that his very method renders his conclusions suspect.

The assumption of exclusive textual dependency among the Synoptics can be readily observed, though not explicitly stated throughout *Tendencies*. Sanders prefaces his analysis of the "form-critical laws" by stating that,

. . . for the sake of convenience, all the lists which compare the Gospels with each other are composed as if the shorter text were always earlier. Thus instances in which Matthew is longer than Mark are listed as Matthean "additions" to Mark, while instances in which Mark is longer than Matthew are listed as Marcan "additions" to Matthew.[59]

Perhaps such a method seems satisfactory upon an initial reading, but following closer inspection it is a highly problematic basis on which to study the tradition. Sanders presents his method of comparison without much reflection, arguing that it "enables us quickly to grasp how often each Gospel is longer than each of the others."[60] This proposed method, which Sanders will indeed follow, reveals yet another instance in which he assumes that the relationship between the Synoptic Gospels is one of exclusive textual dependency.

What Sanders employs for the purpose of "convenience" has consequences that extend far beyond his initial justification for the use of such a method. His listing of the shorter text as "always earlier" is coupled with an assumption that the later (longer) Gospel is textually derivative from the shorter *text* of its parallel. This is confirmed via his subsequent analysis, whereby the Synoptic parallels are studied from an exclusively literary perspective. As an example, in his chapter on "Detail and the Tendency of the Tradition," Sanders compares the Synoptic Gospels with one another to determine if there is a tendency for details to be added or removed during the process of Gospel development. To this end, he subjects the Synoptic Tradition to various examinations, each designed to test his hypothesis. These tests include, among others, "Subjects in one Gospel but not in another," and "Direct objects in one Gospel but not in another."[61] Following each test, Sanders presents a summary of his

---

[59] Sanders, *Tendencies*, 52–53.

[60] Sanders, *Tendencies*, 53.

[61] Although Sanders' list of eighteen tests is too extensive to cite here in its entirety, some other examples include "The use of a noun with a proper name in one Gospel but not in another," and "Prepositional phrases in one Gospel but not in another," see Sanders, *Tendencies*, 152–183.

findings. In the case of the test for "Subjects in one Gospel but not in
another," his results are as follows: [62]

Mt	more explicit than Mk	49 times	Mt:Mk::49:23
Mt	more explicit than Lk	38 times	Mt:Lk::38:26
Mk	more explicit than Mt	23 times	Mk:Lk::21:24
Mk	more explicit than Lk	21 times	
Lk	more explicit than Mt	26 times	
Lk	more explicit than Mk	24 times	

Sanders' summary chart presents all six combinations of ways in which
any two Gospels can be related to one another. The cryptic code on the far
right of the above chart presents in summary fashion the reciprocal
relationship between two Gospels. For example, "Mt:Mk::49:23" means
that Matthew is more explicit than Mark 49 times, and conversely, Mark is
more explicit than Matthew 23 times. Sanders compiles a similar table for
each of his eighteen tests in the above category.

It is now possible to grasp more fully the extent of Sanders
assumptions. In each of the above six relationships listed in the table
above, one must assume that for each comparison, Matthew to Mark,
Matthew to Luke, etc., that the relationship between the texts is one of
direct literary dependency. As mentioned above, if each one of the parallel
passages is indeed the product of direct literary dependency then his
conclusions can be accepted as valid, but what is the case if some of the
parallel passages are not actually the product of textual redaction of a
common source text? Following Sanders' own observation, it is not
possible to derive "tendencies" from any passages that are not textually
derivative of one another.[63]

---

[62] Sanders, *Tendencies*, 155.

[63] Sanders makes another interesting statement in the context of our discussion on
textual dependency. In his "Addendum: Creation of new material," Sanders writes, "In
all the Apocryphal Gospels, most of the material does not appear in the canonical
Gospels, so the very existence of the former is proof of the tendency to create new
material" (*Tendencies*, 61). This is another logical fallacy given his own statements about
"lineal descendents." To make the assertion that he does, one must make the *a priori*
assumption that the canonical Gospel traditions are in fact representative of an "older" or
more "pure" a form of tradition than that contained in the Apocryphal Gospels, and that
the Apocryphal Gospels are textually dependent upon the Synoptic Tradition. Given
Sanders' reliance upon the thesis of Koester, it is not possible to argue as he does. In
fact, one could just as easily argue for the opposite observation of Sanders — that the
canonical Gospels have shortened, or abbreviated the originally longer tradition. If there
was more than one "stream" of tradition then Sanders cannot make such a statement.

It is important to recognize on the one hand that the majority of the parallel pericopes within the Synoptic Tradition are the product of direct editorial interaction with another source text. However, on the other hand, it is also highly likely that there are pericopes within the Synoptic Tradition which appear at first to be the product of textual redaction, but upon further inspection could reflect the existence of a separate, non textually-dependent Jesus tradition that was in circulation among the early Jesus communities. This observation in turn casts doubt upon the entire enterprise in which Sanders is engaged. Therefore, Sanders' methodology and conclusions must be subjected to further analysis before his results can be accepted as valid indicators of any tendencies, or lack thereof, within the Synoptic Tradition.

Despite the above critique of Sanders' *Tendencies,* his work continues to lend valuable insight into the differences between the Synoptic Gospels and as such is to be commended. His comparison between parallel pericopes can be used as a basis for establishing general descriptions about the Synoptic Gospels. His evaluation of the evidence regarding detail and the tendency of the tradition is helpful indeed, for he lists eighteen summary statements that are based upon his comparative study of the Gospels.[64] In the list of statements that correspond to his tests, Sanders concludes, for example, that Matthew is the most explicit in terms of making the subject of a sentence or clause explicit, and that Luke is slightly more explicit than Mark.[65]

Conclusions like these are helpful descriptions of the *differences* between the three Gospels, but are *not indicative of tendencies* within the Synoptic Tradition. This is a vital distinction that must be maintained and upheld given our above observations. For example, it is possible to determine which Gospel contains the greatest occurrence of parataxis — Mark employs the device more than both Matthew and Luke. Therefore, one can rightly conclude that Mark prefers parataxis more than either Matthew or Luke.[66] What we have done in this case is analyze all three Gospels as *separate, static entities* without assuming any particular interrelationship among them. This type of statistical analysis regarding parataxis could be done between any two texts, even between those that deal with divergent subject matter. However, such a study, while helpful, does not lend any insight into the *tendency* of an author to either employ parataxis, or conversely, to remove parataxis and replace it with more varied literary devices. One can only posit such conclusions regarding

---

[64] See Sanders, *Tendencies,* 183–187.

[65] Sanders, *Tendencies,* 183.

[66] Cf. Joanna Dewey, "Oral Methods of Structuring Narrative in Mark," *Interpretation* 43 (1989): 37.

possible tendencies, or lack thereof, if one of the texts in question is demonstrably a literary descendent of the other.

Following Sanders' eighteen summary statements regarding "detail and the tendency of the tradition," he attempts to formulate "tendencies" of the tradition based upon his earlier observations.[67] It is at this point where the discussion shifts towards the issue of Gospel priority. Sanders no longer simply describes the characteristics of each Gospel, but rather he uses his previous analysis to evaluate in turn the merits of Markan, Matthean, and Lukan priority. He is either not aware of, or does not mention the difficulties involved in making such a transition. His summary of the evidence is divided into three categories, each of which is support for the priority of one Gospel over another. For Markan priority, Sanders concludes that his test of "Subjects in one Gospel but not in another" and "Genitive nouns in one Gospel but not in another" provides evidence that Mark is indeed the first Gospel.[68] Here we can see Sanders' method breaking down. How is it that Sanders can argue that the addition of subjects and genitive nouns is evidence for Markan priority? He can do so only if he engages in circular reasoning and assumes that the addition of details is an indicator of later composition based upon the redaction of a prior text. Even if one agrees with Sanders' implicit argument that the Synoptic Gospels are exclusively inter-textually dependent, his evidence cannot be used to demonstrate an issue such as priority, but rather can be used only to show in what ways the Gospels differ from one another.

The move away from simple static descriptions of the Gospels towards conclusions regarding "tendencies" is indicative of Sanders' lack of sensitivity about the oral traditioning process. His misunderstanding of the characteristics of oral performance essentially allows him to ignore the possible influence of oral tradition upon the Synoptic Gospels.

In his opening chapter, Sanders addresses the question of oral tradition and within that context reveals his concept of orality. The concept of oral tradition adopted by Sanders is essentially Bultmannian, and therefore Sanders' work is subject to many of the same shortcomings as is Bultmann's. Both scholars engage in a study of the Synoptic Tradition as exclusively *text*, without regard for the potential difference between oral and literary methods of composition and transmission.[69] This relationship is not implicit; rather, it is stated explicitly by Sanders himself. Regarding the need to discern between the possible difference in tendencies between oral and written tradition, Sanders writes:

---

[67] Sanders, *Tendencies*, 187–189.

[68] Sanders, *Tendencies*, 187.

[69] See ch. 3 for Bultmann's view of oral tradition.

Here the question of oral tradition need not be decided. We investigate written tradition because that is all that is available to us. Many scholars now think that there would have been little difference between written and oral tradition during the first century, however, so that *the tendencies of the one are presumably the tendencies of the other.* We must operate on this presumption, although it cannot be tested. Even if it should be the case that oral tradition was not so rigid as some seem to think, *that does not of itself mean that oral tradition was a great deal different from written tradition,* since written tradition itself was by no means inflexible, as we shall see [italics mine].[70]

In a footnote to the first sentence of the above quote ("Here the question . . . need not be decided"), Sanders approvingly cites Bultmann and his statement regarding the character of oral tradition — "[t]his formulation stands in the closest agreement with that of Bultmann."[71] Sanders also approvingly cites Bultmann's statement regarding the "matter of indifference whether the tradition were oral or written."[72] It is possible to summarize Sanders' argument as follows: 1) Because many scholars think that there is little difference between oral and written tradition, 2) We can investigate the written tradition (all that is available to us) without regard to the question of whether or not the tradition is oral. 3) *Therefore,* the tendencies of the one are presumably the tendencies of the other. 4) This method is supported by the fact that written tradition was itself flexible (as he will conclude following his testing of the Synoptic Tradition).

As we will detail in the next chapter, many of these assumptions have been derived from an early form-critical view of oral tradition which had, and indeed continues to have, a profound impact on how we understand the earliest stages of the Jesus tradition. These assumptions contribute toward a view of Synoptic interrelationships that does not give adequate weight to the dynamism of oral tradition and undercuts the significance of the oral milieu in which the Synoptics were written.

2.4 Two-Source/Four-Document Hypothesis

The problems highlighted above are not only encountered in the work of the proponents of the so-called "alternative" approaches to the Synoptic Problem. Many of the same assumptions and methodological shortcomings underpin the more mainstream work of advocates of the dominant two-source hypothesis. These deep-rooted assumptions commonly manifest themselves through some of the recent work on "Q." This is not surprising

---

[70] Sanders, *Tendencies*, 8.

[71] Sanders, *Tendencies*, 8, n.2.

[72] Sanders, *Tendencies*, 8. Sanders cites, Bultmann, *Synoptic Tradition*, 7.

given the extent to which a text-centered methodology has dominated the study of the Synoptic Gospels. If the use of textual terminology and the assumption of direct literary relationships among the Synoptic Gospels forms the basis for the majority of work on the Jesus tradition, then it would be a small step indeed to extend such a view beyond the immediate context of the Synoptic Gospels to the study of their sources as well. In this case, the study of the sources behind the Synoptic Gospels is done from within an essentially textual paradigm, enabling one to appeal to external, textual sources to account for the similarities and differences between the Synoptics. One can envision how such an approach can naturally lead to an assumption that behind every agreement between the Synoptic Gospels is a *written* text.

B. H. Streeter's "four-document hypothesis" continues to extend its influence upon Synoptic Gospel research. Despite his use of the term *document* in describing his hypothetical sources of the Gospels, his almost one hundred year old theory in some instances represents a more historically sensitive and nuanced view of the origins of the Synoptic Gospels than is often argued today.[73] His awareness of oral tradition and its possible impact upon the formation of the Synoptic Tradition should be reviewed, and in some instances reaffirmed. During the presentation of his hypothesis, Streeter was quick to point out that the term "two-source" hypothesis is potentially misleading for it can lead one to the "unconscious assumption" that the Evangelists used only Q and Mark, or as Streeter labeled it the "Big Two."[74] In his analysis of what he calls the three "unconscious assumptions,"[75] Streeter argues that, "One reason why these erroneous assumptions have held sway so long is that the Synoptic Problem has been studied merely as a problem of literary criticism apart from a consideration of the historical conditions under which the Gospels were produced."[76] Streeter was correct to state that the literary paradigm has had a profound affect upon the study of the Synoptic Problem.

---

[73] Although Streeter's *Four Gospels* is the fuller exposition of his view of Synoptic interrelationships, see his earlier "On the Original Order of Q," in *Oxford Studies in the Synoptic Problem* (ed. W. Sanday; Oxford: Clarendon Press, 1911) and "The Literary Evolution of the Gospels," in *Studies in the Synoptic Problem* (ed. W. Sanday; Oxford: Clarendon Press, 1911).

[74] B. H. Streeter, *The Four Gospels: A Study of Origins* (London: Macmillan, 1924), 227.

[75] According to Streeter, the three false assumptions are: 1) That the Evangelists used no other sources besides Mark and Q, 2) That the "simplest hypothesis" is likely to be the correct solution, and 3) that all similarities between Gospels are to be accounted for by a common source text. See Streeter, *Four Gospels*, 227–230.

[76] Streeter, *Four Gospels*, 229–230.

With regard to the hypothetical source behind the double tradition, Streeter argued against any definitive reconstruction of Q, recognizing that the presence of non-textual sources behind the Synoptics makes the task difficult, if not impossible.[77] The strength of the Q hypothesis rests not on the assertion that it was a physical text, but on the basis of its ability to account *generally* for the double tradition.[78] Even though he argued for a written Q, Streeter felt that the "author" of Q "wrote to supplement, not to supersede, a living oral tradition. Both the longer parables and the Passion story were easy to remember, and every one knew them . . ."[79] In this case, Streeter recognized that the *Sitz im Leben* of the early Jesus movement must remain an important factor in any attempt to understand the developmental process that ultimately led to the Synoptic Gospels. Oral tradition was an important part of this "organic" process of Gospel development, and Streeter did attempt to include it in his model of Synoptic interrelationships. He argued that we must account for the probability that "Jerusalem and Caesarea, the two great Palestinian Churches, and Antioch, the original headquarters of the Gentile Mission, must each have had a cycle of tradition of its own,"[80] and that the influence of this "cycle" of tradition would have continued up to, and even carried on following the composition of the Synoptics.[81]

Oral tradition was *in theory*, a reality that required inclusion in Streeter's model. From this brief summary of Streeter's *The Four Gospels,*

---

[77] Streeter wrote, "The Q hypothesis, however, can be pressed too far. (1) Where the versions of sayings in Matthew and Luke differ considerably, the probability is high that one (or both) of the two versions did *not* come from Q. (2) Matthew probably omitted some sayings of Q which Luke retained, and *vice versa*. (3) Short epigrammatic sayings would be likely to circulate *separately* by word of mouth. Hence all attempts at a reconstruction of Q must be tentative" (*Four Gospels*, 153). Along similar lines, Kümmel suggests that "the exact compass and order of Q is beyond our reach," although he does feel that "some conjectures about its literary character may be advanced" ("In Support of Q," in *The Two Source Hypothesis: A Critical Appraisal* [ed. Arthur J. Bellinzoni; Macon: Mercer University Press, 1973], 234). Recently, Peter Head and P. J. Williams, following their discussion of the sigla used in the *Critical Edition of Q*, conclude that "*the wording of Q can never be reconstructed with any certainty* [italics original]" (Peter M. Head and P. J. Williams, "Q Review," *TynBul* 54:1 [2003]: 125).

[78] See Sanders and Davies, *Studying*, 66, 114.

[79] Streeter, *Four Gospels*, 229.

[80] Streeter, *Four Gospels*, 230. Streeter's view was that these cycles were "church-based."

[81] Streeter suggests that these three cycles of tradition were ultimately incorporated into the final Gospels themselves, and "thus traces of at least three different cycles of tradition, besides the material derived from Mark, are what antecedently we should expect a critical examination of Matthew and Luke to reveal" (Streeter, *Four Gospels*, 229).

we can see that he attempted to account for the influence of external, non-literary sources (i.e., oral tradition) in the production of the Synoptic Tradition, but only gave "lip service" to such a theory. In practice, Streeter did not incorporate into his hypothesis the insight gained from his understanding of oral tradition and the "historical conditions"[82] in which the Synoptic Gospels were written. Although he often referred to the existence of oral tradition, it was quickly replaced by a thoroughly literary approach to the tradition — clearly illustrated by the use of the term "Four Document Hypothesis" to describe Streeter's thesis.[83]

Another important study which continues to exert influence upon current discussions of the two-source hypothesis is J. C. Hawkins' contribution to the *Oxford Studies in the Synoptic Problem* in which Hawkins discussed the use of "unusual words" in each of the Synoptics.[84] He argued that there was a written document behind the so-called double tradition in Matthew and Luke due to two general phenomena: 1) similarity in "unimportant details" and 2) the occurrence of "certain peculiar or very unusual words or phrases in the Synoptic Gospels. Both of these phenomena led Hawkins to the conclusion that Matthew and Luke must have been in some sort of literary relationship with one another.

Hawkins listed several words and phrases that he claims supported his thesis. He pointed to the occurrence of phrases such as ἐν γεννητοῖς γυναικῶν which occurs only five times in the LXX, and grammatical peculiarities like ἱκανός ἵνα that occurs only in the New Testament and not anywhere in the LXX. For Hawkins, and those who continue to cite his work, these unusual phrases would have been replaced by more common words and phrases during the process of oral transmission of the early Jesus tradition.[85] Therefore, he argued that the double-tradition must have been derived from editorial access to a written source text. Hawkins' work has been highly influential, and continues to play a significant role in the ongoing discussion regarding the nature of Q as a text and understandably so. His observations are highly suggestive that there is a common source

---

[82] Streeter, *Four Gospels*, 229–230.

[83] On numerous occasions, Streeter refers to the influence of oral tradition (e.g., *Four Gospels*, xiii, 153, 184–186, 225, 229–230). Despite his recognition of oral tradition, he quickly moves into a section regarding the "overlapping of sources" in which he argues for Mark/Q overlaps from a literary perspective; see Streeter, *Four Gospels*, xiii, 242–246.

[84] John C. Hawkins, "Probabilities as to the So-Called Double Tradition of St. Matthew and St. Luke," in *Oxford Studies in the Synoptic Problem* (ed. W. Sanday; Oxford: Clarendon Press, 1911), 99.

[85] Most studies on the Synoptic Problem still refer to Hawkins' study as strong evidence for the literary relationship between the Synoptic Gospels; see John S. Kloppenborg Verbin, *Excavating Q* (Minneapolis: Fortress Press, 2000), 59.

behind the double tradition, although as is often the case, the evidence can cut in more than one direction.

Given the context of our current discussion regarding the "literary paradigm" there are several points worth considering before we continue to take Hawkins' argument at face value. Although none of these points constitute definitive evidence against Hawkins' thesis, each one of them raises important questions that need to be addressed further.

First, it is important to note that Hawkins' argument was based upon a thoroughly text-centered approach to the tradition. For example, he argued that the lack of *literary* parallels to these "peculiar words" is evidence that they are derived from a text. This is a most interesting argument from silence. It seems rather strained to argue from a *text* that these "peculiar" words are not "oral" in origin. Without any access to the no longer extant oral tradition, why should we come to such a conclusion?

There were several thoroughly literary presuppositions behind Hawkins' argument that led him to conclude as he did. First, Hawkins had to assume that the early Jesus communities would have had no reason or desire to *retain* these unusual words within their oral tradition, and that they would not have served any function within a performance setting. As Jonathan Draper has pointed out, the existence of "peculiar phrases by both these writers [i.e., Matthew and Luke] is not an argument against oral tradition, since the use of metonymic markers is characteristic of its function . . . These words are retained by the oral tradition precisely because of their peculiarity, because they mark out a particular discourse unequivocally."[86] Second, there was also an implicit assumption that oral communication would not be capable of transmitting these "unusual" words without changing them to more popular conventions. As we will explore below in chapters 4–5, given what we know about how oral communication functions and what we know of the early Jesus communities, it is necessary to question this premise behind Hawkins' work. While Hawkins' argument might initially seem quite persuasive, a more detailed examination of his implicit assumptions reveals that his argument is not as "concrete" as is often assumed. Perhaps what we are left with is actually the remnant of oral communication that has been

---

[86] Jonathan A. Draper. "The Sermon on the Plain (Luke 6:12–7:17) as Oral Performance: Pointers to "Q" as Multiple Oral Performance" (Unpublished, private correspondence. Originally presented at the SBL Annual Meeting, Nashville, November 2000), 3. Draper points to the use of these "peculiar phrases" in Zulu praise poems — ". . . where epithets associated with particular historical figures are no longer understood but continue to be passed on verbatim because of their metonymic associations, i.e., the mere mention of the praise name conjures up the person even if its reference is not understood" ("Sermon on the Plain," 3).

retained by the literate authors of the Synoptic texts, not evidence *per se* of literary activity.[87]

On a more secure footing is Hawkins' second major argument concerning what he described as "similarity" or "closeness" of the Matthean and Lukan double tradition.[88] Although he never directly uses the term "verbatim agreement" in his *Oxford Studies* contribution, Hawkins focused on the apparent similarities between the common Matthean and Lukan double tradition and concluded "[t]here are many passages, some of them being of considerable length, in which the similarity, even in unimportant details, between the two Gospels seems too great to be accounted for otherwise than by the use of a document."[89] Hawkins proceeded to divide the double tradition into three categories based upon the level of "probability" that the pericope was derived from the "document Q."[90] According to Hawkins this step was necessary for the double tradition is not characterized by a uniform distribution of "closeness," but varies widely throughout.[91] In his assessment, the way forward was to "omit none of the passages in Mt and Lk as to which there seems to be any appreciable ground for thinking that the document Q can have been their source," and to categorize the "Q material" into three categories based upon the *probability* that they were derived from a written documentary source.

At this stage it must be noted that Hawkins was aware of the danger in collapsing what are two separate arguments into one. With regard to Q, he recognized that there were two distinct arguments: 1) the argument for the *existence* of a written source behind the Matthean and Lukan double tradition, and 2) the argument to determine the *scope*, or boundaries of Q. As we will discuss in the next section, more recent studies on Q continue to appropriate several of the key arguments of Streeter and Hawkins. However, at the same time, they have not given due attention to some of the warnings expressed by both Hawkins and Streeter.

---

[87] We must also be open to the possibility that although oral and written communication share much of the same vocabulary, there could be a subset of vocabulary (slang words, phrases, colloquialisms, etc.) that exists only within the realm of oral communication and as such, might be considered inappropriate for use in written communication. If this is the case then there could be a subset of "oral" vocabulary to which we no longer have access.

[88] Hawkins, "Probabilities," 98, 108.

[89] Hawkins, "Probabilities," 98.

[90] Hawkins, "Probabilities," 98, 109.

[91] Cf. H. F. D. Sparks, *The Formation of the New Testament* (London: SCM Press, 1952), 98: ". . . by no means all of the common material can be assigned with equal confidence to a written (as distinct from an oral) source — the variations between the versions are sometimes very wide."

2.4.1   The Written Text of Q

All "modern" discussion on the Two-Source Hypothesis is built upon the presupposition that the agreements between Matthew and Luke are the primary reason for positing their mutual reliance upon a shared source document.[92] Kloppenborg's discussion on the "Two-Document hypothesis" (N.B. *document*) makes clear the strong emphasis placed on agreement.[93] He lists three major categories of phenomena that necessarily lead one to conclude that the Two-Source hypothesis can best account for the extant Synoptic Tradition: 1) agreements in wording and sequence, 2) patterns of agreements in the triple tradition, and 3) patterns of agreement in the double tradition.[94] Each of these three categories of phenomena is firmly based upon the notion of agreement. It is clear that if one were to remove the phenomena of agreement from the discussion, there would be far less support for the Two-Source hypothesis.[95]

Moving beyond general arguments for the Two-Source Hypothesis, we are faced with a similar situation with regard to the arguments for the documentary status of Q. Kloppenborg argues that there are three constituent arguments for a *written* Q, including "near-verbatim agreement" in certain double tradition pericopes, agreement in relative

---

[92] One can contrast this "modern" view with the pre-Griesbachian use of Gospel harmonies to account for the differences between the Gospels. The production of a Gospel harmony dates back to the very earliest stages of Christianity itself. Tatian's Diatesseron is among the first, but by no means the last harmony produced. Dungan's discussion of St. Augustine and other advocates of the Gospels harmony is helpful. He argues that the earlier harmonies proceeded on the basis of Augustine's assumption that all four Gospels were "uniformly true and without admixture of the slightest degree of error," and that Origen, and to a lesser degree Augustine, understood that the Bible contained both symbolic and literal truth; in this way, "differences and discrepancies among the Gospel narratives were still all true; they just weren't all literally true," see Dungan, *History*, 304.

[93] Kloppenborg, *Excavating Q*, 12–38. Kloppenborg continues to use the term "document" in describing Matthew and Luke's use of a Q "text" and Mark. In this case, his choice of "document" is consistent with how he envisions the production of the Synoptic Tradition. He states his justification for the use of the term *document* as follows: ". . . why do we refer to the Two *Document* hypothesis? It is one thing to argue that Matthew and Luke independently used two *sources*, Mark and another set of sayings and stories; it is another matter to conclude that this second source was a document, with reasonably clear contents and sequence. Because one still occasionally encounters statements to the effect that "Q" might be oral or written, it is crucial to be clear about the data and the arguments that have lead most specialists on Q to conclude that it was a written document" (*Excavating Q*, 9).

[94] Kloppenborg, *Excavating Q*, 12–38.

[95] For an example of just such a conclusion, see Eta Linnemann, *Is There a Synoptic Problem?:Rethinking the Literary Dependence of the First Three Gospels* (Grand Rapids: Baker Book House, 1992).

sequence, and the occurrence of "unusual phrases" in the Matthean and Lukan double tradition.[96] All three of these arguments offered by Kloppenborg derive from the earlier studies of scholars such as Streeter and Hawkins, and by examining how these contemporary arguments have evolved over the latter part of the twentieth-century, we will be in a better position to evaluate some of the strengths and weaknesses of the current "quest" for Q.

Kloppenborg's first argument for the *written* nature of Q is built on a solid foundation. Without devoting much space to this particular question we can make the following comments. The high level of verbatim agreement across portions of the double tradition has understandably led strong support to the notion of a shared source *text* behind at least a significant percentage of the shared Matthean and Lukan tradition. This point has been articulated with sufficient clarity and strength over the years and we find no sufficient grounds to question that overall conclusion.

Unfortunately, the positive conclusion reached over the *existence* of a common source has contributed to the over-confident attribution of much, if not all, of the shared double tradition to the now posited written source text (i.e., Q). This can be seen clearly in much recent work on Q that has been directed towards the reconstruction of its original form as a *text*. *The Critical Edition of Q*[97] is the most recent, and perhaps the ultimate example of just such an attempt within New Testament research. It is far beyond the scope of this study to interact with *The Critical Edition of Q* in detail, but it will serve our purposes here to use the work as an illustration of the extent to which the textual paradigm dominates the discipline. Despite a recognition of the complex interrelationship between oral and written tradition,[98] scholars associated with the *IQP* project feel confident enough to reconstruct a *text* that can account for the *entire* double tradition.[99]

---

[96] Kloppenborg, *Excavating Q*, 56.

[97] James M. Robinson, Paul Hoffmann, and John S. Kloppenborg, *The Critical Edition of Q* (Hermeneia Philadelphia: Fortress Press, 2000).

[98] See John S. Kloppenborg, *The Formation of Q* (Philadelphia: Fortress Press, 1987), 42–51 for his summary of the "oral hypothesis" in a section entitled "Q: Written or Oral?" Kloppenborg only interacts with a caricature of, in his own words, the "oral hypothesis."

[99] After only a few pages in which he presents a cursory summary of oral tradition, he concludes that, "[t]he oral hypothesis must in fact be rejected . . . because there is no evidence that such techniques were in use in primitive Christianity (or in contemporary Judaism for that matter!)" (Kloppenborg, *Formation*, 44). Following his reasons for rejecting the "oral hypothesis," one must question Kloppenborg's understanding of what constitutes "evidence." It is rather ironic that Kloppenborg can assert that his reconstruction of Q is based upon "evidence" — after all, there is no textual witness to

James D. G. Dunn has recently highlighted the danger in making such an assumption. He notes that behind "all" Q scholarship is the working assumption that "Q=q".[100] That is to say, it is problematic to assume that the entire "text" of "Q" consists of nothing beyond what can be reconstructed via the agreements and similarities between Matthew and Luke.[101] We are reminded of the danger in supposing that the authors of Matthew and Luke had no access to the early Jesus tradition apart from a physical, written text.[102] Allen has stated this rather pointedly, ". . . are we to suppose that, *e.g.*, the discourse about the Baptist had never been the subject of teaching in the Christian assemblies, was unfamiliar, and accessible only in a single Greek writing, to which Mt and Lk had to have recourse when they wished to insert it in their Gospels?"[103] Why should we assume that Matthew and Luke incorporated the entire *text* of a possible precursor to the Synoptics?

The only way that it is possible to reconstruct the text of Q (as posited by the *IQP*) is if one assumes both that the Synoptic Gospels are the product of exclusive textual-dependency, and that behind the three Synoptic texts lies another textual source which has been incorporated in its *entirety* by the Evangelists. If those assumptions are not adopted, then it becomes increasingly difficult to engage in any comprehensive attempt to delineate with any specificity the form of "Q." It is not justified to simply assume that all "shared" material between Matthew and Luke derives from

---

the existence of Q, it exists only by means of *inference*. Thus, this is the same as any hypothesis (either oral or literary) that attempts, by inference, to reconstruct a possible scenario by which the Synoptic Tradition was created. It is simply a *non sequitor* to argue that Q scholars are somehow is working with "evidence," while proponents of orality are not.

[100] Dunn, "Oral Memory 2000," 298 writes, "The working assumption that Q=q is one of the major weaknesses in all Q research." Dunn uses this expression (i.e., Q=q) to express the likelihood that there is not a direct one-to-one correspondence between the Q *text* itself and all of the material common to both Matthew and Luke. Therefore, Dunn employs the siglum "Q" to denote the physical *text* to which Matthew and Luke had access, and "q" to designate the collection of material whereby Matthew and Luke overlap in common content. In this case, the text of "Q" overlaps with the body of "q" (i.e., the double tradition) material, and can be envisioned in terms of a venn diagram consisting of two overlapping circles that share material with one another, but, in addition, have material that is unique to each group of tradition. Along these lines, Dunn asks the rhetorical question, "Did Matthew and Luke have no common (oral) tradition other than Q?" ("Oral Memory 2000," 299). Also, along similar lines, cf. Sanders and Davies, *Studying*, 117–118, who writes that this "working assumption" is "the view that *nothing was ever omitted* [from Q] *and nothing was ever created*."

[101] Dunn is not the first scholar to recognize this potential difficulty in Q research, see also C. K. Barrett, "Q: A Re-examination," *Expository Times* 54 (1943): 320.

[102] Dunn, "Oral Memory 2000," 299.

[103] Allen, "Logia," 426.

a common extra-canonical source text. Given these observations, the *Critical Edition of Q* might be more appropriately named the "critical edition of the Matthean-Lukan double tradition." But that is not what is envisioned by the *IQP*; what has been compiled represents an attempt to delineate the scope of the text *behind* the double tradition, not just the text *of* the double tradition itself — there is a significant difference between the two.

We can now observe how this approach contrasts with that of Hawkins and other scholars who specifically cautioned against collapsing the two separate arguments into one. While Hawkins was aware of the need to separate the argument for the existence of a common source text from the argument to determine the scope of the Q source, more recent scholars have moved away from an attempt to do so. The arguments on the "closeness" of the Matthean and Lukan double tradition, which were used by Hawkins to support a written Q, have been equally applied to the question of the scope of a written Q source. The underlying implicit assumption is that evidence for the former is necessarily evidence for the latter. While this is to some extent true, the argument for the existence of a written source does not naturally lead to the conclusion that *all* of the material common to Matthew and Luke is derived from a written source *text*. Hawkins recognized this fundamental distinction, and as we will see below, other more recent Q scholarship has attempted to address this specific issue.

The argument for a written Q has progressed to the point where questions regarding the scope of Q are at times pushed into the margins of the discussion, in preference for discussions on the coherence of Q, the theology of Q, the Q community, etc. We find this approach lacking methodological clarity. These questions, while vital and significant in themselves, must not supplant vital questions regarding the scope of Q. This leads us to ask several questions to which we will return in chapters five and six. What criteria must we employ to determine what does, and what does not belong to "Q"? And more importantly, how should our current knowledge of the oral milieu behind the Gospels inform our approach to the double tradition? It is from this perspective that we must revisit the discussion about verbatim agreement and Q and observe how the current status of Q as a unified text has been established by way of statistical studies on the double tradition and a long-standing reliance upon the "literary paradigm."

2.4.2 *Verbatim Agreement and Q as a "Text"*

Since the time of Hawkins, statistics have continued to play a vital role in source-critical arguments regarding the two-source theory and Q in particular. Theodore Rosché's 1960 article was an attempt to question the validity of the "Q" hypothesis.[104] Therein, Rosché aligned himself with scholars who argued that Q is no longer a viable hypothesis. Among those identified by Rosché are Farrer, B. C. Butler, and L. Cerfaux. Rosché argued that the work of scholars from these "Oxford" and "Matthean" schools has led one to ask whether the Q hypothesis has "outlived its usefulness."[105] In the remainder of his article, Rosché addresses the question of verbatim agreement between Matthew and Luke in the triple tradition, and Matthew and Luke in the double tradition (so-called Q) material.

Following his statistical analysis of the double and triple tradition, Rosché states that "[i]t is improbable *a priori* that Matthew and Luke would have followed one standard of evaluation for the sayings of Jesus found in triple tradition and yet another for sayings of the same Jesus in double tradition."[106] This leads him to question the claim that there was a common written source behind the double tradition. In conclusion, he argues that the "large majority of 'Q' verses have such a low verbal correspondence and no common order that in most cases the agreements are found only among the most minimal skeletal words necessary in order to call these verses 'common' sayings".[107] It is here that Rosché suggests that these "minimal skeletal" words are perhaps best explained as the result of "independent courses of oral, pregospel transmission," and the portions of the double tradition that have a higher percentage of agreement need not be derived from a written source, but "require only the versatility of being easily memorized and freely applied."[108] While Rosché was open to the possibility that the "Q" tradition was not a unified text, subsequent scholars generally have not embraced his particular thesis.

Carlston and Norlin wrote "Once More — Statistics and Q" in 1971 as a response to Rosché's earlier work.[109] Carlston and Norlin's objective was to demonstrate that behind the double tradition is a *unified, written* source. Their primary critique of Rosché was of his methodology. Carlston and Norlin noted correctly that Rosché's comparison of Matthew and Luke in the double tradition with Matthew/Mark and Luke/Mark in the triple tradition was an error in judgment. Subsequently, Carlston and Norlin

---

[104] Theodore Rosché, "The Words of Jesus and the Future of the "Q" Hypothesis," *JBL* 79 (1960).

[105] Rosché, "Words of Jesus," 210.

[106] Rosché, "Words of Jesus," 219.

[107] Rosché, "Words of Jesus," 220.

[108] Rosché, "Words of Jesus," 220.

[109] Charles E. Carlston and Dennis Norlin, "Once More- Statistics and Q," *Harvard Theological Review* 64 (1971).

substitute what they feel is a more useful method — compare Matthew/Luke in the triple tradition with Matthew/Luke in the double tradition. For the authors, this remedy allows for a proper examination of the means by which the Gospel writers edited their source material (i.e., Mark, and Q).

Following this methodological adjustment, Carlston and Norlin observe that the level of agreement between Matthew and Luke in the double tradition is approximately 27% greater than the level of agreement between Matthew and Luke in the triple tradition. Sharon Mattila responded to Carlston and Norlin by pointing out that the double tradition is composed of a greater percentage of sayings material, and therefore one would expect the level of agreement to be greater in the double tradition than it is in the triple,[110] and that the small number of narrative words in the double tradition is statistically too small a sample size from which to draw any sort of meaningful inference regarding the redactional use of narrative words by Matthew and Luke.[111] Carlston and Norlin's recent response to Mattila is that even though their figures for average agreement between Matthew and Luke in the double and triple tradition are substantially higher than those compiled by Rosché, Honoré, Morgenthaler, and others, the percentage of the *difference* remains at approximately 27%.[112] What is noteworthy in this discussion is that the 27% figure cited by Carlston and Norlin is based upon an average percent agreement of 71% for the double tradition and 56% agreement for the triple tradition. Therefore, they arrive at their conclusion that the double tradition has a 26.8% greater verbatim correspondence than the triple tradition.[113] A. M. Honoré's corresponding figures are 39.1% for the double tradition and 30.7% for the triple

---

[110] Sharon L. Mattila, "A Problem Still Clouded: Yet Again-Statistics and 'Q'," *Novum Testamentum* 37:4 (1994): 316. This argument is based on the observation that in both the double and triple tradition, sayings material is transmitted more faithfully than narrative, see Rosché, "Words of Jesus," 212–213. Mattila used this argument despite Carlston and Norlin's statement that "this phenomenon cannot be explained solely on the basis of the greater amount of sayings-material in Q than in Mark, since the correspondence is greater in both narrative and sayings material from speakers other than Jesus as well" (Carlston and Norlin, "Once More," 71–72).

[111] Mattila, "Still Clouded," 316–318.

[112] Charles E. Carlston and Dennis Norlin, "Statistics and Q- Some Further Observations," *Novum Testamentum* 41 (1999): 116–117.

[113] The percent agreement is calculated as follows: (*ave. %agreement in DT- ave. % agreement TT)/ ave. % agreement in TT*, or $(71.0-56.0)/56.0=26.8\%$. For the chart from which these figures are derived, see Carlston and Norlin, "Once More," 71.

tradition, thus he concludes that there is a 27.4% greater verbatim correspondence in the double tradition.[114]

For Carlston and Norlin, the approximately 27% difference (26.8% for C&N, 27.4% for Honoré) between the level of verbatim agreement in the double and triple tradition is evidence that, despite the quite different figures of verbatim agreement, there is a *unified, written* source text behind the double tradition. However, as we will see, it is necessary to question this conclusion. The significance of the similar figures offered by Carlston and Norlin and Honoré goes far beyond what their nearly equivalent 26.8% and 27.4% might suggest. The problem lies with the numbers *behind* the final summary figures. Carlston and Norlin's overall average percent agreement is 71% and 56% for the double and triple tradition respectively. These figures are far higher than those offered by Honoré (39.1%/30.7%), although the percent *difference* between both Carlston and Norlin's and Honoré's figures is almost identical.

Carlston and Norlin's argument is as follows; 1) the level of agreement between Matthew and Luke in the double tradition is greater than that in the triple tradition, 2) Matthew and Luke depend upon a written source document in the triple tradition, therefore 3) the Matthean and Lukan double tradition must also be dependent upon an underlying source *text*. Although this syllogism appears to be sound, there are several mitigating factors that lead one to conclude that Carlston and Norlin's argument is built upon a less than solid foundation.

First, it must be noted at the outset that Carlston and Norlin and Honoré arrive at markedly different statistical results despite studying the same corpus of Synoptic material.[115] Carlston and Norlin's aforementioned approach glosses over the great *disparity* between their results and those of Honoré, preferring instead to focus on the similar *levels of difference* between Matthean and Lukan levels of agreement in both the double and triple tradition. The overall differences in agreement are profound indeed — Carlston and Norlin do not take seriously enough the difference between their 71%/56% and Honoré's 39.1%/30.7%.

If one accepts Carlston and Norlin's high figures for verbatim agreement (71%/56%), then it is understandable to argue, as they do, that there is a written text behind the *entire* double tradition. Their average figure of 71% would strongly suggest that the entire double tradition is derivative from a written source. However, what is relevant here is that the overall level of verbatim agreement in Honoré's study is far lower in every

---

[114] Honorè's figures are calculated as follows: (39.1–30.7)/30.7; see Anthony M. Honoré, "A Statistical Study of the Synoptic Problem," *Novum Testamentum* 10 (1968): 140–144.

[115] Cf. below, §6.2.

instance than that compiled by Carlston and Norlin. Honoré's average calculation of 39.1% is substantially lower than that compiled by Carlston and Norlin, and if his figures were adopted, the strength of the argument for Q's documentary status is significantly weakened. As the overall percentage of agreement in the double tradition drops, one "deprives the Q-hypothesis of its foundation and topples one of the two pillars of the two-source hypothesis".[116] As the overall level of verbatim agreement between the double tradition decreases, the likelihood that all of the shared Matthean and Lukan (non Markan) material is derived from a unified written source text also decreases. It is at that point that we need to reassert the importance of the overall levels of verbatim agreement in the double tradition. While the *relative* difference between the levels of verbatim agreement in the double and triple tradition as proposed by Honoré and Carlston and Norlin is important, both studies cannot be equally used to support the claim of a unified, written text of Q.

The second problem that arises is in regard to the *significance* of the *difference* between the figures compiled by Carlston and Norlin and Honoré. As the average percentage of agreement between Matthew and Luke increases, one can have more confidence in the *significance* of the difference between the figures. Conversely, the lower the average percentage of agreement, the less confident one can be in their significance. An example will serve as a helpful illustration of this important principle. If, in theory, Matthew and Luke were in 100% in agreement with one another in the double tradition and 75% in agreement with one another in the triple tradition, there would be a 33% difference between them ((100%-75%)/75%); and if Matthew and Luke were in 30% agreement with one another in the double tradition and 22% in agreement in the triple tradition, there would once again be approximately a 33% difference between them ((30%-22%)/22%=36%). Again, the same 33% difference is misleading and not indicative of the relationship between the two theoretical sample groups.

While it is clear that the statistics compiled by Carlston and Norlin, Honoré, among others are quite divergent, we have not yet asked ask *why* Carlston and Norlin, Honoré, and others arrived at these widely disparate results for the level of verbatim agreement across the Synoptic Tradition. The "pillar" of verbatim agreement is artificially bolstered by Carlston and Norlin's inflated figures for verbatim agreement (71%/56%).[117] These

---

[116] Denaux uses this phrase in summarizing the work of Thomas Bergemann, see Adelbert Denaux, "Criteria For Identifying Q-Passages: A Critical Review of a Recent Work by T. Bergemann," *Novum Testamentum* 37:2 (1995): 108.

[117] See Carlston and Norlin's summary of the correspondence between Matthew and Luke, Carlston and Norlin, "Once More," 71.

figures are far higher than those compiled by other scholars such as Honoré and Morgenthaler, and this has been duly noted in detailed critiques of Carlston and Norlin's work by Sharon Mattila and in passing by John O'Rourke.[118] As Mattila has noted, the *method* employed by Carlston and Norlin greatly contributes to their elevated figures for verbatim agreement. Carlston and Norlin do not perform their analysis on complete pericopes from the Huck-Leitzmann sections, but rather excise portions of the pericopes and arrive at what Mattila calls a "purified triple tradition" and a "purified 'Q'."[119] What they excise are *sections* of the individual pericopes themselves, including: 1) introductory material in Luke or Matthew, 2) material within a Huck-Leitzmann section which is peculiar to either Luke or Matthew, 3) a summary or generalization at the end of a section which seems to be the work of either Luke or Matthew.[120] Carlston and Norlin justify this approach by stating that they employ the same procedure for *both* the double and triple tradition.[121] It is important to realize that such a method will remove much of the variation in the double and triple tradition, and conceal the substantial differences that are characteristic of the Synoptic Tradition as a whole.[122]

Carlston and Norlin adopt such an approach in an attempt to study the way in which Matthew and Luke *redact* a known source text (i.e., Mark). This in itself is not problematic, but when such a method is used to argue that the source *behind* the Matthean and Lukan common material is a written, unified text, their argument breaks down. As non-common sections and the introduction and conclusions of pericopes are removed, one begins to realize that the argument put forth by Carlston and Norlin is hampered by their operating presuppositions and their method of excising sections of the double tradition that do not fit their intended goals.

---

[118] Mattila's critique of Carlston and Norlin's elevated percentage of verbatim agreement is harsh but justified, despite its overly polemical tone. See Mattila, "Still Clouded," 319–324, and also John O'Rourke, "Some Observations on the Synoptic Problem and the Use of Statistical Procedures," *NovT* 16 (1974): 272.

[119] Mattila, "Still Clouded," 319, 324.

[120] Carlston and Norlin, "Once More," 61–62.

[121] Carlston and Norlin, "Once More," 61.

[122] Carlston and Norlin eliminate "whatever occurs in Luke and Mark only or Matthew and Mark only. The reason for this is evident: we are trying to judge how closely Luke and Matthew correspond to each other (not to Mark) when they use Mark" ("Once More," 62). This method has been adopted by Honorè and others, although such a methodology is only valid if one presupposes that the tradition under examination is derivative from the same source text. If the Matthean and Lukan parallels are actually *traditional* rather than redactional, then such a method would give the false impression that the levels of observed agreement are indications of literary copying.

Carlston and Norlin are to be commended for stating their *a priori* assumptions and methodology at the outset. Their assumptions are stated clearly in their response to Mattila in 1999, and consist of the *de facto* foundations of the two-source theory and includes: Markan priority, the independence of Luke and Matthew, the existence of some source behind the double tradition, and the similar treatment of source material (i.e., Mark and Q) by Matthew and Luke.[123] These presuppositions themselves are not necessarily problematic, but they do play a significant role in how Carlston and Norlin approach the double tradition in the remainder of their study.

Their assumption regarding the source behind the double tradition has allowed them to bypass the question regarding what is and is not legitimate Q material; that is, whether or not a passage has a common textual ancestor, or perhaps is just derived from the oral tradition that was freely circulating around the early Jesus communities of the time. One must be highly cautious and not assume that shared traditions are derivative of a source text until their individual tradition-history has been determined with confidence on a case-by-case basis. In excising all non-common sections from individual double tradition pericopes, Carlston and Norlin have done just that. They have bypassed the necessary precaution of questioning the scope of the material they consider to be derived from a source text, and have removed from discussion the possibility that some of their so-called Q passages might actually come from a source other than a written document.[124]

---

[123] Carlston and Norlin, "Further Observations," 109. Carlston and Norlin emphasize that they define "Q" as the *source* behind the double tradition, not the entire double tradition. However, it is clear that for them, the *source* behind the double tradition is equivalent to all the shared Matthean and Lukan material not found in Mark. Here, we are once again faced with the assumption that "Q = q" which we discussed in more detail in chapter 2, above.

[124] One is faced with a similar situation with regard to the Mark-Q "overlaps" allegedly contained within the tradition. These "overlaps" have been posited due to the observation that at times Matthew and Luke appear to agree *against* Mark; cf. Christopher M. Tuckett, *Q and the History of Early Christianity: Studies on Q* (Edinburgh: T&T Clark, 1996), 34 — "where a different version seems to have been used by Matthew and Luke alone." As such, this hypothesis is formulated in an attempt to maintain the independence of Matthew and Luke. Sanders argues that these "Mark-Q overlaps" are an "Achilles' heel" to the two-source hypothesis (Sanders and Davies, *Studying*, 79; also cf. E. P. Sanders, "The Overlaps of Mark and Q and the Synoptic Problem," *NTS* 19 [1973]: 453). Some argue that this results in a hypothesis that can never be falsified, for it just changes to accommodate any agreements between Matthew and Luke (e.g., Goulder). This is similar to the situation with the criterion of verbatim agreement. Although many so-called "Q" passages do not exhibit high levels of verbatim

2.5 Conclusions and Implications

In this chapter we have focused on the extent to which the early Jesus tradition has been studied from our post-Gutenberg perspective. Our immersion in the world of texts has led to the current state in which the Synoptic Gospels are often perceived as the end products of an editorial process based upon the *a priori* assumption that the relationship between the Gospels is one of *exclusive* inter-gospel textual dependency. Such an approach privileges written texts and textual sources despite the likelihood that the Jesus tradition circulated in oral form among the early Christian communities both prior to the inscription of the tradition in textual form, and subsequently in parallel alongside the inscribed Gospels.

This bias, which is inherent in most Synoptic Gospel and Q research, can be illustrated via the description of oral processes of communication with terms from the nomenclature of textuality, and in the use of strictly editorial language to describe the process by which the Synoptic Gospels were composed. While the use of literary and editorial terms in itself does not necessarily imply a fundamental misunderstanding of the process of gospel formation, it is indicative of how many scholars understand the question of Synoptic interrelationships. Adopting textual terminology only makes it easier to assume that the relationship between the Gospels is one of exclusive literary interdependency, and that behind every similarity between the Synoptic Gospels is a *written* text. All of the following assumptions lead to what is perhaps the most significant difficulty in Synoptic Gospel scholarship: New Testament scholars acknowledge that oral tradition was a significant factor in the development and transmission of the Jesus tradition, but often do not appropriate the implications of such a view when studying the Synoptic Tradition itself.

The current debate regarding the status of Q as a *text* has been, to a large extent, based upon statistical studies on the level of verbatim agreement between the Matthean and Lukan double tradition. These studies have been used to support the thesis regarding the existence of a written source text behind the double tradition, but unfortunately, the positive conclusion reached over the *existence* of a common source has led to the over-confident attribution of much, if not all, of the shared double tradition to the now posited written source text (i.e., Q). We suggested that this is partially due to the over reliance upon statistical studies that have arrived at very high levels of overall verbatim agreement for the double tradition. Once it is recognized that these earlier studies were methodologically flawed, it becomes necessary to revisit the question of

---

agreement, they are included in Q by other means, thereby abandoning the initial reason for positing a hypothetical source first off.

verbatim agreement and the possible role that it might have in determining the scope of a Q document and the possibility that some double tradition passages are not the result of textual redaction of a common source text.

As the overall level of verbatim agreement decreases, the likelihood that the entire double tradition can be attributed to a single, unified source document also decreases. At some point, the strength of the evidence of verbatim agreement between two parallel traditions decreases to a point where it can no longer support a strictly literary approach to the tradition. It is at that juncture where one must explore the possibility that oral tradition has had an impact on the development of the Synoptic Gospels and in particular the Matthean and Lukan double tradition.

Chapter 3

A Brief History of the Problem of Oral Tradition

3.1 Introduction

In the previous chapter we focused on some of the shortcomings inherent in a strictly literary approach to the question of Synoptic interrelationships. It is now necessary to take a step back and reflect on how oral tradition, and its role in the formation of the Synoptic Tradition, has been understood throughout the twentieth century. We shall now focus on previous attempts to counteract the weaknesses of a purely literary approach to the Synoptic Tradition.

In this chapter we will survey the development of New Testament scholarship with regard to the early Jesus tradition's origins in orality and its subsequent transmission within that medium. For the purposes of our current examination we will not attempt to engage in a comprehensive survey of work on oral tradition and the Synoptic Gospels. Such an examination would require a monograph itself and is beyond the scope of this work. Rather, we will use selected works to chronicle the development of thought over the last century. For this approach we will divide the secondary literature into two categories, roughly demarcated by the pioneering work of Albert B. Lord (1960). The influence of Lord's work marked a turn in New Testament research. Prior to the publication of Lord's *The Singer of Tales*,[1] New Testament research was for the most part dominated by an early form-critical view of oral tradition that was based upon the studies of nineteenth-century diffusionist folklorists such as the Brothers Grimm. That is to say, the early form-critical view on how oral tradition functioned was derived from nineteenth-century studies of predominantly *German* folklore traditions. All this was to change following the fieldwork that was begun by the classicist Milman Parry and brought to fruition by Lord following Parry's untimely death. For reasons that will become clear in what follows, we find sufficient justification to use Lord's *Singer* as the demarcation line in categorizing the New Testament work on oral tradition.

---

[1] Albert B. Lord, *The Singer of Tales* (Cambridge: Harvard University Press, 1960).

Works prior to 1960 will be discussed under the category "early form-critical studies" along with the earlier work of Birger Gerhardsson. The rationale behind this decision is twofold. First, Gerhardsson's influential *Memory and Manuscript* (1961) was published within one year of Lord's *Singer* and therefore Gerhardsson most likely would not have had sufficient time to take into account the implications of Lord's influential study. Second, Lord's *Singer* was not intended to be a contribution to New Testament research. Rather, it was a contribution to the ongoing Homeric question that concerned classical scholars. Given both factors, it would be unfair to criticize Gerhardsson for not interacting with Lord's important work.

Following the discussion of the early form-critical studies on oral tradition we shall examine the impact that Lord has had upon the modern view of oral tradition. We will then be in a position to evaluate subsequent New Testament studies in the area. Our examination will survey the following secondary literature in chronological order in an attempt to elucidate the development of some of the more important themes in relation to oral tradition and the formation of the Synoptic Gospels. To begin we shall now turn to the past and examine the highly influential work of the early New Testament form critics.

3.2 Early Form-Critical Studies

3.2.1 Rudolf Bultmann and Martin Dibelius

Martin Dibelius and Rudolf Bultmann are often identified as cofounders of the New Testament form-critical movement which perhaps achieved its finest expression in Bultmann's *Die Geschichte der synoptischen Tradition*.[2] Dibelius' seminal work *Die Formgeschichte des Evangeliums*[3] was also highly influential and it served as a discussion partner throughout Bultmann's work.[4] Bultmann's work to this day is a brilliant example of

---

[2] Bultmann's *Geschichte* has gone through several editions. In particular, Rudolf K. Bultmann, *Die Geschichte der synoptischen Tradition* (Göttingen: Vandenhoeck & Ruprecht, 1931), *Die Geschichte der synoptischen Tradition* (Göttingen: Vandenhoeck & Ruprecht, 1957) .

[3] Dibelius' work has appeared in several editions: Martin Dibelius, *Die Formgeschichte des Evangeliums* (Tübingen: J.C.B. Mohr, 1919), *Die Formgeschichte des Evangeliums* (Tübingen: J.C.B. Mohr, 1933), and *From Tradition to Gospel* (Cambridge: James Clarke, 1971).

[4] Bultmann is critical of Dibelius' emphasis on the sermon as the impetus that led to the development of the gospel tradition. See Bultmann, *Geschichte* (1931), 64, *Synoptic*

meticulous and detailed study of the formation and transmission of the Synoptic Tradition. The impact of these early form-critical pioneers is still strong today in numerous fields of study relating to the New Testament and Christian theology, and served as the driving force "which made an enormous impact and which put scholars to work for decades."[5]

Form criticism is often understood as an attempt to categorize the various gospel traditions into their respective mini-genres. According to Bultmann's definition, "[t]he aim of form-criticism [*sic*] is to determine the original form of a piece of narrative, a dominical saying or a parable. In the process we learn to distinguish secondary additions and forms, and these in turn lead to important results for the history of the tradition."[6] Indeed, his definition is a succinct summary of the process with which he engaged the Synoptic Gospels. Bultmann's aim was threefold: 1) to distinguish secondary forms, thereby 2) determining the "original form" of a tradition. An analysis of the first two points then leads to, 3) "important results for the history of the tradition." This most evident aim of form criticism is still widely embraced today. Currently, many involved in the "third quest" for the historical Jesus have retained principles and methods previously enacted by Bultmann.[7]

Although the categorization of the various gospel traditions is one dimension of the form-critical process, it is not the sole or even primary purpose of the discipline. Through analysis and categorization, Dibelius hopes to "explain the origin of the tradition about Jesus, and thus to penetrate into a period previous to that in which our Gospels and their written sources were recorded. But it has a further purpose. It seeks to make clear the intention and real interest of the earliest tradition."[8]

Tradition, 60. Dibelius in his revised edition (1933) prefers his term "Chriae" over Bultmann's "Apophthegmata," Dibelius, *Formgeschichte* (1933), 149–151.

[5] Sanders and Davies, *Studying*, 126.

[6] Bultmann, *Synoptic Tradition*, 6; "[d]ie ursprüngliche Form eines Erzählungstückes, eines Herrenwortes, eines Gleichnisses zu erkennen, ist eben das Ziel der formgeschichtlichen Betrachtung. Sie lehrt damit auch sekundäre Erweiterungen und Bildungen erkennen und begegnet sich in solchen für die Geschichte der Tradition wichtigen Ergebnisse mit der vorigen Betrachtungsweise" (Bultmann, *Geschichte* (1931), 7).

[7] For but one example, Crossan likens his task to that of a textual "archaeologist" — one who must remove the various layers of the encrusted Synoptic Tradition in a manner analogous to that of an archaeologist removing layers from a tell in order to uncover earlier, more primitive layers. In this case his self-defined task is quite analogous to Bultmann's attempt to remove layers of tradition from the Synoptic Tradition in order to arrive at what he views as the pure forms in which the tradition originated. For a fuller description of Crossan's methodology, see, *The Historical Jesus: The Life of a Mediterranean Jewish Peasant* (San Francisco: HarperSanFrancisco, 1991), xxvii–xxxiv.

[8] Dibelius, *Tradition to Gospel*, v.

Similarly for Bultmann, form criticism does not simply "consist of identifying the individual units of the tradition according to their aesthetic or other characteristics and placing them in their various categories." Rather, it is to "rediscover the origin and the history of the particular units and thereby to throw some light on the history of the tradition before it took literary form".[9] In this respect, both Dibelius and Bultmann understood their purpose not as the simple genre classification of individual traditions, but rather as a means by which they could increase our understanding of the earliest stages of the early Jesus tradition.

The "analytical" method employed by Bultmann and the "constructive" method of Dibelius required that they reconstruct the earliest beginnings of the early Christian church and the process by which the Jesus tradition was formulated and transmitted. Dibelius recognized that it is not possible to trace the development of the Jesus tradition without formulating some basic propositional statements regarding the nature of the early church. His method of *Formgeschichte* requires "reconstruction and analysis."[10] It was his reconstruction of the early church, or his "model," that would form the basis for his further analysis.

Throughout his *Synoptic Tradition*, Bultmann acknowledges the workings of oral tradition and oral communication. After assigning the formation of the controversy dialogues to the work of the Palestinian church, he then proceeds to discuss the extent to which these traditions are products of oral or written tradition. Bultmann felt that passages such as Mark 2:1-12, 15-17, 7:1-23, and 10:2-12, among others, reached their present form in the written tradition. On the other hand, he also suggested that passages such as Mark 3:1-5, 10:17-30, and 12:13-17 might have been shaped "orally," and that in many other cases either scenario is possible.[11] While not passing judgment on all of the texts, it is apparent that Bultmann is open to the possibility that many passages could have their roots in oral tradition.

In their attempt to describe this "oral shaping," Dibelius and Bultmann develop "laws of transmission" which are then used to trace what Dibelius describes as the "development" of the Jesus tradition.[12] Both form critics

---

[9] Bultmann, *Synoptic Tradition*, 4.

[10] Dibelius, *Tradition to Gospel*, v.

[11] Bultmann, *Synoptic Tradition*, 48.

[12] Although Dibelius and Bultmann approach their respective studies with different methodologies, their use of the term "laws" with respect to the development of the tradition is strikingly similar. For Dibelius' use of "laws of transmission," see Dibelius, *Tradition to Gospel*, 4. For Bultmann's use of the term, see Bultmann, *Synoptic Tradition*, 6. The typical use of the phrase "development of tradition" (and similar variants) is to describe the growth or expansion of the tradition. See esp. Dibelius, *Tradition to Gospel*, 27, 160.

use the term law/laws throughout their respective works to describe the process of tradition development that they believe culminated in the writing down of the Gospels.[13] Several examples will illustrate their understanding of the term.

Bultmann begins his study by outlining three primary tools which he feels are available to the form critic. His first tool is to observe how Matthew and Luke have used the sources which were at their disposal. This leads Bultmann to develop a set of "laws" which he will use to analyze further the Synoptics. These laws then enabled him to "infer back to an earlier stage of the tradition than appears in our sources."[14] In a similar fashion, Dibelius states, "What took place previously was the formation and the growth of small separate pieces out of which the Gospels were put together . . . [t]o *trace out those laws*, to make comprehensible the rise of these little categories, is to write the history of the Form of the Gospel."[15]

For both Dibelius and Bultmann, the term "law" is used to imply that a regular and predictable process of tradition development and transmission existed within the early church.[16] At the beginning of chapter 2 (Sermons), Dibelius refers to the "law" which regulates the "spreading of reminiscences."[17] He writes,

Fixation is only to be accepted where the handing down takes place either in the regulated activity of teaching and of learning, or under the control of immanent laws . . . we must inquire (1) as to *the motive* which caused the spreading of the reminiscences . . . and (2) as to *the law* which governed their spreading and which helped to form and to preserve what had been said. If there is no such law, then the writing of the Gospels implies not an organic development of the process by means of collecting, trimming, and binding together, but the beginning of a new and purely literary development.[18]

---

[13] At the start it is important to question the very use of the term "law" to describe a process as intricate and complex as that of Synoptic Gospel development. The use of the term "law" derives from Newtonian principles (i.e., laws) that are thought to both govern and describe our physical universe. One must question the use of such terms and principles for the study of the New Testament.

[14] Bultmann, *Synoptic Tradition*, 6.

[15] Dibelius, *Tradition to Gospel*, 4.

[16] Bultmann, *Synoptic Tradition*, 6.

[17] Dibelius, *Tradition to Gospel*, 11.

[18] Dibelius, *Tradition to Gospel*, 11; "Fixierung muß aber in unserem Prozeß vorausgesetzt werden, wenn wir wirklich die Evangelien oder ihre Quellen aus der Gemeindetradition entstanden denken. Nach beidem wäre also zu fragen: nach dem Motiv, das die Verbreitung von Erinnerungen veranlaßte, obwohl Sinnen und Sehnen der Menschen auf die Zukunft gerichtet war; und nach dem Gesetz, das über dieser Verbreitung waltete und das Erzählte formen und konservieren half. Wenn es dieses Gesetz nicht gibt, dann bedeutet die Niederschrift von Evangelienbüchern nicht einen

Dibelius assumes that the writing down of the gospels is simply an *extension* of the process of tradition development. If there is no law "governing their spreading," then Dibelius feels that the gospels are "a new and purely literary development." He assumes that there is a predictable, almost *linear process* of tradition formation that led to the development of the gospels. We can better elucidate the early form critics' understanding of the term "law" with two further examples.

First, Dibelius feels that traditions were "handed down in isolation . . . [o]nly gradually were they taken up into the broader connections in which they were preserved, either clearly defined or edited from a literary standpoint."[19] He later reinforces the same premise — "The stories contained in the Synoptic Gospels . . . were first handed down in *independent* stories. Folk tradition as contained in the Gospels could pass on Paradigms, Tales, and Legends, but *not a comprehensive description of Jesus' work* [italics mine]."[20] *Independence* and *isolation* is an appropriate summary of this "law" of transmission.

Second is Dibelius' "law" regarding what happened to those stories during the time of their "independence." During this time Dibelius envisions mostly growth and expansion. There are many occasions in *From Tradition to Gospel* where the term "development" is used to imply the occurrence of either expansion or growth of the tradition.[21] This particular view of tradition transmission led Dibelius to view the formation of the Gospels as "the collecting of a tradition that had grown 'wild' and that had been consciously corrected . . ."[22] According to Dibelius, "[t]he apocryphal Gospels have apparently preserved such [wild] collections."[23]

---

organischen Fortgang des Prozesses durch Sammlung, Rahmung und Verbindung, sondern den Anfang eines neuen, rein literarischen Werdens. Wenn es jenes Motiv nicht gibt, dann ist überhaupt nicht zu begreifen, wie literaturscheue Menschen eine Tradition schaffen konnten, die Vorstufe der kommenden literarischen Produktion war" (Dibelius, *Formgeschichte* (1919), 5–6).

[19] Dibelius, *Tradition to Gospel*, 156.

[20] Dibelius, *Tradition to Gospel*, 178.

[21] See *Tradition to Gospel*, 27, 29, 160–161, 264–265. Also, there are a few examples where Dibelius mentions the "conservatism" of the tradition (*Tradition to Gospel*, 270–271, 289, 293). It is important to note that all of these occurrences occur near the end of his book during his closing remarks. In this context these statements take on an apologetic purpose. Dibelius is attempting to maintain a balance within his presentation, but it is quite incompatible with the whole of his argument. He spends the vast majority of the book discussing the development (i.e., growth/embellishment) of the tradition and only makes a few passing comments on the "conservative" tendencies within the tradition. If Dibelius saw these tendencies, they most certainly did not affect his arguments throughout his book.

[22] Dibelius, *Tradition to Gospel*, 4.

[23] Dibelius, *Tradition to Gospel*, 4.

Bultmann's understanding of orality also affects how he views the development and transmission of received tradition. In the opening pages of *Synoptic Tradition*, he summarizes Dibelius' work with an explanation of his thought process by which "it was necessary to inquire what account could be given of the *individual units of the tradition*, and how the tradition passed from a fluid state to the fixed form in which it meets us in the synoptics and in some instances even outside them."[24] It is Bultmann's agreement with Dibelius that will form the basis for his method throughout the book. He is quite concerned with establishing that his primary goal is to discern the *"general tendency of the tradition."*[25] According to Bultmann, "we may with certainty detect on the part of the sources an *expansion of an original saying by addition"*.[26]

In order to discern the "general tendency of the tradition," it is necessary to understand the way in which tradition was transmitted in early Christian circles. That is, in order to describe the actual process of tradition transmission, one must attempt to describe how material is presented and transmitted via the *oral* medium. However, Bultmann does not do this in the *Synoptic Tradition*. Rather, he avoids the difficulty by stating that the distinction between the oral and literary characteristics of the tradition is an inconsequential matter, or in his own words, "relatively unimportant."[27] The following four excerpts from his work illustrate this tendency. They are listed in order of their appearance in the *Synoptic Tradition*:

1) While Bultmann acknowledged the presence of oral tradition in the process of tradition formation[28], it is interesting to note that in the same paragraph he also dismissed the importance of distinguishing between the two stages of development:

This means, in my view, that we can firmly conclude that the formation of the material in the tradition took place in the Palestinian Church . . . [f]or this reason I think the question how far such formulations took place in an oral or written stage of tradition to be relatively unimportant. [29]

---

[24] Bultmann, *Synoptic Tradition*, 3.

[25] Bultmann, *Synoptic Tradition*, 93.

[26] Bultmann, *Synoptic Tradition*, 89. Also Bultmann, *Synoptic Tradition*, 88, "The issue is not what judgment is made upon one particular instance, but only whether we have to reckon with a tendency of the tradition to enlarge upon older sayings."

[27] Bultmann, *Synoptic Tradition*, 48.

[28] Bultmann, *Synoptic Tradition*, 48.

[29] Bultmann, *Synoptic Tradition*, 48; "Das lässt sich nun m. E. mit Sicherheit feststellen, dass die Formung des Stoffes überwiegend in der palästinensischen Urgemeinde erfolgt ist — sowohl die der einheitlichen Konzeptionen wie die der andern Stücke. Das zeigt die Parallelität der Rabbinengeschichten wie auch der Gedankengehalt der Probleme und der Argumente, in denen nur selten hellenistischer Geist zu spüren ist

2) While discussing the "Form and History of the Logia,"[30] and in particular Matt 5:44–48, Bultmann offers another example: "How far, in all these examples the oral tradition has been at work, or how far the written, is a question which neither can be decided, nor is of chief importance".[31]

3) In dealing with the miracle tradition Bultmann presents numerous Palestinian and Hellenistic parallels to the Synoptic traditions, he writes,

. . . In this regard it is further of importance to ask at what stage the Tradition was enriched by the addition of miracle stories, and to a less degree whether it took place in the oral or written stage. No doubt both have to be accepted, but here as elsewhere this distinction is in my view relatively unimportant for the gospel Tradition, since the fixing of the tradition in writing was in the first place a quite unliterary process. Much more important is the distinction between the Palestinian and Hellenistic stages of the Tradition.[32]

4) All three of the previous excerpts foreshadow the statement that Bultmann makes in the opening sentence to part three of his book, "There is no definable boundary between the oral and written tradition, and

---

wie Lk 6,5 D und in dem späten Anhang Mk 7,20–23. Dabei halte ich die Frage, wieweit solche Formung in der mündlichen oder in der schriftlichen Tradition erfolgt ist, für relativ nebensächlich. Beide Stufen der Tradition kommen in Betracht" (Bultmann, *Geschichte* (1931), 49–50).

[30] Bultmann, *Synoptic Tradition*, 81–108.

[31] Bultmann, *Synoptic Tradition*, 88.

[32] Bultmann, *Synoptic Tradition*, 239; "Wichtig ist dabei aber ferner die Frage, in welchem Stadium die Tradition durch den Zuwachs von Wundergeschichten bereichert wurde; und zwar weniger die Frage, ob das im mündlichen oder im schriftlichen Stadium der Fall war. Beides ist zweifellos anzunehmen; aber wie sonst ist auch hier dieser Unterschied für die evangelische Tradition m. E. relativ bedeutungslos, da ja auch die schriftliche Fixierung zunächst ganz unliterarisch war. Viel wichtiger ist die Unterscheidung des palästinensischen und des hellenistischen Stadiums der Tradition" (Bultmann, *Geschichte* (1931), 253–254). Cf. Bultmann, *Synoptic Tradition*, 6, where following his "laws of transmission," Bultmann writes, "Moreover it is at this point a matter of indifference whether the tradition were oral or written, because on account of the unliterary character of the material one of the chief differences between oral and written traditions is lacking." This view of the non-literary character of early Christianity was based upon the earlier work of Franz Overbeck which argued that Christian literature proper began with the second-century writings of the church fathers, see Franz Overbeck, *Über die Anfänge der patristischen Literatur* (Basel: Benno Schwabe, 1882). For Dibelius' comments on Overbeck see *Formgeschichte* (1933), 5. Güttgemanns, in his response to classical *Formgeschichte*, devotes a chapter to Overbeck's view of the early Christian writings as *Urliteratur* (Erhardt Güttgemanns, *Offene Fragen zur Formgeschichte des Evangeliums: Eine methodologische Skizze der Grundlagenproblematik der Form- und Redaktionsgeschichte* [BEvT 54; Munich: C. Kaiser, 1970], 106–118).

similarly the process of the editing of the material of the tradition was beginning already before it had been fixed in a written form."[33]

In conclusion, we can discern from our survey of the early form critics the following two categories with which they had major difficulties. The first and most apparent area of difficulty is in their understanding of the process of tradition formation and transmission. Bultmann and Dibelius posited that the following characteristics were descriptive of the oral traditioning process. First, there was a period of time in which the Jesus tradition existed in oral form. Second, the *"general tendency of the tradition"* is towards growth, expansion,[34] and at times creation *ex nihilo*. This tendency implied a progression in a rather linear fashion from simplicity to complexity as the tradition evolved from a fluid, oral form to a more fixed, written form.

The linearity that the early form critics envisage is based upon the premise that the development of the tradition progressed in a linear fashion from simplicity to complexity, from short, disconnected stories to a larger, connected narrative. The difficulty is that this observation depends upon the unbroken movement of the tradition from its oral origins to its literary form. But if the style and method of tradition transmission differs in its oral and literary forms, or the tradition itself oscillates back and forth from text to oral tradition, then the early form-critical argument loses its force. We shall examine some of the differences between the oral and literary paradigm in more detail following our survey of Lord's work.

Therefore, in sum, the difficulty in the theses of Bultmann and Dibelius lies not in their acknowledgment of the process of oral tradition formation — which is correct — but rather in their misunderstanding of the character of oral tradition and how the tradition was transmitted in its pre-textual, oral stage. Given their lack of interest in the question regarding the medium in which the tradition was transmitted, it is not surprising that the discussion developed in the way that it has. Bultmann accepted the oral character of the tradition, but was not sure how to deal with the material as orally transmitted. His uncertainty about how oral tradition functioned in the context of tradition formation and transmission led him ultimately to abandon any genuine pursuit of the role of orality in the development of the Synoptic Gospels.[35] He therefore dealt with orality in a rather peripheral manner and the question of its possible impact upon the development of the Jesus tradition effectively dropped out of the discussion. Orality then became an unimportant side issue and was

---

[33] Bultmann, *Synoptic Tradition*, 321.

[34] Bultmann, *Synoptic Tradition*, 93.

[35] Cf. Güttgemanns (*Offene Fragen*) who suggested that there was no way to reconstruct an earlier "oral period" from the literary texts.

replaced by a more literary approach to the Jesus tradition. Much is the same with Dibelius. He envisioned the Synoptic Gospels as the natural extension of the process of oral transmission. He understood the progression from orality to literacy as did Bultmann — it was simply the transcription of oral tradition into the textual medium.

3.2.2 Birger Gerhardsson

Birger Gerhardsson's work *Memory and Manuscript: Oral Tradition and Written Transmission in Rabbinic Judaism and Early Christianity* was the next important work to follow that of Bultmann and Dibelius. Although *Memory and Manuscript* (1961) was published after Lord's *Singer* (1960), understandably, Gerhardsson's work does not reveal any insights gained from Lord's work. Both works were published within a short period of time, and Lord's *Singer* was not concerned with the New Testament itself. Since Gerhardsson was most likely not aware of the recently developed oral theory,[36] or he chose not to incorporate Lord's findings, we will survey Gerhardsson's work from within the perspective of *early form-critical* New Testament research. In many respects Gerhardsson proposes a model of tradition formation and transmission almost diametrically opposed to that of Bultmann and Dibelius.

His major goal is to ask "what was the technical procedure followed when the early Church *transmitted,* both gospel material and other material".[37] In this respect Gerhardsson attempted to take earlier form-critical scholarship's acknowledgment of the oral origins of the tradition to the next level by addressing the question of *how* the material was transmitted. He is to be commended for recognizing the importance of this endeavor,[38] even if his conclusions have been questioned by many scholars and do not seem to account for the cultural setting of nascent Christianity nor the extant evidence itself.[39]

For Gerhardsson, rabbinic Judaism can provide us with the answer for how the tradition was transmitted. He attempts to demonstrate that

---

[36] As we will deal with in more detail later, the terms "oral theory" and "oral-formulaic theory" are often used synonymously to refer to Lord's thesis regarding the process by which an oral singer composes/performs an epic. See the §3.2.2 for more detail on this process.

[37] Gerhardsson, *Memory and Manuscript,* 14–15.

[38] Robert Culley also realized that this was an important endeavor. In 1963 he asked the question, "[w]hat is the process involved and how does it happen?" ("Approach," 113). He recognized that it simply was not enough to presuppose that oral tradition functioned in the way proposed by Old Testament scholars like Gunkel and others.

[39] For a critique of Gerhardsson and how he deals with the extant evidence see Kelber, *Oral and Written Gospel,* 23.

Jerusalem was the center of early Christianity[40] and that Jesus formed a type of rabbinical "academy" that included his disciples as the recipients, possessors, and transmitters of the authentic tradition.[41] The process of tradition transmission involved the recording of Jesus' teachings and sayings in notebooks[42] which would later serve as an *aide-mémoire*. Mechanical memorization from written aids coupled with an authoritative teacher (Jesus) formed the "technical procedure" envisaged by Gerhardsson.[43] Throughout this process the "reverence and care for the *ipsissima verba* of each authority remains unaltered."[44]

Unfortunately, Gerhardsson's appeal to rabbinic methods of memorization and transmission is open to criticism on several points. Although it is beyond the scope of our inquiry to interact in detail with his thesis, we can comment on some of the more pertinent matters. The most common objection to Gerhardsson's thesis is that of his possible anachronistic reading of the rabbinic material back into nascent Christianity. The process of tradition transmission to which Gerhardsson appeals derives from the more formalized rabbinic Judaism of the tannaitic and amoraic periods. Thus, the proposed historical analogy is several centuries removed from the time of Jesus, and understandably must be used with great caution, if at all. Second, and perhaps more telling is the fact that the early Christian church quickly moved beyond its Judeo-centric Palestinian roots to become a multi-ethnic movement that rapidly spread throughout the Roman Empire, thus raising questions regarding the applicability of a predominantly rabbinical model for understanding early tradition transmission. Even if the tradition did begin and was fostered

---

[40] Gerhardsson, *Memory and Manuscript,* 216–217.

[41] Gerhardsson, *Memory and Manuscript,* 85. Several other scholars have also argued along similar lines. Riesner (*Jesus als Lehrer: eine Untersuchung zum Ursprung der Evangelien-Überlieferung* [WUNT II 7; Tübingen: Mohr Siebeck, 1984], cf. "Jesus as Teacher and Preacher," in *Jesus and the Oral Gospel Tradition* [ed. Henry Wansbrough; JSNTSup 64; Sheffield: Sheffield Academic Press, 1991]) has examined the Jesus tradition from the perspective of didactic practices which were in place prior to the period which was examined by Gerhardsson. Byrskog, a former student of Gerhardsson, has examined the role of Jesus as the only teacher in his monograph on the Matthean community (*Jesus the Only Teacher: Didactic Authority and Transmission in Ancient Israel, Ancient Judaism and the Matthean Community* [Coniectanea Biblica: New Testament Series 24; Stockholm: Almqvist & Wiksell International, 1994]). Byrskog, *Only Teacher,* 22–23, attempts to go "one step further" than Gerhardsson and Riesner and ask ". . . if there were situations in which the authority of a person considered in some way to be a teacher — whether alive or not — constituted the essential identity marker for the settings of transmission."

[42] Gerhardsson, *Memory and Manuscript,* 105, 157.

[43] Gerhardsson, *Memory and Manuscript,* 81.

[44] Gerhardsson, *Memory and Manuscript,* 130–131.

within the setting envisioned by Gerhardsson, the transmission of the tradition did not cease there. The tradition continued to be transmitted by others outside of that original setting. The rapid expansion of the early Christian church beyond its Palestinian roots requires that we examine how the tradition would have been transmitted in those wider circles. Third, the traditions transmitted by the rabbinical schools to which Gerhardsson appeals were contained within a recognized body of "sacred" material (although loosely collected) that previously existed for a substantial period of time, while the early Christian movement did not come to understand its received collected *textual* tradition as "sacred" until later in the second century C.E.[45] Fourth, there is no extant evidence that would suggest that Jesus formed a structured school around his teachings.[46] There is no evidence of any formal education of Jesus' disciples, or even of Jesus himself. If anything, the canonical evidence regarding the educational level of the apostles would point in the other direction.[47]

---

[45] In this case we are using "sacred" to describe the status given to a religious text within the cultic context of communal worship. Robert Culley credits Sigmund Mowinckel with relating the notion of verbatim transmission of a "fixed text" to the recognition of the "text" as sacred scripture ("Approach," 114). This is important in understanding the development and transmission of the early Jesus tradition. In the case of the early Jesus material, it is difficult to accept that the early Christians would have considered a *written text* of the Jesus tradition something to be revered (i.e., sacred) from the very beginning of the movement. While it is clear that there was reverence for Jesus traditions (e.g., last supper, passion narratives, etc.), it is highly unlikely that the *physical text* containing the traditions became revered and therefore protected from corruption until a fully developed manuscript tradition was underway. This makes it increasingly difficult to accept the process envisaged by Gerhardsson in his *Memory and Manuscript*.

[46] Regarding the Gospel of Mark, Botha suggests "Mark is not Hochliteratur. Not only the common, unliterary style and the closeness of the Gospel to popular, unpretentious writings, but also the lack of liturgical elements and the inadequate (nonexistent to my mind) indications of a format or official situation are determinative" (J. J. Botha, "Mark's Story of Jesus and the Search for Virtue," in *The Rhetorical Analysis of Scripture* [ed. Stanley E. Porter and Thomas H. Olbricht; JSNTSup 146; Sheffield: Sheffield Academic Press, 1997], 162).

[47] Cf. Acts 4:13. There have been many proposals as how to interpret the phrase ὅτι ἄνθρωποι ἀγράμματοί εἰσιν καὶ ἰδιῶται. First, as a *hapax legomenon* within the New Testament, ἀγράμματοί has been interpreted to mean "uneducated" (Joseph A. Fitzmyer, *Acts of the Apostles* [The Anchor Bible 31; New York: Doubleday, 1998], 302), "unschooled" (Luke Timothy Johnson, *The Acts of the Apostles* [Sacra Pagina 5; Collegeville, Minn.: Liturgical Press, 1992], 78), and a person lacking formal scribal training in the law (C. K. Barrett, *A Critical and Exegetical Commentary of the Acts of the Apostles* [International Critical Commentary; Edinburgh: T & T Clark, 1994], 233–234; cf. Ben Witherington III, The Acts of the Apostles: A Socio-Rhetorical Commentary [Grand Rapids, Mich.: Eerdmans, 1998]: 195–196). However, as pointed out by Barrett, *et al.*, in classical literature, the term ἀγράμματοί primarily denotes one who is illiterate (cf., Xenophon, *Memorabilia* 4.2.20). Thomas J. Kraus, "'Uneducated', 'Ignorant', or

For the purposes of this study, the final and perhaps most profound difficulty in Gerhardsson's thesis is with respect to his envisioned differences between oral and written transmission. Despite the wide chasm between Bultmann and Dibelius' laws of growth and expansion and Gerhardsson's thesis of stability and fixity, one striking similarity rises above their disagreements. Gerhardsson approaches oral transmission from a *textual perspective*. Although he does not seem to be aware of it, his approach is not unlike that of Bultmann, who, as we have already seen, also lacks concern for the differences between the two types of media. Werner Kelber summarizes this observation:

How firmly Gerhardsson saw the oral Torah underwritten by textual authority is manifested by his consistent application of literary terminology to oral speech in such expressions as "oral text," "collections of oral textual material," "oral passages of text," "oral literature," "memory-texts," "repetition-texts," and the like . . . In the end, there exists no substantial difference between the processes of oral versus written transmission: both are empowered by the same mechanism of mechanical memorization.[48]

Kelber is correct to note this trend towards "blurring the lines" between orality and literacy evident throughout *Memory and Manuscript*. There was little if any progress made toward understanding better how oral tradition functioned in the context of early Christian tradition transmission during the time between Bultmann/Dibelius and Gerhardsson. Despite the fundamental difficulties of the early form-critical model of tradition transmission, the model would continue to exert its strong influence upon New Testament studies for the first half of the twentieth century, and its shortcomings would not begin to be addressed until the 1960's.

3.2.3 Summary

As we draw to the close of our brief survey of the early pioneers of form-criticism, we must recognize that many, if not all of the above preconceptions regarding the character of oral tradition and the process of oral transmission were formed *apart from the insight of any significant sociological studies*. More recent sociological and anthropological field work in the area of oral composition and transmission has yielded important information that was not available to the early form-critics and subsequent New Testament scholars. We are now able to critique better

---

Even 'Illiterate?' Aspects and Background for an Understanding of ΑΓΡΑΜΜΑΤΟΙ (and ΙΔΙΩΤΑΙ) in Acts 4.13," *NTS* 45 (1999), 434–449, in his examination the term ἀγράμματοί in Greek documentary papyri, has suggested that the term can be translated as "illiterate" if one does not connect a "modern understanding of illiteracy" with that from the New Testament period ("Uneducated," 441–442). See also Kelber, *Oral and Written Gospel*, 21.

[48] Kelber, *Oral and Written Gospel*, 8.

past scholarship and formulate new theories into the development of the Synoptic Tradition. Subsequently, as we shall see, we must modify and at times abandon many of the early form-critics' concepts of oral tradition and tradition-transmission. Long held concepts such as a "pure" original and equating tradition development with growth and expansion (e.g., Bultmann, Dibelius) must be revisited in light of more sociologically informed studies of orality. Likewise, concepts such as stability and linearity of traditions (e.g., Gerhardsson) must also be questioned. To consider further these and other issues we must we must now turn to the work of Milman Parry and Albert Lord, who represent the transition away from early form-critical Synoptic research to the more sociologically informed post-1960 studies on Synoptic orality.

3.3   Post-1960 Studies on Oral Tradition

3.3.1   Evolution of a Discipline

The recent interest in oral tradition and the study of the "oral mind" by scholars across a wide variety of disciplines, could very well lead one to assume that orality has been at the fore of the discussion for many decades or even centuries. However, this is not the case. As will become evident, the recent interest in orality is a product of the second-half of the twentieth century. The genesis of what is often called the "Parry-Lord theory" can be found in the work of Milman Parry who attempted to determine how an epic was performed by oral poets.[49] His primary question was to determine whether an epic resulted from the performance of a text memorized verbatim, or if the epic was the product of a performance which was created at the time of its delivery. Although interested in the Homeric epic, his quest led him to study the process of epic performance in Yugoslavia due to the absence of an applicable setting in modern-day Greece. Yugoslavia provided Parry with a glimpse into an earlier time in which oral composition was commonplace and thrived within a setting of primary orality.

Parry was the evolutionary link between the traditional understanding of Homer as a literary author in the modern sense of the term, and the contemporary understanding of Homer as an oral composer who worked with a long-standing oral tradition.[50] His work led him to the conclusion

---

[49] See Alan Dundes, preface to *The Theory of Oral Composition* (ed. John Miles Foley; Bloomington: Indiana University Press, 1988), ix.

[50] Interestingly, Josephus (b. 37/38 C.E.) anticipated the revolution that would begin to take place seventeen centuries later among Homeric scholars. He wrote: "Even of that date [of the Greeks' acquisition of literacy] no record, preserved either in temples or on

that the Homeric epics were not originally composed *ex nihilo* by a literary genius, but were performed by an oral poet. Parry's conclusions were profound; Walter Ong credits Parry with the discovery that "virtually every distinctive feature of Homeric poetry is due to the economy enforced on it by oral methods of composition,"[51] and that Homer had stitched together prefabricated parts to form his epic from which only a small percentage of the words therein were not parts of formulas which were a necessary part of oral composition.[52] Parry's fieldwork provided him with the opportunity to apply anthropological insight into the Homeric question, but due to his untimely death in 1935 he was only able to publish one work in which he engaged the results of his Yugoslavian fieldwork.[53] Fortunately, the progress made by Parry was carried forward by his co-worker and at the time, student, Albert B. Lord. Lord had participated with Parry in field research which would later be established as the *Milman Parry Collection of Oral Literature* at Harvard University.

Lord not only continued where Parry left off, but shifted the focus towards a comparative approach between the Serbo-Croatian epic and other oral traditional material. In his most influential work *Singer of Tales* (1960), Lord briefly applied his now fully expressed oral theory to other non-Homeric works such as *Beowulf, La Chanson de Roland, Digenis Akritas*, and as we will see later, further expanded his approach to include the Synoptic Gospels.[54] According to J. M. Foley, the oral theory

---

public monuments, could now be produced; seeing that it is a highly controversial and disputed question whether even those who took part in the Trojan campaign so many years later made use of letters, and the true and prevalent view is rather that they were ignorant of the present-day mode of writing. Throughout the whole range of Greek literature no undisputed work is found more ancient than the poetry of Homer. His date, however, is clearly later than the Trojan war; *and even he, they say, did not leave his poems in writing* [italics mine]" (Josephus, *C. Ap.* 1:11–12; *trans.* Thackeray). Josephus continues to describe how the works of Homer were preserved in songs (i.e., lyric poetry), and put together (συντεθῆναι) at a later stage. According to Josephus, this is why there were a number of variations (τὰς διαφωνίας) in them. It is noteworthy to observe that even in Josephus' time there was speculation over the character of Homer's works and whether they were the product of a literary author, or an oral poet. One must take into account the apologetic purpose of Josephus' account, but nevertheless it is interesting to note that some people in antiquity were interested in the same questions that have been asked by contemporary classicists.

[51] Ong, *Orality and Literacy*, 20–21.

[52] Ong, *Orality and Literacy*, 22–23.

[53] Milman Parry, "Whole Formulaic Verses in Greek and Southslavic Heroic Song," *Transactions of the American Philological Association* 64 (1933): 179–197.

[54] For *Beowulf* see Lord, *Singer of Tales,* 198–202, for *La Chanson de Roland* see Lord, *Singer of Tales,* 202–207, and for *Digenis Akritas* see Lord, *Singer of Tales,* 297–220.

developed by Lord has been applied to no less than one hundred different language traditions.[55] Foley describes fifteen hundred of the eighteen hundred bibliographic entries in his *Oral-Formulaic Theory and Research: An Introduction and Annotated Bibliography* as "stem[ing] directly from the work of Parry and Lord."[56] It is appropriate to conclude that the vast majority of current work on oral epic composition is directly attributable to the work of Parry and Lord.

What is most important for the discipline of New Testament research is that, for the first time since Bultmann and Dibelius, true progress was made regarding fundamental questions of tradition formation and transmission. Lord's field research in the former Yugoslavia provided important data, the analysis of which would provide valuable insight into the Synoptic Tradition. No longer would presuppositions and assumptions regarding the oral character of the Synoptic Tradition be based on pure speculation or predominantly German folktales. The findings of such research prove to be profound: the assumptions and "laws of transmission" first posited by the form-critics can no longer stand without substantial correction or abandonment. A brief summary of Lord's findings will allow us to critique better the work of Bultmann, Dibelius, and Gerhardsson, and also provide us with a means for evaluating more recent work in the field.

3.3.2   The Contribution of Albert Lord

Lord's extensive field work enabled him to make detailed observations regarding the process of oral composition of epic poetry. He demonstrated that oral epic performance was not the delivery of a memorized text,[57] but rather it was a process by which traditional formulas employing mnemonic devices were presented via a "reflexive action."[58] The discovery of "formulas" used in composition led to the coining of the term "Oral-Formulaic Theory" to describe this process of composition-in-performance.

Lord observed that the performer makes use of set phrases that assist in the performance of any given song. These set phrases form the vocabulary from which the singer can draw inspiration and ultimately utilize in

---

[55] John Miles Foley, *The Theory of Oral Composition: History and Methodology* (Bloomington: Indiana University Press, 1988), 57.

[56] Foley, *Oral Composition*, xiii.

[57] Albert B. Lord, "The Gospels as Oral Traditional Literature," in *The Relationships Among the Gospels: An Interdisciplinary Dialogue* (ed. William O. Walker Jr.; San Antonio: Trinity University Press, 1978), 37.

[58] Albert B. Lord, "Memory, Fixity, and Genre in Oral Traditional Poetries," in *Oral Traditional Literature: A Festschrift for Albert Bates Lord* (ed. John Miles Foley; Ohio: Slavica Publishers, 1980), 451.

performance. The verbal content of a performance is not planned out in meticulous detail like a well-crafted written piece of literature, but is composed spontaneously as it is performed.[59] In this setting, musical accompaniment was required to enable the poet (performer) to maintain a sense of rhythm and flow.[60]

Lord's insight into the process of oral performance can be very helpful for understanding the character of the Synoptic Tradition. Of the many questions raised by Lord's work, his research forces us to question the search for the *ipsissima verba Jesu* that is at the very center of much contemporary third-quest historical Jesus research.[61] The concept of a "pure form" (*reinen Gattung*) of Jesus material is a *leitmotif* that runs through all of the early form-critical work on the Gospels. While our attention is quickly drawn towards the early form-critics such as Bultmann and Dibelius,[62] we must recognize that Gerhardsson also argued for the existence of a pure form of Jesus material which was consciously preserved by the early Jesus movement. He felt that the formal process of tradition-transmission was capable of preserving the *ipsissima verba Jesu* which would then be consciously memorized and studied. For Gerhardsson, this was possible, in part, to the existence of eyewitnesses who could hold others accountable for the correct transmission of the received tradition.[63] In this envisioned scenario, an *active or conscious* process of transmission guaranteed that important material would not be forgotten nor transmitted incorrectly.

Lord has argued that the modern concept of a "word for word and line for line" rendition is foreign to those who live in a predominantly oral

---

[59] It is important to note that this process of "improvisation" (as it is often described) can be misleading. The performer does not simply "make up" the song as he/she goes along, but is drawing from a pre-existing collection of phrases and content. Thus, the performer functions within a structure that insures the relative stability of tradition, and the performance is "by its very nature traditional" (Culley, "Approach," 121).

[60] Lord, *Singer of Tales,* 126, observes that even without the aid of musical accompaniment a singer could dictate an oral composition to a scribe but in doing so, the composition was affected. Forcing an oral poet to perform outside of a traditional musical setting would result in "a mixture of prose and verse, parts of verses interspersed with parts of prose sentences and *vice versa*."

[61] This approach is typified by the work of the Jesus Seminar; see Funk and Hoover, *Five Gospels.*

[62] See Dibelius, *Tradition to Gospel,* 143, 240 and Bultmann, *Synoptic Tradition,* 6 for their concept of "original form."

[63] Gerhardsson, *Memory and Manuscript,* 280. Gerhardsson's reference to eyewitnesses was preceded by both Vincent Taylor — "eyewitness preservation" (*The Formation of the Gospel Tradition* [London: Macmillan & Co., 1933], 208), and Dibelius — "relative trustworthiness" due to eyewitnesses (*Tradition to Gospel,* 61–62, 293).

milieu,[64] and that "oral traditional narrative . . . has no fixed original."[65] In this case, the performance of a tradition is not the verbatim reproduction of previously memorized material, but rather a fresh "re-creation"[66] of the story on every occasion. Lord comes to this conclusion based upon his study of multiple retellings of the same story by one individual. In each case, the retelling of a story was a unique one-time creation and never repeated verbatim. After presenting three versions of the *Song of Baghdad* sung by Salih Ugljanin, Lord concludes that,

Salih had not memorized this passage. He remembered, unconsciously, the elements that make it up and, to some extent, the order of the elements . . . Not memorized, not improvised either, not even exactly repeated, but presented in "more or less the same words," while expressing the same essential ideas. The text is not really fixed, yet because the essential ideas have remained constant, it is "more or less fixed."[67]

---

[64] Lord recounts a conversation with a singer who claimed he could listen to a song and after an hour he could "give every word and not make a mistake on a single one . . ." Upon further questioning, the same singer said that "if I were to live for twenty years, I would sing the song which I sang for you here today just the same twenty years from now, word for word." Lord demonstrates that their concept of "word for word, and line for line" is in reality a foreign concept for people of a predominantly oral culture. They "do not know what words and lines are" (Lord, *Singer of Tales*, 26–28). This is illustrated by the observation that though the singers do not achieve "word for word" accuracy when re-performing traditions, they nevertheless claim to be able to do so. Lord demonstrated that is was due, in part, to the concept of the term "word" among the oral performers of Yugoslavia. John Miles Foley, *How to Read an Oral Poem* (Chicago: University of Illinois, 2002), 17-18 elucidates this matter further, and writes: "[f]or the three *guslari* [singers] a *reč* [word] is not a string of black letters bounded by white spaces or something enshrined in a dictionary, but rather a unified utterance — never as small and partial as what we mean by a word but large and complete enough to have idiomatic force as a speech-act. Thus a phrase that occupies a regular section of the ten-syllable line, like 'he/she was drinking wine,' qualifies as a functional vocabulary item within the language of epic singing." The claim to have the ability to reproduce traditions "verbatim" is due to the performer's concept of "words." Foley suggests that oral performers "think and compose with these 'bigger words'," and that this must play a significant role in the process of interpretation and the attempt to derive meaning from performances (*How to Read*, 18) .

[65] Lord, "Gospels," 37.

[66] Leander E. Keck, "Oral Traditional Literature and the Gospels: The Seminar," in *The Relationships Among the Gospels: An Interdisciplinary Dialogue* (ed. William O. Walker Jr.; San Antonio: Trinity University Press, 1978), 120. Also Culley, "Approach," 119–120: "A fixed text is not recited but the work is created anew each time it is performed. Traditional oral literature of various kinds is transmitted by this process in which the essential outline of the work and many or all of the details are repeated but never in exactly the same way."

[67] Lord, "Memory, Fixity," 453.

His work forces one to question the usefulness of the concept of an "original form," and subsequently to ask whether the *ipsissima verba Jesu* sought after by many scholars is attainable.[68]

Lord's work also has implications regarding the development of the Jesus tradition. Bultmann and Dibelius both worked with what Werner Kelber describes as an "evolutionary model" of tradition transmission.[69] They believed that early "pure forms" evolved and grew as they were repeatedly transmitted throughout the early Christian communities. As we noted previously, this concept of a linear progression from simplicity to complexity was a foundational assumption of the form-critical method. Lord addresses this important question in his research and concludes that, "if we are dealing with oral traditional literature, it is not *necessarily* true that the longer text is later than the shorter, although it may be."[70] Each re-creation of a story can result in *either* expansion or contraction.[71] There is no universal direction or tendency within the tradition that can be attributable to the oral traditioning process of tradition formation.[72] Although Gerhardsson did not agree with the early form-critical assumptions regarding growth and expansion, he did envisage a linear, continuous, fixed process of tradition transmission that must be questioned given Lord's work on oral performance.

Lord's study of the process of oral composition and performance also has had an important impact on the early form-critics' understanding of the pre-Synoptic grouping of the Jesus tradition. Bultmann and Dibelius both concluded that the oral traditions concerning Jesus circulated in an independent and isolated state.[73] This was a natural corollary to their understanding of linear growth and expansion. If the material originated as

---

[68] This of course raises other questions; among many is the question regarding the "first performance" of any particular saying by Jesus himself. There was indeed a "first" time that Jesus uttered any saying or parable, but how does this help us with our understanding of the early, oral origins of the tradition? Hypothetically speaking, could not Jesus' one-hundredth retelling of a story more closely fit our criteria for authenticity than, let us say, his first telling of the same story? If so, then our observations regarding the "re-creation" of traditions must impact upon our understanding of the early Jesus tradition. Why are we still attempting to discover "authenticity" when, according to Lord's research, we cannot even speak of an "original" version?

[69] Kelber, *Oral and Written Gospel,* 191.

[70] Lord, "Gospels," 42.

[71] Lord comes to this conclusion based upon his oral-traditional study of the Synoptic Gospels. See Lord, "Gospels," 90.

[72] While Sanders' *Tendencies* was an attempt to question the early form-critical "laws" of tradition transmission (see above, ch. 2), from an "oral tradition perspective," one should not expect there to be any type of overall, universal direction or tendency within the Synoptic Tradition.

[73] Dibelius, *Tradition to Gospel,* 156, 178.

disjointed, isolated sayings, then it is possible to argue for the tendency toward growth and expansion simply by looking at the Synoptic Gospels themselves — the mere existence of a connected, relatively orderly narrative would be evidence of such tendencies. But, on the other hand, if the individual stories originally circulated within larger groupings of material, then the whole notion of growth and expansion becomes more difficult to support for the tradition itself took its earliest form as a structured performance sequence. This is another area in which the research of Lord has benefited our understanding of the character of the oral tradition itself. He has demonstrated that the primary compositional unit of orally transmitted material was not the abstract, isolated saying, but a *block*, or *sequence* of material.[74] Units were interconnected together from the very beginning stages of the tradition. Isolated proverbs and wisdom sayings were always incorporated within blocks, or sections of material.

3.3.3 Subsequent Studies on Orality

As seen above, the comparative approach of Lord was based upon observed oral performances and the dictation of epics among the former Yugoslavian people. Some more recent works that are indebted to Lord and Parry have taken the next logical step; to relate what we know about oral tradition and transmission to the larger perspective of how the "oral mind" functions.[75] These studies, which begin from a more sociological/anthropological perspective attempt to place the study of oral tradition within the larger context of its relationship with that of textuality.

Walter Ong has been perhaps the most visible proponent of this type of approach. His *Orality and Literacy* continues to have a major impact on various disciplines. While not in itself a work in Biblical Studies, it has had a profound impact on the field of New Testament research. *Orality and Literacy* represents a departure from Lord's strict analysis of specific epic traditions to a more widely applicable psychology of orality and literacy. His attempt is helpful in that he seeks to describe over-arching principles of oral communication that transcend chronological time and cultural distinctions. Ong's primary thrust is twofold. 1) He attempts to create a cohesive account of the psychodynamics at work in individuals who have not been influenced by the introduction of literacy into their societies.[76] According to Ong, an individual lacking any exposure to literacy communicates in a radically different manner than does a literate

---

[74] Lord, "Gospels," 59.

[75] See below, ch. 5 for more specifics on the "oral mind" of antiquity.

[76] See Ong, *Orality and Literacy*, 31–77 for his chapter entitled "Some Psychodynamics of Orality."

person. Memory and verbal communication, among other things, function in a significantly different manner. The operative principles of our literate world do not necessarily apply in the world of non-literacy.[77] 2) Ong also presents what he considers to be the effects of the transition from the world of "primary orality"[78] to that of "secondary orality."[79] These transitional effects are powerful and permanent. Once an individual has been introduced to literacy, there can be no return to his or her pre-literate existence.[80]

[Humans are] beings whose thought processes do not grow out of simply natural powers but out of these powers as structured, directly or indirectly, by the technology of writing. Without writing, the literate mind would not and could not think as it does, not only when engaged in writing but normally even when it is composing its thoughts in oral form. More than any other single invention, writing has transformed human consciousness.[81]

The transformative effects of literacy have profound effects upon how our mind works and functions. His proposed principles are wide-ranging and cover the entire spectrum of human experience. For Ong, literacy has a dramatic impact upon all human communication and thought processes.

---

[77] In terms of the early Jesus tradition, this observation forces one to consider the extent to which current literary methods of analysis and interpretation are applicable to our study of the Synoptic Gospels. If the Gospels are highly oral in character, then a strictly literary approach to the tradition imposes an inappropriate interpretative framework upon the tradition. Werner Kelber echoes this concern, and subsequently wrote his book "out of a concern for what seemed to me a disproportionately print-oriented hermeneutic in our study of the Bible" (*Oral and Written Gospel*, xv).

[78] Ong, *Orality and Literacy*, 6, defines "primary orality" as a culture comprised "of persons totally unfamiliar with writing."

[79] "Secondary orality" essentially describes our present culture. Ong writes, ". . . at the same time, with telephone, radio, television and various kinds of sound tape, electronic technology has brought us into the age of 'secondary orality' . . . it is essentially a more deliberate and self-conscious orality, based permanently on the use of writing and print, which are essential for the manufacture and operation of the equipment and for its use as well" (*Orality and Literacy*, 136).

[80] Ong is indebted to the foundational work of Havelock on the transition from orality to literacy. Havelock's work on Plato and the development of the alphabet has led him to conclude that the development of the technology of the alphabet (which in his estimation is an invention of the Greeks ca. 700 B.C.E., *Literate Revolution*, 15) is the impetus which gave rise to higher conceptual thought processes and "modern" history. He writes, "The true parent of history was not any one 'writer' like Herodotus, but the alphabet itself. Oral memory deals primarily with the present; it collects and recollects what is being done now or is appropriate to the present situation" (*Literate Revolution*, 23). Modern philosophy and other abstract forms of thought are only possible in a post-alphabetic culture which has sufficiently incorporated written language into its cultural ethos. For Havelock, the shift from orality to literacy is profound and transformative in every way.

[81] Ong, *Orality and Literacy*, 78.

Since the early Jesus tradition was both "born and raised" within a culture of high residual orality, and at the same time subject to the powerful influence of literacy, what consequences does that have for the Jesus tradition? If we study orally composed material in the same way that we would study a written text, then we are in danger of misinterpreting the tradition, and likely to draw improper inferences from the material.[82]

Contemporary New Testament studies on the oral foundations of the Jesus tradition must consider the work of Ong and that of his successors who have emphasized the complex cultural milieu in which all the New Testament documents were written. The primary oral setting of the first century C.E. demands that we re-evaluate the process of tradition development and transmission in the early Christian church. As we now look to evaluate more recent work on the oral origins of the Synoptic material, we must do so with respect to the foundational work of Lord and Ong.

3.3.4   Charles Lohr (1961)

In the same year that Gerhardsson's *Memory and Manuscript* was published (1961), Charles Lohr wrote "Oral Techniques in the Gospel of Matthew."[83] Lohr was the first scholar to apply the newly developed oral theory to a study of the New Testament Gospels.[84] His work is illustrative, for the weaknesses therein reveal that it would take many years before the impact of the oral theory would have its full effect upon the study of the Synoptic Gospels. Many of Lohr's difficulties stem from the fact that the application of the oral theory upon varied disciplines was still in its infancy and did not have the chance to impact fully New Testament research.

Throughout Lohr's article he refers to the term "oral literature" to describe a body of orally transmitted material.[85] As we suggested above in

---

[82] As previously noted, this fundamental concept of the distinction between oral and literary compositional processes eluded Bultmann, Dibelius, and Gerhardsson.

[83] Lohr, "Oral Techniques," 403–435.

[84] See Foley, *Oral Composition*, 84.

[85] Lohr, "Oral Techniques," 411–412, 408–409, 414, 425. Lohr does not seem to be aware of the difficulty in using such a term. For a more recent use of the term "text" see David E. Aune, "Prolegomena to the Study of Oral Tradition in the Hellenistic World," in *Jesus and the Oral Gospel Tradition* (ed. Henry Wansbrough; JSNTSup 64; Sheffield: JSOT Press, 1991), 97. Robert Culley uses the term "oral text" several times in his work ("Approach," 115, 117), and then acknowledges the "contradiction" in using such terms to describe the subject of his study ("Approach," 118). Culley discusses the work of Bascom, "Verbal Art," 248, who suggests that the term "verbal art" be adopted when referring to orally composed/transmitted material. The term "art" seems to be a rather

chapter two, this is more than just a question of semantics. The indiscriminate use of the term "text" when referring to a body of orally composed/performed material can betray a lack of sensitivity toward the different dynamics at work in the formation of material within both mediums. In the case of Gerhardsson, we noted that the indiscriminate use of the term "text" revealed his lack of sensitivity to the dynamics of oral performance and how the medium itself might have exerted influence upon the development of the Jesus tradition. We now note that the same difficulty is also evident in Lohr's work.

Lohr argues that Matthew's "grouping together like materials is most obvious in Mt's collection of . . . the sayings of the Lord into five extensive sermons, each marked by the same formula, 'When Jesus had finished this discourse' (7:28; 11:1; 13:53; 19:1; 26:1)."[86] Lohr attributes this grouping to Matthew's use of oral compositional techniques — "It is very clear that these discourses have not simply grown; they have been built up by design, and stamped each with a character of its own, determined by its place in Mt's outline."[87] While Lohr is correct in recognizing Matthew's grouping of material into various discourses, his work suffers from the inference he draws from such an observation. Lohr suggests that the grouping is the result of oral composition techniques, but he is most likely pointing out the redactional grouping of the various sayings traditions within the gospel. Editorial arrangement of passages, or as Lohr writes, "its place in Mt's outline," is not evidence of oral techniques of composition. Rather, these passages, cited by Lohr, represent a more visual approach to organization than would be expected in an orally organized piece of tradition, and are most likely products of editorial activity. Eric Havelock considers this characteristic of textuality to be "language managed visually on architectural principles."[88] The linearity and temporal functions of the redactional work of Matthew are not themselves products nor indicators of oral transmission.[89]

Lohr continues to misunderstand the process behind the development of the Synoptic Tradition. He argues that Mark failed to retain traditional

---

peculiar way to describe the early Jesus tradition, so, understandably, the term "verbal art" has not won many, if any, converts.

[86] Lohr, "Oral Techniques," 421.

[87] Lohr, "Oral Techniques," 421.

[88] Havelock, *Literate Revolution*, 9.

[89] Chronological flow and progression are characteristics sought after by moderns who have been exposed to the organizational abilities of a text. Even if an oral performer desired to deliver a chronologically "accurate" account he would most likely not succeed — "If he were to try to proceed in strict chronological order, the oral poet would on any given occasion be sure to leave out one or another episode at the point where it should fit chronologically and would have to put it in later on" (Ong, *Orality and Literacy*, 143).

compositional techniques. His evidence for this view is his observation that "Mt made a skillful use of the devices of oral style to assure the continuity and interconnection of the materials of his Gospel. By carefully arranging the elements of the narrative he has made them all serve a single purpose."[90] Once again this "careful arranging" of the elements has its origins in a more redactional-literary technique than an oral-compositional technique. Lohr then concludes that Mark's "little concern for unity of style and over-all arrangement" is the reason that Mark "failed" and subsequently Matthew returns to a more "traditional manner of composition."[91] His view of Mark "failing" to retain traditional compositional techniques is misguided. The "little concern for unity of style and over-all arrangement" is proof of *precisely the opposite* of what Lohr wants to demonstrate.[92] What he observes in Mark is actually evidence of the higher residual orality of Mark as distinguished from the more literary Matthew. Matthew is indicative of the greater time span between the oral origins of the text and the later literate productions of the early Christians. Once again, Lohr's work reminds us of the fundamental misunderstanding of the oral compositional process that was responsible for the development and transmission of the Jesus tradition. While Lohr's attempt was informed by the principles of the so-called oral theory, he did not grasp fully its implications for the Synoptic Tradition. In sum, Lohr approached oral tradition from a fully textual perspective and assumed that Matthew *edited* his oral traditional material as he would have edited a text.

3.3.5 Ernest Abel (1971)

Abel begins his article "The Psychology of Memory and Rumor Transmission and Their Bearing on Theories of Oral Transmission in Early Christianity"[93] with a perceptive critique of the early form-critics such as Bultmann and Dibelius along with members of the "Scandinavian school" such as Riesenfeld and Gerhardsson. He notes that the discrepancies (i.e., inconsistencies) within the Synoptic Tradition do not seem to be compatible with "a rigidly controlled school for oral transmission"[94] as

---

[90] Lohr, "Oral Techniques," 434.

[91] Lohr, "Oral Techniques," 434.

[92] Ong writes that a "consciously contrived narrative" is not the result of oral composition, but rather is a product of today's "literate and typographic culture[s]" (*Orality and Literacy*, 141).

[93] Ernest L. Abel, "The Psychology of Memory and Rumor Transmission and Their Bearing on Theories of Oral Transmission in Early Christianity," *Journal of Religion* 51 (1971): 270–281.

[94] It is necessary to note that an assumption that oral tradition functioned only within a "rigidly controlled school of oral transmission" is just as mistaken as assuming that all

envisaged by Riesenfeld and Gerhardsson.[95] Although Abel's critique of Riesenfeld and Gerhardsson is valid, he does not deal with the more important issue of these inconsistencies and their importance for evaluating the potential level of "residual orality" within a text. Inconsistencies are not only helpful for questioning the thesis of Gerhardsson, but can be an important factor in determining the extent to which a text is orally influenced.

Inconsistencies within a communicative work result from the dynamic tension between the aural and visual senses. The aural character of orally performed material is a most elementary observation but deserves treatment nonetheless. Havelock reminds us that oral communication *ipso facto* is composed with the aid of the mouth.[96] This fundamental characteristic of oral communication is also the source of the medium's greatest weakness. Once a spoken word fades to silence it no longer exists.[97] Unless a word is spoken anew, it cannot be returned to for verification or confirmation. In an oral setting, the message is delivered and then disappears forever. This is in contrast to the visual word which once inscribed on a writing medium can be reviewed and revisited at any time. Given these differences, it is only natural that the frequency and severity of inconsistencies within a text will vary according to the medium in which it was composed. Therefore, inconsistencies within our extant Gospel texts are to be expected given the oral origins of the tradition itself. Extreme concern for coherence and consistency only develops after a collection of material has had sufficient time to develop and be transmitted

---

texts were fixed and stable. See Larry W. Hurtado, "The Gospel of Mark: Evolutionary or Revolutionary Document?," in *The Synoptic Gospels: A Sheffield Reader* (ed. Craig A. Evans and Stanley E. Porter; Sheffield: Sheffield Academic Press, 1995), 200 for his observation that texts were not "fixed" in the proper sense of the term until after the Gutenberg printing press.

[95] Abel, "Psychology," 272. Harald Riesenfeld, *The Gospel Tradition* (Philadelphia: Fortress Press, 1970), 74 attributed the inconsistencies within the tradition to the dynamic tension between 1) The firm elements of tradition, and 2) The evangelist's intention from a theological point of view to edit and systematize the material handed down.

[96] Apart from the physical apparatus of the human vocal cords, lungs, mouth, tongue, etc., no oral communication can take place. As air passes over the vocal cords they produce a "vibrating column of air which is also started or stopped . . . by the action of lips, palate, tongue, and teeth" (Havelock, *Literate Revolution*, 80).

[97] Ong illustrates this "temporary" quality of vocal speech with an analogy between sound and image. He argues that a fixed image can still be viewed, but if a sound is stopped, the result is silence (*Orality and Literacy*, 32). Despite Ong's fallacious analogy (both sound and light are in reality both waves which, unless generated continuously, do not project either sound or an image), he illustrates his point nonetheless — oral communication is based upon the temporary characteristic of verbal speech.

within the sphere of textuality.[98] Since neither the sender nor the receiver of an orally transmitted tradition has the ability to go back and review or "scan" an oral performance, a performance is likely to retain inconsistencies or errors that might have been removed otherwise.[99]

Abel also devotes a small section of his article to the applicability of modern psychological studies in understanding the oral transmission of the Jesus tradition. He validates the use of these wide-ranging oral-formulaic studies due to the fact that they were "conducted with different material and under varying circumstances, the results of each are basically in accord, indicating that they are indeed dealing with basic psychological processes as relevant today as they would be in first-century Christianity."[100] Of course, the observation that the contemporary studies are "in accord" with on another does not necessarily lead to the conclusion that they are applicable for our research. As is probably apparent by now, we feel that contemporary studies on orality are applicable to our area of interest, but we must not minimize the danger of anachronism that threatened the thesis of Gerhardsson.[101] What makes contemporary studies on orality applicable is not only the fact that their results are in accord with one another, but also, more significantly, that the studies have been conducted among peoples who still retain a high level of residual orality. The similar results of these highly diverse studies suggests that what is being described is an oral-traditioning process that to a large extent transcends ethnic, cultural, and religious boundaries.[102] Cultures that

---

[98] This process can help explain why there was an increasing attempt to smooth out differences and inconsistencies within the Jesus tradition over time. As the Jesus tradition became increasingly evaluated as a *text*, the visual process of scanning had profound effects upon the tradition itself. Continual scanning of a text would enable a reader to pick out discrepancies and inconsistencies within a text which would not be noticed during an oral performance. This same tendency affects all readers and students of the New Testament (or any other work of literature). It would be very unlikely that the inconsistencies within any given gospel would be "discovered" following the *initial* reading of the text. It is only after repeated re-readings that the discrepancies come to the surface. Therefore, it would not be difficult to imagine the process of visual scanning leading to the production of gospel harmonies such as Tatian's Diatesseron.

[99] Jack Goody, *The Domestication of the Savage Mind* (Cambridge: Cambridge University Press, 1977), 128. Goody discusses the process of visual "scanning" which is enabled by the visual examination of a physical text.

[100] Abel, "Psychology," 272.

[101] Later we will discuss the difference between Gerhardsson's use of rabbinic sources and recent New Testament scholarship's use of twentieth century sociological research.

[102] For more on this see below, ch. 5.

develop apart from the great influence of literacy and remain highly oral are not prone to rapid change and cultural progress.[103]

Abel correctly disagrees with the early form-critics' concept of the evolutionary development of the Synoptic Tradition, arguing that it is based upon the observation of how the apocryphal gospels compare to the Synoptics (esp. Mark), and in turn, how the Synoptics might compare to the oral tradition that preceded them.[104] He then labels this progression as "(a) the assumption that the changes which are likely to occur in oral transmission are viewed as similar to those which occur in the written documents, and (b) the idea that the added details in the written tradition are regarded as fanciful."[105] It is interesting then to note that Abel embraces Vincent Taylor's concept of the tradition becoming smaller and losing details over time.[106] Although Abel is quick to critique early form-critical assumptions regarding the tendency of the tradition, his thesis suffers from the same difficulty of linearity; he has just turned the linearity in the opposite direction to that of the "general tendency of the tradition" argued by Bultmann and Dibelius. Linearity, as we have already discussed is not the norm in oral communication, but rather oscillation, or in Kelber's colorful words, oral tradition is "a pulsating phenomenon, expanding and contracting, waxing and waning, progressing and regressing. Its general behavior is not unlike that of the stock market, rising and subsiding at more or less unpredictable intervals, and curiously interwoven with social and political realities".[107]

In his conclusion, Abel makes clear that he does not fully realize the oral theory's implications for any attempt to determine the authentic, verbatim words of Jesus. He still seeks the "authenticity of the material"[108] when perhaps the best we can hope to achieve is chronological proximity to the time of Jesus' ministry.

---

[103] See Ong, *Orality and Literacy*, 41. He appeals to the "conservative or traditionalist" state of the oral mind. Cultures of high orality must remain non-progressive in their thought processes or else they risk the chance of forgetting or losing "what has been learned arduously over the ages" (Ong, *Orality and Literacy*, 41). Gerhardsson notes this same tendency in the educational processes of early Rabbinic Judaism, see *Memory and Manuscript*, 77. Also, see Jack Goody and Ian Watt, "The Consequences of Literacy," in *Literacy in Traditional Societies* (ed. Jack Goody; Cambridge: Cambridge University Press, 1968), 30–34.

[104] Abel, "Psychology," 275.

[105] Abel, "Psychology," 275.

[106] Abel, "Psychology," 275–277.

[107] Kelber, *Oral and Written Gospel*, 32.

[108] Abel, "Psychology," 280–281.

Abel also addressed the question of genre that developed from his psychological studies of African culture.[109] While it is important to focus on "rumor transmission," he does not examine other genres such as parable, proverb, etc., and ask whether or not his findings are applicable to these forms as well.

Abel is to be commended for his attempt to integrate sociological insights into the discussion on gospel formation, but in the end his work leaves several questions unanswered. We are led to ask whether the process of "rumor transmission" best reflects the way in which the Jesus tradition was transmitted in its earliest forms. Does the genre "rumor story" provide us with an accurate means to classify the majority of the Jesus tradition? We must ask if there maybe another genre which might give us a more well-balanced insight into the question of early Christian tradition transmission. Although we will explore these questions in a later chapter, it will suffice to suggest at this point that the model envisioned by Abel is not adequate given the recent advances in oral studies. It is once again clear that the newly developed oral theory had not sufficiently impacted New Testament scholarship, including that of Abel himself.

3.3.6 Albert Lord (1978)

We will not spend much time surveying Lord's specific contribution to the Synoptic Problem for the previous summary of his contribution highlights the important findings of his research and, in addition, we will interact with Lord's thesis in more detail later.[110] What we will do here though, is elucidate the more important contributions that Lord makes to our discussion based upon his study of the Synoptic Problem. In his "The Gospels as Oral Traditional Literature," Lord takes a fresh approach to the question of the Synoptic Problem. His insight is valuable because of his ability to study the Synoptic Gospels without any preconceived notions of interdependency or textual interrelationships.[111]

---

[109] Abel, "Psychology," 276.

[110] See below, §5.4.

[111] Keck, "Oral Traditional Literature," 105, in his summary of the seminar writes, "Lord could do what professional students of the New Testament cannot do but often wish they could: read the texts as though they had just discovered them with no staked-out positions to defend." Keck goes on to write, "In short, the seminar provided a probably unprecedented opportunity for New Testament students to test what they think they know about oral tradition and the Gospels" (Keck, "Oral Traditional Literature," 105).

Lord argues that the Synoptic Gospels are "three oral traditional variants of the same narrative and non-narrative materials".[112] His preliminary observations are that

The fragmentation [of sequence] would seem to indicate that the third gospel [the one not in agreement] does not recognize the passage in the other two as a unit but does know the elements of the passage. On the other hand, the correspondences in two or more of the Gospels are an indication that the relevant passage was recognized as a unit by more than one of the gospel writers. One would be tempted to conclude that the relationship among the Gospels was one of written documents were it not for two decisive phenomena. First, there are many instances where elements of a sequence are scattered sporadically in one or more Gospels. Second, there is less verbal correspondence than I would expect in a manuscript tradition. I find it unusual for a writer to choose passages from several documentary sources as if from a buffet.[113]

Throughout his paper, Lord highlights many important characteristics of orally performed material that are important for a proper understanding of the pre-textual origins of the Jesus tradition. Of his observations, several derive from his earlier *Singer of Tales* and are presented by way of summary: 1) There is no "fixed original" in oral traditional "literature," but each retelling "is in reality composition of the same story by someone else in the tradition".[114] 2) The shorter form of a tradition is not in itself evidence of the "comparative age of any given text."[115] 3) The gospels contain "several instances of duplication of multiforms" which are "peculiarly an oral traditional phenomenon."[116]

In addition to the above three points, Lord discusses what, for our purposes, is a vital question. As was the case with Ernest Abel, Lord recognizes that genre is one of the key issues in the oral traditioning process. He alludes to the role of genre in determining the stability of traditions — "One might ask whether a *fixed* unwritten or oral original is

---

[112] Lord, "Gospels," 90.

[113] Lord, "Gospels," 59–60.

[114] Lord, "Gospels," 37. Also, cf. Lord, *Singer of Tales*, 99–123.

[115] Lord, "Gospels," 44. Lord presents a hypothetical story to illustrate this point: "Envisage, if you will, a tradition of return songs that open with the prisoner shouting in his dungeon. A singer, who knows a song about the capture of a hero on his wedding night, at one time began his return story with the narrative of an attack and capture. Other singers continued to tell the return story without a preceding account of capture. In this case, therefore, there are texts without the capture that are later than texts with it" (Lord, "Gospels," 43). Lord also gives an example of the possibility of a longer tradition being shortened because it was no longer relevant to the story as a whole; see Lord, "Gospels," 43.

[116] Among Lord's examples of these multiform traditions are "the appointing, commissioning, and reporting of the seventy in Luke bears the hallmark of a duplication of the similar actions or passages concerning the Twelve," and also the "striking multiforms of the healing of blind men" ("Gospels," 90).

possible . . . it is possible for short forms in oral tradition, such as incantations, riddles, proverbs, or sayings, to be comparatively stable, if not actually 'fixed'."[117] Lord recognizes that genre is an obvious, but often overlooked aspect of tradition transmission. This is a question which we will address in a later chapter.[118]

3.3.7 Werner Kelber (1983)

Werner Kelber has written more extensively than any other New Testament scholar on the question of oral tradition and the Gospels.[119] His work is heavily influenced by contemporary studies on orality, in particular that of Walter Ong.[120] Kelber wrote his book out of "a concern for what seemed to me a disproportionately print-oriented hermeneutic in our study of the Bible,"[121] and spends the remainder of his book "uncovering" the oral character of Mark which, in his view, has been obscured over the last two-thousand years on account of the "literate revolution" that has transformed and forever changed how human beings think and interact with their surroundings. According to Kelber, "Mark's writing manifests a transmutation more than mere transmission."[122]

In chapter five of his *Oral and Written Gospel*, Kelber addresses what he labels "textuality as disorientation."[123] The "oral legacy has been deracinated and transplanted into a linguistic construct that has lost touch with the living, oral matrix" in which "[s]ayings and stories are rescued, but at the price of their transportation into and, we shall see, transformation by a foreign medium."[124] In emphasizing the transformation of oral tradition by its incorporation into a text, Kelber does not take into serious account the dynamic interaction between orality *and* textuality at work in the culture within which the gospel of Mark was composed, even though he is fully aware of this phenomenon.[125] Joanna Dewey and others have critiqued Kelber on this very point, arguing that Kelber's view of

---

[117] Lord, "Gospels," 37.

[118] For more on the question of genre and how it affects our approach to the Synoptic Tradition see below, §5.4.

[119] Among Kelber's many works in the area of oral tradition and the New Testament are "Mark and Oral Tradition," *Semeia* 16 (1980), *Oral and Written Gospel,* and "From Aphorism to Sayings Gospel and from Parable to Narrative Gospel," *Foundations & Facets Forum* 1 (1985).

[120] Ong contributed the preface to Kelber's *Oral and Written Gospel*, and Kelber relies heavily on Ong for his understanding of the dynamics between orality and literacy.

[121] Kelber, *Oral and Written Gospel,* xv.

[122] Kelber, *Oral and Written Gospel,* 91.

[123] Kelber, *Oral and Written Gospel,* 91–105.

[124] Kelber, *Oral and Written Gospel,* 91.

[125] Kelber, *Oral and Written Gospel,* 15.

"radical discontinuity" must be modified due to the "overlap between orality and textuality"[126] that existed for a period of many centuries and which, according to Ong, extended into the seventeenth century.[127]

Ultimately, Kelber goes to great lengths to demonstrate that the author of Mark intentionally created his gospel as a "countersign" to the oral gospel being transmitted throughout early Christian circles,[128] and that Mark's negative view of the disciples is indicative of his antagonism towards oral authorities, or the "guarantors of the tradition."[129] Kelber argues that the destruction of the Jewish temple in 70 C.E. was the impetus that led to the creation of the Gospel of Mark. The loss of "the center" led to "awakening doubts about oral, heroic christology and distrust toward oral authorities."[130] We agree with Kelber's assessment of the importance of the Jewish War for the creation of Mark, but must differ with his interpretation of significance of the event. It is more likely that the Jewish War led Mark to write his gospel to *preserve* the tradition, not to counteract and transform it. Given the breakdown in the local communal life which resulted from the destruction of Jerusalem, the traditional societal structures in which the oral Jesus tradition circulated would have been destroyed. In regard to Mark's negative view of the "guarantors of the tradition," if one accepts that the text of Mark would have been read aloud to congregations and therefore received in the form of an oral re-telling, then one must attempt to account for Mark's motives and intentions when writing his account.

If we follow Kelber's thesis regarding the creation of the Gospel of Mark, we are confronted by a paradox that seems difficult to explain. According to Kelber, Mark's animosity towards the disciples reflects his attempt to discredit them as "oral authorities" of the gospel. Kelber also suggests that Mark "shunned" the "oral legacy" by inscribing his gospel,[131] and demonstrated his hostility toward the sayings traditions[132] by *not* incorporating them in his gospel as extensively as did Matthew and Luke

---

[126] Dewey, "Oral Methods," 33.

[127] Havelock, *Literate Revolution*, 10 argues that the "intimate partnership between oral and written practice" continued for at least three hundred years after the development of literacy among the Greeks. He dates literacy to approximately 430–400 B.C.E. to correspond with the "introduction of letters at the primary level of schooling" (Havelock, *Literate Revolution*, 27). Ong notes that residual orality existed until the seventeenth century. He uses the 1610 Douay Version of Gen 1:1 to illustrate the "additive" characteristic of orally composed material (*Orality and Literacy*, 37).

[128] Kelber, *Oral and Written Gospel*, 79–80.

[129] Kelber, *Oral and Written Gospel*, 97.

[130] Kelber, *Oral and Written Gospel*, 210.

[131] Kelber, *Oral and Written Gospel*, 91.

[132] Kelber, *Oral and Written Gospel*, 101.

in their respective works.[133] Therefore the paradox is established: why would Mark *write a document* which he knew would then be re-circulated throughout the early churches via the very mechanism and medium of orality which he was against?[134] In addition, if Kelber is able to observe antagonism against oral authorities within the gospel of Mark, we must also conclude that the original readers of Mark would have seen such antagonism even more clearly.[135] Therefore, we must ask how such antagonism would have been received by the early Christian communities. If the early Christian communities did discern such a negative evaluation of oral authorities within Mark, how can one account for the use of the Markan text by the authors of Matthew and Luke? It seems unlikely that Matthew and Luke would be willing to incorporate, and at many times without alteration, the text of Mark if they were conscious of Mark's active antagonism towards the "oral authorities."[136] Our tentative conclusions make it difficult to accept such a theory, and we must therefore conclude

---

[133] There is another more straightforward explanation for the paucity of sayings material in Mark. The existence of collections of sayings material (e.g., *Gos. Thom.*, Q, etc.) illustrates that the early Christian communities already had access to sayings material. Therefore, it is likely that the absence of sayings material in Mark is not due to Mark's apprehension (Kelber: "reservation") towards the genre, but to the simple fact that the Gospel authors not feel the need to repeat sayings material that was already commonly known and accepted as authoritative by their intended audience. For a similar situation regarding Paul's use of Jesus material, see below, ch. 4.

[134] Here, the point of critique is based on the *medium* of delivery. Since ancient texts were most frequently *heard* by an audience (see below, §3.3.9, §4.5), from the perspective of the *hearer,* the tradition functioned as another oral performance.

[135] Here, attempts to read Mark as a subversive narrative contrast with the plain agenda of the author. Stephen C. Barton, "Can We Identify the Gospel Audiences?," in *The Gospels for All Christians* (ed. Richard Bauckham; Grand Rapids: Eerdmans, 1998), 184 is correct to suggest: "it is *a priori* far more likely that he [Mark] is concerned to pass on the tradition in a way that will summon his readers to faith and . . . true discipleship rather than to engage in acts of subtle literary character assassination designed to undermine the leaders of neighboring churches."

[136] The natural question regarding the use of Mark by Matthew and Luke is — why incorporate so much of a text that you disagree with? The incorporation of the Markan text is not done in the context of widely accepted methods of presentation and refutation (e.g., rabbinical halakic disputes), but rather the material is incorporated without any reference to its source. Evidence of refutation most likely would be present within Luke and Matthew if they were indeed *reacting negatively* toward Mark. Also, why would Mark be canonized if, in a culture that so emphasized oral communication, the author seemed to be against the very foundational principles of their society? One would need to assume that the early church quickly "forgot" Mark's original subversive intentions and that Matthew and Luke were no longer aware of Mark's intention when they wrote their respective works.

that Kelber is pushing a valuable thesis too hard.[137] We must heed the advice of Havelock who warns against "a flaccid compromise between the oral and the literate" when studying a culture which is fully a "product of a dynamic tension."[138]

When all is said and done, Kelber's contribution remains, to this day, the single most important and influential work on oral tradition and the composition of Mark and Q. Although many scholars have pointed out, and rightly so, some of the difficulties in his bold and progressive thesis, the basic tenets of his work remain intact. His questioning of the "literary paradigm" is still valid today, and one is still forced to take account of his work when dealing with the formative stages of the early Jesus tradition.

3.3.8 Joanna Dewey (1989)

Joanna Dewey attempts to demonstrate that "the Gospel of Mark as a whole — not just its individual episodes — shows the legacy of orality, indeed that its methods of composition are primarily oral ones."[139] Her "Oral Methods of Structuring Narrative in Mark"[140] is informed by the works of Ong, Havelock, and Kelber, and she applies the oral theory to the whole of Mark. It is from the perspective of the "overlap" between orality and literacy that she attempts to argue for the oral composition of Mark. While acknowledging Kelber's contribution to the field, she perceptively critiques the dichotomy he constructs between orality and literacy. Following Havelock and Ong, she notes that the transition from orality to literacy within the gospel tradition took place over "decades if not centuries."[141] Subsequently, she rightly understands that writing during the time of the composition of the Gospels was highly influenced by oral compositional styles, and therefore one should expect to observe "oral

---

[137] We recognize and agree with Havelock's statement that "a novel thesis requires a restricted emphasis to be put across" (Havelock, *Literate Revolution*, 9), but Kelber has pushed the pendulum too far in arguing his thesis.

[138] Although Havelock's statement is in the context of the literate revolution in Greece, his observations are none the less valid for the Middle East during the time of Jesus (*Literate Revolution*, 9).

[139] Dewey, "Oral Methods," 33.

[140] Dewey, "Oral Methods," 32–34.

[141] Dewey, "Oral Methods," 33. Dewey follows Havelock, *Literate Revolution*, 10. Also, J. D. Harvey summarizes the various positions on the transition from orality to literacy (*Listening to the Text: Oral Patterning in Paul's Letters* [Grand Rapids: Baker Books, 1998], 35–40), but the dates he attributes to Havelock do not correspond with those given by Havelock himself. Harvey places Havelock's "craft-literacy" at 600 B.C.E. (cites Havelock, *Literate Revolution*, 10), but Havelock actually defines "craft-literacy" as, "the period ending about 430 B.C. from that which succeeded it" (*Literate Revolution*, 10).

techniques of composition" in the writing of a Gospel.[142] Her observations provide a helpful corrective to the earlier position of Kelber.

Her major contribution to the study of the possible oral origins of the gospel of Mark is that she attempts to analyze the oral structure of the gospel as a whole and not the individual pericopes within.[143] During her study she repeatedly applies Ong's "further characteristics of orally based thought and expression"[144] to the structure of the Markan text. Following Ong's "additive rather than subordinative" characteristic,[145] Dewey demonstrates that extensive use of the word καί often serves an "additive" function within the text, and she suggests that this characterizes oral composition and transmission. She notes that "[o]f the thirteen pericope introductions in Mark 1–2, eleven begin with καί. Only Mark 1:1, the opening of the Gospel, and 1:14, the beginning of Jesus' public ministry, do not."[146] Mark does not use καί to present his pericopes in a diachronic sequence of events, but rather presents his material in a more synchronic fashion as though not necessarily bound to the linear, chronological framework that is so highly valued by the contemporary literate mind. Dewey also argues that the lack of order in the Markan narrative, often attributed to the author's "'simple' writing style or to his incorporation of sources," is more likely the "natural consequence of his oral narrative technique."[147]

Dewey also makes a significant contribution to the debate regarding the interrelationship between orality and literacy during the time of Gospel composition. She recognized the importance of maintaining a proper balance between both media and in the conclusion to her study wrote, "[f]inally, or perhaps first of all, we must develop a media model for the Gospel of Mark and early Christianity in general. We need a better understanding of how oral and written media work both together and in opposition to each other in the early Christian mixed media situation."[148]

---

[142] Dewey, "Oral Methods," 33.

[143] Of Dewey's work on Mark the following are of particular interest: "Mark as Aural Narrative: Structures as Clues to Understanding," *Sewanee Theological Review* 36 (1992), "Oral Methods," "From Oral Stories to Written Texts," in *Women's Sacred Scriptures* (ed. Pui-Lan Kwok and Elisabeth Schüssler Fiorenza; Maryknoll: Orbis, 1998).

[144] Ong, *Orality and Literacy*, 37.

[145] Ong, *Orality and Literacy*, 37.

[146] Dewey, "Oral Methods," 37. In addition, of the 11,099 words in the shorter version of Mark (1:1–16:7), the word καί appears 1069 times, or 9.6% of the total word count. This is higher than the percentage of either Matthew or Luke.

[147] Dewey, "Oral Methods," 37–38.

[148] Dewey, "Oral Methods," 44.

3.3.9   Paul Achtemeier (1990)

Paul Achtemeier's "Omne Verbum Sonat: The New Testament and the Oral Environment of Late Western Antiquity"[149] follows Dewey's work by one year, and like Dewey relies heavily on both modern orality studies (e.g., Havelock, Ong, Foley) and New Testament studies on orality (e.g., Kelber). Achtemeier's major accomplishment in his article is to turn the focus of the orality/literacy question on the interrelationship between writing and reading. He addresses at least one aspect of the question posed previously by Dewey regarding the relationship between oral and written media in early Christianity. Achtemeier argues that both reading and writing operate on principles of oral communication and aural reception. In his summary on writing he argues that:

> The oral environment was so pervasive that no writing occurred that was not vocalized. That is obvious in the case of dictation, but it was also true in the case of writing in one's own hand. Even in that endeavor, the words were simultaneously spoken as they were committed to writing, whether one wrote one's own words or copied those of another . . . In the last analysis, dictation was the only means of writing; it was only a question of whether one dictated to another or to oneself.[150]

This is an important aspect of the problem of oral tradition and the Gospels. As we have previously seen, the early form-critics struggled with the distinction between oral and written tradition, and later scholars such as Kelber proposed a strong distinction between both media. Achtemeier's work forces us to question any thesis which maintains a strong dichotomy between orality and literacy.

Achtemeier did not restrict his study to ancient writing techniques, but also examined reading in antiquity, and concluded that personal reading was also vocalized and not undertaken in silence as is expected today.[151] If Achtemeier's thesis is correct, then even writing in antiquity would retain "residual orality" (Ong) and reading would be a predominantly *aural*, not visual practice. In sum, Achtemeier suggests that all interaction with literature was mediated via aurally spoken words, and

> [w]hat we want to look for . . . are verbal clues that, by being heard (not seen!), would have aided the listener in understanding the organization of the kind of complex writings

---

[149] Paul J. Achtemeier, "Omne Verbum Sonat: The New Testament and the Oral Environment of Late Western Antiquity," *Journal of Biblical Literature* 109:1 (1990): 3–27.

[150] Achtemeier, "Omne Verbum Sonat," 15. Also, Ong, *Orality and Literacy*, 157 notes that even in Medieval Europe, people "continued the classical practice of writing their literary works to be read aloud."

[151] Achtemeier, "Omne Verbum Sonat," 3–27. Also, see Ong, *Orality and Literacy*, 131.

that are found in the NT, clues that helped the hearer determine when one unit of thought had ended and another begun.[152]

The most readily apparent application of Achtemeier's thesis is to the Synoptic Problem. He argues that the "inconsistencies one can find, say, in the Gospel of Mark are more likely to be due to the orality of that document, and hence the need to provide oral clues for its understanding, than to its author's combination of various written sources."[153] His point is valid even though Achtemeier's well-informed study betrays a slight misunderstanding of the implications that the oral theory has on the Synoptic Problem. He is correct to observe that the oral origins of the Gospels can account for some of the inconsistencies and problems in the Synoptics better than a strictly literary dependency model, but his explanation for the inconsistencies is lacking.[154]

3.3.10 Øivind Andersen (1991)

Øivind Andersen's contribution to Henry Wansbrough's Jesus and the Oral Gospel Tradition deserves mention here for he successfully encompasses the findings of contemporary studies on orality into a single essay.[155] His work addresses many of the important areas of oral tradition that previously have been ignored or treated superficially by some of the previously surveyed scholarship.

Andersen gives attention to several important issues regarding the oral compositional process. He addresses the possibility of different levels of change (i.e., deviation from verbatim rendition) for various different genres of material,[156] something that has not been widely addressed in our survey thus far. He also refers to what he calls the "*literization* of oral tradition."[157] He argues that "oral tradition either may be (and in primary oral societies by necessity *is*) fully oral or may take on literate characteristics even as it remains oral, if it is surrounded by and under the

---

[152] Achtemeier, "Omne Verbum Sonat," 20.

[153] Achtemeier, "Omne Verbum Sonat," 25.

[154] *Contra* Achtemeier, inconsistencies are not necessarily the result of a conscious attempt to "provide oral clues for its understanding." "Oral clues" often include techniques such as redundancy, inclusio, and other mnemonic devices, but do not in themselves account for "inconsistencies." Oral composers/performers do not consciously create difficulties and discrepancies within a body of material, rather, the observed inconsistencies often derive from the inability of an oral performer to review, or "scan" back through a live performance and smooth out the difficulties therein — methods which are clearly available to editors working with a physical text.

[155] Øivind Anderson, "Oral Tradition," in *Jesus and the Oral Gospel Tradition* (ed. Henry Wansbrough; JSNTSup 64; Sheffield: JSOT Press, 1991), 17–58.

[156] Anderson, "Oral Tradition," 28.

[157] Anderson, "Oral Tradition," 49.

influence of literate culture."[158] This leads him to the conclusion that it is difficult if not impossible to discern oral from written composition.[159]

Andersen has moved away from the optimism of earlier New Testament scholars such as Lohr, and his conclusion reflects the complex interaction between orality and textuality as suggested by Dewey and presented in more detail by Achtemeier. This is perhaps among the reasons that Dewey did not look to comment on the orality of Mark at the pericope level, but focused instead on the structural indicators of orality within the overall structure of the canonical text. Andersen's study raises the question of whether or not it is possible to discern oral compositional indicators at the individual pericope level of the gospel text. Have orality and textuality become so intertwined within the Gospel tradition that it is no longer possible to distinguish them from one another?[160] This is one question that has not yet been resolved, but demands further attention.

3.3.11 Kenneth Bailey (1991)

Kenneth Bailey's "Informal Controlled Oral Tradition and the Synoptic Gospels"[161] is an attempt to explore, in his own words, the "concrete reality of our own experience of more than three decades of life and study in the Middle East among communities of great antiquity that still preserve in oral form much of what is important to them."[162] Bailey recognizes that sociology and anthropology can make a significant contribution towards the development of a model of early Christian tradition-transmission.

His study begins with a brief but helpful survey of the early form-critics and the Scandinavian school typified by Riesenfeld and Gerhardsson. He concludes that the form-critical school of Bultmann can be characterized by the term *informal uncontrolled* oral tradition. It is *informal* in the fact that it has "no identifiable teacher nor student and no structure within which material is passed from one person to another," and *uncontrolled* because the community "was not interested in either preserving or controlling the tradition."[163] In contrast, Bailey characterizes the Scandinavian school as *formal controlled* oral tradition. In this case, it is *formal* "in the sense that there is a clearly identified teacher, a clearly identified student, and a clearly identified block of traditional material that

---

[158] Anderson, "Oral Tradition," 49.

[159] Anderson, "Oral Tradition," 50.

[160] Kelber wonders whether "oral forms have become textualized beyond recognition" (*Oral and Written Gospel*, 44).

[161] Kenneth E. Bailey, "Informal Controlled Oral Tradition and the Synoptic Gospels," *Asia Journal of Theology* 5:1 (1991): 34–54.

[162] Bailey, "Informal Controlled," 35.

[163] Bailey, "Informal Controlled," 36.

is being passed on from one to the other," and it is *controlled* "in the sense that the material is memorized (and/or written) and identified as "tradition" and thus preserved intact."[164]

Bailey proposes that the early Christian tradition-transmission is best described as "a third phenomenon with a unique methodology all its own . . . unknown in New Testament circles and has never been analyzed" — *informal controlled* oral tradition.[165] This informal controlled process represents a median position between that of Bultmann and Gerhardsson, one that Bailey equates with C. H. Dodd. According to the model proposed by Bailey, there was "no set teacher and no specifically identified student" and yet the community did have boundaries and limitations that functioned to control the content of the tradition.[166] The "seated community exercises control over the recitation of the tradition,"[167] thereby keeping a system of "checks and balances" on the tradition and preventing its uncontrolled growth or expansion.

Bailey's work is significant for any inquiry into the earliest stages of the Jesus tradition. His work takes seriously the character of "living tradition" and as such has the potential to shed helpful light on a discussion of how the early Jesus movement handled and transmitted the traditions both about Jesus and from Jesus. Bailey is among the first New Testament scholars in recent times to take seriously the character of oral tradition as reflected in the nature of the agreements and disagreements within the Synoptic Tradition, and as such, we will return at a later point in the discussion to a more detailed analysis of his model.

3.3.12 Barry Henaut (1993)

We have been able to discern a clear progression in thought from Lord's *Singer* to that of Bailey. Barry Henaut's work however, is a reaction against the growing awareness of the role of oral tradition in the formation of the Gospel tradition. Henaut's primary concern is to question "[t]he ability to infer from written Gospel texts an underlying 'oral' substratum," and to seek "what factors are necessary to demonstrate literary independence between versions of a saying."[168] Although there is much with which to interact in Henaut's work, we will have to limit our probe to the issues most relevant to the current discussion.

Henaut's underlying methodology is based upon one's ability to discern redaction within a tradition. He asserts that before attributing any material

---

[164] Bailey, "Informal Controlled," 37.
[165] Bailey, "Informal Controlled," 39.
[166] Bailey, "Informal Controlled," 40.
[167] Bailey, "Informal Controlled," 42.
[168] Henaut, *Oral Tradition*, 26.

to the influence of oral tradition "we must begin with a careful application of redaction criticism to determine whether any theological and literary consideration of the Gospel author have been at work."[169] The results of such an inquiry then enable one to make an assessment regarding the possible oral substratum behind a Gospel tradition. For Henaut, this method is justified because of the strong support for the thesis of literary dependence between the Synoptic Gospels which is "determined on the basis of the pattern of agreements based upon the entire Gospels."[170] He argues that the aforementioned thesis of Lord in his *Gospels as Oral Traditional Literature* is flawed for this very reason:

> a textual relationship between two passages has to be established not on a verse-by-verse basis, but by an extensive examination of all the textual data. Two texts which initially look like independent oral variants might actually, upon closer examination, be shown to share a textual relationship once adequate allowance has been made for the redactional and literary concerns of each author.[171]

This statement reveals several methodological and presuppositional shortcomings in his attempt to question the role of oral tradition in the formation of the Synoptic Tradition. Throughout Henaut's work it is clear that he approaches the question of oral tradition from a *strictly literary perspective*. In addressing the question of textual dependency within the Gospel tradition, Henaut appeals to the work of Streeter and those who have argued for the two-source hypothesis. For Henaut, the work of these scholars is evidence that a thesis of gospel *independence* is untenable. Therefore, Lord's thesis regarding the Gospels is deemed a "mistake."[172] As we noted above in chapter 2, there are two separate arguments involved in the question of inter-gospel textual dependency.[173] Henaut is *correct* to suggest that the extant evidence strongly suggests that some thesis of gospel inter-dependence is required to explain the various phenomena such as verbatim agreement and pericope order. However, he then goes beyond what the evidence can support and intertwines the basic supposition of literary dependency together with his argument for a specific solution to the question (i.e., two-source hypothesis), coupled with an assumption that evidence for the former (i.e., literary dependency) supports his wider thesis regarding oral tradition. This is not the case however, for the two arguments are not necessarily interrelated. The fact that there is evidence for literary dependency and redaction within the Gospel tradition in no

---

[169] Henaut, *Oral Tradition*, 63.

[170] Henaut, *Oral Tradition*, 109.

[171] Henaut, *Oral Tradition*, 113.

[172] Henaut, *Oral Tradition*, 113.

[173] The two arguments are 1) the argument for the existence of "Q" and 2) the argument for the "scope" of Q. See above, ch. 2.

way supports the claim for an *exclusively* literary solution to the question of Gospel interrelationships.[174] Henaut has either consciously or unconsciously shifted the argument towards one that polarizes orality against literacy, at which point he then seeks evidence for such literary activity within the tradition.

Time and time again throughout his study, Henaut frames the discussion in these "either/or" terms. He strongly criticizes Kelber for positing a strong distinction between oral and literary tradition and summarizes Kelber's work as positing a "deep chasm between the two media,"[175] a harsh choice of words which Kelber himself does not employ. Henaut then proceeds to detail the non-distinctive characteristics of oral tradition and writes:

We have seen the complete absence of distinctive and unique ground rules for orality. Certainly scholars can identify a number of hallmarks of oral expression and catalogue a variety of variations on the theme of repetition. None of these, however, can be ascribed exclusively to the oral medium. Each of the oral techniques identified, which serve a particularly useful function in the oral medium, finds a natural home in textuality.[176]

Thus we can make sense of his following assessment of the historical situation behind the formation of the Gospel tradition: "[w]e cannot assume that a Synoptic Tradition is guaranteed an oral history."[177]

This conclusion is congruous with Henaut's summary of the "oral argument." He suggests that the following argument has been employed when scholars have attempted to argue for "oral tradition" in the Gospels: "features A, B and C are proper to the oral medium; texts 1, 2 and 3 display characteristics A, B and C; hence texts 1, 2 and 3 were at one point oral."[178] Henaut is correct to argue that lack of *definitive* characteristics of oral tradition makes a *dogmatic* appeal to the oral origins of a tradition a tenuous exercise. However, Henaut employs the converse of the same syllogism when arguing his own case for literary redaction. That is, *he assumes that any evidence of redaction is a priori evidence for the exclusively literary origins of a tradition.* The syllogism not explicitly expressed but upon which Henaut's whole argument is based is as follows: features A, B and C reflect the theological concerns of a given author, texts 1, 2 and 3 display characteristics A, B and C; hence texts 1, 2 and 3 are the result of literary redaction of a textual source. Here his argument is established as an "either/or" dichotomy, one with which he takes issue

---

[174] See above, ch. 2.

[175] Henaut, *Oral Tradition*, 73.

[176] Henaut, *Oral Tradition*, 116.

[177] Henaut, *Oral Tradition*, 74. See below, §3.3.12 for an evaluation of Henaut's assertion.

[178] Henaut, *Oral Tradition*, 65.

when employed by those in favor of the "oral argument." Two examples will serve to illustrate this *Tendenz* within Henaut's work.

First, Henaut points to the incongruity of the Markan narrative (Mark 4:33–34) and argues that it fits "perfectly within Mark's literary and theological perspectives."[179] He then uses Neirynck's *Duality in Mark*[180] as evidence that this characteristic is an "essential" aspect of Markan style. Unfortunately, he avoids discussing the fact that duality is also a predominant characteristic of *oral composition*. Given his own criteria for distinguishing oral from literary tradition, he would have to accept that the Markan phenomenon of "duality" is not specifically literary in origin, and as such, its presence cannot be used to argue for Mark's use of duality as a literary device. The argument for "non-exclusive" criteria must be employed in both directions, not just as a means to discount the possibility of an oral pre-history to Gospel traditions. Henaut's appeal to the presence of duality in Mark is also not capable, in and of itself, of supporting a thesis of Markan redaction.

Second, and perhaps more telling, Henaut repeatedly appeals to the presence of common Markan phraseology and syntax as evidence of literary redaction. He assumes that any evidence of Markan influence on the final form of the text excludes the possibility that the tradition might have been derived from oral tradition.[181] While Henaut feels confident that one can discern Markan influence upon the final form of the Gospel, his observations are not evidence for that which he wishes to demonstrate. Rather, the evidence of Markan influence upon the text *simply highlights the difficulty in discerning redaction from initial composition*, and forces us to examine some fundamental presuppositions regarding the value of redaction criticism for this task at hand.

Henaut assumes that evidence of theological themes, language, etc., within a text is a definitive indicator that literary processes are at work, but this is not necessarily the case. If we assume, and rightfully so, that the early Jesus tradition circulated around in individual Christian communities for a period of time before its inscription into a text, and that the gospel authors were participating members of their respective communities, it would be expected that at least some of the distinctive language and

---

[179] Henaut, *Oral Tradition*, 165.

[180] Frans Neirynck, *Duality in Mark: Contributions to the Study of the Markan Redaction* (Louvain: Louvain University Press, 1972).

[181] This is not unlike Goulder's approach, whereby he suggests that all the features characteristic of Luke's Gospel are attributable to the author's redactional activity. Tuckett, in summarizing Goulder's work on Luke (Christopher M. Tuckett, *Luke: A New Paradigm* [JSNTSup 20; Sheffield: JSOT, 1989]), suggests: ". . . the whole of his [Goulder's] massive two-volume work is an attempt to show that Luke's version is at every point LkR [Lukan redaction] when different from Matthew" (*Q*, 23).

theological themes found in the extant text would have been introduced to the tradition prior to its incorporation in a text — that is, during the oral transmission of the tradition. This means that we should expect the process of community regulation and tradition transmission to have exerted influence on the tradition prior to its inscription. Therefore, we must ask *when* the theological emphases and distinctive linguistic features were stamped onto the tradition. Just because these features exist does not necessarily indicate that *textual redaction* took place. The entire premise behind Henaut's work overlooks this important distinction between literary redaction and initial composition.

Last but not least, Henaut misunderstands how oral tradition functioned in a culture that highly valued oral communicative processes. He asserts that "each oral telling is a new performance, highly dependent upon its context. Variation, rather than stability, is the desirable norm."[182] Here Henaut assumes that there are no controls inherent within the oral tradition, and that the variable character of oral tradition abounds unchecked as depicted by Bailey's term "informal uncontrolled" oral tradition. As was illustrated by Bailey's work, and as we will examine in a later chapter (§5.4), this view of oral tradition must be questioned given what we now know about how oral tradition functions within traditional cultures.

In conclusion, Henaut's study, while elucidating several important aspects of the problem, falls short from what it hopes to demonstrate. While more could be added to the above, it is clear that his attempt to dismiss the possible influence of oral tradition in the formation of the Synoptic Tradition is based upon a thoroughly *literary model* of Synoptic interrelationships which in turn dictates how the remainder of the discussion unfolds. He appropriates a traditional two-source model of Synoptic interrelationships through which he filters all the data. In asserting that one cannot assume an oral pre-history behind the text, and by appropriating a methodology that privileges a highly literary approach to the tradition, it is not surprising that he arrives at the conclusion that there is no "oral layer" behind the Gospels, and that everything can be explained by means of literary redaction.

3.3.13 Richard Horsley & Jonathan Draper (1999)

Horsley and Draper's *Whoever Hears You Hears Me*, is perhaps the most stimulating attempt of late to interact with the Q tradition from the perspective of oral tradition, in particular that of performance theory. Horsley and Draper devote a significant portion of their book to

---

[182] Henaut, *Oral Tradition*, 130.

questioning recent approaches to Q, and they argue that those approaches need to be re-evaluated given recent advances in sociology and anthropology. They question "the major assumption that . . . Q can and should be dealt with as if it were a written text, as opposed to oral tradition."[183] Subsequently, they hope to explore the alternative that "in the predominantly oral communication environment of antiquity, Q was an oral-derived text that calls for interpretation as it was performed orally before groups of people."[184]

In chapter seven, entitled "Recent Studies of Oral-Derived Literature and Q," Horsley surveys the more significant work undertaken on orality over the last one hundred years, and focuses particular attention on the work of Foley and his theory of metonymic referencing which can be defined as "a mode of signification wherein the part stands for the whole."[185] In relation to orally-oriented communities, Horsley suggests that Q functioned as a libretto,[186] whose performance referenced extra-textual tradition with which its hearers would resonate. In this scenario, the tradition functions within a greater complex of meanings of which all the hearers are aware. For Horsley and Draper, this concept of metonymic referencing provides the hermeneutical key · to unlock the socio-cultural/political milieu behind the Q tradition. Properly understood, the Q discourses would have "resonated metonymically with Israelite popular tradition, in interaction with but over against the official tradition."[187]

Having established the methodological framework from which to study the Q tradition, Draper addresses the question of "Recovering Oral Performance From Written Text in Q."[188] In his chapter, Draper attempts to delineate a model of oral communication which is based upon the social linguistic theory of M. A. K. Halliday.[189] He focuses on the elements that

---

[183] Richard A. Horsley and Jonathan A. Draper, *Whoever Hears You Hears Me: Prophets, Performance, and Tradition in Q* (Harrisburg: Trinity Press International, 1999), 3.

[184] Horsley and Draper, *Whoever*, 3.

[185] John Miles Foley, *Immanent Art: From Structure to Meaning in Traditional Oral Epic* (Bloomington: Indiana University Press, 1991), 7.

[186] Horsley suggests that we must "appreciate and understand Q as a libretto that was regularly performed in an early Jesus movement" (*Whoever*, 174).

[187] Horsley and Draper, *Whoever*, 174. Horsley and Draper build upon the distinction between the "great tradition" and the "little tradition" as detailed in the two works of J. C. Scott (*Domination and the Arts of Resistance: Hidden Transcripts* [New Haven: Yale University Press, 1990], and *Moral Economy of the Peasant* [New Haven: Yale University Press, 1977]).

[188] Horsley and Draper, *Whoever*, 175–194.

[189] M. A. K. Halliday, *Language as Social Semiotic: The Social Interpretation of Language and Meaning* (Baltimore: University Park Press, 1978).

constitute a communicative event, in particular, its register, which is comprised of the field, tenor, and mode of discourse.[190] Despite Draper's full acknowledgement of the complex interrelationship between oral and written media,[191] he feels that the differences between the oral and literate registers allow for the identification of "oral performances surviving within written texts." In this instance, the work of Dell Hymes and Foley is foundational, and provides the way forward for the task of discerning oral performance in the reconstructed text of Q.[192] Draper proceeds to utilize Hymes' method of "measured verse" in an attempt to test the thesis that Q "consisted of orally performed discourses which have been separately inscribed in text by Matthew and Luke."[193] Following the application of Hymes' method upon Q 12:49–59, Draper concludes that "[t]his measured text immediately indicates that this is the residue of oral performance."[194]

In assessing Horsley and Draper's contribution to the current discussion we must reflect primarily on their approach to the Q tradition. What is significant is that Horsley and Draper have taken seriously for the first time the potential implications that contemporary performance theory has for studying the reconstructed Q text. Recognizing Q as an "orally-derived text" represents to some extent a paradigm shift in the modern discussion on Q. Their study shows how one can gain insight into both the development of the tradition and its subsequent interpretation by focusing on a dimension of the text that has not been given adequate attention due to an overly literary approach to the double tradition. There is much to gain from their appropriation of insights derived from modern performance theory. Horsley and Draper have opened up the discussion and have pushed the boundaries of Q research beyond the limits imposed by a strictly literary approach to the tradition.

---

[190] Draper offers the following definitions: field — "represents what is taking place and where it is taking place. It refers to the event which occasioned the communication and its setting"; tenor — "represents the relational aspect of communication: who is speaking to whom, the class dynamic, and the aspect of domination"; and mode — "represents the means of communication (what channel of communication is adopted, such as oral or textual), genre, and form" (*Whoever*, 182).

[191] Horsley and Draper, *Whoever*, 183.

[192] Horsley and Draper, *Whoever*, 183. Also see John Miles Foley, *How to Read an Oral Poem* (Chicago: University of Illinois, 2002), 47 where he states that oral compositions "bear a telltale compositional stamp" even though they currently exist only in the form of written texts.

[193] Horsley and Draper, *Whoever*, 187.

[194] Horsley and Draper, *Whoever*, 189.

3.3.14 J. D. G. Dunn (2000–2003)

Dunn has recently argued that the early Jesus tradition exhibits the fixity and flexibility indicative of oral traditioning processes in Middle Eastern society.[195] One of his aims is to revisit the notion that the Jesus tradition in its earliest form was *oral* tradition. To this end, Dunn surveys some previous work done on oral tradition, beginning with Bultmann and Gerhardsson, and including Lord, Kelber, and most importantly, Bailey. Dunn draws heavily on Bailey's "Informal Controlled Oral Tradition and the Synoptic Gospels," and observes a process of tradition formation and transmission in the Synoptic Tradition analogous to Bailey's anecdotal description of contemporary Middle Eastern society.[196] He proceeds to examine several double and triple tradition passages with a view towards their *fixed* and *flexible* characteristics. Dunn suggests, during the course of his investigation, that the variation within the pericopes under examination is reflective of their indebtedness to the oral-traditioning process described by Bailey, where traditions are changed (i.e., flexible) during their retellings, but remain within the bounds established by the individual communities. Thus, for example, in his examination of the Lord's Prayer (Matt 6:7–15//Luke 11:1–4), Dunn suggests that the variation within the prayer is attributable to the "living liturgy of community worship,"[197] and that one should not jump to the conclusion that the only access that Matthew and Luke had to the prayer was through a written "Q".[198] Dunn continues his examination of other pericopes along similar lines and among his conclusions he suggests:

the combination of stability and flexibility positively cried out to be recognized as typically oral in character. That probably implies in at least some cases that the variation [within the tradition] was due to knowledge and use of the same tradition in oral mode, as part of the community tradition familiar to Matthew and Luke. And even if a pericope was derived from Mark or Q, the retelling by Matthew or Luke is itself better described as in oral mode, maintaining the character of an oral retelling more than of a literary editing.[199]

---

[195] Dunn has addressed the topic on more than one occasion over the last several years; "Oral Memory 2000," 287–326, "Jesus in Oral Memory: The Initial Stages of the Jesus Tradition," in *Jesus: A Colloquium in the Holy Land* (ed. Doris Donnelly; New York: Continuum, 2001), 84–145, "Altering the Default Setting: Re-envisaging the Early Transmission of the Jesus Tradition," *NTS* 49 (2003): 129–175, and chapter 8 in his *Jesus Remembered* (Grand Rapids: Eerdmans, 2003).

[196] Dunn, "Oral Memory 2001," *passim*.

[197] Dunn, "Oral Memory 2001," 108.

[198] Dunn, "Oral Memory 2001," 108.

[199] Dunn, "Oral Memory 2001," 128.

3.4 Conclusion

We have come a long way in our brief but necessary survey of the role that oral tradition has played in both early form-critical thought and in more recent work as well. Our chronological survey has revealed a progression from the linear, evolutionary theses of Bultmann and Dibelius to a more robust synthesis of the oral theory as evidenced in some of the more recent works of Dewey, Achtemeier, and Andersen. With the exception of Henaut, the scholars examined above struggled to come to terms with what has been an ever-changing and moving target. That is, despite the difficulty in dealing with the problem of oral tradition, they recognized that it was an integral part of the transmission of the early Jesus tradition, and as such, required due attention. Of course, some attempts were stronger than others, and we can note that the theories regarding oral tradition have tended to improve over time. The evolutionary model of tradition transmission might not apply to the Jesus tradition itself, but it has typified the way in which New Testament scholars have appropriated the recent work of sociologists, anthropologists, and folklorists — the study of oral tradition *has* evolved and changed for the better over the course of the last forty years since the publication of Lord's *Singer*.

In many respects, the last decade of the twentieth century proved to be the most profitable for the inquiry into how oral transmission might have functioned in the early Jesus communities. Bailey's "Informal Controlled Oral Tradition" (1991) in many respects set in motion the current discussion, and Horsley and Draper's work (2000) brought to the fore several important insights from performance theory that they applied to their study of Q. We ended our survey by examining the recent work of Dunn (2000–2003) and his attempt to take seriously the implications of Bailey's earlier study. He has moved the discussion forward and we will return to discuss his model in more detail in chapters five and six. We must now move forward and build upon these important studies in an attempt to understand better the development and transmission of the Synoptic Tradition.

Chapter 4

Oral Communication and Written Texts

4.1 Introduction

When we read and study the New Testament, and in particular the early Jesus tradition in both its canonical and extra-canonical forms, we do so from within a particular socio-historical perspective. This current perspective has been affected in no small manner by the physical processes involved in the production of texts themselves, beginning with the initial inscription of the Jesus tradition into textual form, and continuing throughout the two millennia of the Christian church.

The scribes that were responsible for the careful copying and reproduction of the earliest New Testament documents were fortunate enough to have been in a position to observe the ascension of the Jesus tradition from its humble origins as an orally proclaimed gospel to its status as an authoritative, inscribed text.[1] On the other hand we are not nearly as fortunate. We are forced to address the difficult questions regarding the earliest stages of the Jesus tradition from both a chronological and cultural distance via nothing but the fixed literary tradition that remains. We must attempt to reconstruct a world that is disparate from our own and one to which we have great difficulty relating.

Following the elevation of Jesus-texts to their place as sacred *script*-ure, the Jesus tradition became ever increasingly bound to the rigid constraints that are inherently characteristic of texts and fully developed manuscript traditions.[2] This developing process of textual "rigidity" was gradual and

---

[1] The process of canonization was the direct result of a "consciously literary culture" (Philip R. Davies, *Scribes and Schools: The Canonization of the Hebrew Scriptures* [Library of Ancient Israel Louisville: Westminster John Knox, 1998], 9). Davies correctly notes: *"copying and archiving are the very stuff of canonizing . . .* [a] work becomes canonized (a) by being preserved by copying until its status as a classic is ensured; and (b) by being classified as belonging to a collection of some kind" (*Canonization*, 9).

[2] This is not to suggest that texts are *always* fixed, but that they are more likely to be transmitted without substantial change *if desired*. Aune is correct when he writes, "the notion that oral tradition is flexible and written tradition is fixed (or even that oral tradition can be fixed and written transmission even more fixed) is a thoroughly modern

began with the production of texts on papyri and parchment, reaching its pinnacle as a "fixed" text only following the invention of a machine that we have now come to take for granted — the printing press. Following the invention of the moveable-type printing press by Gutenberg, the Jesus tradition would no longer be subject to the potential influx of errors — and hence instability — that was an inevitable consequence of the earlier scribal process of creating and copying texts. Thus, the transformation was now complete. The highly valued but flexible communal-based traditions of early Christianity have now become concrete, fixed texts, and the New Testament texts that are currently studied and expounded upon by members of the theological academy, are thoroughly the products of the relatively recent invention of movable type.

This fundamental and quite profound transformation has not been without consequence for our approach to, and study of the New Testament texts. As we noted above, this fundamental shift in emphasis has had a significant impact on the ways in which we study and evaluate the tradition. Recovering the lost oral/aural dimension behind the New Testament texts requires us to explore the extent to which the world of antiquity, for many centuries both prior to and following Jesus, was one dominated by oral communication.

In this chapter we shall examine the complex relationship in antiquity between oral communication and written texts. We will interact with a wide range of primary source material through a diachronic approach in an attempt to formulate a composite picture of how oral tradition was viewed in antiquity by the tradents of the tradition itself. No attempt will be made to deal with the source material in a comprehensive manner. Rather, we shall focus on several key areas in an attempt to illuminate by way of illustration the *perceived* value of oral communication and written texts in antiquity and the extent to which oral tradition was used in the production of ancient texts. In so doing, we shall note the extent to which oral

---

assumption which is not supported by the evidence," see David E. Aune, "Oral Tradition and the Aphorisms of Jesus," in *Jesus and the Oral Gospel Tradition* (ed. Henry Wansbrough; JSNTSup 64; Sheffield: JSOT Press, 1991), 240; cf. Larry W. Hurtado, "The Gospel of Mark: Evolutionary or Revolutionary Document?," in *The Synoptic Gospels: A Sheffield Reader* (ed. Craig A. Evans and Stanley E. Porter; Sheffield: Sheffield Academic Press, 1995), 200. For an extended discussion of this characteristic of texts see the helpful work of Parker, *Living Text*, Bart D. Ehrman, *The Orthodox Corruption of Scripture : The Effect of Early Christological Controversies on the Text of the New Testament* (New York: Oxford University Press, 1993), and E. J. Epp, "The Multivalence of the Term "Original Text" in New Testament Textual Criticism," *HTR* 92 (1999). The concept of a "fixed" text does not apply to the early period of the Gospels; such a concept only develops once the inscribed tradition has become sacred to the extent that the text itself becomes an object of veneration.

tradition was integral to all aspects of life in ancient Mediterranean society and then conclude by exploring the implications of such a view.

4.1.1   Humans as "Oral" Communicators

Human beings are "oral/aural" beings. Such an assertion may seem overstated, but upon further inspection the merits and benefits of such an observation are apparent. It is almost paradoxical that the only time humans are free from any conscious biases or culturally conditioned behavior is at the very beginning stages of their human development. Born with a "clean slate," human beings do not have the immediate ability to communicate in any *meaningful* sense of the term. Communication is limited to the ability to convey primal needs such as food, warmth, sleep, etc. As a child develops, she or he will become mindful of the constant intercommunication between other humans, and will gradually become aware that humans communicate in order to achieve their wants and desires, or conversely, to express their dislikes and fears. In this context it is important to realize that the universal experience of all infants is that they learn to communicate *aurally*, by example, not visually by writing and reading. All humans must be taught to read and write via instruction, while verbal communication and aural reception are intuitive and result from the natural process of human interaction. Eric Havelock summarizes this characteristic of *homo sapiens* as follows:

> The biological-historical fact is that *homo sapiens* is a species which uses oral speech, manufactured by the mouth, to communicate. That is his definition. He is not, by definition, a writer or reader. His use of speech, I repeat, has been acquired by processes of natural selection operating over a million years. The habit of using written symbols to represent such speech is just a useful trick which has existed over too short a span of time to have been built into our genes, whether or not this may happen half a million years hence.[3]

Havelock makes an astute observation, and it has consequences for our understanding of how the human mind functions with regard to oral communication. Across the broad spectrum of human culture, writing remains the exception, and not the norm, for it is only in our current electronic culture[4] that we operate with the modern notion of literacy as the cultural norm. Apart from modern Western society, the oral legacy of our ancestors remains strong and oral communication reigns as the

---

[3] Havelock, *Literate Revolution*, 50.

[4] Thomas E. Boomershine, "Biblical Megatrends: Towards a Paradigm for the Interpretation of the Bible in Electronic Media" (Society of Biblical Literature Seminar Papers: Society of Biblical Literature, 1987), 144–157 uses this term to describe our late twentieth century Western civilization.

predominate mode of human discourse.[5] Ong points out that of the three thousand spoken languages today, only seventy-eight of those language groups have produced literature in the common sense of the word.[6] Such a radical discord between spoken language and the "written word" would increase if we were to move back further into the distant past. It is still shockingly apparent that for the majority of residents in the Western world, literacy remains the quantitative litmus test for determining the level of both individual and societal intelligence. Despite more recent awareness of the fallacious use of such a criterion, the "literate mind"[7] remains an integral part of the Western worldview, and we must agree with Ong that we tend to perpetuate continually the notion that writing is the basic, or primary form of language.[8]

4.1.2 Cultural Primacy of "Oral" Communication

In addition to the primacy of individual interpersonal oral communication, we must consider the primacy of group based, or corporate oral communication. We can safely assert that oral communication preceded written communication within an ancient societal context.[9] Our current Indo-European languages have a long lineage, the evolution of which can be traced back over the last several millennia. The roots of contemporary English can be traced back primarily to Latin and Greek; Greek owes its history to the more primitive Linear-B, and the development of the vowels which distinguishes Greek from its less developed antecedents is likely due to the Greeks attempt to emulate their Phoenician neighbors.[10] As we venture back in time, retracing the evolutionary development of written language, it becomes apparent that functional literacy came into use relatively late in our history as *Homo sapiens*.[11]

---

[5] Foley writes, ". . . writing is recent and literature is rare. On the other hand, as far as we know all peoples have composed and transmitted oral traditions . . . [e]ven today the majority of the planet's inhabitants use oral traditions as their primary communicative medium, a fact obscured by modern Western egocentrism" (Foley, *How to Read*, 25).

[6] Ong, *Orality and Literacy*, 7.

[7] Ong, *Orality and Literacy*, 5.

[8] Ong, *Orality and Literacy*, 5; cf. Davies, *Canonization*, 16.

[9] The very use of the now popular term "pre-literate" assumes this observation.

[10] Havelock argues that the cultural contact between the Greeks and Phoenicians, on the account of trade, led the Greeks to try and emulate the Phoenician system of vocalization (*Literate Revolution*, 10).

[11] According to Richard E. Leakey and Roger Lewin, *Origins: What New Discoveries Reveal About the Evolution of Our Species and Its Possible Future* (London: MacDonald & Jane, 1979), 141, 168, Homo Sapiens have existed for approximately fifty thousand years. Foley bases his chronology of the development of writing systems on a one-hundred thousand year time period (*How to Read*, 23-24).

4.1.3   Early Use of Writing

4.1.3.1   Commerce and Trade

The relatively recent development of "functional writing" is closely related to the economic and social consequences of the *Homo sapiens'* transition from loosely associated groups of roaming hunter-gatherers to the firmly established agrarian groups which would begin to form the basis of the modern *polis*. Larger communities that remained in one location were in a position to develop an economic infrastructure — one that resulted from the newfound ability to produce surplus food in large enough quantities to serve as a viable commodity to be used for trade and commerce. It was this ability to produce excess food that represented a dramatic departure from their hunter-gatherer ancestors who could at best maintain a subsistence existence as nomads, having to follow the food as it migrated throughout the seasons, and eating from what the land had to offer. This fundamental difference between land-based agrarian groups and their itinerant predecessors led to the development of an economy, and thus writing.[12] From available evidence it seems likely that this economic necessity was the impetus that led to the development of the earliest forms of writing.[13]

4.1.3.2   Societal Organization

Although commerce and trade played a vital role in the development of writing, it is difficult to assess the specific extent to which it did encourage the development of writing due to the scarcity of relevant evidence. On the other hand, we do have significant grounds on which to base the assertion that the need for societal organization encouraged the proliferation of written scripts and texts. As noted above, as humans began to settle down in larger, non-nomadic groups an increased need developed for a way by which society could be structured and governed. The universally appropriated means for instituting and perpetuating such structure and order in society has been, and will always be the creation and enforcement of laws. Therefore, it should not be surprising that some of the earliest uses for writing were for these very purposes.

---

[12] So Davies, *Canonization*, 17 — "[w]riting was first used to record economic transactions: receipts, letters, or records, and had little or no use beyond this."

[13] Estimates vary regarding the dating of the earliest forms of scripts. Ong suggests that cuneiform is the first of the scripts to be invented and assigns it a date of ca. 3500 B.C.E. (*Orality and Literacy*, 85–86). More recent studies have posited a date of 3200 B.C.E. for Egyptian script traditions, and a later date of 3100 B.C.E.. for cuneiform. For these estimates and a further chronology of the development of scripts see Foley, *How to Read*, 23-24 which draws upon the work of Peter D. Daniels and William Bright, eds., *The World's Writing Systems* (New York: Oxford University, 1996) .

We need look no further than the ancient Fertile Crescent from which many of the earliest writing systems derive. The ancient Babylonians, Assyrians, Hittites, and Sumerians all present us with written law codes that date back to the very development of functional writing systems. Of the more well known examples is the Code of Hammurapi (CH) and the Laws of Eshunna (LE) which cover a variety of concerns from everyday life including issues such as commerce, physical violence, and interpersonal relations.

The category of commerce forms a significant portion of these extant law codes. In particular, the laws address common concerns often related to the broad category of agriculture. Some examples include the hire of a wagon (LE 3–5) and a donkey/rider (LE 10), the renting of fields (CH 42–47), and the buying and selling of fields (CH 40–41) or property (LE 38–39). Also entailed are laws concerning the rate of interest on loans (LE 18A-21; CH 88–91) and the issue of debt collection and loans in general (CH 98–102, 104–106, 113–115).

Laws regarding physical violence or injury to others also occupy a significant percentage of the content therein. Particular issues of violence are addressed, such as the loss of, or damage to the nose, eye, tooth, ear, and even includes provision for a slap on the face (LE 42). With regard to these laws, the concern is for the character and extent of retribution for the act of violence. Accordingly, the laws typically detail financial compensation, or, in the case of the CH, the principle of *lex talionis* is detailed and expanded — "eye for eye" (CH 196), "bone for bone" (CH 197), "tooth for tooth" (CH 200), and even an "ox for ox" (CH 245).[14]

The more extensive laws in the Code of Hammurapi also govern relational issues such as inheritance (CH 168–184), adoption of children (CH 185–193), and the treatment of slaves (CH 15–20; cf. LE 40, 49, 50–52).

The early use of writing systems to detail laws for societal organization can also be observed within the Hebrew Bible, in particular in the fundamental importance given to the Torah and its laws and regulations. The emphasis on written law begins early in the Hebrew Bible (Exod 17:14; 34:27), and is attributed to God himself (Exod 34:1; 32:15–16). The laws not only derive from Yahweh, but they are the "work of God" (אֱלֹהִים מַעֲשֵׂה), having been inscribed on stone tablets with his own hand (Exod 34:1; 32:16), and others write and record these laws for future generations.[15] Subsequently, these laws became one of the fundamental means for structuring all aspects of Hebrew society, from birth to death. There are many similarities between the earlier LE and CH and the Torah:

---

[14] Cf. Biblical parallels: Gen 9:6, Exod 21:12, 23–25, Lev 24:21.
[15] Josh 8:32; 24:6.

both law codes detail many specific regulations that cover the diverse spectrum of human experience. What we can therefore conclude is that within the geographical region that encompassed the ancient civilizations of Mesopotamia and Israel, writing was established initially as a means by which one could organize and structure groups of people as they developed into more populous collectives.

4.1.4   Greek Concept of Written and Unwritten

The development of written laws to serve an organizational purpose indicates indirectly that these now inscribed and codified laws existed in earlier oral forms. Such an observation is an intuitive premise based upon the assertion that all ancient cultures began as oral cultures, only later to develop writing systems which could be used to publicly display and re-proclaim what a king or leader had previously stated. In fact, we have many examples of both oral and written laws coexisting side by side with one another. In the case of the aforementioned Babylonian law codes, the laws were inscribed on eight-foot tall tablets for the purpose of public display.[16] They were inscribed versions of previously proclaimed laws which were written for all the public to see (cp. Andocides, *De mysteriis* 84) and therefore served as a legal reference when disputes arose between two or more parties. One could no longer claim ignorance regarding the laws, as could possibly be the case prior to their inscription. Therefore, there was an antecedent oral law tradition that eventually led to a written law tradition, each existing in conjunction with the another. There was a similar situation among the Jews and even the Greeks, both of whom were fully capable of producing highly sophisticated works of literature. Both the Jews and Greeks supported and sustained an oral corpus of laws and traditions which would continue in that form long after they were incorporated into written works of literature.

We can see an example of this two-fold distinction within Greek literature over a period of several centuries. In a brief survey of this phenomenon, we will explore three major categories of oral and written law that can be discerned via primary sources. We will see that in the case of the extant Greek literature, there was indeed the recognition that laws existed in both an oral (unwritten)[17] and inscribed (written) form. Such a recognition supports the claim that early writing served to supplement and record that which already existed in oral form, and that oral

---

[16] Samuel A. Meier, "Hammurapi," *The Anchor Bible Dictionary* 3: 39–42.

[17] In Lysias, *In Andocidem* 10, unwritten laws are described as those whose author is unknown.

communication remained the fundamental medium for interpersonal and intercommunity dialogue.

4.1.4.1 Both Written and Unwritten

The development of written laws and traditions took place alongside the promulgation of oral laws and traditions. As written laws became more abundant there was a clear distinction between the two media of transmission, but that distinction did not immediately lead to the abandonment of the earlier oral laws in favor of their later written counterparts. On one particular occasion Plato (ca. 428–347 B.C.E.) recounts a dialog between Socrates and a stranger, in which is described two types of law, both written and unwritten (γράψαντι καί ἄγραφα) (Plato, *Politicus* 295e-296a). In this case, both types of law are grouped together and equal in authority, apart from any concern for their medium of transmission (cp. Plato, *Respublica* 563d-563e). The dialogue continues with a summary statement equating laws inscribed upon tablets (γράψαντασὲν) with unwritten ancestral customs (ἄγραφα πάτρια) (Plato, *Politicus* 295e-296a). The authority of the unwritten laws seems to be taken for granted and the actual content of the written and unwritten laws is also assumed to be more or less the same (Plato, *Leges* 793a-793b). Aristotle also argues that good laws will produce a good society, and therefore he advocates the enforcement of both written and unwritten laws (Aristotle, *Ethica nichomachea* 1180b:1; Aristotle, *Politica* 1319b-1320; cp. Lysias, *In Andocidem* 10). In this same context, Plato argues that the written laws are simply *summaries* of the previous ancestral customs, and therefore are to be acknowledged as normative. Thus, the Athenian argues that the unwritten law is effective in keeping men from having sexual intercourse with their brothers, sisters, and even children (Plato, *Leges* 838a-838b). Both written and unwritten laws exist, and both types serve an important role in society.

4.1.4.2 Written Law

In this category there is a distinction between written and unwritten (oral) laws, with an emphasis on the legal basis for enforcing written laws. Andocides (ca. 440–390 B.C.E.) recounts how written laws act as a protection against the abuse of citizens. He emphasizes that all laws are to be applied equally to all citizens (Andocides, *De mysteriis* 89), and that "in no circumstances shall magistrates enforce a law which has not been inscribed (ἀγράφῳ)" (Andocides, *De mysteriis* 1.85–86). Thus for Andocides, people cannot simply prosecute one another out of malice; charges must be based upon the violation of a written law (Andocides, *De mysteriis* 1.89). Thucydides (ca. 460–400 B.C.E.) also implies that oral and written laws differ with respect to their enforceability. He distinguishes between the laws which are on the statute book (Thucydides, *Hist.* 1.40.3) and therefore enforceable, and those which are unwritten (ἄγραφοι) but the transgression of which results in disgrace (Thucydides, *Hist.* 1.40.3). Therefore, there is a clear distinction between two types of laws, written and unwritten, and a recognition that these two categories exist alongside one another. In the case of the Greeks, written law clearly had the advantage of enforceability.

4.1.4.3 *Unwritten Law (Natural, Moral, or General Law)*

The concept of written and unwritten law has also been expressed through what has been described as natural law. Xenophon provides us with valuable insight into the concept of natural law in recounting a dialogue between Socrates and Hippias. In this dialogue, Socrates questions Hippias and asks him if he knows what is meant by unwritten laws (ἀγράφους ... νόμους) (Xenophon, *Memorabilia* 4.4.19). Hippias responds that unwritten laws are 1) observed in all countries[18], and 2) made by gods, not men (Xenophon, *Memorabilia* 4.4.19).[19] This Greek notion of a natural, universal law has also influenced later Jewish thought, in particular that of Philo, who also speaks of an unwritten, natural law which is unwritten (ἀγράφῳ) yet "intuitively learnt."[20]

In addition to natural law, Greek authors frequently associated this natural law with universal morality, essentially tying together the two concepts. Demosthenes (ca. 384–322 B.C.E.) contrasts that which is not only in the law (οὐ μόνον ἐν τοῖς νόμοις) with both the unwritten laws (τοῖς ἀγράφοις νομίμοι) and the moral sense of humanity (Demosthenes, *De corona* 275). Similar logic can be found in Demosthenes' contemporary, Aristotle. Aristotle repeatedly associates the unwritten laws with natural, or moral law.[21] For Aristotle, the unwritten law has the following characteristics: it is, 1) universally recognized (Aristotle, *Rhetorica* 1368b), 2) based upon nature (Aristotle, *Rhetorica* 1373b), 3)

---

[18] They are also described as a universal law (πανταχοῦ νομίζεται), Xenophon, *Memorabilia* 4.4.20.

[19] These unwritten laws are described as universal, and therefore, by definition must be obeyed by all people. Therefore, Hippias' response to Socrates is that the "unwritten law" forbidding parents from having sexual intercourse with their children is *not* a universal law because it is broken (παραβαίνοντας) by some people (Xenophon, *Memorabilia* 4.4.20).

[20] Philo, *De Abrahamo* 16, trans., LCL.

[21] For one example see Aristotle, *Ethica nichomachea* 1162b.20, where Aristotle specifically contrasts unwritten/law with moral/legal.

inexplicit (Aristotle, *Rhetorica* 1374a),[22] 4) never changing (Aristotle, *Rhetorica* 1375a-1375b),[23] 5) goes beyond the written law (Aristotle, *Rhetorica* 1374a). Given these characteristics, what is perhaps most significant is that for Aristotle there is *greater merit* in obeying the "oral," or unwritten law, than there is in obeying the written, or explicit law. This is due to the fact that written laws entail compulsion and obligation, while the unwritten laws do not. Therefore, according to Aristotle transgression is greater if it is against the written law, and conversely, it is better to obey the unwritten law (ἀγράφοις) for it is done apart from coercion.

At this point we must conclude that for Aristotle and his fellow Greeks, there were two corpora of laws: unwritten and written. While written laws were firmly established in ancient Greece, they existed in conjunction with an unwritten body of rules, customs, regulations, and moral guidelines, all of which played an integral role in their society. *The Greeks felt that these unwritten, universally accepted guidelines were important, even though they were not inscribed.* Due to the noncompulsory character of unwritten "law," there was *greater merit* in obeying that which was universally accepted by the whole of Greek society.

4.1.5 Jewish Concept of Written and Unwritten

The concept of a written and unwritten collection of laws and traditions was not confined to ancient Greece, but played an integral role in ancient Judaism as well. As mentioned above, as was the case with the ancient Greeks, Jewish notions of written and unwritten law (Torah) can be traced back to the very beginnings of Judaism itself.

The Hebrew canon makes it clear that the Torah was given to Moses (Exod 19–20),[24] and Moses writes down the law (Exod 24:4), presumably to ensure the obedience of future generations.[25] In this case the mandate to Moses is significant for it demonstrates that there was a desire to connect the law with Moses himself, and in so doing, to establish an early date for the inscription of the laws, thereby giving authority to the written laws themselves. This desire to assert the authority of the written law is reinforced apart from the Hebrew Bible. Within the *Pseudepigrapha* there is also an account describing the antiquity of writing, this time with respect

---

[22] This is implied from Aristotle's description of the explicit characteristic of written law in contrast to the inexplicit characteristic of unwritten law.

[23] Compare this with Josephus' description of the Greeks, whereby he describes them as always changing their unwritten customs (ἀγράφοις χρώμενοι), Josephus, *C. Ap.* 2.155.

[24] See 2 Chr 34:14; Ezra 7:6; Neh 8:1, 10:29, John 1:17.

[25] Note the similarities between Biblical mandate to inscribe the laws with the older CH and LE.

to Enoch who is described as "the first who learned writing and knowledge and wisdom, from (among) the sons of men . . . And who wrote in a book the signs of the heaven according to the order of their months . . . This one was the first (who) wrote a testimony and testified to the children of men throughout the generations of the earth" (*Jubilees* 4:17–18). This description of Enoch reinforces the Jewish notion that their written laws date back to the very origins of their society.

From these accounts it is clear that the novel medium of writing was appropriated by the Jews for several important reasons. As was the case for the Greeks, writing was used initially as a means for inscribing laws to help organize and structure society. This use of writing was accepted as the principle means by which God revealed his desire for his chosen people. At a later date, other Jewish writers reinforced the importance of this medium by linking its initial use to the highly revered patriarch, Enoch.

4.1.6 Interaction between Two Media

Following this brief survey we can make several important observations based upon the ancient notion of oral and written laws. There is strong evidence to suggest that ancient cultures, and in particular the Greeks and Jews, had a clear notion of the difference between oral and written collections of laws and traditions. Writing began as a novel way by which one could make visible and accessible the laws which were previously heard only within the context of oral communication and from the public performance of a king before his people. Over time the growing collection of laws did not immediately lead to the dismissal of the antecedent oral corpus. Both collections of laws and traditions existed alongside one another for many centuries, and in the case of the Jews, culminated with the writing down of the Mishnah in about 200 C.E. Further, we will show that during this time there were instances when oral traditions were held in higher regard than their written counterparts.[26]

Although the above evidence only deals with a limited range of source material it does provide us with an example of the problems we face when

---

[26] According to Neusner, the Leviticus Rabbah "turns matters around and treats the written Torah exactly as if it were part of the Oral Torah, right along with the Mishnah" (Jacob Neusner, *The Oral Torah* [San Francisco: Harper & Row, 1986], xv). Also, the Babylonian Talmud explicitly states that "you are not to pass on sayings [received] in writing by word of mouth; you are not to pass on sayings [received] by word of mouth in writing," *Git.* 60b (trans. Millard). Millard summarizes this saying as an "official" policy on the transmission of the Mishnah, and that "writing was banned not only for the Oral Law but for almost everything with religious content." Subsequently, Millard shows that, despite this prohibition, the Oral Torah was written down, and thus, this prohibition was an ideal in word, not a reality in deed (Alan R. Millard, *Reading and Writing*, 191–192).

attempting to unravel the complex interrelationship between oral and written media. We have a clear distinction between these media, but we also must realize that both media interacted with one another, each having a mutual impact on the other. Given this possible difficulty, we must be careful to avoid oversimplifying the problem by juxtaposing orality against literacy in an antithetical manner, or as has been done in the past, by using one in contradistinction to the other.[27] Such an approach does not take into consideration the intricate nature of the interrelationship between orality and literacy, something which has been emphasized particularly in the last decade of the twentieth century.[28] If we are to progress in our understanding of the earliest stages of the Jesus tradition, we must be willing to take an integrative approach to the extant texts, one that acknowledges both its literary and oral dimensions. It is just such an approach that we will take during the remainder of this chapter. In the sections that follow we will explore in more detail the relationship between ancient texts and the world of ancient oral communication.

4.1.7 Literacy, Texts, and Education

As we make our way through history from the development of primitive writing systems to the invention of the highly refined Greek alphabet, we must address, however briefly, the setting within which the New Testament Gospels developed. Our task is complicated by the complex transitional period which was fully underway during the first-century C.E. The transition between an "oral culture" and the fully "literate culture" of the post-Gutenberg era was not immediate, but was the consequence of a long period of change occurring over the period of approximately 5,500 years.

Scholars have used various terms to categorize and describe the stages of development along this evolutionary timeline. Ruth Finnegan contrasts the two ends of the orality-literacy spectrum as "Type A" and "Type B" cultures. Her two categories are helpful for they contrast in a succinct form the differences between an "oral" and a "literate" culture. She describes a "Type A" culture as having the following characteristics: 1) small-scale . . . homogeneous, 2) "oral," dominated by tradition at least and probably also by religion and ascribed kinship, 3) unself-conscious, 4) perhaps more organic and close to nature than ourselves, 5) certainly

---

[27] This has been the claim most often levelled against Kelber, in particular against his *Oral and Written Gospel*. It is noteworthy to point out that Kelber has not done much to soften this impression (either justified or not) in the recent reprint (1997) of his important work. It is also helpful to note that scholars have taken extreme positions on both ends of the orality-literacy spectrum.

[28] See above, ch. 3, in particular the work of Achtemeier and Andersen.

untouched by mechanization, advanced technology, and mass culture.[29] These characteristics are contrasted with those of a "Type B" culture: 1) literate, 2) dominated by the tradition of the written word, 3) secular and rationalistic, 4) oriented towards achievement and individual development, 5) highly mechanized, 6) perhaps bound together by artificial rather than natural links, 7) with a well developed technology.[30] Other scholars have used their own terms to convey characteristics similar to those of Finnegan. Ong uses the term "oral"/"radically oral", Havelock "pre-literate," and Boomershine "oral" — all these are similar to Finnegan's "Type A." On the other hand, Ong uses "secondarily oral," Havelock uses "type-literate," and Boomershine uses "print" to describe cultures similar to Finnegan's "Type B."[31]

Regardless of the nomenclature used to describe the various stages of human literacy, the aforementioned scholars have all recognized that the process of acquiring written language and using it as the lens through which all human thought and experience is viewed, was slow, gradual, and occurred over a period of millennia, not decades. For our purposes, the writing of the Gospels occurred during this pivotal transitional period. Ong describes the period beginning at 100 C.E. as a "manuscript" culture that began to interact with texts on a new level.[32] It is no coincidence that Ong's date corresponds with the ascendancy of the New Testament documents to their established position as authoritative *texts*. Ong's observations no doubt have been influenced (and rightly so) by the

---

[29] Finnegan, "How Oral?," 52.

[30] Finnegan, "How Oral?," 52.

[31] None of the terms used by Ong, Havelock, and Boomershine correspond to one another in detail, but they are all similar enough to be used for comparison. Boomershine uses the term "electronic" to refer to the culture at the end of the 20th century while Havelock's work was completed prior to the "electronic revolution" and thus does not create a new category for our current culture. See Harvey, *Listening to the Text*, 38 for a summary of the chronology and dates of Havelock, Boomershine, and Ong.

[32] One must be cautious when using the term "manuscript" culture to uniquely define the post 100 C.E. era. It is clear that the early Christians did participate to a certain extent in a "manuscript" culture with regard to LXX and other sacred writings of the period. A cursory examination of Paul's letters reveals a significant level of indebtedness to a textual tradition. However, as we will address below in §4.5, there is uncertainty as to the extent to which Paul was citing a fixed manuscript of the LXX or recalling the tradition from his memory. In either case, Ong's date of 100 C.E. is best understood as referring to a point in time when the transition took place from a predominately oral culture to one where an emphasis was on the printed text. This is not to suggest that prior to this time there were no manuscript traditions from which both the Jews and Christians could draw. Rather, a complex confluence of factors following 100 C.E. led to the situation where the text would become, over time, an authoritative and fixed tradition which would have prominence over an ongoing oral tradition.

Christian manuscript tradition that began as a result of the increased desire to produce "sacred texts" to meet the various needs of Christian life during the first few centuries of the Christian era. This insatiable desire for Christian texts manifested itself in the increased emphasis on texts as the only source for reliable Jesus tradition — a position that would become later in the 20th century a fundamental characteristic of many Christian movements.[33]

The long-running manuscript tradition which has now become a fully print-oriented tradition has unduly influenced how we read and interpret the NT texts. We must continually keep in perspective the recent studies on ancient literacy rates and educational standards of antiquity. Although some recent scholarship has attempted to demonstrate that literacy was more widespread than often envisaged,[34] the consensus remains that the vast majority of people in antiquity, including the Jews in Roman Palestine, were at best marginally literate.[35] Raymond Person identifies the disparity between modern and ancient rates of literacy as the cause for the large cultural gap between the modern Biblical scholar and the ancient world of Israel.[36] As for ancient Judea and Galilee, the estimation of literacy rates varies, but by all recent accounts remains far below even minimal acceptable levels within contemporary Western society,[37] and was

---

[33] I am referring in particular to contemporary evangelical Christianity with its strong emphasis on the written word, often to the neglect of unwritten tradition and contemporary prophecy.

[34] In particular, Millard, *Reading and Writing*, 157–184. Also, see Loveday C. A. Alexander, "Ancient Book Production and the Circulation of the Gospels," in *The Gospels for All Christians* (ed. Richard Bauckham; Edinburgh: T&T Clark, 1998), 87, where she describes a "commercial booktrade," whereby copyists and booksellers earned income from the production and sale of texts.

[35] Horsley points out that despite the low estimations of literacy levels, scholars "continue to trust generalizations about high rates of Judean or diaspora Jewish literacy that preceded recent critical studies of literacy in antiquity" (*Whoever*, 127). Also see *Hearing the Whole Story: The Politics of Plot in Mark's Gospel* [Louisville: Westminster John Knox, 2001], 53–55). Hezser, in her recent comprehensive work on Jewish literacy (*Jewish Literacy in Roman Palestine* [TSAJ 81; Tübingen: Mohr Siebeck, 2001]), emphasizes the form and function of literacy in Roman Palestine. Although she suggests that it is not possible to determine the precise literacy rate among Jews of the time, she does agree with Bar-Ilan's view that the rate of Jewish literacy must have been *lower* than the literacy rate among Romans during the first centuries C.E. (Hezser, *Jewish Literacy*, 496–504).

[36] Raymond F. Person, "A Rolling Corpus and Oral Tradition: a Not-so-literate Solution to a Highly Literate Problem," in *Troubling Jeremiah* (ed. A. R. Pete Diamond, Kathleen M. O'Connor, and Louis Stulman; JSOTSup 260; Sheffield: Sheffield Academic Press, 1999), 263–271.

[37] William V. Harris, *Ancient Literacy* (Cambridge: Harvard University Press, 1989), 114 suggests that fewer than 10% of the population were literate; cf. Meir Bar-Ilan,

"concentrated in the political and cultural elite."[38] The lack of widespread literacy was also highlighted by the low educational standards of antiquity, a situation with which the early tradents of the Jesus tradition must have been familiar. Martin Hengel summarizes the situation as follows:

With the possible exceptions of Luke and the author of Hebrews, the New Testament authors ... had no deeper acquaintance with secular Greek writing. They either completely lacked real Greek education, obtained through well-known "classical literature," as in the case of Mark, Matthew or John (and probably also Paul), or their knowledge was very fragmentary. As a rule the New Testament authors came from the synagogue training of the Greek-speaking Jewish community of Palestine and the Diaspora ... Moreover, it was not literature which had the greatest missionary effect in the first and second centuries, but Jewish and Christian preaching, oral discussions and personal testimony in word and action, encounters which led to participation in the synagogue services or meetings of the Christian community.[39]

In addition to the relatively low levels of literacy in Roman Palestine, there were problems concerning the individual ownership of texts and access to writing instruments and writing media (papyrus, parchment, etc.). The economic conditions in the first-century were far from favorable. There was severe economic hardship, heightened by the great strain placed on the agrarian-oriented society.[40] The size of individual land holdings continued to decrease, while the tax burden increased. These were two among many factors that contributed to a financial climate in which owning texts was a luxury that few could afford. Texts were expensive to produce,[41] and the

---

"Illiteracy in the Land of Israel in the First Centuries C.E.," in *Essays in the Social Scientific Study of Judaism and Jewish Society* (ed. Simcha Fishbane, Stuart Schoenfeld, and A. Goldschlaeger; New York: KTAV, 1992), 46–61. Also, see Horsley and Draper, *Whoever*, 125–127, for a succinct summary of scholarship on ancient rates of literacy. Horsley presents the following summaries based upon recent work ancient literacy rates: 1% Mesopotamia; 5–10% classical Athens; 3% Roman Palestine.

[38] Horsley and Draper, *Whoever*, 127.

[39] Martin Hengel, *The "Hellenization" of Judaea in the First Century After Christ* (London: SCM Press, 1989), 55.

[40] The economic strain on the Galilean populous was great during the time of Jesus, leading Horsley to argue that *social banditry* was a dominant feature of first-century Galilee (Richard A. Horsley, *Bandits, Prophets, and Messiahs* [San Francisco: HarperSanFrancisco, 1988]). While Freyne disagrees with Horsley's conclusions, he agrees that poverty "was a basic fact of life" (Seán Freyne, *Galilee, Jesus and the Gospels* [Philadelphia: Fortress Press, 1988], 160).

[41] Millard acknowledges the high cost of acquiring texts, but suggests that the costs "would not put books out of the reach of the reasonably well-to-do" (*Reading and Writing*, 165). However, in light of the desperate economic situation envisaged by Horsley and Freyne, *et al.*, Millard's "reasonably well-to-do" must have comprised a very limited number of people — widespread ownership of texts was likely limited.

subsistence-level existence of the average person would make the individual purchase and ownership of texts an uncommon practice.[42]

Beyond these economic factors, one would need to envisage a social situation in which individuals had a self-perceived *need* to own texts personally. Individual participants in both local Jewish synagogue life and early Galilean Christianity would have had no need to own texts personally. The time-honored traditions so dear to both of these religious groups would have been intertwined with all facets of their lives, and their primary interaction with texts would have taken place within the context of public communal worship.[43] Thus, private ownership of texts was not necessary to have access to the tradition.[44] Any additional clarification or teaching on a written text would have been mediated through a *viva vox*,[45] and would not require direct access to a privately owned text. These criteria are extensive, and it is unlikely that a member of the agrarian class would have had either the economic means or social impetus to own texts. Given the above observations, it is highly likely that the private ownership of texts remained within reach of only those members of the economic and religious elite.

The lack of widespread literacy coupled with the financial inability to purchase or create texts meant that for the majority of people in first-century Palestine, the primary access to the early Jesus tradition was by way of the universally appropriated vehicle of spoken speech. In the next section we will explore further how oral communication was the dominant means for human interaction. Whether by means of oral proclamation or

---

[42] Millard presents several examples of the cost of producing texts, including that of a man in Egypt during the first-century who paid two drachmae for a copy of a letter; the projected cost of producing a scroll of Isaiah (6–10 denarii); and the estimated cost of the Chester Beatty codex ($\mathfrak{P}^{45}$) of the Gospels and Acts (44 drachmae), see Millard, *Reading and Writing*, 164–166. With regard to Torah scrolls, Hezser, *Jewish Literacy*, 146 suggests that the cost of their production was "exceedingly high, preventing the large majority of Jews from owning such scrolls privately."

[43] Hezser, *Jewish Literacy*, 452 suggests, "[i]n early Christian communities religious texts were mostly read when members gathered for worship." Gamble suggests that this practice was influenced by the similar practice of Torah reading in synagogue (Harry Y. Gamble, *Books and Readers in the Early Church: A History of Early Christian Texts* [New Haven: Yale University Press, 1995], 205–208).

[44] It is a similar situation even within later Rabbinic Judaism, whereby the primary access to the texts was through the public reading and aural reception of the text. Horsley, *Hearing the Whole Story*, 54–55 notes that the passages often cited to support the notion that ancient Jewish communities were "largely literate," actually depict the oral recitation and the *hearing* of pupils. This enabled the tradition to become "engraved on their souls . . . and guarded in their memory" (Josephus, *Ant.* 4.210, 16.43; Josephus, *C. Ap.* 2.175, 178, 204; Philo, *Legat.* 115, 210).

[45] See below, §4.4.2 for more on the *viva vox*.

aural reception, the interface between humans and tradition has been, and will always be the spoken word. Texts for the most part functioned indirectly in the tradition-transmission process, requiring a human mediator to bridge the gap between the seen and the heard word.

4.2   Oral Origins of Traditions and Texts

4.2.1   Oral Origins of Tradition

For heroes have the whole earth for their tomb; and in lands far from their own, where the column with its epitaph declares it, there is enshrined in every breast a record unwritten with no tablet to preserve it, except that of the heart (Thucydides, *Hist.* 2.43.3).[46]

Here we are addressing what is almost an *a priori* assumption in modern Jesus research: the Jesus tradition began as spoken voice, not written text. As far as we know, Jesus never wrote a book or left any autographs of any kind; the closest example of which we have in the gospel account of Jesus writing in the sand (John 8:6, 8:8),[47] and even in that case it is more likely that he was illustrating his point by drawing pictures or shapes rather than writing in Hebrew, Aramaic, or even Greek script.[48] Consequently, we are faced with the unavoidable paradox of having to study Jesus via a mediator, that is, texts which are at best second-hand accounts of his life and ministry. This realization is important and should impact the way in

---

[46] See also, Prov 3:3: "Do not let loyalty and faithfulness forsake you; bind them around your neck, write them on the tablet of your heart (כָּתְבֵם עַל־לוּחַ לִבֶּךָ)"; also, Jer 17:1: "The sin of Judah is written with an iron pen; with a diamond point it is engraved on the tablet of their hearts (עַל־לוּחַ לִבָּם), and on the horns of their altars."

[47] Even the authenticity of this solitary account of Jesus writing is debatable, and does not occur in the earliest manuscripts (e.g., $\mathfrak{P}^{66,75}$, א). Bruce M. Metzger, *A Textual Commentary on the Greek New Testament* (Stuttgart: Deutsche Bibelgesellschaft, 1994), 188 states that, "the case against its being of Johannine authorship appears to be conclusive," and that "it [John 7:53–8:11] is obviously a piece of oral tradition which circulated in certain parts of the Western church and which was subsequently incorporated into various manuscripts at various places" (Metzger, *Textual Commentary*, 188).

[48] Despite his assumption that Jesus was able to write, Bernard suggests that, ". . . it is probable that on this occasion He was only scribbling with His finger on the ground, a mechanical action which would suggest only an unwillingness to speak on the subject brought before Him . . ." (*The Gospel according to St. John* [Edinburgh: T&T Clark, 1928], 719). Raymond Brown surveys the debate and concludes that the simplest possibility is that "Jesus was simply tracing lines on the ground while he was thinking . . ." (*The Gospel according to John* [Garden City: Doubleday, 1966], 334) and surmises, "if the matter were important enough, the content of the writing would be reported" (*John*, 334).

which we analyze what remains in the form of texts. Such a view of the origin of the tradition is supported by the early church fathers of the first several centuries.

4.2.2 Papias

Papias (ca. 60–130 C.E.)[49] has attracted much attention over the history of New Testament scholarship despite the fact that none of his writings have been preserved to this day. His "Exposition of the Lord's Logia" (Eusebius, *Hist. eccl.* 3.39.1) existed in five volumes, none of which survive, leaving us only with fragments existing in the work of other church fathers.[50] Many scholars have focused their work on Papias, at times using the scarce remaining evidence as a foundation for their thesis. The estimation of Papias' worth for unravelling the complexity of the Synoptic Problem varies, from those who view Papias as definitive evidence for their thesis, to those who feel that what he says has little, if any relevance to the issue at hand.[51] It will be helpful to state at this stage

---

[49] It is difficult to date the writings of Papias, although the most common date given is between 100–150 C.E. Hengel dates Papias' writings to c. 120–135 (*Die johanneische Frage. Ein Lösungsversuch* [WUNT 67; Tübingen: Mohr Siebeck, 1993], 77) and Körtner to c. 110 (Ulrich H. J. Körtner and Martin Leutzsch, *Papiasfragmente. Hirt des Hermas* [Schriften des Urchristentums 3; Darmstadt: Wissenschaftliche Buchgesellschaft, 1998], 30–31). Harnack dated them to the later period of c. 140–160 (Adolf von Harnack, *Geschichte der altchristlichen Litteratur bis Eusebius. Zweiter Theil: Die Chronologie* [Leipzig: J. C. Hinrichs, 1897], 357).

[50] See Körtner and Leutzsch's critical edition of the Papias fragments for more detailed discussion on the background and history of the Papias tradition (*Papiasfragmente*). Papias' work has been preserved mainly in the writings of Eusebius (*Hist. eccl.* 3.39) and Irenaeus (*Adversus haereses* 5.33.3–4). Other fragments are located in the works of Apollinaris of Laodicea and Andrew of Caesarea (Andrew of Caesarea, *On the Apocalypse* ch. 34, serm. 12; Andrew of Caesarea, *On the Apocalypse* on Rev 12:7–9).

[51] Reicke places much emphasis on the testimony of Papias and possible eyewitnesses to Jesus (*The Roots of the Synoptic Gospels* [Philadelphia: Fortress, 1986], 46–47). On the other hand, Sanders argues that the Papias tradition is not evidence for the view that the "Jesus tradition was memorized and preserved orally" (*Studying*, 142). He establishes a firm dichotomy between what he labels "oral history" and "oral tradition" — relating the former with the statements of Papias. Subsequently, Sanders argues that the Papias tradition cannot be used to support a "believable environment in which extensive teaching material was precisely transmitted" (*Studying*, 142). This strong dichotomy appears to be constructed to refute Gerhardsson's model of transmission, but in so doing, Sanders makes many unsubstantiated assumptions regarding the process of oral transmission. In particular, that "first-century Jews did not sit around campfires telling and re-telling stories" (*Studying*, 142), and "we should not think that Jesus lived in a pre-literate society where everyone memorized everything. Documents abounded" (*Studying*, 141). Alan Millard has gone to great lengths to demonstrate that documents did abound

that it would be misguided to place too much emphasis on the implications
of the Papias tradition in matters peripheral to our central argument (e.g.,
Papias' relationship to Q, the Synoptic Problem, etc.); rather, we will only
use Papias to help support the broad thesis encompassed in this current
chapter.

In brief summary, the Papias tradition supports other available evidence
regarding the origins of the Jesus tradition. In particular we must look at
Papias' statements regarding the role and function of the disciples
Matthew and Mark in the reception and subsequent transmission of the
Jesus tradition. Papias attributes the source of the Jesus tradition to
remembered speech, not written and read texts.[52] Regarding Mark, Papias
describes the process of gospel production as one of Mark recalling what
he remembered of Peter's preaching and then writing that down —
Μάρκος μὲν ἑρμηνευτὴς Πέτρου γενόμενος, ὅσα ἐμνημόνευσεν,
ἀκριβῶς ἔγραψεν, οὐ μέντοι τάξει τὰ ὑπὸ τοῦ κυρίου ἢ λεχθέντα ἢ
πραχθέντα (*Hist. eccl.* 3.39.15),[53] and that he tried not to omit or falsify
anything — ἑνὸς γὰρ ἐποιήσατο πρόνοιαν, τοῦ μηδὲν ὧν ἤκουσεν
παραλιπεῖν ἢ ψεύσασθαί τι ἐν αὐτοῖς (*Hist. eccl.* 3.39.15).[54] This
statement by Papias has received much attention, and has often been
approached from the perspective of apologetic; that Papias' account states

during the time of Jesus (*Reading and Writing*), but as we have seen thus far in this
chapter, they did not replace oral communication as the primary medium through which
the Jesus tradition was transmitted. Following her survey of ancient epigraphical
evidence for Israelite literacy, Susan Niditch, *Oral World and Written Word: Ancient
Israelite Literature* (Library of Ancient Israel; Louisville: Westminister/John Knox,
1996), 59 concludes: "[a]ll of these examples [epigraphic evidence] thus find their place
on the oral-literate continuum, and all of these examples of literacy in ancient Israel do
not in the least overturn the suggestion that Israelites live in a world heavily informed by
the oral end of the continuum as I and others have defined it." To draw a strong
dichotomy between oral history and oral tradition does not take seriously the ability for
individuals and communities to transmit traditions in a controlled, informal manner, as
envisaged by Bailey ("Informal Controlled," 34–54).

[52] Jens Schröter has emphasized memory as a key component for studying the Jesus
tradition. He suggests that one can only understand the historical Jesus from the
perspective of how he was *remembered* by the early Christians (*Erinnerung an Jesu
Worte. Studien zur Rezeption der Logienüberlieferung in Markus, Q, und Thomas*
[WMANT 76; Neukirchen-Vluyn: Neukirchener Verlag, 1997], 465–466, 482–483; "The
Historical Jesus and the Sayings Tradition: Comments on Current Research," *NeoT* 30
[1996]: 153–158).

[53] Bart D. Ehrman, *The New Testament and Other Early Christian Writings* (New
York: Oxford University Press, 1998), 364 — "Mark, having become Peter's interpreter,
wrote down accurately everything he remembered, though not in order, of the things
either said or done by Christ."

[54] Lohr, "Oral Techniques," 434 argues that this statement of Papias "reveals to us a
significant aspect of the oral style."

that Mark "did not go wrong" because he wrote down a saying as he remembered it and tried not to omit anything.[55] Other scholars go further in arguing that Papias' main reason for writing his account was to exonerate Mark of all responsibility for the contents of his gospel.[56] Dungan summarizes Papias as follows: "Don't accuse Mark of wrongdoing. Mark was just the interpreter of Peter and faithfully copied down whatever Peter said. He didn't falsify or omit anything."[57] Abel also suggests that Papias is defending Mark, in arguing that Mark "made no mistake in omitting or falsifying anything which he heard"[58] because he was following Peter in adapting his material to fit the current needs of the moment (Eusebius, *Hist. eccl.* 3.39.15).[59] Regardless of Papias' motivation for writing what he did about Mark, his statements are helpful for they help us understand the process by which the Jesus tradition was transmitted during its earliest stages of development.

Papias also writes of his own interaction with the Jesus tradition. He describes a process of tradition transmission based upon oral communication. He would inquire carefully about the words of the elders (τοὺς τῶν πρεσβυτέρων ἀκέκρινον λόγους), specifically seeking a living testimony from those who had information about what was said by Jesus.[60] Papias mentions several by name: Andrew, Peter, Philip, Thomas, James, John, Matthew, Aristion, and the elder John (Eusebius, *Hist. eccl.* 3.39.4). This process of inquiry was intentional, for Papias writes that he "did not think that information from books would profit me as much as information from a living and abiding voice" (ζώσης φωνῆς καὶ μενούσης, Eusebius, *Hist. eccl.* 3.39.4).[61]

---

[55] E.g., Lohr, "Oral Techniques," 434.

[56] Dungan, *History*, 20.

[57] Dungan, *History*, 20; ὥστε οὐδὲν ἥμαρτεν is best translated as "did not do anything wrong" rather than "sin" (cf. Koester, *Ancient Christian Gospels*, 32–34).

[58] Abel, "Psychology," 273–274.

[59] See Reicke, *Roots*, 46.

[60] Compare this statement of Papias with other early statements about the words of Jesus (τῶν λόγων τοῦ κυρίου); Acts 20:35; *1 Clem.* 13:1.

[61] The significance of this statement by Papias has not been ignored. Andrew Walls sees the Papias tradition as an apologetic defense of some works that claimed to be reliable. Therefore, Walls argues that Papias is concerned about "the quality of the source, not whether it is oral or written" ("Papias and Oral Tradition," *VC* 21 [1967]: 139). Richard Glover's bias against orality runs deep as is apparent in a footnote in his work on the *Didache* — "[w]hy has so much stress been laid on the idea that Jesus' teaching was long preserved in none but oral form? If Jewish scholars made a fetish of burdening their memories in preference to using paper and ink, Gentiles did not. Besides, we have Papias' assurance that one of Jesus' own immediate followers committed his teaching to paper . . . surely the oral tradition idea is overdone" ("Didache's Quotations," 22). All of this is put into proper perspective by Loveday Alexander, see "The Living

Similarly, Papias describes Matthew as composing (συνετάξατο)[62] the oracles of Jesus (τὰ λόγια) in the Hebrew language ('Εβραΐδι διαλέκτῳ),[63] presumably from his hearing the preaching and teaching of Jesus himself.[64] Therefore, putting aside some of the more difficult implications of Papias' statements for the Synoptic Problem, we can at this point be confident in asserting that in the eyes of Papias, the early church and the gospel writers' primary, and most reliable access to the Jesus tradition was through oral accounts of the teaching and ministry of Jesus.

4.2.3 Apostolic Access to Oral Accounts

Apart from Papias there is additional evidence that points to the oral origins of the tradition, and suggests that the formulation and preservation of the early Jesus tradition was indebted deeply to the process of oral performance and proclamation. Clement of Alexandria, in his description of the process of gospel formation[65] states, as does Papias, that Mark followed Peter for a long period of time and remembered his sayings

---

Voice: Scepticism towards the Written Word in Early Christianity and in Graeco-Roman Texts," in *The Bible in Three Dimensions: Essays in Celebration of Forty Years of Biblical Studies in the University of Sheffield* (ed. D. J. A. Clines, S. E. Fowl, and S. E. Porter; JSOTSup 87; Sheffield: Sheffield Academic Press, 1990), 221–247, who demonstrates that Papias' statement concerning the *viva vox* is not unique, but rather one of many similar statements by Papias' contemporaries. We will treat the implications of the *viva vox* below (§4.4.2).

[62] "put in order together" perhaps is a more suitable translation for the Greek (συντάσσω, LSJ).

[63] This term is used in the NT to refer to Aramaic (Acts 21:40; 22:2; 26:14), and again in the fourth century (Eusebius, *Hist. eccl.* 3.39.16; Epiphanius, *Haer* 1.198.13; Basil of Caesarea, *Enarratio in prophetam Isaiam* 8.212). The same is true here.

[64] Streeter does not address the significance of the Papias tradition for understanding the oral origins of the tradition and the process by which it was transmitted; rather, he is narrowly concerned with the meaning of λόγια and the identity of Papias' πρεσβύτερος 'Ιωάννης (*Four Gospels*, 17–22). Streeter, in identifying the elder John with the Fourth Gospel (*contra* Taylor, *Formation*, 188), argues that Papias is concerned with the issue of apostolic authority, in particular, that "Gospels like Matthew and Mark, which were at times in conflict with it [i.e., the Gospel of John], were no more directly apostolic than itself" (*Four Gospels*, 21). According to Reicke (*Roots*, 46), Papias "wanted to say that Matthew also collected quotations and narratives, available to him in the form of living oral units." Koester also gives merit to the thesis that τὰ λόγια possibly refers to Q, "circulating as a document under the authority of Matthew" (*Ancient Christian Gospels*, 166), while Kloppenborg summarizes that Papias' testimony is "no longer treated as credible in respect to Q" (*Excavating Q*, 73). Also, see Kloppenborg, *Excavating Q*, 78–80 for a current summary of the debate on Papias and Q.

[65] Clement places the gospels with the genealogies first (Matthew and Luke), followed by Mark, and finally by the "spiritual gospel" (πνευματικὸν ποιῆσαι εὐαγγέλιον) of John (Eusebius, *Hist. eccl.* 6.14.5).

(μεμνημένον τῶν λεχθέντων, Eusebius, *Hist. eccl.* 6.14.6). Eusebius also describes Mark as a follower of Peter, and that Mark had received his material via oral tradition (Eusebius, *Hist. eccl.* 2.15). Eusebius also recounts Irenaeus' statements in regard to the sacred Gospels (τῶν ἱερῶν εὐαγγελίων), that Mark transmitted (παραδέδωκεν) things which Peter had preached, and adds that Luke wrote what Paul had preached (Eusebius, *Hist. eccl.* 5.8.2–4). This is indeed what Luke himself implies in his prologue when he emphasizes that which was handed down (παρέδοσαν ἡμῖν) from eyewitnesses (αὐτόπται) (Luke 1:2).[66]

Eusebius also recounts Irenaeus' statements about Polycarp, how Polycarp interacted with "John and the others who had seen the Lord," and how he "remembered their words, and what were the things concerning the Lord which he had heard from them, and about his miracles, and about [his] teaching." Irenaeus continues by stating that Polycarp had received these traditions from eyewitnesses (ὡς παρὰ τῶν αὐτοπτῶν τῆς ζωῆς τοῦ λόγου παρειληφώς), and that Irenaeus himself listened eagerly to these things and made notes of them, "not on paper but in my heart" (οὐκ ἐν χάρτῃ ἀλλ᾽ ἐν τῇ ἐμῇ καρδίᾳ) (Eusebius, *Hist. eccl.* 5.20.7).[67] Sanders quickly discounts the significance of this, and argues that this passage (and the previous passage from Papias) is not evidence "that the Jesus-material was memorized and preserved orally."[68] Sanders points out that Irenaeus "does not say that he was trained to remember what Polycarp taught," but rather that "old men can remember what they experienced as children."[69] He then concludes his assessment of this section by stating, "[t]here is no evidence from this passage that, around the turn of the first century, there was a body of memorized oral tradition for Christians to draw on. There were occasional reminiscences (Polycarp had met "eyewitnesses"), not a carefully controlled body of orally transmitted texts."[70] We must agree with Sanders, that this text does not demonstrate the existence of a

---

[66] For but one of numerous examples, "Luke's own perception of the oral period is that the process of the transmission of the materials was carried out by eyewitnesses" (Robert H. Stein, *Gospels and Tradition: Studies on Redaction Criticism of the Synoptic Gospels* [Grand Rapids: Baker, 1991], 45).

[67] See also, *1 Clem.* 2:8; Jer 17:1, 31:33; Prov 3:3, 7:3; and in particular, 2 Cor 3:1–3, where Paul writes, ἡ ἐπιστολὴ ἡμῶν ὑμεῖς ἐστε, ἐγγεγραμμένη ἐν ταῖς καρδίαις ἡμῶν, which is not written in ink, rather is written with the "spirit of the living God" (πνεύματι θεοῦ ζῶντος), not upon tablets of stone (λιθίναις), but ἐν πλαξὶν καρδίαις σαρκίναις.

[68] Sanders and Davies, *Studying*, 142.

[69] Sanders and Davies, *Studying*, 143.

[70] Sanders and Davies, *Studying*, 143.

"carefully controlled body" of oral tradition,[71] but that is not our concern. What we must state however, is that the Papias tradition is valuable and significant for our study; we must be open to the possibility that the informal retelling of communal traditions which Sanders discounts as unimportant, is indeed capable of sustaining and propagating reliable accounts within the community controls inherent in highly oral cultures.[72] Papias provides us with a window through which we can get a glimpse of the earliest processes of tradition formation and transmission, regardless of whether or not they should be classified as either oral tradition or oral history.[73]

4.2.4   Jewish Oral Accounts

Within Judaism there are numerous examples of a similar emphasis on the oral origins of tradition. Here, the Mishnah is an illustrative text, providing important insight into the place of oral tradition within what would become rabbinic Judaism following the destruction of the Jerusalem temple in 70 C.E.

Earlier, we noted that there was a desire within Jewish circles to attribute the writing down of laws to the early patriarchs such as Moses and Enoch. Such an emphasis on the written Torah within Judaism can lead one to the false assumption that the written Torah antedates the Oral Torah, and subsequently, that the Oral Torah is a less authoritative and significant body of material. Neusner suggests that we should not be "confused and think that written Torah goes back to Sinai, while Oral Torah derives from a much later period."[74] As Neusner points out, it is not only the written Torah that goes back to Sinai, but the Oral Torah as well. According to the Mishnah, the Oral Torah was handed to Moses on Mount Sinai and then handed down in succession to Joshua, the elders, the prophets, and finally to the "Men of Assembly" who were responsible for

---

[71] It appears that Sanders is reacting specifically against Gerhardsson's thesis of a formal, controlled process of tradition-transmission analogous to that typified by the later rabbinical movement.

[72] See Jan Vansina, *Oral Tradition: A Study in Historical Methodology* (Chicago: Aldine, 1965) and more recently Samuel Byrskog, *Story as History — History as Story: The Gospel Tradition in the Context of Ancient Oral History* (WUNT 123; Tübingen: Mohr Siebeck, 2000) for the argument that oral cultures can indeed preserve and transmit reliable history. We need not assume that formal, controlled, verbatim memorization is the only means through which we have access to reliable tradition.

[73] W. Sanday, in an early study of Papias and Q argues that Papias' λόγια is an appropriate description of the Q source, and that "we have in the statement of Papias about St. Matthew a bit of solid and trustworthy history" ("A Plea for the Logia," *ExpTim* 11 [1899]: 472–473).

[74] Neusner, *Oral Torah*, viii.

the development of rabbinic Judaism.[75] While we must be careful to distinguish between a rabbinic and historical reconstruction of the origins of the Oral Torah, it is significant that the Mishnah details the importance of oral tradition in the process of tradition transmission. The Mishnah, in its own *self-perception*, describes its constituent traditions as being handed down in oral form alongside the written Torah until their inscription in approximately 200 C.E.[76]

The presence of the Jewish concept of the dual Torah (both oral and written) indicates that there was a body of tradition that was different, or at least distinct, from the written Torah that was claimed to have been given by God at Sinai, and written down by Moses.[77] The Mishnah depicts this oral collection within the dual Torah as originating with God, "If a law comes to hand and you do not know its nature, do not discard it for another one, for lo, many laws were stated to Moses at Sinai, and all of them have been embedded in the Mishnah" (*y. Ḥag.* 1:7b). It is also depicted as originating "from the mouth of the Almighty" (*b. ʿErub.* 54b) in verbal form; note, not from an inscribed text. Therefore, the Mishnah's inscription of previously oral material is, in its own *self-perception*, the record of traditions that have been passed down, generation to generation, since the time of Moses.[78] These traditions originate from an oral proclamation and are passed down via oral processes within the Jewish context of a teacher-disciple relationship.[79]

---

[75] *m. ʾAbot* 1:1; see Neusner, *Oral Torah*, vii.

[76] See also Neusner, *Oral Torah*, vii.

[77] Gerhardsson summarizes the Oral Torah as "the interpretation of the written Torah — an interpretation given by God on Sinai!" (*Memory and Manuscript,* 82). Although one might question Gerhardsson's conclusions regarding the transmission of the Jesus tradition, his work does indeed support the notion that the distinction between written and unwritten tradition was not only acknowledged, but that it was even supported and at times upheld as normative. Within the Mishnah there is a striking realization that both groups of traditions exist, and that they should be preserved and transmitted exclusively within their respective media. One example will suffice here: "*K*. R. Yohanan and R. Yudan b. R. Simeon — One said, 'If you have kept what is preserved orally and also kept what is in writing, I shall make a covenant with you, and if not, I shall not make a covenant with you'. *L*. The other said, 'If you have kept what is preserved orally and you have kept what is preserved in writing, you shall receive a reward, and if not, you shall not receive a reward'" (*y. Ḥag.* 1:7). See Günter Stemberger, *Introduction to the Talmud and Midrash* (Edinburgh: T&T Clark, 1996), 31–44 for a discussion of the Oral Torah and oral tradition within rabbinic Judaism.

[78] Martin Jaffee argues that the rabbinic methods of oral instruction were intended to reproduce an original giving of the oral law from Moses to his disciples ("Writing and Rabbinic Oral Tradition: On Mishnaic Narrative Lists and Mnemonics," *Journal of Jewish Thought and Philosophy* 4 [1994]: 143–144).

[79] See *m. ʿEd.* 8:7; *b. ʿErub.* 54b.

4.3   Oral Sources for Texts

4.3.1   Texts Composed from Oral Accounts

If the earliest interaction with the Jesus tradition was by way of oral communication, then it likely follows that these oral accounts and traditions would be used as sources for the production of texts. As the early Christian movement began the process of writing comprehensive *bioi* about their founder,[80] it would be most natural for them to draw upon the rich reserve of communal traditions and stories to create their accounts.

We can find several helpful illustrations regarding this tendency to use oral sources when compiling or writing narratives. The pseudepigraphic *Letter of Aristeas* contains a description of its own compositional process. The author states with confidence that "a trustworthy narrative has been compiled" (*Let. Aris.* 1) which was based upon a personal meeting between Philocrates, Eleazar the high priest, and himself. The meeting itself arose from Philocrates "hearing a personal account" (*Let. Aris.* 1). Likewise, Philo of Alexandria describes the process by which he wrote his *De vita Mosis*. In his prologue Philo claims he will "tell the story of Moses as I have learned it" (*Mos.* 1.1.4), and that his sources are the sacred books (βίβλων τῶν ἱερῶν), the wisdom which Moses has left behind, and most importantly, the elders of his nation (τοῦ ἔθνους πρεσβυτέρων). Therefore, he summarizes his compositional process: "I always interwove what I was told with what I read . . ." (*Mos.* 1.1.4).

The above description of the compositional process as recorded by Philo and also in the *Letter of Aristeas* is strikingly similar to that described by Luke in his prologue (Luke 1:1–4). Luke's desire to compile an orderly (ἀνατάξασθαι) account parallels Aristeas' claim to have compiled a "trustworthy" narrative (*Let. Aris.* 1). Philo, Aristeas, and Luke all claim to have been aware of the existence of both oral and written sources, and all three authors claim to have incorporated oral traditional sources in their respective narratives (Philo, *Mos.* 1.1.4; *Let. Aris.* 1; Luke

---

[80] At this stage it is not necessary to determine the proper genre in which to place the Gospels' accounts. For now it will suffice to appropriate the work of Richard Burridge in classifying them as *bioi*, see Richard A. Burridge, *What Are the Gospels? A Comparison with Graeco-Roman Biography* (Cambridge: Cambridge University Press, 1992), and specifically his summary (*What Are the Gospels*, 254–255). As for the term "comprehensive," this is used to describe how the narrative accounts of the Gospels differ from the more disconnected logia of the hypothetical "Q" or even that of the *Gospel of Thomas*. Whether or not the Gospels are *sui generis* is not of concern here. Rather, what is important is that regardless of their genre, the Gospels do represent an attempt (for the first time?) to gather together the Jesus tradition in a coherent, logical, and orderly narrative (cp. Luke 1:1–4).

1:2). These similarities are not simply narrative devices used programmatically in the creation of prologues,[81] but indicate that for both the author and recipient (reader/hearer), oral traditions were accepted as valid sources for texts,[82] even those that might be concerned with historical reconstruction.

Luke is not the only ancient writer to have drawn from oral sources when researching and writing a text. Among the Greeks we can examine their two most influential historians, Herodotus and Thucydides. Their works are quite different from one another despite the fact that they were both historians concerned primarily with writing an historical account of the recent wars among the Greeks. Although they differed in both content and style, they agreed in regard to their selection of source material. Both Herodotus and Thucydides had access to oral sources, and used them during the writing of their respective works. Oral sources can account for up to eighty percent of Herodotus' material, and he mentions those oral sources by name on at least three occasions (Herodotus, *Hist.* 3.55.2; 4.76.6; 9.16.1).[83] Thucydides also incorporated oral reports into his historical account:

And with regard to my factual reporting of the events of the war I have made it a principle not to write down the first story that came my way, and not even to be guided by my own general impressions; either I was present myself at the events which I have described or else *I heard them from eye-witnesses whose reports I have checked with as much thoroughness as possible.* Not that even so the truth was easy to discover: different

---

[81] See Loveday C. A. Alexander, "Luke's Preface in the Pattern of Greek Preface Writing," *NovT* 28 (1986): 63–64, also Loveday C. A. Alexander, *The Preface to Luke's Gospel: Literary Convention and Social Context in Luke 1:1–4 and Acts 1:1* (SNTSMS 78; Cambridge: Cambridge University Press, 1993). She notes that despite the similarities between Luke's preface and other parallels, the great variation suggests that there is not one specific predecessor to Luke's prologue but rather that "he is composing freely, but in a certain style and within a certain pattern which is distributed widely throughout the scientific tradition" ("Preface," 64). Alexander feels that Luke did not deliberately choose to use a "scientific preface-style," but rather, his work should be considered as an example of a "formal" style of Greek writing ("Preface," 65–66).

[82] Stein writes that both Luke and Theophilus "were aware of, and at least in the case of Luke, acquainted with both the written and the oral traditions" (*Gospels and Tradition*, 46).

[83] Herodotus mentions Archias of Sparta (*Hist.* 3.55.2), Tymnes at Oblia (*Hist.* 4.76.6), and Thersander of Orchomenos (*Hist.* 9.16.1). John Maricola writes that Herodotus "presents his work as a collection of oral traditions, and his method is frequently to allow native spokesmen to present their case: 'the Persians say', 'the Egyptians say'" (John Maricola, *Herodotus: The Histories* [London: Penguin, 1996], xviii).

eye-witnesses gave different accounts of the same events, speaking out of partiality for one side or the other or else from imperfect memories [italics mine].[84]

Thucydides emphasizes his access to reliable *oral accounts* when writing his historical work (cp. Thucydides, *Hist.* 1.138.6; 2.5.5–6; 2.48.2; 3.88.3; 6.2.2), although he does not cite them by name specifically as does Herodotus.[85]

In addition to the specific references to oral sources within the nonbiblical literature, many scholars have come to a similar conclusion regarding both the Hebrew Bible and the New Testament, although, as we have already noted, the implications of this fundamental premise have not always been taken seriously.[86]

4.3.2 The Didache's Oral Origins

There is also a strong likelihood that the *Didache* is highly indebted to oral sources and the processes of oral communication. The debate has often centered on the question of its possible dependency upon the Synoptic Gospels, in particular the nature of the relationship between the *Didache* version of the Lord's Prayer (8:2) and the Synoptic parallels in Matthew (6:9–13) and Luke (11:2–4). Also of concern is the multiply attested "Two Ways" doctrine in *Didache* 1–5 and *Barnabas* 18–20. In both cases, some scholars have argued that these traditions in the *Didache* are not derivative of the Synoptic Gospels, but rather derive from a shared oral tradition that circulated freely among the early Christian communities of the time.[87] As for the Lord's Prayer, Rordorf argues that it is based upon the "oral form of the prayer in use in his community,"[88] and Koester rightly states that "it is unlikely that a Christian writer would have to copy from any written

---

[84] (Thucydides, *Hist.* 1.22; trans. Warner) — τὰ δ᾽ ἔργα τῶν πραχθέντων ἐν τῷ πολέμῳ οὐκ ἐκ τοῦ παρατυχόντος πυνθανόμενος ἠξίωσα γράφειν, οὐδ᾽ ὡς ἐμοὶ ἐδόκει, ἀλλ᾽ οἷς τε αὐτὸς παρῆν καὶ παρὰ τῶν ἄλλων ὅσον δυνατὸν ἀκριβείᾳ περὶ ἑκάστου ἐπεξελθών. ἐπιπόνως δὲ ηὑρίσκετο, διότι οἱ παρόντες τοῖς ἔργοις ἑκάστοις οὐ ταὐτὰ περὶ τῶν αὐτῶν ἔλεγον, ἀλλ᾽ ὡς ἑκατέρων τις εὐνοίας ἢ μνήμης ἔχοι.

[85] See Aune, "Prolegomena," 77.

[86] Gunkel's view regarding the oral origins of the text has been "widely accepted" and should not be confused with what Robert Culley calls the "modern" problem relating to the "presuppositions of the literary criticism which Gunkel accepted and employed" ("Approach," 113). This is quite similar to the current New Testament consensus regarding the oral origins of the Jesus tradition, see chapter 3, above.

[87] For an extensive examination of both of these parallel traditions, see Huub van de Sandt and David Flusser, *The Didache: Its Jewish Sources and Its Place in Early Judaism and Christianity* (CRINT 5; Assen: Van Gorcum, 2002).

[88] Willy Rordorf, "Does the Didache Contain Jesus Tradition Independently of the Synoptic Gospels?," in *Jesus and the Oral Gospel Tradition* (ed. Henry Wansbrough; JSNTSup 64; Sheffield: JSOT Press, 1991), 422.

source in order to quote the Lord's Prayer."[89] The liturgical character of the prayer along with its use in early Christian worship is indicative of its indebtedness to oral tradition.[90] Rordorf, in his work on the *Didache*, argues that the "Two Ways" section "has preserved a Jesus tradition independently of the Synoptic Gospels [i.e., oral tradition],"[91] although he avoids the question of the relationship between the "Two Ways" tradition found in both *Didache* 1–5 and the alleged "Q" source.[92] Rordorf also likens his findings to that of Niederwimmer, who argues that the "Two Ways" section of the *Didache* derives from oral tradition.[93] Apart from that specific question there is the more general question regarding the sources behind the book as a whole.

Ian Henderson argues that the *Didache* is described best as "oral" and on several occasions it reveals a "suppression of literate sensibility,"[94] although he does recognize that its author might have made use of some written sources for the "Two Ways" section (*Did.* 1–5).[95] Although he allows for the possibility of written sources, his thesis is that the *Didache* "remains a book essentially about the normativity of various kinds of speech, a text which, though written and dependent on written sources, takes in itself no cognizance of writing."[96] He summarizes his argument for an "oral" *Didache* with the following three points: 1) It embodies to an unusual extent an oral poetic/compositional sensibility. The book is centered, topically and symbolically on oral categories, to the "exclusion of literary metaphors and literary argumentative logic,"[97] and that the *Didache* relies on oral conversational techniques. 2) It is oral in that its argument depends on an oral attitude towards harmonizing apparently divergent voices. The *Didache* "is not only orally written; it is *about*

---

[89] Koester, *Ancient Christian Gospels*, 16.

[90] Sandt states, ". . . there is no need to assume that the Didache is dependent on the gospel of Matthew, for it is most unlikely that the (Christian) editor of this unit in the Didache would have needed Matthew's text in order to reproduce the prayer. On the contrary, it makes more sense to assume that he is citing the liturgical, that is, the oral form of public prayer" (*Didache*, 294–295). Cf. Hans Dieter Betz, *The Sermon on the Mount. A Commentary on the Sermon on the Mount, Including the Sermon on the Plain* (Hermeneia; Minneapolis: Fortress, 1995), 371.

[91] Rordorf, "Didache," 411.

[92] Rordorf, "Didache," 411.

[93] Kurt Niederwimmer, *Die Didache* (Kommentar zu den Apostolischen Vätern 1; Göttingen: Vandenhoeck & Ruprecht, 1989), 108.

[94] Ian Henderson, "Didache and Orality in Synoptic Comparison," *JBL* 111 (1992): 297, 305.

[95] Henderson, "Didache and Orality," 293.

[96] Henderson, "Didache and Orality," 293.

[97] Henderson, "Didache and Orality," 305.

orality, as a normative hermeneutical strategy."[98]   3) Further elements
within the *Didache* suggest "the relative probability of social-historical
exposure to milieus in which the cultivation of conversational oral
tradition is imaginable."[99]

4.3.3   Other Early Christian Literature

In addition to the *Didache*, there are other early Christian texts that have a
strong connection to the oral communicative processes indicative of their
time.[100] Dennis MacDonald has argued that the story of Thekla's divine
avoidance of death during her captivity was first told orally prior to its
inclusion in the *Acts of Paul*.[101] In summary, MacDonald presents three
reasons for his view regarding the oral origins of the Thekla tradition.
First, he argues that the story is "full of folkloric commonplace —
beautiful nubile women, frustrated lovers, journeys, perils, and miraculous
rescues — and that it conforms to commonly recognized conventions of
oral narrative." Second, that "Thecla's popularity was in no way dependent
on the reception of the *Acts of Paul*," and third, "Tertullian knew of some
who told the story to legitimate the right of women to teach and baptize"
(Tertullian, *Bapt.* 17.5).[102] MacDonald asserts that "Thekla was popular in
the imaginations of early Christians," and that the Pastoral Epistles seem to
be aware of, and reacting against the oral circulation of these legends
concerning Thekla.[103] If this is indeed the case, then we have another clear
example of an oral account being used as source material for a text.

---

[98] Henderson, "Didache and Orality," 305.

[99] Henderson, "Didache and Orality," 305.

[100] Koester has argued extensively throughout his career that the scriptural citations
contained within the writings of the early church fathers were not derived from the
gospel texts in their attested forms (*Apostolischen Vätern*). Given that the Synoptic
Gospels were written prior to the existence of any authoritative, and/or fixed textual
tradition, it would be less likely that they were citing verbatim other preexisting
Christian texts. It took a significant period of time before the early Christian texts and
Gospels achieved a status that could be described as both fixed and authoritative, and
thus worthy of citation *as texts*.

[101] Dennis Ronald MacDonald, "From Audita to Legenda: Oral and Written Miracle
Stories," *Forum* 2:4 (1986): 16–17.

[102] All three points from MacDonald, "Audita to Legenda," 16–17.

[103] Dennis Ronald MacDonald, "Thekla, Acts of," *ABD* 6: 443–444. MacDonald
argues that the stories dismissed as "tales told by old women" (1 Tim 4:7) are in fact
those concerning Thekla (*The Legend and the Apostle: The Battle for Paul in Story and
Canon* [Philadelphia: Westminster, 1983]).

4.3.4 Conclusion

Our above survey highlighted the role of oral sources in the production of ancient texts. We can now conclude by stating with confidence that the production of ancient texts involved the incorporation of oral sources in addition to whatever other textual sources were at hand. Oral sources were an indispensable element that contributed to the writings of the Greek historians, the Pseudepigrapha, the Mishnah, and early Christian literature like the *Didache* and the *Acts of Paul*.

4.4 Oral Performance and Written Texts

Performance is at the very center of oral cultures. Cultures that rely heavily on oral communication for the transmission and preservation of their self-identity must continually perform and re-perform the same traditions over and over. In this case, anything worth remembering is worth performing, and indeed must be performed or will soon be lost and unrecoverable.[104] This fragile characteristic of oral performance is among the primary reasons why many cultures eventually utilize the technology of writing to preserve important communal traditions. As we shall see in this section, oral performance is often related to the production of written texts. This provides us with additional evidence that the processes of oral communication had a profound impact on both the content and structure of ancient texts.[105] Here we shall examine examples in which texts claim to be written as a result of direct contact with an oral performance.

We return, once again, to one of the earlier examples of written texts. We can discern the remnants of oral performance from extant examples of ancient Mesopotamian texts. The aforementioned legal codes (CH, LE) were inscribed following their proclamation by the king. They were often inscribed in a public place, possibly at the town gate and included a list of those who witnessed the proclamation and inscription.[106] This concept of the "living" presence of the king is reinforced further by examples from Hittite treaties that begin with "Thus says," in reference to the ongoing presence of the king in each re-proclaiming of the text.[107]

---

[104] This is a universal characteristic of all primary oral/residually oral cultures. See below on the characteristics of orally transmitted material.

[105] Even "modern" texts have been impacted significantly by the demands of the oral medium. See Ong, *Orality and Literacy*, 25–27.

[106] Alan R. Millard, "Oral Proclamation and Written Record: Spreading and Preserving Information in Ancient Israel," in *Michael* (ed. Yitzhak Avishur and Robert Deutsch; Tel Aviv: Archaeological Center Publications, 1999), 239.

[107] Millard, "Oral Proclamation," 239.

In addition, we have many similar references within the extant Sumerian and Akkadian letters. The majority of letters focus on the interaction between kings, or between a king and one or more of his subjects. We are not interested in the content of the letter *per se*, but more on the way in which they relate to oral performance.

Among the ANE texts is a Sumerian letter from King Ibbi-Sin which begins; "To Puzur-Numushda, the governor of Kazallu *speak*; thus *says* your king Ibbi-Sin" (ANET, p.480). Note that in this case the preface of the written letter includes the recipient and more importantly the curious phrase "thus *says* your king Ibbi-Sin [italics mine]." This use of the present tense indicates that the letter is designed to function as a substitute for the living presence of the king himself. The king has "performed" the content of the letter to a scribe who subsequently inscribed his oral performance into a text which would, at a later time, be re-proclaimed to its intended recipient.

As was often the case in antiquity, written communication was a vehicle for speech rather than a visual abstraction that could communicate silently apart from a messenger. Throughout the ANE and other ancient cultures, letters were written as a transcription of a prior oral performance. The Mari and Amarna letters illustrate this characteristic of ancient texts. There are numerous textual references to what were previously communicated events. For example, ". . . *saying to me*: I will send him by ship to the king" (ANET, p. 485; EA, no. 245, 25–30), "But *I answered them*: May the god of the king, my lord, preserve me from making war against the people . . ." (ANET, p. 485; EA, no. 250, 15–25), "[a]nd thus the two sons of Lab'ayu *spoke*: 'Be hostile to the king . . .'" (ibid., 40–45), "To the king, my lord, my pantheon, my Sun-god, *say* . . . Now he seeks two thousand (shekels) of silver from my hand, *saying to me*: 'Give me thy wife and thy children, or I will smite!'" (ANET, p.486; EA, no.270).[108] It quickly becomes apparent that these letters are inscribed transcriptions of prior oral performance.[109] They are meant to be heard, not read. When a messenger recited these letters, the inscribed text became a living oral *performance*. The letters are not created with a concern for the past, but rather are designed to re-enact past events with a sense of immediacy that is only achievable through the aural reception of an oral performance.

The *Testaments of the Twelve Patriarchs* provides us with additional evidence of this function of texts. Once again the text describes its own function as one of presenting the reader/hearer with a "copy of the words"

---

[108] cf., ANET, p.484, RA, XIX, p.100; ANET, p.485, EA, no. 244; ANET, p.485, RA, XIX, p.97; ANET, p.486, EA, no.270.

[109] Ong, makes a similar point regarding early written poetry, which he states is at first a "mimicking in script of oral performance" (*Orality and Literacy*, 26).

of a particular patriarch. These indicators typically occur at the beginning of the books, often in the opening verse. Several of the testaments begin with the formula "a copy of the words of . . ." (ἀντίγραφον λόγων . . .), followed by the name attributed to the testament itself, for example, "a copy of the words of Simeon . . ." (*T. Sim.* 1:1). This same formula is repeated in several of the other testaments (*T. Levi* 1:1; *T. Jud.* 1:1; *T. Iss.* 1:1; *T. Dan* 1:1), and occurs with a slight variation in others, where the phrase "a copy of the testament . . ." (ἀντίγραφον διαθήκης . . .) replaces the previous formula (*T. Reu.* 1:1; *T. Zeb.* 1:1; *T. Naph.* 1:1).[110]

In each of the testaments in the *T. 12 Patr.*, the reference to prior oral performance extends far beyond the introductory formula, and is present throughout the text. In the *Testament of Simeon*, the preface is written from the perspective of a third-person narrator until chapter two where there is a sudden shift from third to first person at the point where Simeon takes on the role of narrator.[111] The account then progresses from that point and one can envisage the hearer of the text feeling as though she or he were actually hearing Simeon himself.

This dimension of oral performance is made even more explicit in several of the other testaments. In the *Testament of Levi*, the narrator prepares the stage for Levi by explicitly stating that "when they [his sons] were gathered together *he said* (εἶπε) to them" (*T. Levi.* 1:2). A similar setting is constructed in Judah — "when they [his sons] gathered together and came to him, *he said* (εἶπεν) to them" (*T. Jud.* 1:2), Issachar — "He called his sons to him and *said* (εἶπεν) . . ." (*T. Iss.* 1:1), Dan — "Assembling his clan, he said (εἶπεν) . . ." (*T. Dan.* 1:2), Naphtali — "when his sons were gathered together (*T. Naph.* 1:2) . . . he began *to say* (λέγειν) to his sons (*T. Naph.* 1:5).[112] In each of the above there is a conscious gathering of people together, and a subsequent performance to the group.[113] What is noteworthy is that there is a conscious switch in narration, from a third to first person perspective. This shift indicates that the text is *presenting itself* as a written account of previous verbal interaction.[114] In this case, the text reveals its intended function, anticipates

---

[110] Cf. *T. Job* 51:1–4, where the author attributes his access to the tradition to an "oral interaction" between Job and the "holy angel" — "[I] heard the magnificent things, while each one made explanation to the other."

[111] Gray, "Repetition," 300 describes the sudden shift of person as one indication of prior oral performance.

[112] Cf. *T. Job.* 1:4; *T. Issac* 1:4.

[113] If one grants the premise that Jesus chose/collected his twelve disciples to form a group around him, we have a similar historical situation to that of the gathering/performing as envisioned in the *T. 12 Patr.*

[114] This is of course not to assume that the words of each patriarch have been recorded verbatim, but does indicate that oral performance was an integral part of the

an oral retelling, and accordingly assumes that it would be retold verbally to an audience. Such is the way of the ancient text — it is not transcribed orality, not a text to be read silently, but a performance to be re-enacted in the presence of an audience. Each subsequent reader (i.e., performer) of the text takes on the character and persona of its respective patriarch, thereby conveying not only the content of the message, but appealing to the authority and presence of the patriarch himself.

Additional clues reveal the close connection between oral performance and written text, in particular, the high frequency of words belonging to the semantic domain of oral communication and aural reception. Performance oriented words such as "speak," "say," and "tell" are used rather than visually oriented words related to the silent reading and visual interaction with a text. Also prominent are words such as "hear," and "listen," which indicate the intended aural reception of the inscribed text. The testament of Naphtali contains a succinct summary of this characteristic of *T. 12 Patr.* as a whole: "Then he [Naphtali] began to *say* to his sons, '*Listen* (ἀκούσατε), my children, sons of Naphtali, *hear* your father's words (ἀκούσατε λόγους πατρός ὑμῶν)" (*T. Naph.* 1:5).

The Hebrew Bible also contains many references to oral performance, and it is often associated with the production of the Biblical texts themselves. We find specific reference to this phenomenon within the prophetic tradition, particularly in the book of Jeremiah.[115] The implied narrator of Jeremiah indicates that the book is the product of previous oral performances by the prophet himself. As was the case with Moses, YHWH instructs Jeremiah to write in a book all the words spoken to him (Jer 30:2; 36:2). The genesis of the initial prophetic content is credited to YHWH and passed down to Jeremiah via oral processes.[116] The origin of the tradition is attributed to an audible voice within the context of oral performance. Although this oral performance attributed to YHWH is admittedly of a different character than that between two humans, it is illustrative nonetheless, for it shows the perceived importance of these oral processes in both vertical and horizontal relationships.

---

transmission and subsequently was presented as an ideal witness, or testimony to the life of each patriarch; see Gray, "Repetition," 300. This evidence helps illustrate the *perceived importance* of oral performance and oral tradition during the late second-temple period.

[115] This phenomenon is found elsewhere in the Hebrew Bible. For example, in 2 Chr 35:25, Jeremiah is said to have uttered a lament for Josiah, and that "singing men and women" have spoken of Josiah, and that these traditions have been written in the Laments (כְּתוּבִים עַל־הַקִּינוֹת). Also, see *T. Job* 51:1–4.

[116] There is an association of the words of YHWH with those of Jeremiah, so that Jeremiah functions as the "mouth" of the Lord (Jer 25:13).

The second link between oral performance and written text is in the mode, or method, of transferring the tradition from the tradent to an inscribed text. In the case of Jeremiah, that process is described as one of dictation from the prophet himself to a scribe.[117] Baruch is associated with the inscription of the prophetic performance by way of Jeremiah's dictation, and thus, according to the text's self-description, it is the result of the verbal process of dictation. As was the case with the above ANE texts, the dictation and subsequent inscription of prior oral performance is a way by which the authority and presence of Jeremiah can be conveyed via a text. These examples convey a sense of the important place occupied by oral processes in antiquity; and that oral performance is often related to the production of written texts.

We can thus summarize this section by stating that orality had a great impact on each stage of the process of tradition formation and transmission. It is possible to discern the existence of *implicit orality* and *implied performance* within written texts. While this does not enable us as such to "uncover" the original oral performance, or allow us to argue conclusively for the oral origins of texts (e.g., *T. 12 Patr.*), it does enable us to understand the great significance that oral communication had in ancient society. Given the great interaction between oral performance and written texts, we must not be surprised to find that the content, organization, and structure of texts often exhibits legacy characteristics which are indicative of their origins in oral communication. In the next section we will explore the extent to which the reception of ancient texts was often via the medium of spoken voice, and thus, were *aurally received*.

4.5 Reading Aloud

When we approach the study of ancient texts, and in particular, their mode of reception, we must take into consideration several important social factors before we can feel confident enough to reconstruct a plausible setting for such activity. Apart from issues related to the level of literacy among the highly agrarian populations, which we will address later, we must uphold the notion that in antiquity, reading was primarily a *social activity*. Ong notes that reading tended to be an activity that involved the public reading of a text to a group of people.[118] The group could consist of an extended family, or perhaps the local community, depending on the

---

[117] See Jer 36:4, 6, 17–18, 28, 32; 45:1.

[118] Ong, *Orality and Literacy*, 131; also George Steiner, *Language and Silence: Essays on Language, Literature, and the Inhuman* (New York: Athenaeum, 1967), 383.

content and importance of the work. Such a public context indicates that the primary access to texts was through an oral performance; not private, personal reading that would require "a home spacious enough to provide for individual isolation and quiet."[119] Given the physical parameters of the ancient house and the social class of the majority of Jesus' followers, it is difficult to envisage the average first-century home as a suitable context for private, individual reading. In sum, we must realize that oral/aural factors influenced all aspects of the production and reception of ancient texts.[120]

If we grant the premise that private, silent reading was not the predominant means for interacting with a text, we must consider that with few exceptions, texts were read aloud, and functioned orally. We are reminded of the previously discussed work of Achtemeier in his "Omne Verbum Sonat," in which he demonstrates that reading was an aural activity, not a visual interaction with a text[121], and therefore essentially *functioned* as oral transmission.[122] Oral reading of texts was not only done within a group setting, but was also the *de facto* means for the private reading of texts intended for individuals.[123] Thomas Boomershine concludes that "silent reading was, if it existed in the first century, an

---

[119] Ong, *Orality and Literacy*, 131. Archaeological evidence from the first-century C.E. suggests that most Palestinian homes could be divided into two primary categories ("simple house," "courtyard house"). The "simple house" was the most common type of dwelling. According to Guijarro, the size of these homes varied from 20 to 200m², although "most of them were very small" (Santiago Guijarro, "The Family in First-Century Galilee," in *Constructing Early Christian Families: Family as Social Reality and Metaphor* (ed. Halvor Moxnes; New York: Routledge, 1997), 50). These homes were often enlarged to accommodate siblings and their new families. The courtyard home was the other most popular type of home in first-century Palestine. This type of home consisted of several smaller houses which shared a common courtyard. In either case, it would be difficult to envision the type of privacy required to engage in personal, private reading. For more on this see L. E. Stager, "The Archaeology of the Family in Ancient Israel," *BASOR* 260 (1985): 17–18.

[120] Alexander, "Book Production," 86 highlights the aural factors involved in the production of texts. She states that "the primary means of publication in Greco-Roman antiquity was *oral performance*."

[121] Achtemeier, "Omne Verbum Sonat"; Michael Slusser, "Reading Silently in Antiquity," *JBL* 111 (1992): 499. Even Frank Gilliard, who challenges the extent to which Achtemeier argues for an exclusive verbalization of written texts, concludes that there is abundant evidence that the culture of late Western antiquity is one of "high residual orality," see Frank D. Gilliard, "More Silent Reading in Antiquity: Non Omne Verbum Sonabat," *Journal of Biblical Literature* 112 (1993): 694.

[122] Øivind Andersen rightly classifies "the reading aloud of a text as oral transmission, though admittedly of a less 'pure' nature than if the text in question had been learnt by heart or if no writing was involved at all" ("Oral Tradition," 26).

[123] Achtemeier, "Omne Verbum Sonat," 15–17.

extraordinary and disrespected idiosyncrasy. Private reading aloud was more frequent but, because of the scarceness of texts, remained a luxury available to relatively few individuals."[124] Likewise, Shemaryahu Talmon argues that "all reading was aloud, and most probably intoned, in a sing-song voice."[125]

We have previously summarized Lord's work on the Homeric question, in particular, with respect to the oral origins of the Homeric epics. The works of Homer provide us with another glimpse into several aspects of the relationship between oral performance and written text. They are a good example of the difficulty inherent in the study of highly "oral" texts. The epics confront us in the form of written texts, but the traditions therein are demonstrably oral in origin. There is little doubt that the Homeric epics were intended to be read aloud following their inscription, and thus it is not surprising that they exhibit characteristics of orally composed and aurally received material. Lord recognized this characteristic of Homeric epic, and brought to the fore the realization that the extant texts are densely packed with formulae that derive from the tradition's pre-textual existence in the form of orally performed sagas. Oral compositional devices such as ring composition and parataxis can be found throughout the epics, and the metrical hexameter exhibited throughout aids in both the composition/recitation and reception thereof.[126] What can be ascertained from Homer is quite significant; that is, it is clear that the epics are texts, but served as handmaidens to aurality.[127] The epics circulated orally for a]long period of time before they were eventually inscribed in a text, and following that transition were read aloud and performed in public settings,

---

[124] Thomas E. Boomershine, "Peter's Denial as Polemic or Confession: The Implications of Media Criticism for Biblical Hermeneutics," *Semeia* 39 (1987): 53–54. Boomershine draws attention to Augustine's surprise at Ambrose' silent reading of a text (Augustine, *Conf.* 6.3.3) .

[125] Shemaryahu Talmon, "Oral Tradition and Written Transmission, or the Heard and the Seen Word in Judaism of the Second Temple Period," in *Jesus and the Oral Gospel Tradition* (ed. Henry Wansbrough; JSNTSup 64; Sheffield: JSOT Press, 1991), 150. This method of vocalization was what Lord encountered in his Yugoslavian field work, see *Singer*.

[126] For parataxis in Homer see James A. Notopoulos, "Parataxis in Homer: A New Approach to Homeric Literary Criticism," *Transactions of the American Philological Association* 80 (1949): 1–23. Roland Meynet, *Rhetorical Analysis: An Introduction to Biblical Rhetoric* (JSOTSup 256; Sheffield: Sheffield Academic Press, 1998), 172–177 suggests that parataxis is one of the three characteristics of Hebrew rhetoric. He then proceeds to suggest that the New Testament authors "have followed — consciously and/or unconsciously — the laws of composition of Hebrew rhetoric" (*Rhetorical Analysis*, 176).

[127] Talmon comes to the same conclusion with regard to the Hebrew Bible ("Oral Tradition," 150).

thereby functioning within the realm of oral communication.[128] The Greeks themselves recognized that this was the case and that Homer was composed for the *ears*, and not the eyes.[129] Isocrates' describes two kinds of pleasure, that of the myth, and that of contests and action. Homer's myth is presented for the *ears*, while the contests and action of other poets are for the benefit of the eyes.[130] Aristotle, working with the categories of tragedy and epic, states that the quality of an epic can be discerned by reading it aloud,[131] and Lycurgus indicates that Homer's epics were of such great cultural worth that they were read aloud during the Panathenaea.[132]

The Biblical evidence also agrees with the premise that oral presentation and aural reception were integral to all facets of interaction with written texts. For many centuries following the formation of the Christian canon and the production of the Bible text, its message reached its intended recipients via oral speech.[133] George Kennedy notes that "very

---

[128] Edgar Conrad argues that the written texts of the Old Testament formed the basis for the oral proclamation of the tradition; see "Heard But Not Seen: The Representation of 'Books' in the Old Testament," *JSOT* 54 (1992): 45–59.

[129] There are countless references to eyes and ears in Greek literature. Although it demands a study on its own, a few points can be made here. At times "ears" and "eyes" are mentioned together in a collective manner to refer to experiencing something with all of one's senses (e.g., Xenophon, *Cynegeticus* 1.4; Aeschines, *Speeches (Against Ctesiphon)* 3.255; Lysias, *Olympiacus* 2.1), at other times they are used in a specific manner to highlight the difference between the auditory and visual senses (Plato, *Respublica* 530d; Diodorus Siculus, *Bibliotheca historica* 14.60.7) , and most importantly, as we will discuss later, eyes and ears are sometimes mentioned in the context of trusting one sense over another.

[130] "Wherefore we may well admire the poet Homer and the first inventors of tragedy, seeing that they, with true insight into human nature, have embodied both kinds of pleasure in their poetry; for Homer has dressed the contests and battles of the demigods in myths, while the tragic poets have rendered the myths in the form of contests and action, so that they are presented, not to our ears alone, but to our eyes as well (μὴ μόνον ἀκουστοὺς ἡμῖν ἀλλὰ καὶ θεατοὺς γενέσθαι)" (Isocrates, *Ad Nicoclem* 48, *trans.* Norlin) .

[131] Aristotle, *Poetica* 1462a.1.

[132] Lycurgus, *Against Leocrates* 102. Lycurgus also states that Homer is more valuable for instruction for his works give "life lessons" that affect one's heart, while laws (i.e., written laws) only state what must be done. The Panathenaea was a festival held in Athens every four years, dedicated to Athena (Paul Brooks Duff, "Processions," *The Anchor Bible Dictionary* 5: 469–473).

[133] Boomershine insightfully observes, "[t]he irony of the current state of biblical studies is that the recognition of public reading as the intended medium of ancient literature has been known for decades. It has become virtually a commonplace in the study of medieval literature. But in the study of much earlier biblical literature, *this recognition has received little or no attention* [italics mine]" ("Peter's Denial," 54).

few early Christians owned copies of the Bible and some did not know how to read."[134] Kennedy has touched on an important point, but has been too gracious in his assessment of levels of literacy in antiquity. It is likely that that very few Christians outside the religious and academic elite possessed the ability to read, and therefore most people would not be able to experience the written text without a mediator who would present it to them in an oral form.[135] This is a very significant observation, of which we can easily lose sight in our present print culture. Both the Hebrew Bible and the New Testament were produced in a highly oral culture, and both were written with the expectation that they would be read aloud.

The Hebrew Bible and Apocrypha are packed with references to aural reception, and Talmon has pointed out that this emphasis "pervades all strata of the Biblical literature."[136] Baruch read aloud to the people all the prophetic utterances of Jeremiah following their inscription in a book (Jer 36:6). The celebration of the covenant renewal ceremony entailed the public reading of the Torah before the people, at which all those who could "hear with understanding" were present (Neh 8:2).[137] Special provisions were in place for this public recitation, including a special wooden platform erected specifically for the occasion. There are numerous other instances of aural reception of texts within the Biblical tradition, and they can be divided into several categories based on the intended recipient(s) of the text. Among the categories include texts read aloud before: 1) a King,[138] 2) people in the Lord's House (בֵּית יְהוָה),[139] 3) Israel, or the assembly of Israel,[140] and 4) a group of people.[141] There are also many other instances of the oral reading of texts that do not fit into one of these categories, but are clear examples of aural reception nonetheless.[142] Along with the clear evidence of oral reading of texts, there is no evidence of

---

[134] George A. Kennedy, *New Testament Interpretation Through Rhetorical Criticism* (Chapel Hill: University of North Carolina Press, 1984), 5–6.

[135] See above, §4.1.7.

[136] Talmon, "Oral Tradition," 152.

[137] The covenant renewal ceremony was to take place on the first day of the seventh month. Horsley places much emphasis on the concept of covenant renewal, in particular he describes Q 6:20–49 as a covenant renewal discourse, see *Whoever*, 195–227.

[138] 2 Kgs 22:8–13, 16–18; 2 Chr 34:18, 24, 30; Esth 6:1; Jer 36:21–24; Dan 5:17; 3 Macc 1:12; Ezra 4:18.

[139] Jer 36:6; Bar 1:14.

[140] Josh 8:35; 1 Macc 14:19; Deut 31:11.

[141] Bar 1:3; 1 Macc 5:14; 1 Esd 9:41; Exod 24:7; Neh 8:18; Jer 36:10–19.

[142] There are examples of reading aloud in front of nobles (1 Esd 3:13), from individual to individual (e.g., Zephaniah to Jeremiah, Jer 29:29), before those who can understand (Neh 8:3), and to one's family (4 Macc 18:6).

private, personal reading within the Hebrew Bible, and only ambiguous references to the practice in the Apocrypha.[143]

Further evidence for reading out loud can be ascertained via a study of ancient letters and the means by which they were both written and received. M. McGuire in his work on ancient letters and letter carriers concludes that "the ancients habitually read everything aloud."[144] Dictation was the typical means for writing a letter, as is evident in ancient letters as well as in the Pauline corpus;[145] and as we saw above, within the Hebrew Bible there are accounts of texts being produced as the result of the dictation from an author to a scribe.[146] This observation coheres with what we know about scriptural citations and allusions within Paul's letters. Paul does not cite consistently either the MT or the LXX, and at times his citation is not clearly identifiable at all (e.g., 1 Cor 2:9).[147] It is likely that this non-uniform use of "source material" can, to some extent, be attributed to the likelihood that Paul was not citing from a written text that was in front of him at the time of composition,[148] but rather, Paul was

---

[143] There are what is best described as *ambiguous* references to reading within the Apocrypha (i.e., those that are not conclusive evidence for either aural or private reading). In the prologue to Sirach, the author addresses "those who read" without reference to the aural or visual nature of the activity. The author of 2 Macc indicates that "we have aimed to please those who wish to read, to make it easy for those who are inclined to memorize, and to profit all readers" (2 Macc 2:25). Also ambiguous are: 2 Macc 6:12; 1 Esd 2:26–30; 3:13; 2 Esd 14:45.

[144] M. R. P. McGuire, "Letters and Letter Carriers in Ancient Antiquity," *Classical World* 53 (1960): 150.

[145] Achtemeier, "Omne Verbum Sonat," 15. For dictation in the Pauline corpus, see Rom 16:22 — ἐγὼ Τέρτιος ὁ γράψας τὴν ἐπιστολὴν ἐν κυρίῳ. It is also noteworthy that Paul notes his "poor" handwriting when writing his own letters (Gal 6:11). This suggests that Paul himself might not have been a proficient scribe.

[146] Particularly in Jeremiah, where the prophet claims to have dictated all the "words of the Lord" (אֶת־דִּבְרֵי יְהוָה, Jer 36:6).

[147] See D. Moody Smith, "The Pauline Literature," in *It is Written: Scripture Citing Scripture* (ed. D. A. Carson and H. G. M. Williamson; Cambridge: Cambridge University Press, 1988), 266 for more on the "source" behind Paul's citations. Smith lists 105 citations/allusions from Paul, and he distinguishes between citations from the LXX, MT, LXX/MT (agrees with LXX and the underlying MT). Interestingly, Smith labels 37 citations/allusions as neither in agreement with the LXX nor the MT, and another 27 that agree with neither the LXX nor MT but are close to the LXX. Thus, 64 out of 105 citations/allusions (61%) cannot be equated with either the LXX or MT, and therefore remain ambiguous. Smith also notes that Paul "seems to exercise great freedom" when incorporating scripture in his letters ("Pauline Literature," 266).

[148] Jaffee writes, ". . . the written text was useful as a mnemonic aid, not a crutch. Neither Paul nor the Sages had writings before them as they composed their discourses" ("Figuring Early Rabbinic Literary Culture: Thoughts Occasioned by Boomershine and J. Dewey," *Semeia* 65 [1994]: 71; cf. Horsley and Draper, *Whoever*, 140). Achtemeier

recalling OT texts with which he was well acquainted.[149] Thus, from that perspective, the eclectic character of Paul's scriptural citations/allusions is due to the variable character of previously remembered tradition which he received either via a previous aural hearing, and/or from the personal instruction he claimed to receive at the feet of Gamaliel (Acts 22:3 — παρὰ τοὺς πόδας Γαμαλιὴλ). In either case, the character of Paul's scriptural citations/allusions is a possible indication that his main vehicle for receiving tradition was ultimately oral speech.[150]

Apart from the question of Paul's scriptural citations or allusions, there are additional New Testament references to the oral recitation and aural reception of texts. There are three references in Acts to the aural reception of texts within the context of public worship. Acts 13:27 depicts the aural reading of the words of the prophets each Sabbath, and similarly, Acts 15:21 refers to the reading aloud of Moses' law within the context of the local synagogue worship. In Acts 15:30–31, the congregation (τὸ πλῆθος) is gathered together and then presented with the letter from the Jerusalem

---

attributes the difficulty in discerning Paul's "sources" to the fact that references were "much more likely to be quoted from memory than to be copied from a source" ("Omne Verbum Sonat," 27), and likewise, "the assumption that Paul is laboriously quoting a source he has in front of him is overwhelmingly likely to be false" ("Omne Verbum Sonat," 27). Ong also notes that quotations functioned quite differently in antiquity due to the inability to ever "look up" a textual reference in any meaningful sense of the term (*Orality and Literacy*, 31).

[149] Smith does not mention the possibility that Paul could be citing his "scripture" (i.e., the Torah) from memory, and consequently, that this could account for some of the difficulty in determining the "source" of his material. When dealing with the "nature and definition of the OT Paul cites" ("Pauline Literature," 266–267), he approaches the question from a strictly textual perspective, and without any sensitivity to the cultural milieu in which Paul lived. The discussion revolves exclusively around the question of which source *text* (LXX, MT) was used by Paul. James D. G. Dunn, *The Theology of Paul the Apostle* (Edinburgh: T&T Clark, 1998), 172 rightly summarizes that Paul's adaptation of scripture "would have been wholly characteristic for the time"), but he does not ask the question relevant for this discussion — from what source did the "adaptation" take place? For our purposes, we must ask whether the adaptation was of a written text that was in front of Paul during the composition process, or, if Paul adapted a remembered tradition that he had in his "textual memory." If the second option is correct, then what appear initially to be non-verbatim citations from a theoretically set text (i.e., LXX, MT), are actually natural variations of remembered traditions, fully consistent with what we know of highly oral cultures, and thus, not necessarily deviations from a sacred, written text.

[150] Along similar lines, Person, in his study of the differences between the LXX and MT versions of Jeremiah suggests that many of the variants are best understood as resulting from the variegated character of oral performance and transmission ("Rolling Corpus," 269–271). He concludes, ". . . the changes that occurred between LXX-Jer. and MT-Jer. were primarily 'oral' in character with some 'literate' variants along the way" ("Rolling Corpus," 271).

council. What is significant here is that the congregation is depicted as having *read* (ἀναγνόντες) the letter, without any specific indication that the reception is aural. It is difficult to envision each individual congregational member reading the text by him/herself, and therefore, the context suggests that the letter was read, that is *heard*, by the gathered congregation.[151] The story of Philip and the Ethiopian Eunuch (Acts 8:26–40) contains another example of aural reading. Initially, the eunuch is depicted as reading the text, without any indication that his reading was either aloud or silent (Acts 8:28). Shortly thereafter, Philip *hears* the eunuch reading aloud the text of Isaiah (Acts 8:30), implying that there was an initial assumption that the text was read aloud. Furthermore, if we assume that the eunuch was alone in his chariot, we have an indication that even the private reading of a text was done in an audible voice.

The Synoptic Gospels contain many references to reading, most of which are included within Matthean citation formula. In all of these instances, the formula does not address the question regarding the medium of reception (i.e., aural or visual), but rather is concerned with establishing the framework for the appeal to scriptural authority, typically within the context of a controversy dialogue with the Pharisees (Matt 12:5 par. Mark 2:25 par. Luke 6:3; Matt 19:4, 21:16, Matt 21:42 par. Mark 12:10, 26), Sadducees (Matt 22:31), or others (Luke 10:26). It is clear that these references reflect Matthean redactional concerns and therefore are not helpful evidence for our current question regarding aural reception of texts.

The testimony within the Pauline corpus[152] is more or less in agreement with what we have seen up to this point. On more than one occasion Paul instructs the churches with whom he corresponds to read his letter before their members (1 Thes 5:27; Col 4:16), and even instructs the Colossians to exchange letters with the church at Laodicea (Col 4:16) so it can be read

---

[151] There is a similar situation in the Hebrew Bible involving the finding of the book of the Law and Josiah's reformation (2 Kgs 22:8–23:3). Here, King Josiah *hears* the book read to him aloud (2 Kgs 22:10) and tears his clothing upon *hearing* the words of the law (2 Kgs 22:11). Following this, King Josiah is depicted as having read (silently) the words of the law (2 Kgs 22:16), and again later, as having *heard* the words of the Lord (2 Kgs 22:18–19). In this situation, we have a significant indication that reading and hearing were synonymous and aural reception of a text is *described as reading*. Orality was so prevalent that although silent reading is depicted, it remains subordinate to aural reception. The concept of "visual reading" has not yet been distinguished from the aural hearing of a text.

[152] For our current purposes, it is not necessary to enter into the debate regarding the authenticity of the letters commonly attributed to Paul — the current argument does not depend on their status. Therefore, we include Colossians and the Pastoral Epistles in this survey.

before both groups. Paul also instructs Timothy in 1 Tim 4:13 to be attentive to the reading (τῇ ἀναγνώσει), exhortation (τῇ παρακλήσει), and teaching (τῇ διδασκαλίᾳ,); all of which are instructions given to Timothy in the context of his ministry activity. There are a few ambiguous references to reading (2 Cor 1:13; 3:2; 3:15), but given what we have surveyed thus far, those references are understood best as assuming an aural reception of a publicly read text.

In sum, we have argued that the primary interface between texts and their intended recipients was audible speech. Throughout the greater Judeo-Christian tradition (Hebrew Bible, NT, Pseudepigrapha, Apocrypha) there is overwhelming evidence that texts were read aloud to their recipients, and therefore functioned as oral communication. Interpreted in light of the above-presented textual evidence, the few ambiguous references to reading in the tradition are almost certainly further examples of vocalized reading. In the ancient world, it was assumed that reading was to be vocalized, and examples of silent reading are few, and altogether non-existent within the greater Judeo-Christian tradition.

4.6 Ancient Perceptions of Oral Traditions and Texts

We must now pause to reflect on the significance of the above regarding oral tradition and the processes of oral communication. As suggested above, the textual sources describe a setting within which aurality was the primary means for interacting with texts. Oral sources were used in the production of ancient texts, and the texts themselves were read aloud, retaining their oral/aural character. We were able to discern the remnants of oral performance within the texts, in what we termed *implicit orality*, and *implied oral performance*. Such an observation raises questions regarding the perceived value of texts and oral traditions in the ancient world. How were texts perceived? Were oral accounts and oral tradition perceived as equal in value to written texts? Or, did either oral tradition or texts have a greater perceived value than the other? To these questions we now turn.

4.6.1 Hearing as Instrument of Learning

Due to the lack of primary "oral source material," we must look for implicit evidence via a survey of the extant textual sources. Of particular interest is the emphasis on *hearing* as the means for learning and understanding. Xenophon describes the advantages of hunting with a horse; instead of seeing with two eyes and hearing with two ears, the rider can now "gather evidence with four eyes and *learn* with four ears"

(Xenophon, *Cyropaedia* 4.3.21). The ears are the instruments of *learning*; the eyes are simply used to gather evidence. Xenophon also associates the ears with *memory* (Xenophon, *Anabasis* 3.1.26), and in a similar fashion, Aeschylus associates the ears with *understanding* (Aeschylus, *Prometheus vinctus* 445).[153]

The *Testament of Reuben* contains an illustrative description of the value attributed to hearing and speech. Chapter 2 juxtaposes seven "spirits of deceit" (πνευμάτων τῆς πλάνης) against seven other spirits that are given to man. The third spirit is that of "hearing" (ἀκοῆς) through which comes "instruction" (διδασκαλία) (*T. Reub.* 2:5), and the fifth spirit is the "spirit of speech" (πνεῦμα λαλιᾶς) with which comes "knowledge" (γνῶσις) (*T. Reub.* 2:6). Both of these spirits have very positive connotations, compared to the second spirit of "seeing" (i.e., with the eyes) which is associated with the *negative trait of desire*.[154] In this case, verbal speech and the auditory senses are held in high regard, corresponding to what we discussed previously regarding aurally received texts.

As we move forward in time towards the period of the early church fathers, much has remained the same with respect to attitudes toward hearing and learning. Clement of Alexandria comments on Rom 10:17 — "faith comes from what is heard, and what is heard comes through the word of Christ," and in so doing, creates an analogy between a ball game and the process of teaching and learning (Clement of Alexandria, *Stromata* 2.6). Clement uses his analogy to assert that reliable teaching is the product of faith, which in turn contributes to the process of learning. In his assertion, Clement notes that the means of receiving the "word of the lord" (ῥῆμα κυρίου, *Stromata* 2.6.25) is through *hearing*, which he describes as a natural, or native process (ὑπάρχουσα φυσική, *Stromata* 2.6.26).[155] The whole process of teaching and learning is made possible through heard speech, not read texts.

Augustine also hints at the perceived importance of learning through hearing. When he was twenty years old, Augustine recounts that he had

---

[153] Although there are many similar Biblical passages (e.g., Ps 115:5–6; 135:16; Isa 6:10; 32:3; 35:5: 43:8; Jer 5:21; Ezek 12:2; Matt 13:13–16; Mark 8:18; Acts 28:26–27; Rom 11:8), they are all examples of synonymous parallelism, using multiple senses to highlight the total lack in perceiving YHWH'S purposes. As such, these Biblical passages are not illustrative for our aims here.

[154] This is evident from an examination of the seventh spirit of "procreation and intercourse," which is described as the means by which sin enters through the desire for pleasure (*T. Reub.* 2:8–9).

[155] Also, within the *Pseudo-Clementine* literature, Peter is described as being "satisfied" with Clement and writes, "he satisfied me, . . . showing that the truth is more manifest to the ear by the discourse of the prophet than things that are seen with the eye" (*Ps.-Clem.* Homilies 1:20, *trans.* Thomas Smith).

read a copy of Aristotle's *The Ten Categories*, a book for which he had great respect on account of the status attributed to it by his teacher at Carthage (Augustine, *Conf.* 4.15.28). In a rather boastful manner, Augustine describes how he read Aristotle's book by himself and understood it. He contrasts his ability to understand the book with the others who, despite receiving *oral* instruction from tutors, were scarcely able to understand the book. Augustine wonders at the significance that the others "could tell him no more about it [the book] than I had acquired in the reading of it by myself alone" (Augustine, *Conf.* 4.15.28, *trans.* Outler). It is clear that Augustine is contrasting the ideal educational setting within which the others learned against his unorthodox approach to learning, which entailed the private reading of Aristotle's book.[156] The impact of Augustine's statement is only grasped when one realizes that the other students are learning through the time-honored pedagological principles that have been in place for centuries, while Augustine's method represents a novel approach to learning.

We must also address the question of the perceived value of texts within an educational system that relied heavily on oral pedagogical methods. Much work has already been done in this area, and we need only present a brief summary of previous scholarship. Loveday Alexander has written on the use of the term *viva vox*, and we will present her findings as additional support for what we have observed thus far in this chapter.[157] Alexander groups her primary source material into six categories. They are as follows, with reference to a few representative examples: 1) the proverb,[158] 2) rhetoric,[159] 3) the crafts,[160] 4) the schools,[161] 5) philosophical

---

[156] This should not be considered evidence contrary to the above argued section on reading aloud. It should be noted that this private reading described by Augustine is *not* necessarily silent reading, which at this point in history is still a cultural anomaly. We are reminded of Augustine's bewilderment over Ambrose's *silent* reading (Augustine, *Conf.* 6.3.3) . In that passage, Augustine notes that Ambrose's "voice and tongue were silent" (Augustine, *Conf.* 6.3.3, *trans.* Outler), and this causes Augustine to speculate about reason for Ambrose's bizarre behavior. In the end, Augustine surmises that, "whatever his motive was in so doing, it was doubtless, in such a man, a good one" (Augustine, *Conf.* 6.3.3, *trans.* Outler).

[157] See Alexander, "Living Voice," 221–247.

[158] "There may well be truth in the saying current among most craftsmen, that reading out of a book is not the same thing as, or even comparable to, learning from the living voice," Galen, *De compositione medicamentorum secundum locos* 6.

[159] "that 'living voice', as the saying goes, provides more nourishment," Quintilian, *Inst.* 2.2.8; "the 'living voice', as the common saying has it, is much more effective," Pliny, *Epistulae* 2.3.

[160] "I blame the earliest writers on the forms of plants, holding it better to be an eyewitness by the side of the master himself and not to be like those who navigate out of books," Galen, *Temp. med.* 6, preface.

esotericism, and 6) Papias and Clement.[162] Following her survey of the various references to the *viva vox*, Alexander concludes that, "there is in the schools a strong tendency to see written texts as secondary to and subordinate to oral instruction. It is the "living voice" of the teacher that has priority: the text both follows that voice (as a record of teaching already given) and stands in a subordinate position to it."[163] In antiquity, it is this personal, oral instruction that is associated with orthodox teaching and the "truth."[164]

In summary, ancient teaching and learning were once again integrally connected with oral communicative processes. Hearing was the accepted and preferred means for learning, and oral communication in the form of the *viva vox* was often than held in higher esteem than written texts.

4.6.2 Texts as "Holy Writings"

The ease with which the ancients appropriated oral communication for teaching and learning is not surprising given the extent to which oral communication pervaded all aspects of society. On the other hand, texts remained a cultural enigma for many centuries, and were not immediately trusted by the masses. Reading and writing remained the exception, and were not the norm in ancient society; thus books, and writing in general, retained a semi-magical quality that typified their lofty and often-perceived inaccessibility.[165]

Ancient inscriptions functioned differently than one would expect today. Greg Woolf suggests that we must recognize the monumental character of inscriptions, and that, at times, they were inscribed for their

---

[161] "However, you will gain more from the living voice and from sharing someone's daily life than from an treatise," Seneca, *Epistulae morales* 6.5.

[162] Earlier we focused on Papias' statements from the perspective of *remembered speech* (see above, §4.2.2). Here we are more concerned with Papias' preference for the "living voice" (ζώσης φωνῆς καὶ μενούσης, Eusebius, *Hist. eccl.* 3.39.4) *over* that of texts.

[163] Alexander, "Living Voice," 244.

[164] In addition to Alexander's texts we have another text that associates "truth" with receiving personal instruction within a teacher/student relationship. Eusebius cites Irenaeus' description of how Polycarp was instructed by the apostles and had been acquainted with many people who had seen Christ. It is this personal instruction, presumably oral, that makes Polycarp a more reliable and true witness than the other "heretics" (i.e., Valentinus and Marcion) (Eusebius, *Hist. eccl.* 6.14).

[165] See Hezser, *Jewish Literacy*, 209–226. She suggests that the Torah was viewed by the rabbis as "the written form of the Divine name holy," and that they "objectified the text of the Torah and (religious) writing *itself* [italics mine]" (Hezser, *Jewish Literacy*, 226). See also, Davies, *Canonization*, 18.

aesthetic value more than for their ability to communicate information.[166] Ancient Mesopotamian law codes were inscribed on tablets and displayed for all people to see, despite the fact that only 1% of people in ancient Mesopotamia were literate, and thus able to read the laws themselves.[167] Similarly, in ancient Israel, the inscription of the Decalogue takes on a greater significance than the mere preservation of the laws themselves. We must assume that the ancients would have been able to remember ten relatively simple laws. Therefore, we must understand the inscription of the laws (texts) from within the perspective of ancient perceptions of texts and of writing in general. The descriptions of the inscription of the Decalogue are illustrative of ancient perceptions of texts. Whenever the Hebrew Bible depicts the creation of the tablets and the inscription of the Decalogue, it is always surrounded by events marked by supernatural activity, often within a highly sacred or cultic setting.

Prior to the first "oral" presentation of the law (Exod 20), Mt. Sinai has already been deemed sacred (Exod 19), and cannot be climbed or even touched (Exod 19:12–13). The text also depicts YHWH as accompanying Moses in the form of a cloud (Exod 19:9), and his entrance on the scene proceeded by thunder, lightening, and a trumpet blast; all of which made the people in the camp fearful (Exod 19:16). An altar to YHWH has been constructed (Exod 20:22) and the chronology of the annual festivals has been established (Exod 23:14–19). Immediately prior to the introduction of the tablets is the covenant initiation ceremony whereby Moses dashed sacrificial blood upon the altar and the people (Exod 24:8). It is within this context that Moses received the tablets containing the laws of the covenant (Exod 24:12). Moses and the elders saw YHWH, although only Moses ascended further up the mountain to receive the tablets (Exod 24:15) amidst the glory of YHWH that appeared before the people of Israel in the form of fire.

After Moses' encounter with YHWH, he is given the two tablets (presumably to bring down to his people) that are described as originating

---

[166] Greg Woolf, "Monumental Writing and the Expansion of Roman Society in the Early Empire," *Journal of Roman Studies* 86 (1996): 24–29. Woolf also suggests that monumental inscriptions may have taken on a symbolic form that even illiterates could recognize, and that they served to "assert the place of individuals within society" ("Monumental Writing," 29; also, Rosalind Thomas, *Literacy and Orality in Ancient Greece* [Cambridge: Cambridge University Press, 1992], 86). Hezser suggests that "[e]ven the illiterate may have recognized recurrent formulas and abbreviations" in public inscriptions (*Jewish Literacy*, 361).

[167] See Millard, *Reading and Writing*, 154–184 for his summary of the question of ancient literacy. The estimated rates of literacy were even lower in ancient Egypt than they were in Palestine, where only members from the very elite ranks of society were able to read and write; see Millard, *Reading and Writing*, 156.

from the "finger of God" (Exod 31:18). Given the sacred nature of the tablets (as well as the law of the covenant itself), the smashing of the two tablets by Moses (Exod 32:19) represents far more than a purely symbolic breaking of the covenant, but rather, signifies the destruction of a "holy object" itself — one that has taken on a special significance beyond that of the content inscribed upon the stone.[168]

The second giving of the tablets to Moses is also surrounded by events and circumstances that promote the sacred status of the tablets. In this case, the law has already been given to the people, and therefore, the second set of tablets is not associated with the sacred giving of the law itself. Once again the giving of the physical tablets (note: not the content of the law) is associated with the sacred Mount Sinai. No one is permitted to ascend into the presence of YHWH, and even the livestock are not permitted to graze in front of the mountain. Following Moses' descent with the two new tablets, his face shone from his encounter with YHWH (Exod 34:29–35), thus highlighting the sacred nature of the encounter between Moses and YHWH.

This "sacred" character of the covenant tablets within the Hebrew Bible is made more explicit within other extra-canonical Judeo-Christian texts.[169] Within Jubilees there are several references to "heavenly tablets," all of which highlight their sacred status. This attributed status has now extended beyond the two tablets on which were inscribed the Decalogue to include what appears to be the whole Torah. Jubilees 4:32 depicts the murder of Abel and the subsequent "righteous judgment" that led to Cain's death by a stone. The author of Jubilees associates this 'judgment' with what has been ordained in the "heavenly tablets." Additional reference to this phrase occurs in the commentary on Noah before the flood is unleashed on the earth, in which the judgment of the sinful has been "written in the heavenly tablets" (Jub 5:13), and following the flood, where the section on the ordination of the feasts and festivals uses the term "heavenly tablets" on several occasions. The passage itself also uses "heavenly tablets" as an inclusio, bracketing the introduction (Jub 6:17) and conclusion (Jub 6:31)

---

[168] There is a similar view of text as "holy objects" among more recent Middle Age societies. For an example from the British Isles, one need look no further than the Lindisfarne Gospels to understand this ancient view of texts. The ornate decoration and meticulous attention to detail ensured that the copy of the *text itself* was as valued as the message therein.

[169] See Pieter J. J. Botha, "Greco-Roman Literacy as Setting for New Testament Writings," *Neotestamentica* 26 (1992): 209 for this characteristic of texts in the Greco-Roman world.

of the section itself; thereby emphasizing the otherworldly nature of the tablets.[170]

The pseudepigraphic *Ascension of Isaiah* and the *Testament of Moses* also contain references to this view of texts. In *Ascension*, Isaiah is depicted as having seen books presented to him by angels (9:22). These books were "not like the books of this world" (9:22) although they had writing in them, and later Isaiah makes Hezekiah vow that he would "not allow any man to copy these words [from the vision]" (11:39). It is clear that the book referred to in the *Ascension of Isaiah* is almost "magical" in that it contains writing, but possesses a supernatural dimension which defies description and prohibits its copying. The *Testament of Moses* clearly attributes to texts a sacred status — "[y]ou shall arrange them, anoint them with cedar, and deposit them in earthenware jars in the place which (God) has chosen from the beginning of the creation of the world . . ." (*T. Mos* 1:17). These objects of veneration are to be protected and set apart as holy. We can now see that the development of the Jewish tradition has placed increased significance upon the sacred nature of texts — not less. The sacred status attributed to the stone tablets in Exodus has now extended beyond the "autographs" inscribed by YHWH himself; thus, we can note how this view of texts was extensive, and reflective of common perceptions of, and attitudes towards texts and writing in general.

4.7 Conclusion

This section completes our survey on literacy and texts. It is now necessary to recapitulate what we have covered above. We have shown how low rates of ancient literacy were indicative of the general inability to interact directly with texts. Few people could read texts, and even fewer could write themselves. Texts were not commonly owned by individuals, and were not easily accessible for the majority of ancients. Those who were able to interact directly with texts did so via the long-standing methods of oral communication. Texts were *heard* rather than *read* silently, composition was typically by way of dictation, and oral performance and ancient texts were closely related to one another — functioning as both a *source* for texts, and as the *impetus* for writing the text in the first place.

---

[170] The phrase "heavenly tablets" occurs 28 times in Jubilees and is distributed throughout the text. Many of the references to the term are accompanied with by term "ordained" (4:32, 5:13, 6:17, 6:30–31, 6:35, 16:3, 16:29, 18:19, 28:6, 30:9, 30:22, 31:32, 32:10, 32:16, 33:10, 49:8).

Despite the proliferation of texts during the time of the creation of the Gospels, they did not supplant oral communication, but were often viewed as *less valuable* than tradition that could be acquired through the oral/aural interaction with other eyewitnesses (αὐτόπται). In addition to all of these factors, ancient texts were often perceived as "holy objects" worthy of veneration and reflected the ancient perceptions of texts — mysterious, inaccessible, divinely authored, and sacred. None of these attitudes towards texts would be compatible with modern concepts of texts and literacy.

It is now possible to return to the questions regarding *textual dependency* that we posed previously in chapters two and three. We suggested that a more careful analysis of the ways in which oral communication and written texts worked in conjunction with one another could help us evaluate the merits of an *exclusively literary* model of Synoptic interrelationships. From the above model, we can offer some tentative answers to that question. As we have observed, oral communication was so interwoven into the fabric of ancient society that it affected *all aspects* of life. As such, it is difficult to envisage a strictly editorial compositional situation where an isolated author would be able to collect the various manuscripts of "Jesus traditions," sit down at a large work area, open up the various codices and scrolls containing source material, and work *without the benefit and input of oral tradition*.[171] Individual elements of that model are feasible, but even *if* a comprehensive suitable environment can be reconstructed, we cannot avoid the inevitable:

---

[171] This is, for the most part, how Mack envisions the writing of the Gospel of Mark. Mack writes, "it [Mark] was composed at a desk in a scholar's study lined with texts and open to discourse with other intellectuals. In Mark's study were chains of miracle stories, collections of pronouncement stories in various states of elaboration, some form of Q, memos on parables and proof texts, the Scriptures . . . and other literature representative of Hellenistic Judaism" (*A Myth of Innocence: Mark and Christian Origins* [Philadelphia: Fortress Press, 1988], 321–323). Goulder's work equally suffers from a mechanistic, highly literary view of Gospel production. He envisions Luke working through the non-Markan sections of Matthew 1–12 and 23–25, and then moving *backwards* through Matthew from chs. 22–13 to glean material that he missed earlier ("On the Order of a Crank," in *Synoptic Studies* [ed. Christopher M. Tuckett; JSNTSup 7; Sheffield: Sheffield Academic Press, 1984], 121). Derrenbacker's critique of Goulder's view of Luke's compositional technique is applicable here: "One reason, I think, that the Synoptic Problem remains a 'problem' has to do with most scholars' unimaginative and anachronistic conceptions of the Synoptic evangelists as first-century writers in the Greco-Roman world. Most Synoptic source critics seem to imagine a literary world for the Gospel writers characterized by extensive literacy, ample access to writing materials, the proliferation of writing desks that allow an author to have visual contact with written sources, and, generally, a conception of a literary environment not too different from our own age of information technology" ("Writing Practices," 61); cf. Tuckett, *Q*, 28–31.

ancient authors, even the most "literary" ones at that, *interacted with oral traditions* when composing their works. Therefore, we are forced to conclude that any solution to the Synoptic Problem that does not take into serious account the influence of oral tradition in the compositional process must be deemed inadequate. The rigid models of Synoptic interrelationships that we examined earlier in chapter two must be re-evaluated from within the historical model offered above.[172]

Any model of Synoptic interrelationships which is constructed apart from the historical realities of antiquity will remain no more than an intellectual exercise — an artificial construct that does not reflect the complex milieu of first-century Palestine. The question of Synoptic interrelationships cannot be studied as a strictly literary phenomenon for the simple sake of convenience. If we are to move beyond the thoroughgoing literary paradigm that has dominated New Testament scholarship for much of the last century, we must attempt to develop a realistic model of Synoptic interrelationships that takes into account how tradition was transmitted within a culture so indebted to the processes of oral communication. In developing such a model, it is necessary to explore, in more detail, how oral communication functioned in antiquity.

---

[172] Farmer's approach is among those particularly susceptible to this line of critique (see above, ch. 2). He forces the discussion into an exclusively literary paradigm and does not attempt to account for the influence of oral tradition on the process of Gospel formation. As Parker has forcefully stated, those who appeal to these "two-dimensional diagrams" to solve the Synoptic Problem are assuming that the Gospel authors were working with "published editions" of source texts and that "there is a single point of contact between two texts, for example, the single contact when Matthew copied Mark, and there was and end of the matter" (*Living Text*, 121). Parker asserts, and correctly so, that there is the need for a "third dimension" which "represents a series of contacts between texts each of which may have changed since the previous contact . . ." (*Living Text*, 121). This complex process of multiple contacts extended beyond literary sources to include "oral tradition, and any other sources that might have been available" (*Living Text*, 121). Once one recognizes the sheer complexity of the historical process of Gospel composition, it is difficult to envision its solution in any overly simplistic terms. Along similar lines, Barrett suggests, "it is simpler to suppose that Matthew and Luke in collecting their material used traditions which were similar but not identical than that they each had identical copies of one source (a supposition sufficiently improbable on geographical and historical grounds), which in the case of one of them was contaminated with a parallel version" ("Re-examination," 322).

Chapter 5

Characteristics of Oral Communication

5.1 Introduction

In the previous chapter we developed an ancient media model by focusing on the *self-perceived* value of oral communication and the relationship between oral communication and written texts. It is therefore fitting that we now attempt to describe to some extent how that model functioned in practice. The media model we developed in chapter four is limited in its ability to describe in full the complex relationship between orality and literacy in antiquity. This is due in part to the fact that, as we will see below, our model was an inferential *model* which was derived from a study of *texts* from antiquity. It should be no surprise at this stage in the discussion that such a model will have its inherent limitations.[1] To rephrase this limitation in terms of our current discussion, we have approached the question of the relationship between "oral communication and written texts" from a literary perspective. We have probed into ancient texts in an attempt to uncover what is, in the apt words of Ong, an evanescent phenomenon.[2] We are simply at a marked disadvantage when it comes to studying the entire phenomenon of oral communication in the ancient world, and therefore we must examine alternative ways in which we can supplement the earlier model and subsequently enrich our understanding of the earliest stages of the Jesus tradition.

Since it is no longer possible to study the early Jesus tradition in its originally transmitted oral form, one must search (look? — listen?) elsewhere in an attempt to understand better how orality functioned in antiquity. In order to understand the difficulty that lay before us as we try to untangle the Gordian Knot that is "oral tradition," we must once again remind ourselves of some previous attempts at uncovering the "oral dimension" behind the canonical New Testament.

---

[1] Havelock perceptively notes, "How can a knowledge of orality be derived from its opposite? And even supposing texts can supply some sort of image of orality, how can that image be adequately verbalized in a textual description of it, which presumably employs a vocabulary and syntax proper to textualization, not orality?" (*Muse*, 44).

[2] Ong, *Orality and Literacy*, 31–32.

The "oral dimension" behind the canonical New Testament has been recognized by many scholars over the years. Rhetorical criticism has been particularly helpful in this respect, and although its practicioners are not directly concerned with oral tradition, their work has led to an increased awareness of how the now silent texts were once related to their oral performance and subsequent aural reception. Much work has been done on rhetoric in Paul, and many scholars have approached the Synoptic texts from a similar perspective.

Most scholars who have examined the New Testament tradition in search of "residual orality" have done so via the characteristics of oral commuication which have been derived from contemporary orality studies. The process typically begins with the compilation of a list of linguistic features and structural characteristics thought to derive from oral communication or oral performance. Subsequent attention is then directed toward the presence, or lack thereof, of these features in the texts under examination. In turn, it is then often suggested that the presence of these features might indicate that the tradition is indebted to the process of oral communication. This overarching methodology has manifested itself in two distinct approaches to the New Testament texts.

The first approach has been concerned with the possible pre-textual history of New Testament tradition. Scholars such as Lord, Ong, Havelock, Kelber, among others, generally have explored the effect of oral communication on the pre-textual, or performance-history of a tradition and matters related to the "oral mind" of antiquity. Lord was concerned with how the extant Homeric epics reflected their performance history prior to their inscription in the form of a text. His fieldwork in the former Yugoslavia was intended to help him understand how the Homeric texts lived in oral performance, and how oral performance techniques played an integral role in shaping and forming the extant Homeric texts. He later utilized the same approach in his examination of the Synoptic Tradition. Likewise, Kelber, in building upon the work of scholars such as Lord and Ong, has been concerned about the ways in which orality and oral commuication have affected and shaped the extant gospel of Mark and Q. These approaches utilize recent orality studies and emphasize how tradition is transmitted and how the dynamics of oral performance can effect the formation and subsequent inscription of traditions within texts.

The second approach also utilizes recent orality studies, but is concerned with a different set of questions. John Harvey's *Listening to the Text* (1998) and Casey Wayne Davis' *Oral Biblical Criticism* (1999) are but two works which utilize this second approach to the question of "orality." Harvey's work is an attempt to examine Paul's use of "oral patterning" in his letters from a perspective informed by recent orality studies.[3] Harvey summarizes what he feels are important works in oral studies, including those of Lord, Ong, and Kelber. His summary of previous work on orality is sound and his study is helpful, but the inference he draws from these studies requires further examination.

Harvey examines how Paul intentionally utilized rhetorical patterns during the composition process. A great deal of attention is directed towards the chiastic structures within the Pauline epistles, and it is suggested that these were designed to meet the rhetorical goals of Paul himself. Harvey's principle methodology consists of seeking rhetorical devices in Paul's letters, and in turn seeing this as evidence of "oral patterning." His observation regarding the presence of structural patterns and rhetorical devices in Paul's letters is valid, but the question is whether they really provide evidence for the letters' "oral" character.

Many of the examples of highly structured "oral patterning" studied by Harvey (e.g., extended chiasmus) would most certainly have been the result of a highly refined *literary* process of letter writing, one that would be capable of structuring a rhetorical argument in a detailed manner not possible in a strictly oral setting.[4] Thus, while the *reception* of Paul's letters was aural, the composition process involved a level of detail and precision that would most likely be attainable only through the highly refined visual examination of a text. Therefore, the detailed survey of scholarship on orality undertaken by Harvey in his introductory chapters has only limited value for understanding the process by which Paul wrote his letters to the various New Testament congregations. The process of tradition transmission depicted by orality scholars simply does not apply to the context within which Paul wrote his letters. While such an observation does not diminish the importance of Harvey's work, one needs to be

---

[3] Harvey, *Listening to the Text,* "Orality and Its Implications for Biblical Studies: Recapturing an Ancient Paradigm," *Journal of the Evangelical Theological Society* 45:1 (2002).

[4] A quick glance through Harvey's book reveals example after example of highly structured use of rhetorical patterning which are best understood as literary in origin. In his chapter 9 on Galatians, Harvey cites several previous attempts to outline the entire book as an extended chiasmus. Of note is the extensive chiastic structure suggested by John Bligh, *Galatians in Greek: A Structural Analysis of Paul's Epistle to the Galatians* (Detroit: University Press, 1966). Although Harvey disagrees with Bligh's structural analysis of Galatians, he includes this discussion under the heading "Readily Apparent Oral Patterns" (*Listening,* 219). Harvey does question the usefulness of these "extended chiasms," but does not give enough attention to the issue of whether these structural features are best understood as examples "oral patterning," or, if they should be understood as excellent examples of a highly *literary* use of language. The extensive patterning detailed by Harvey is more likely attributable to literary processes of composition whereby the author of the tradition has a text in front of him, and can "scan backward" (Goody, *Savage,* 128) through the text to correct, emend, delete, etc.

careful and not draw inappropriate conclusions from the presence of these rhetorical and structural patterns.

Harvey's recognition of the rhetorical function of the patterning in the Pauline corpus is helpful for interpretative and exegetical issues, but that patterning in and of itself is not a valid indicator of the letter's indebtedness to "orality." A literary creation written to be heard (i.e., Harvey's view of Paul's letters) is not indebted to the dynamics of orality in the same manner as an orally performed tradition which is eventually inscribed in a text (i.e., Lord's view of Homer).

Therefore, Harvey's work is better described as a study of the intended *aural reception* of the textual tradition; not the "oral patterning" stage of initial composition or performance. In other words, Harvey examines how Paul intentionally composed his letters so that they might achieve their maximum impact when they were *heard* by their intended recipients.[5] The process which is envisioned by Harvey is more akin to the process of publication by oral performance.[6] Harvey's work leaves open the question as to when, or if, "orality" had an influence upon the written tradition, and one is left to question the extent to which the Lord-Parry theory of composition-in-performance applies to Paul's compositional procedure. Therefore, despite the progress made in rhetorical criticism and "oral biblical criticism"[7], there remains some confusion over the applicability of recent orality studies for understanding both the presence and function of the rhetorical features in texts, and there remains ambiguity over what the presence of these characteristics signifies. In essence, we are still left with the question of what it means for a text to be indebted to "orality," and how we are to interpret the existence of these characteristics within extant texts.

When examining any text for evidence of oral communication, it is important to recognize that structural features in a text such as chiasmus, inclusio, ring composition, and others, also exist in *texts which are not*

---

[5] In this sense, Davis' *Oral Biblical Criticism* is similar in its aims and objectives. However, it must be stated that Davis, in contrast with Harvey, seems to recognize the distinction between these two stages of tradition-transmission, and his overall his work is more carefully nuanced than that of Harvey.

[6] McLuhan, *Gutenberg Galaxy*, 84–86.

[7] See Casey Wayne Davis, *Oral Biblical Criticism: The Influence of the Principles of Orality on the Literary Structure of Paul's Epistle to the Philippians* (JSNTSUP 172; Sheffield: Sheffield Academic Press, 1999), 29–62 for his description of the discipline of "oral biblical criticism." Davis' goal for "oral biblical criticism" is to "seek to demonstrate the extent to which these principles [i.e., principles of orality] affected the form, style, diction, scope and interrelationships of the literary (or oral) units in this letter" (*Oral Biblical Criticism*, 11).

derivative from the processes of oral transmission and communication.[8] This is a crucial point that must be restated given the way in which these structural devices have been used in past and even recent studies on orality. In the 1991 volume *Jesus and the Oral Gospel Tradition*, Wansbrough summarized in his introduction to the collection of essays that, "[w]e have been unable to deduce or derive any marks [in the canonical Gospels] which distinguish clearly between an oral and a written transmission process."[9] The same remains true today; at this point in time there are no indicators which can definitively demonstrate either an oral or written prehistory of any given tradition which now exists in only textual form, although, we also must be open to the possibility, albeit remote, that there are definitive indicators within the texts that have yet to be found.[10]

Likewise, there is the difficulty in *proving* that the Synoptic Gospels are textually dependent on one another or upon a common textual ancestor. In evaluating the *likeliness* of intertextual dependency within the Synoptic Tradition, one examines characteristics, or features which can be observed by means of a careful comparison of one or more texts. Among these characteristics are those often mentioned in support of the existence of Q; verbatim agreement, argument from order, alternating primitivity, etc.

---

[8] Harvey's summary of "orality" is followed by a chapter in which he proceeds to catalogue and describe the various forms of "oral patterning in the Greco-Roman world" (*Listening*, 61–82) followed by another chapter on "oral patterning in the Hebrew Scriptures" (*Listening*, 83–96). In both of these chapters Harvey operates under the assumption that these structural patterns (inversion, ring-composition, transposition and contrast, etc.) are *oral* without inquiring whether they are *distinctively* oral. These features also exist in thoroughly "literary" compositions; therefore one must be cautious in labelling them "oral" without further clarification as to what is envisioned by such a term. On the other hand, Davis, *Oral Biblical Criticism*, 62 recognizes this danger, and states "[o]ral biblical criticism is not intended to focus solely on oral/aural clues to composition while ignoring features common to both oral and literary material. The method recognizes characteristics of oral compositions (not just oral characteristics)." Even here, there remains ambiguity over the difference between an "oral composition" and "oral characteristics." Davis must be commended for recognizing the inherent tension that exists in any attempt to catalog and describe the presence of oral characteristics within texts. Davis concludes his discussion on his method by stating that the difference between his method and that of literary linguistic analysis is one of "degree" not of substance (Davis, *Oral Biblical Criticism*, 62).

[9] Wansbrough, "Introduction," 12.

[10] Foley notes that "[i]n the early going some specialists believed that the mere density of such patterning could serve as a litmus test, that it constituted 'proof' of the actual orality or writtenness of a manuscript poem — whether the text in hand was originally an oral performance or not. We now claim much less, but at the same time something much more fundamental: that these features signal a background in oral poetry, though they don't magically reveal the precise story behind any given text" (Foley, *How to Read*, 48).

Strictly speaking, it is important to realize that these "formal proofs" for Markan priority and the existence of Q are not "knock down" arguments that are beyond reproach. Each of these classic arguments has been subjected to rigorous examination, and some have not stood the test of time.[11] Several of the classic arguments for the two-source hypothesis can no longer be accepted in their originally proposed forms.[12]

We are therefore confronted with a difficult situation, relief from which does not seem imminent at this time. If it is not possible to argue conclusively for an oral origin of individual traditions within extant texts, what *can* one demonstrate?[13] It seems clear that, although it is not possible

---

[11] In particular, the classical arguments for Markan priority have been the subject of extensive examination. For some scholars, the observation that Matthew and Luke appear to follow Mark's ordering of pericopes is no longer considered to be *clear-cut* evidence for Markan priority; rather, it has been suggested that such phenomena simply demonstrate that Mark is in some sort of literary relationship with the other two Gospels. For an example of this line of reasoning see Sanders and Davies, *Studying*, 87, Goodacre, *Case Against Q*, 22, and B. C. Butler, *The Originality of St. Matthew: A Critique of the Two-Document Hypothesis* (Cambridge: Cambridge University Press, 1951), 62–71. For a detailed discussion on the argument of order, see David Neville, *Arguments From Order in Synoptic Source Criticism: A History and Critique* (New Gospel Studies 7; Leuven: Peeters, 1994), also *Mark's Gospel — Prior or Posterior?: A Reappraisal of the Phenomenon of Order* (JSNTSup 222; Sheffield: Sheffield Academic Press, 2002). Of course, the standard two-source hypothesis remains the consensus view of New Testament specialists, although it is often presented in modified form to account for the large number of so-called "minor-agreements" between Matthew and Luke. For example, see Udo Schnelle, *Einleitung in das Neue Testament* (UTB für Wissenschaft Göttingen: Vandenhoeck & Ruprecht, 1994), 205–206, where he accepts the view of a *Deuteromarkus* which is posited to account for the large number of minor agreements — "Die für die Zweiquellentheorie grundlegende Annahme der Markuspriorität wird durch Deuteromarkus ledigliche modifiziert, indem nun eine Erklärung für den größten Teil des Markussondergutes und die 'minor agreements' angegeben werden kann" (*Einleitung*, 206). In addition, the very multiplicity of solutions to the Synoptic Problem is evidence in itself that the arguments supporting these theses are not as conclusive as some would hold.

[12] This can be illustrated by the category of tradition referred to as Mark-Q overlaps. Here is a classic case of an original thesis (i.e., the independence of Matt/Luke) that could be sustained given the initial formulation of the Markan priority/Q hypothesis. However, In order to maintain such a view of independence, the category of Mark/Q overlaps has been employed in an attempt to explain why at times Matthew and Luke appear to use a different form of a pericope that is also paralleled in Mark (e.g., the temptation, Matt 3:11–12 // Mark 1:7–8 // Luke 3:16–17). Goodacre has pointed out that this is a problematic approach to the problem, for it is a highly circular argument that simply assumes what it hopes to prove (i.e., Q); see Goodacre, *Case Against Q*, 54.

[13] Although Foley warns of the difficulty in making any definitive judgements about the "oral origins" of any given "manuscript poem," he does however argue that through an examination of the two types of evidence — "direct accounts and structural symptoms" — one can make overall judgements about texts which he categorizes as

to produce a clear-cut argument for the oral prehistory of any particular tradition, it *is* possible to shift the weight of the evidence in one direction or another, thereby achieving all that could be expected in historical reconstruction.[14] One way in which it is possible to evaluate the weight of the evidence is through an examination of the characteristics of oral communication.

Once the characteristics of oral communication have been described, it is indeed possible to see their presence or absence in the textual tradition. The presence of "oral characteristics" within a written text, while not definitive indicators of orality, can be considered to be *consistent* with those of a tradition that has been transmitted orally.[15] That is, the more oral characteristics a text contains, the *more likely* that the tradition is derivative from the processes of oral communication.[16] Conversely, the

---

"Voices from the Past" (Foley, *How to Read*, 47-49). Foley includes the New Testament in this category, and suggests that these types of traditions "were composed according to the rules of the given oral poetry. They bear a telltale compositional stamp" and that the structural symptoms "signal a background in oral poetry" and as such can be labeled "oral poetry" and examined as such. For all of this see Foley, *How to Read*, 47-49. See Foley, *How to Read*, 46, 50 for his inclusion of parts of the New Testament and Hebrew Bible into the category "Voices from the Past."

[14] There has been interest in this very question with regard to formal proofs for the Synoptic Problem. Several scholars have referred to the work of Popper (*The Logic of Scientific Discovery* [London: Hutchinson, 1959]), most notably Goulder ("Is Q a Juggernaut?," *JBL* 115 [1996]: 675–676). Goulder argues that the "usefulness" of any particular hypothesis of Synoptic relationships is tied integrally to the extent to which is can be falsified ("Juggernaut," 675–676). We must agree with Christopher Tuckett's response to this charge against the viability of the Q hypothesis — "no theory about the Synoptic Problem is falsifiable in the strict sense" ("Existence of Q," 40, also *Q*, 1–39). See also John S. Kloppenborg Verbin, "Goulder and the New Paradigm: A Critical Appreciation of Michael Goulder on the Synoptic Problem," in *The Gospels According to Michael Goulder: A North American Response* (Harrisburg: Trinity Press International, 2002), 35–40 for a helpful critique of Goulder's insistence on the criterion of falsifiability.

[15] An appropriate analogy for this type of reasoning can be found in a court of law. In the course of examining the forensic evidence for the death of an individual, a lawyer (solicitor) might probe a medical investigator regarding the cause of death of the victim. The medical examiner would then proceed to show how the wound on the victim was *consistent* with that produced perhaps by a knife, gun, etc. In this case, the examiner does not "prove" the cause of death, but that the evidence is *consistent* is often enough to persuade a jury or judge to convict the defendant. See Tuckett, *Griesbach Hypothesis*, 13–15 for his discussion on the "criterion of coherence" with regard to solutions to the Synoptic Problem.

[16] Henderson, in summarizing Ong's "characteristics" of orality states, "such criteria clearly differentiate some texts and subtexts from others and generate at least plausible hypotheses of oral influence on the selected texts. They cannot, however, serve as independent   criteria   for   a   pre-literary,   technically   oral   composition   or

less oral characteristics a text contains, the *less likely* the traditions therein are derivative from an oral milieu, or it might also indicate that they have been thoroughly "textualized" beyond recognition.[17] Such an approach to the textual tradition that might be described as a *via negativa*, whereby one can use oral characteristics within a text to make general judgments about the likelihood, or *possibility* of a tradition being the product of a strictly literary process, or perhaps the product of an author working in "oral mode" from either a previously written text, or by directly incorporating an aurally received tradition into a text.[18] Therefore, it is possible to discern the balance between the visual and aural senses that exists in extant texts.[19] One need not hesitate from examining the oral characteristics within literary documents just because they do not provide definitive, clear-cut criteria for determining oral from literary tradition. As in any historical discussion, one must often be content with reaching a certain level of *probability* rather than certainty,[20] and it is important to stress that in any discussion regarding the relationship between orality and Synoptic

---

transmission . . . they are essentially relative criteria, useful for comparing texts within a continuum" ("Didache and Orality," 294).

[17] See Kelber, *Oral and Written Gospel,* 44.

[18] Dunn uses the term "oral mode" to account for the possibility that an author might have made direct use of an aurally received tradition, or that an author might have taken a previously received textual tradition and "re-oralized" it, that is, reused it as one would re-perform a tradition prior to incorporating it into his text; see Dunn, "Oral Memory 2001," 101; Dunn, "Default Setting," 157, 163, 167. Used in this manner, the term "oral mode" is an appropriate way to describe the complex interaction between orality and literacy.

[19] The term "balance between the . . . senses" is an apt description of the tension that exists between oral performance and written texts. Ian Henderson expresses this as the balance between oral and literary "sensibilities" ("Didache and Orality," 295), and Havelock uses the phrase "dynamic tension" in a similar fashion (*Literate Revolution,* 9). Dewey has used this method of discerning the "balance between the senses" to study Mark and concludes that "the Gospel of Mark as a whole — not just its individual episodes — shows the legacy of orality, indeed that its methods of composition are primarily oral ones" ("Oral Methods," 33). The earlier work of Ernst Abel is helpful in comparison for he approached Matthew from a similar perspective, and concluded that Matthew was *more* "oral" than Mark or Luke (*contra* Dewey, Kelber, *et al.*). Abel focused on the highly structured patterning in Matthew and argued that its presence was evidence of the Gospel's oral character. As detailed in an earlier chapter, many of the detailed organizational features in Matthew's Gospel that were studied by Abel would be understood better as indications of the *literary* character of Matthew (see above, ch. 1).

[20] Lord expresses this as such: "It may not be possible in the case of many of our medieval texts to know with certainty whether we are dealing with an oral or a written product, but we may reach a high degree of *probability* in our research . . ." (*Singer of Tales,* 220).

textuality, the problem cannot be expressed as either oral or literary, but rather as a question of *degree*.[21]

5.2   Towards a Model of Tradition Transmission

When attempting to develop a cogent model of early Christian tradition-transmission, one must eventually address the question of how oral tradition functioned in antiquity. The process behind the development of such a model begins with an extant text, and as attempts are made to press back further into the tradition-history of the text, there will come a point before which it is not possible to probe without discussing the question of oral tradition. This has led practitioners of form criticism to make underlying assumptions or assertions about how oral tradition functioned in practice, in an attempt to construct this model of tradition-transmission.

Toward that end, there are two ways by which one can form a model of oral transmission. First, one can reconstruct an *inferential* "media model" of the early Christian movement by working with the extant Synoptic texts, and use them in interaction with other written sources contemporary to the time of the Synoptic texts' inscription. It is then possible to *infer* what characterized the pre-textual Jesus tradition. This methodology seems both logical and feasible at first, but quickly breaks down upon further inspection. The primary difficulty with such an approach is that, in the end, it is thoroughly circular. For example, Bultmann, in order to dissect the Synoptic Tradition in the way in which he did, needed to assume that the process of literary transmission was essentially equivalent to the process of oral transmission,[22] and that oral tradition followed a linear path of expansion and growth which thereby enabled him to reconstruct the earliest forms of any given tradition.[23] This assumption of linearity allowed Bultmann to examine the later extra-canonical Gospels in order to *infer* how the tradition developed from its earliest oral forms to that

---

[21] Finnegan, *Oral Literature in Africa*, 18. Henaut seems to miss this point throughout his *Oral Tradition and the Gospels*. Henaut's work on Mark 4 illustrates his confusion between the notion of a recoverable *ipsissima verba Jesu* and the presence of oral tradition behind Mark. In arguing that there is no demonstrable oral tradition behind Mark's account, Henaut embraces an "either/or" approach to the tradition. He does not take into consideration the notion that motivational changes to a tradition also take place *prior to the tradition's inscription into textual form*. Therefore, evidence of redaction in Mark only suggests that Mark's author was an active participant in a Christian community prior to writing those traditions in a text. The question of *when* those changes took place is still unresolved.

[22] Bultmann, *Synoptic Tradition*, 6, 48, also, cf. above, chs. 1, 2.

[23] See Sanders, *Tendencies*, 8–11.

inscribed in the Gospel texts.[24] In addition, Bultmann also assumed that the medium of transmission did not exert any influence upon the development of the tradition itself.[25] Building upon such assumptions, it was possible to for him to understand the pre-Synoptic period of oral transmission by studying the *literary texts* of the Synoptics.

The second approach to the question of how oral tradition functioned in practice can be summed up as an interdisciplinary approach to the tradition. It is this second approach that has not yet been explored fully, and can lend fresh insight into the problem at hand. With this approach, an appeal is made to the work of scholars in other non-Biblical fields of research such as folklore, sociology, and anthropology. These approaches recognize that New Testament scholarship can benefit greatly from complementary fields of research, and subsequently gain insight into how the early Jesus tradition was transmitted prior to its initial inscription in a text.[26]

This interdisciplinary approach has become commonplace as evidenced by the recent impact that alternative methodologies such as social-scientific criticism have had on the field of New Testament studies. Although social-scientific criticism is a relatively recent arrival on the scene, its roots are based in the earlier historical-critical work of late 19th and early 20th centuries. As noted in an earlier chapter, Bultmann, Dibelius, Gerhardsson, and Taylor all attempted to describe the earliest stages of the Jesus tradition. Although each scholar had their own approach to the tradition, and, despite arriving at quite different conclusions, they all worked under the assumption that extra-Biblical insights derived from complementary fields such as folklore, sociology and anthropology could provide important clues into the process of tradition transmission.[27] These scholars appealed to models of transmission that

---

[24] See above, ch. 2, for the discussion on this aspect of Bultmann's approach to the Synoptic Tradition.

[25] Contrast this approach with that of Paul Ricoeur who emphasizes the importance of the medium of discourse: "human discourse is not merely preserved from destruction by being fixed in writing, but that it is deeply affected in its communicative function . . . A kind of short-cut occurs between the meaning of discourse and the material medium. Then we have to do with literature in the original sense of the word. The fate of discourse is delivered over to littera, not to vox" (*Interpretation Theory: Discourse and the Surplus of Meaning* [Fort Worth: Texas Christian University Press, 1976], 28).

[26] In this respect, the currently embraced "social-scientific criticism" has been willing to embrace interdisciplinary research and has for the most part contributed significantly towards the reconstruction of a viable social setting for the early Jesus movement.

[27] Bultmann was influenced by studies on German folklore and rabbinic writings, Taylor's model was partially derived from studies undertaken on his own university students, and Gerhardsson looked toward Rabbinic Judaism for insight into the technical procedure which governed early Christian tradition transmission.

were derivative, not from the Synoptic texts themselves but from anachronistic, contemporaneous sociological and/or folklore studies.

In sum, although in an ideal setting it would be preferable to work with the Synoptic texts alone, it is not possible to do so. Any attempt to understand the oral milieu behind the development of the Synoptic Tradition requires input from extra-Biblical sociological and/or folklore studies. The form critics, both early and more recent, recognize the need to consult with interdisciplinary studies while developing a working model of early Christian tradition transmission. The difficulty with the theses of both Bultmann, Taylor, *et al.* lies not in their interaction with sociology or folklore studies, but rather in their misapplication of these studies. This leads to the question of the relevance of an appeal to anachronistic studies to elucidate the way in which oral tradition functioned in the early Jesus movement.

5.3   Twentieth-Century Studies on Oral Communication

For the better part of the twentieth-century, New Testament scholars have looked for a contemporary society that could be studied with a view towards any insight it might lend towards understanding better the socio-cultural dynamics of the early Jesus movement. The quest for such a "holy grail" has thus far eluded researchers who have not been able to find a culture that closely parallels that in which the New Testament Gospels were written.

There are of course many complex factors that make it difficult to find a useful contemporary parallel to first-century Palestinian society. As noted in chapter four, first-century Palestinian culture was both highly oral and highly literate at the same time. Although texts were commonplace, they did not supplant oral communication but were at times even considered less important than the oral traditions that circulated in conjunction with their inscribed counterparts. Texts abounded, but few people were literate enough to interact directly with texts. Palestine was also ethnically diverse, and the early Jesus movement was representative of that diversity. In addition, the early Jesus tradition was transmitted in multiple languages, most certainly Aramaic and Greek, and possibly Hebrew as well.[28] Coupled with other factors specific to the time (first-century) and place (Palestine), it is clear that finding an appropriate contemporary parallel

---

[28] Regarding the possibility that Jesus spoke Hebrew, see J. A. Emerton, "The Problem of Vernacular Hebrew in the First Century A.D. and the Language of Jesus," *JTS* 24 (1973): 1–23.

culture to compare with early Christianity is a difficult, if not impossible task.

5.3.1 The Question of Anachronism

The lack of a perfect parallel to the socio-cultural setting of first-century Palestine, while frustrating, should not dissuade us from exploring the great body of research gathered from the study of various cultures from around the world, particularly during the latter decades of the twentieth-century. Most of this global research has not been conducted by New Testament specialists, but rather by scholars in other unrelated fields with different aims and goals in view.

With regard to the early Jesus tradition, all twentieth-century fieldwork is by definition anachronistic, and this has led some to question the relevance of recent sociology and/or folklore studies. Indeed, the problem of anachronism has been recognized by both scholars who embrace such fieldwork and those who have raised objections regarding its possible applicability to the Jesus tradition. Although there is no simple answer to this particular problem, it is possible to make a few preliminary observations relating to the question of anachronism.

The "significance" of anachronism when evaluating a historical or cultural parallel to first-century Palestine varies greatly depending upon the specific parallel itself, and what one is trying to demonstrate. As will become clear in what follows, the force of the charge of anachronism is proportional to the level of detail that one attempts to gain from a comparison of two parallels.

First, there is the question of the specific parallel itself. When studying an ancient historical event or cultural setting, the following guideline can be helpful:

the *more closely* a parallel is tied to a specific cultural practice among a specific people-group at a specific time and place, the *more problematic* it is to use a non-contemporaneous parallel to interpret the events or settings under examination.

We can use the work of Gerhardsson to illustrate this type of parallel.[29] In evaluating the usefulness of the proposed parallel suggested by Gerhardsson, it is necessary to ask whether there was continuity between the two different settings and contexts, or, whether the parallel to which he appeals is too closely tied to a specific cultural practice at a particular time. The criticism often expressed against him is that his use of second/third century rabbinic pedagogical methods to understand nascent Christianity must be deemed anachronistic and therefore, his thesis is often

---

[29] Gerhardsson, *Memory.*

judged to be unpersuasive.[30] In this case, the parallel (Rabbinic Judaism) is quite a specific phenomenon. The pedagogical methods studied by Gerhardsson were confined to a relatively small, specific group of people located in a specific geographical location. In addition, the destruction of the temple in 70 C.E. had a profound impact upon the subsequent transmission of Jesus tradition. The instability brought on by the destruction of the temple would have had an impact that extended far beyond the disruption of their cultic practices alone. Community life would have been severely affected, leading to a possible disruption of the means by which tradition transmission took place. These factors, among others, compounded the significance of the time span between the two parallels. Here, although the chronological gap between nascent Christianity and emerging Rabbinic Judaism is relatively short, perhaps a century or two, the problem of anachronism can be quite significant.

Second, there is the question of the level of inference one attempts to draw from a comparison of two proposed parallels. Once again, Gerhardsson attempted to draw a detailed portrait of tradition transmission in early Christianity by comparing it with a rabbinic model.[31] He was not content with a general comparison between the two systems, but rather attempted to construct a detailed picture of the former (early Christianity) based upon inference from the latter (Rabbinic Judaism). Given the

---

[30] Here, several of the early, critical book reviews of Gerhardsson's *Memory and Manuscript* have been highly influential. See Morton Smith, review of Birger Gerhardsson, *Memory and Manuscript, JBL* 82 (1963): 169–176. It would appear that Neusner's view has changed since his initial review of *Memory*. In his preface to the 1998 reprinted edition of *Memory and Manuscript* Neusner withdraws his earlier criticism and attributes his original harsh polemic to the influence of Morton Smith on his earlier career. See Jacob Neusner, Preface to *Memory and Manuscript: Oral Tradition and Written Transmission in Rabbinic Judaism and Early Christianity; with Tradition and Transmission in Early Christianity*, by Birger Gerhardsson (Grand Rapids: Eerdmans, 1998), xxv-xlvi.

[31] Neusner states that Gerhardsson did not try to do this, but rather that Gerhardsson "invokes the Rabbinic writings to provide an example, a model, a possibility — not a record of exactly how things were in the time of the Evangelists" ("Preface to Memory and Manuscript," xxv), and then proceeds to discuss "paradigmatic versus historical thinking" ("Preface to Memory and Manuscript," xxxii-xlvi). Neusner suggests that Gerhardsson's work must be viewed within a "paradigmatic" framework, and that as such, provides the reader with an "occasion for comparison and contrast" ("Preface to Memory and Manuscript," xlvi). Neusner is correct to note that there is merit with both a historical and paradigmatic approach. The difficulty however, is that Gerhardsson's model is far too specific and detailed to be abstracted from Rabbinic Judaism and then applied to nascent Christianity. Can Gerhardsson's work be considered a "paradigm" of how tradition is generally transmitted and received? It would appear that Neusner's recent affirmation of *Memory and Manuscript*, while appreciated, is not sufficient to overcome the charge of anachronism often levelled against Gerhardsson.

specific historical setting of Rabbinic Judaism and the detailed level of inference that Gerhardsson attempted to draw from the rabbinic model, it is not surprising that for the most part, his thesis has not won many converts.[32]

In contrast to the example of Gerhardsson, there is also the situation where the charge of anachronism is less significant in determining the merits of a thesis. In this scenario, a parallel can be used to elucidate another historical context despite a chronological gap between the two settings. It is possible to express loosely this principle as the converse of the above-mentioned statement on anachronism:

the *less closely* a parallel is tied to a specific cultural practice among a specific people-group at a specific time and place, the *less problematic* it is to use a non-contemporaneous parallel to interpret the events or settings under examination.

To rephrase the principle in positive terms, the more widely applicable a phenomenon is among diverse people-groups, the more useful it is, and subsequently less problematic to apply it to the Jesus tradition through a diachronic approach. It is from this perspective that recent fieldwork in the area of oral tradition can be insightful for an inquiry into the earliest stages of the Jesus tradition.

It would be difficult to find many common elements in the various people-groups that have been studied by sociologists and folklorists. The subjects of the various studies reside in different geographical locations, are ethnically distinct, participate in varied cultic systems, speak different languages, etc. The single most striking characteristic of these cultures is that they remain highly dependent upon oral communication; it functions as the primary means of tradition transmission. In these cultures, oral communication is used to establish and perpetuate a sense of individual and corporate identity. It is used to teach the young and exhort the elderly; to maintain and at times challenge the *status quo*;[33] it can persuade and dissuade, and is capable of reaching people from all walks of life — both the poor peasant and the rich leader or king. Oral tradition clearly operates in such varied contexts and among such varied peoples that the parallels from field studies would easily fit into the "less closely" tied category

---

[32] Among those who agree with Gerhardsson are those often associated with the so-called Scandinavian school (e.g., Riesner, Byrskog, etc.). Also, D. Hagner has endorsed (correctly) Gerhardsson's work as an important corrective to the work of the *Jesus Seminar*. See Hagner's preface to the Gerhardsson's recently released *The Reliability of the Gospel Tradition* (preface to *The Reliability of the Gospel Tradition*, by Birger Gerhardsson [Peabody: Hendrickson, 2001], vii-xvi).

[33] See Scheub's collection of South African folklore which describes how oral tradition was used to combat apartheid (*The Tongue is Fire* [Madison: University of Wisconsin Press, 1996]).

mentioned above; thereby, making the issue of anachronism less significant.

What is most significant here is that these field studies in oral tradition describe phenomena that manifest themselves in strikingly similar ways despite their varied cultural contexts. These similarities suggest that these phenomena are not necessarily tied to specific cultural practices, nor are they associated with a specific people-group at a specific time and place. Such diversity suggests that any similarities regarding the way in which oral tradition functions *could* be significant. If oral communication functions so similarly in disparate societies, this could then indicate that the processes of oral communication are linked to some extent to human physiology and are not only cultural manifestations specific to a particular location at a specific time.[34] If this is the case, these field studies could provide helpful insight into the way in which the Jesus tradition was initially proclaimed and subsequently transmitted. It will now be necessary to examine, even if briefly, some of the insights gained from such interdisciplinary studies on oral cultures.

5.3.2   The "Oral Mind" of Antiquity

Folklore specialists have carried out field research in virtually all cultures that place importance on oral communication and remain "rooted" in an oral milieu. Fieldwork has been undertaken in almost all areas of the world; Africa,[35] Australia,[36] Europe,[37] North and South America,[38] Asia,[39] the Middle East, and elsewhere. The significance of these varied studies is not found in their chronological proximity to the time of Jesus nor in their geographical proximity to first-century Palestine, but in their great similarity *despite* their cultural and geographical diversity.

---

[34] There is of course an ongoing debate between the different "schools" of folklore; evolutionary, diffusionist, etc. For a more detailed discussion, see Okpewho, *African Oral Literature*, 6–7.

[35] Harold Scheub, *African Oral Narratives, Proverbs, Riddles, Poetry and Song* (Boston: G. K. Hall, 1977), Harold Scheub, *The World and the Word : Tales and Observations From the Xhosa Oral Tradition* (Madison: University of Wisconsin Press, 1992).

[36] David Unaipon, *Legendary Tales of the Australian Aborigines* (Carlton: Melbourne University Press, 2001).

[37] Katharine M. Briggs and Ruth L. Tongue, eds., *Folktales of England* (London: Routledge, 1965).

[38] Alan Dundes, *The Morphology of North American Indian Folktales* (Helsinki: Academia Scientiarum Fennica, 1964).

[39] Wolfram Eberhard, ed., *Folktales of China* (New York: Washington Square Press, 1973).

The similarities between these cultures has been so striking in fact, that some scholars have been able to construct a composite picture of how humans function as oral communicators, independent of any particular socio-cultural setting. The work of Ong and Havelock has, once again, been highly influential in this respect. Ong's model of the "oral mind,"[40] and Havelock's emphasis on the transformative effects of literacy upon the development of human civilization, [41] have been quite helpful in addressing the question of the relevance of recent sociological and folklore studies. They have demonstrated that it is possible to construct a coherent picture of how oral culture functions, and that humans have communicated in principally oral terms for the whole of our existence. The similarities between these recently studied people-groups is helpful for they suggest that the human mind has not, since the development of the printing press, had sufficient time to change fundamentally the way in which we communicate. We are still predominantly oral communicators and will remain so for the foreseeable future. In sum, there is continuity on a *general level* between the way in which highly oral societies function today and how they would have functioned in the time of Jesus. Interdisciplinary studies can be a helpful means by which one can understand better the way in which oral tradition functioned in antiquity. As long as one maintains modest expectations, these studies can be helpful in establishing *general characteristics* of oral communication.[42]

Before we can address the general characteristics of oral communication, it is necessary to explore the rationale behind the insights offered by Ong, Havelock, and others. Most of these insights into the way in which oral cultures function have been the result of the ongoing fieldwork of folklorists who have conducted extensive studies on oral cultures from all parts of the world. Due to the great influence that folklore studies have had on the question of tradition transmission, it is necessary to address the use of the term "folklore" in studying the Jesus tradition, and to explore the potential significance of these studies for our current study.

---

[40] See Foley, *Oral Composition*, 95 for a succinct summary of Ong's work.

[41] Havelock, *Literate Revolution*, 50. See above, ch. 4.

[42] It is important to avoid using Ong's description of the "oral mind" as a means for conclusively determining orality with extant texts. Ian Henderson expresses this well: "Such criteria clearly differentiate some texts and subtexts from others and generate at least plausible hypotheses of oral influence on the selected texts. They cannot, however, serve as independent criteria for a pre-literary, technically oral composition or transmission or even for an inimitably "oral style": they are essentially relative criteria, useful for comparing texts within a continuum" ("Didache and Orality," 294).

5.4 Folklore Studies and the Synoptic Tradition

5.4.1 Use of the Term "Folklore"

It is important to address briefly the history of the use of the term "folklore," with particular reference to its use and abuse in the field of Biblical Studies. The use of the English term "folklore" can be traced back to William J. Thoms in 1846,[43] although the term itself has several German antecedents, including, *Volkskunde* (Josef Mader; 1787), *Volkslied* (Herder; 1778), and *Volksmärchen* (J. K. A. Musaus; 1782).[44] All of these terms are related to the concept of *das Volk*, which sprung forth from Europe during the late eighteenth and early nineteenth centuries. The concept arose as a response to Rationalism and the Enlightenment and focused upon raditions which are derived from the "common people" of everyday society.

Although the use of the English term "folklore" dates back to 1846, it is its use by both Hebrew Bible and New Testament scholars that influences how the term is currently understood and interpreted. As noted above,[45] Gunkel's work on the Hebrew Bible was important for he was one of the first scholars to recognize the significance of oral tradition and the implications of folklore research on the study of the canonical tradition.[46] In his view, biblical literature was the product of evolving folklore — primitive traditions that developed and were later integrated into narrative accounts which were not able to "completely shed beliefs and practices from earlier stages."[47] Turning toward the New Testament, Bultmann's formulation of his "laws of transmission" was based, in part, upon the folklore studies of the Grimm Brothers. His view of the Gospels as *Kleinliteratur* was closely related to his overall assessment of the process of Gospel development itself. As was the case with Gunkel, Bultmann envisioned an evolutionary model of tradition formation in which the *Kleinliteratur* developed and the "pure forms" were embellished and

---

[43] William J. Thoms, "Folklore," in *The Study of Folklore* (ed. Alan Dundes; Englewood Cliffs: Prentice-Hall, 1965), 4–6.

[44] For all of this see Dan Ben-Amos, "Folklore in the Ancient Near East," *Anchor Bible Dictionary* 2: 818.

[45] See above, ch. 1.

[46] See Robert C. Culley, "Oral Tradition and Biblical Studies," *Oral Tradition* 1 (1986): 34 for a summary of Gunkel's view of oral tradition.

[47] Ben-Amos, "Folklore in ANE," 818–828. Ben-Amos suggests that J. G. Frazer's *Folk-Lore in the Old Testament* espouses this view. Ben-Amos summarizes Frazer by stating that he "interprets the OT itself as being folklore," while Dundes cites a critique by Moses Gaster in which Gaster commends Frazer for he ". . . doesn't make the bible Folklore" (Alan Dundes, *Holy Writ as Oral Lit: The Bible as Folklore* [Lanham: Rowman & Littlefield, 1999], 1).

improved upon, eventually culminating with the Synoptic texts. Bultmann's demythologizing program was also linked with his view of the "non-literary" character of the Synoptic Tradition, and subsequently, his view of folklore.[48] From that point forward, for better or worse, his overall form-critical view of the formation of the Synoptic Gospels became inexorably connected with the term "folklore."

There is great difficulty in superimposing an early form-critical evolutionary view of the development of the Synoptic Tradition upon the term "folklore." The theses of these early form-critics has met with resistance over the last century, due largely in part to their views on the historicity of the canonical tradition. Such criticism subsequently has had an adverse impact on how the term "folklore" has been understood and applied to the Synoptic Gospels. That is, the criticism against the early form-critical view of Synoptic origins has, by way of association, been applied to the term "folklore" and has led to the current situation whereby the term is understood primarily in negative terms in both Hebrew Bible and New Testament scholarship.[49]

As will become clear in the discussion that follows, the term "folklore" need not be associated with the specific theses of the early form critics. A

---

[48] See above, ch. 3.

[49] This negative bias towards folklore can be discerned in Wellhausen's work on the Hebrew Bible. Wellhausen appropriated an evolutionary model of Biblical development, and saw folklore as part of the oral stage that preceded the inscription of the Biblical texts. He felt that folklore was historically unreliable and therefore, the historical value of any extant canonical tradition could be determined by means of its separation from this "oral stage" (*Prolegomena to the History of Israel* [Gloucester 1973], 296, 334–35, 336–37, 341). Hebrew Bible scholars continue to react negatively to the term folklore, and have at times gone to great lengths to separate the Biblical tradition from "folklore." Thus, one still reads rather negative assessments of the relevance of folklore traditions for elucidating the Biblical text. For example, Walter Moberly downplays the value of "folklore" in studying the Sinai tradition in Exodus and describes it as such: "The possibility of oral tradition bears directly upon the question of historicity. Oral tradition tends to make the historical value of a tradition comparatively limited. Although oral tradition can preserve material accurately and unchanged, it can also change it beyond recognition" (*At the Mountain of God* [JSOTSup Sheffield: JSOT Press, 1983], 144–145). Behind such a view of folklore is an assumption that texts are stable and fixed while oral tradition is fluid, variable and therefore not capable of preserving historical information. Several scholars have addressed the ability of oral tradition to preserve history and have shown that such assumptions are not true. In particular see the valuable work of Byrskog (*Story*) who takes seriously the implications of eyewitnesses in the transmission and preservation of the early Jesus tradition. For folklore/oral tradition see Jan Vansina, *Oral Tradition as History* (Madison: University of Wisconsin Press, 1985). The situation in New Testament research is similar. Here, the so-called "Jesus Seminar" has an equally negative assessment of the value of folklore/oral tradition, see Funk and Hoover, *Five Gospels*, 25–30.

proper understanding of the term will be beneficial for an interdisciplinary approach to the Synoptic Tradition. It is now necessary to re-examine the concept of "folklore" with a view toward understanding how it relates to the question of Gospel genre.

5.4.2   Folklore and the Question of Genre

Before proceeding further in our discussion of folklore, it is necessary to address some preliminary matters. The first and most important question that needs to be addressed is "what is folklore?" In many respects, the most helpful approach to understanding the term folklore is by means of an apophatic definition. Folklore does *not* mean "non-historical" or "fairy-tale"; *nor* does it mean tradition created *de novo* from an over zealous imagination; *nor* is it the product of prophetic utterances or ecstatic experiences.[50] Folklore *could include* all of these elements, but the term should not be used as a descriptive catch phrase to describe specifically these types of traditions.[51] For this reason alone, the term folklore should not be interpreted from the pejorative perspective of modern twenty-first century reader expectations.

If the term "folklore" is to be useful for Synoptic studies, it must be understood within the broader discussion concerning Synoptic Gospel genre. Many proposals have been put forth regarding the question of Gospel genre. For the most part, these proposals have been based upon the relationship between the Synoptic Gospels and various literary genres of antiquity. This approach is fully justified for the Synoptic Gospels in their final forms *are* literary works. However, given our previous discussion on the relationship of ancient texts to oral tradition, we must ask whether there are other genres which can lend insight into our understanding of the Synoptics. Several scholars have approached the question of Gospel genre from an alternative, non-exclusively literary perspective. As we shall explore below, these approaches are helpful in counterbalancing an extreme literary reading of the Synoptic Gospels.

Several scholars have questioned the usefulness of a strictly literary approach to the question of gospel formation, noting that the question of oral performance is integrally linked with the question of genre and interpretation. Dewey and others have wrestled with this question and have

---

[50] In particular see M. Eugene Boring, *Sayings of the Risen Jesus: Christian Prophecy in the Synoptic Tradition* (Cambridge: Cambridge University Press, 1982).

[51] In this respect the term "folklore" is akin to the term "myth." Both terms have suffered from their association with previous scholarship. "Myth" has suffered from its association with the demythologizing program of Strauss/Bultmann, and "folklore" has suffered from its association with the early form-critical school, in particular that of Bultmann. Neither term should be understood as inherently negative.

attempted to account for the great interaction between orality and literacy as evidenced in antiquity.[52] If we heed their advice and avoid dealing with the question of Synoptic Gospel genre from a *strictly literary* perspective, we will be prepared to understand the contribution that folklore brings to the debate.[53] As it is not feasible to interact in detail with the great breadth and depth of folklore research in the limited space allotted for this project, we will focus instead on a selected number of highly influential scholars who can contribute important insights to the study of the early Jesus tradition.

Alan Dundes is an influential scholar who has spent more than the last forty-years engaged in folkloric research, and although he is unknown to most New Testament scholars, he has made a significant impact in the folklore community. Dundes has written on a variety of topics, and has studied the folklore of many diverse cultures.[54] Of the great range of topics he has researched, his recent work on the Bible has the most direct potential impact on the question at hand.

In *Holy Writ as Oral Lit*, Dundes explores both the Hebrew Bible and the New Testament from his perspective as a folklorist. Dundes argues that many previous Biblical scholars have looked for folklore *in* the Bible. He refers to the early three-volume work of J. G. Frazer entitled *Folklore in*

---

[52] The idea of a "mixed media model" has been increasingly adopted by New Testament scholars and Susan Niditch has approached the Hebrew Bible from this perspective. She argues that ancient Israelite literacy can be described as a continuum which extends from an "oral end" to a "literate end." Subsequently, Hebrew Bible traditions must be understood according to their relative position on that continuum rather then attempting to label them either "oral" or "literary"; see chs. 5, 6 in Niditch, *Oral World*, 78–98 (cf., Finnegan, "How Oral?," 59–60). Niditch summarizes these two chapters on the oral/literary continuum by stating that "[e]xploring the interplay between orality and literacy is essential to understanding the social contexts of reading and writing in a traditional culture" (*Oral World*, 98). Catherine Hezser's recent comprehensive work on Jewish literacy suggests a similar approach to that of Niditch. In her conclusion on Israelite *literacy*, Hezser asks "How does our image of ancient Judaism change, if one has to reckon with a largely oral, ritual, and symbolic transmission of Jewish religious knowledge and the veneration of the Torah as a sacred object amongst the populace?" (*Jewish Literacy*, 503).

[53] It important to note that adopting a mixed "media model" of Gospel formation does not preclude studying the Gospels from a literary-critical perspective. Dewey herself has interacted extensively with Mark from a literary perspective as well; see David M. Rhoads, Joanna Dewey, and Donald Michie, *Mark as Story: An Interpretation to the Narrative of a Gospel* (Minneapolis: Fortress Press, 1999); and also her Ph.D. dissertation; Joanna Dewey, *Markan Public Debate : Literary Technique, Concentric Structure, and Theology in Mark 2:1–3:6* (Chico: Scholars Press, 1980).

[54] Dundes has been a highly prolific scholar and has worked with folklore from numerous ethnic people-groups, in particular North American Indians (*Morphology*).

the Old Testament (1918)[55], whereby Frazer demonstrated that there are numerous folklore parallels to Old Testament traditions.[56] Dundes points to a review of Frazer's work by Moses Gaster. In reviewing Frazer's work, Gaster comments: "It is refreshing to find now a master in the science of Folklore trying his hand and bringing Folklore to the Bible and not making the Bible Folklore."[57] Dundes objects to Gaster's statement on the premise that folklore is not contained *in* the Bible, but that the Bible itself *is* folklore.[58] Dundes continues by examining a range of Biblical scholarship on both the Hebrew Bible and the New Testament, and concludes in summary:

> Although it is true that many scholars have acknowledged that both the Old and New Testaments were originally in oral tradition before being written down, they have, in my opinion, failed to carry that admission to its logical conclusion. In effect, the nod to prior oral tradition consists largely of lip service. Yes, there was initial oral tradition, but then these scholars go on to consider the bible as a purely religious or literary text, totally ignoring the possible debt to oral tradition . . . I maintain the Bible consists of *orally transmitted tradition written down*. Certainly there were collations, "literary" emendations, and editorial tampering, but the folkloristic component of the Bible remains

---

[55] James G. Frazer, *Folklore in the Old Testament: Studies in Comparative Religion, Legend and Law* (London: Macmillan, 1918).

[56] Also, see Frazer's classic comparative work on the "fall of man" myths in Genesis and those from other cultures throughout the world ("The Fall of Man," in *Sacred Narrative*. Edited by Alan Dundes. Berkeley: University of California Press, 1984. Repr. pages 45–77 in *Folklore in the Old Testament*. [London: 1918], 72–97).

[57] Moses Gaster, "Folk-Lore in the Old Testament," *Folk-Lore* 30 (1919): 72, cited in Dundes, *Holy Writ*, 1. In another work, Dundes examines the so-called "hero pattern" which has been outlined by Hahn (1876) , Rank (1909) , and Raglan (1934) ; see Alan Dundes, "The Hero Pattern and the Life of Jesus," in *In Quest of the Hero* (Otto Rank, Lord Raglan, and Alan Dundes; Princeton: Princeton University Press, 1990), 179-223. Dundes notes that the hero pattern has been tested against a wide spectrum of mythic and historical figures in antiquity, including, but not limited to: Perseus, Oedipus, Heracles, Romulus, Bellerophon, Apollo, Zeus, Moses, and even Abraham Lincoln. However, Dundes notes that there has been a hesitation to examine the extent to which Jesus fits the "hero pattern." According to Dundes, this hesitation is due in large part to the supposition — although incorrect — that the "heroes" were fictional characters and not historical figures ("Hero Pattern," 179-182). Thus, for example, Lord Raglan intentionally avoided applying his "hero pattern" to Jesus because "he had no wish to risk upsetting anyone" (Dundes, "Hero Pattern," 180).

[58] Dundes, *Holy Writ*, 1. Interestingly, Ben-Amos reads Frazer's work differently than Gaster in suggesting that Frazer "interprets the OT itself as being folklore" ("Folklore in ANE," 2:818–820). Dundes is not alone in categorizing the Bible as folklore. Botha argues that "Mark's text should be understood as a folk narrative. Reading it otherwise is a subtle yet powerful distortion (modernization) of the text" ("Virtue," 160).

in plain sight even if blind scholars have failed to recognize it as such [emphasis original].[59]

In addressing the definition of "folklore," Dundes makes it quite clear that the term is "not a synonym for error or fallacy,"[60] and that "to identify or label a verbal account as folklore says nothing one way or the other as to the historicity of that account. Some folklore is historically accurate; some is not. Each instance has to be examined on an individual basis."[61] Also important for Dundes is that folklore exists in both oral and written forms. For Dundes, the distinction between oral and written is unnecessary, for "oral transmission is a common but not absolutely essential factor in defining folklore. There is written folklore as well as oral folklore. Moreover, the same criteria that apply to oral folklore are also applicable to written folklore."[62] Subsequently, he objects to the form-critical work done on the New Testament which attempts to separate oral tradition from the written tradition in order to excise the secondary layers from the text and thereby "reconstruct the original (read "historically bona fide") facts."[63] According to Dundes, such work is founded on the false premise that folklore ceases to be folklore once it is written down–"[i]t is not enough to acknowledge that the Bible was in oral tradition before being written down with the assumption that once written down, folklore ceases to be folklore."[64]

Dundes proceeds to bring his expertise in folklore to bear upon the Biblical text. He approaches the Bible as a folklorist, interested in examining the internal structure and content of the text without passing historical judgments on the accounts therein. To that end, Dundes examines many Hebrew Bible traditions including those on the "flood," the "fall," genealogies, and the Decalogue. From the New Testament he examines traditions such as healing stories, tomb visitation accounts (Matt

---

[59] Dundes, *Holy Writ*, 19–20.

[60] Dundes, *Holy Writ*, 2.

[61] Dundes, *Holy Writ*, 10–11.

[62] Dundes, *Holy Writ*, 5.

[63] Dundes, *Holy Writ*, 12. This of course is not simply a problem with the early-form critics; many other more recent studies also fall into this category (e.g., Crossan, *Historical Jesus*; Kloppenborg, *Excavating Q*, etc.).

[64] Dundes, *Holy Writ*, 9. Dundes cites Douglas Knight as an example of this type of reasoning: "*a tradition ceases to be such at that point at which it is removed . . . from its normal context in life and is entered into a written composition*" (Knight 1975:27; emphasis in original). Dundes argues that this is a "faulty premise. An oral proverb once written down does not then magically cease to be a proverb. Once a proverb, always a proverb! A legend once written down does not stop being a legend. The point is that if the Bible was once folklore, why is it not still folklore? Just because it was written down does not automatically negate its original folkloristic nature" (Dundes, *Holy Writ*, 9).

28:1; Mark 16:1–2; Luke 24:1, 9–10, John 20:1), feeding miracles (Matt 14:15–22//Matt 15:32–39//Mark 6:35–45//Mark 8:1–10), among others.

Throughout Dundes' exposition he points out that "virtually every major event in both the Old and New Testaments exists in at least two versions."[65] Dundes then proceeds to document extensively his claim that the Biblical tradition exhibits the following characteristics of folklore: *variation in number, name, and sequence*.[66] These three characteristics are the hallmarks for folklore, and in turn for oral communication. For Dundes, the presence of these three types of variation is *prima facie* evidence that the Bible is folklore. Folklore functions as a genre within which other more specific sub-genres can be included. Dundes includes legend, myth, proverbs, curses, and folktales as sub-genres of folklore, all of which can exist in both oral and written forms.[67] Following Dundes' broad definition of the folklore genre, it is clear that the Gospels *can* be included therein. The question therefore is *how useful* is such a designation for the Gospels?

In order to determine the usefulness of such a designation, it is necessary to look at the potential benefits and disadvantages of adopting the term "folklore" as a genre. There are several important positive corollaries in adopting Dundes' broad category of folklore. First, the designation of folklore brings to the fore the existence of variability in the canonical Jesus tradition, a point which will be examined more fully in a subsequent chapter.[68] Second, it helps elucidate the close connection that

---

[65] Dundes, *Holy Writ*, 5.

[66] Although not an exhaustive list, the following are some of the traditions examined by Dundes — *Variation in number*: OT — the "flood" (Gen 8:3, 6), the "fall" (Gen 1–2), genealogies in Ezra 2:7–16/Neh 7:12–21, the Decalogue, exile to Babylon (Jer 52:28//2 Kg 24:11, 14//2 Kg 24:16); NT — healing of a blind man (Matt 20:29–34//Luke 18:35–42, tomb visitation accounts (Matt 28:1; Mark 16:1–2; Luke 24:1, 9–10, John 20:1), feeding miracles (Matt 14:15–22//Matt 15:32–39//Mark 6:35–45//Mark 8:1–10), Peter's denial (Matt 26:34, 73–75//John 13:38, 18:26–27//Luke 22:34, 59–62). *Variation in name*: OT — song of Moses/Miriam (Exod 15:1//15:20–21), King David's order to carry out a census (2 Sam 24:1//1 Chr 21:1) and results of census (2 Sam 24:9//1 Chr 21:5), descendants of Caleb (1 Chr 2:19//1 Chr 2:46//1 Chr 2:50); NT — listing of Apostles (Matt 10:2–4//Mark 3:14, 16–19//Luke 6:13–16//Acts 1:13), ascension accounts (Luke 24:50–51//Acts 1:9, 12). *Variation in sequence*: OT — creation accounts (Gen 1:25–27//Gen 2:7, 18–19); NT — temptation (Matt 4:1–11//Luke 4:1–13), Satan entering Judas at last supper (Luke 22:1–4, 7, John 13:2, 26–27).

[67] Dundes, *Holy Writ*, 13. In the context of a discussion on the relationship of Myth to folklore Dundes states that "Myth is one genre out of several hundred genres of folklore" (*Holy Writ*, 2). For an extended list of the many sub-genres of folklore see Alan Dundes, *The Study of Folklore* [Englewood Cliffs: Prentice-Hall, 1965], 5.

[68] This is important, for many recent studies have attempted to downplay the variability of the tradition instead emphasizing the level of verbatim agreement between

the extant texts have to their oral milieu. Third, as suggested by P. J. J. Botha, utilizing such a designation for the Gospels allows a different set of questions to be asked of the text and can lead to a better understanding of what is intended by the author.[69] Dundes' insistence that the Gospels are derivative from oral communicative processes suggests that one is not mistaken to seek a better understanding of the pre-textual oral tradition-history behind the textual tradition. Finally, Dundes' association of the Bible with folklore suggests that we can gain insight into the transmission of the early Jesus tradition and the process by which the textual tradition came into being by examining previously collected folklore.

Despite the insights offered by Dundes' provocative thesis, several important questions remain unanswered and even avoided if one adopts Dundes' approach in an uncritical manner. Dundes makes it clear that he is aware of several pertinent questions regarding the extant Synoptic texts, but he either downplays or dismisses the issues as unimportant in his overall thesis. He acknowledges the question of intertextual dependency (i.e., the Synoptic Problem) in his *Holy Writ*. For Dundes, this is a problem that exists but is dismissed as one best left to those "better qualified to investigate such issues."[70] Clearly, this cannot be judged acceptable since many of those concerned with the question of Gospel genre are also concerned with the question of Synoptic interrelationships. Dundes also leaves unaddressed several additional problems that are a concern for those dealing with the question of Gospel origins. His work does not address questions on the origin of the tradition, but is rather concerned with reading the texts in their final form.[71] By so doing, Dundes is able to distance himself from a difficult subject that is of great interest for Gospel scholars and general readers alike. Also, Dundes does not address in any respect questions regarding the historicity of the tradition. Understandably, one of his aims was to avoid intentionally the question of historicity, but this lessens the impact and potential significance of his study. Finally, Dundes does not address the question of tradition transmission. Since he is

---

the Synoptic Gospels. It is often argued that the variation within the tradition can be accounted for by means of literary redaction of one or more sources (see ch. 3). Not enough emphasis has been made of the variability within the tradition. See below, chapter six, for a test case on this characteristic of oral communication.

[69] Botha, "Virtue," 162–164. Botha uses "folkloric legend" to indicate "that Mark is not simply fiction" ("Virtue," 162–163). Understood correctly, "legend" refers to traditions that have their basis in historical events, as opposed to *folktale*, which is fictional in origin. See Dundes, *Holy Writ*, 18. It is to be noted that Botha's work specifically addresses the Gospel of Mark, although most of his observations can be applied equally to either Matthew or Luke.

[70] Dundes, *Holy Writ*, 24.

[71] Dundes, *Holy Writ*, 24.

only concerned with the final form of the tradition, vital questions regarding how the tradition was transmitted and the process by which the tradition became "textualized" go unanswered. While technically, these aforementioned questions might not concern contemporary folklorists who have their own aims and objectives, they are highly relevant for the New Testament scholar and cannot be entirely isolated from what Dundes is attempting to accomplish.

In sum, Dundes' work is helpful in that he has established a category by which one can compare the vast amount of folklore scholarship with the texts of the Synoptic Gospels. The designation of the Synoptic Gospels as folklore is a helpful heuristic tool that provides an additional basis from which one can approach the tradition.[72] Although Dundes glosses over several issues important to New Testament scholars, his work is helpful in that it reinforces the premise that the Biblical tradition is fully the product of ancient methods of authorship and therefore must be analyzed as such. Following the lead of Dundes, it is now necessary to explore the insights derived from folklore and sociological studies, and to seek how they might inform our understanding of the transmission and development of the Synoptic Tradition.

5.4.3   Characteristics of Oral Tradition

If folklore is accepted as a heuristic category from which one can understand and interpret the Synoptic Tradition, then one can look towards the insights gained from field studies of highly oral people-groups. The strength of Dundes' work is that he provided a means by which one can categorize the characteristics of oral communication. His primary thesis was that the majority of significant events in the Bible occur in more than one version. This is a fine example of the redundant use of traditions. The presence of multiple versions of these stories met one of Dundes' criteria for labelling the Bible as folklore. It is possible to divide the characteristics of oral communication into two major categories, each of which will be explored below.

5.4.4   Redundancy

Redundancy is perhaps the most pervasive characteristic of oral communication. In orally oriented cultures one can not help but note that

---

[72] This is not, of course, to suggest that the Gospels should *only* be understood through the genre designation of "folklore" — previous designations, in particular that of *bioi*, remain central for understanding the overall narrative aims of the Gospel authors and the function of the final form of the text.

redundancy occurs in variegated forms and is utilized in the composition and transmission of all traditions. Many scholars have observed that this characteristic is one of the key manifestations of orally composed/performed traditions.[73] Included within the category of "redundancy" are many of the *non-definitive* characteristics mentioned above, all of which are present in both orally composed/transmitted material as well as thoroughly literary productions.[74]

Redundancy exists on many different levels within traditions, at both the "microscopic" and "macroscopic" scale. At the microscopic level, one can observe the repetition of key words or phrases within individual traditions. Lord noted that within the Homeric texts were the repetition of key formulaic phrases, or as he labeled them, "noun-epithet" formulas such as "wide-eyed Athena."[75] These repetitive features were one of the key points that led Lord to the conclusion that the Homeric texts were originally orally composed and transmitted epics that were inscribed later on in their performance-history.[76] According to Lord, these redundant phrases were generally not the result of a conscious choice by the performer. Rather, they were employed on a more subconscious level, drawn upon from the recesses of the performer's memory during a performance and used as a "reflex action in rapid composition."[77]

---

[73] There are many scholars in both NT studies and Folklore studies that have noted the centrality of this characteristic. For a starting point see Gray, "Repetition," 289–303.

[74] See Henaut, *Oral Tradition, passim.* Despite his rather negative assessment and depiction of the "orality" argument, he correctly notes that most of the examples highlighted by scholars looking for oral tradition are not definitive one way or the other — "we have seen the complete absence of distinctive and unique ground rules for orality. Certainly scholars can identify a number of hallmarks of oral expression and catalogue a variety of variations on the theme of repetition. None of these, however, can be ascribed exclusively to the oral medium. Each of the oral techniques identified, which serve a particularly useful function in the oral medium, finds a natural home in textuality" (*Oral Tradition,* 116).

[75] Lord, *Singer of Tales,* 65. Other scholars such as Okpewho have extended the study of the formula to other non indo-European cultures such as sub-Saharan Africa. Okpewho who argues for the existence of an African epic also uses the phrase "noun-adjective combination" whereby a noun such as a proper name is used in conjunction with a patronymic or qualitative identification (e.g., "Dugo the Owl"). For more see Isidore Okpewho, *The Epic in Africa: Toward a Poetics of the Oral Performance* [New York: Columbia University Press, 1979], 138–140.

[76] Lord observed the use of these "noun-epithet" formulas in the performances he collected in his fieldwork (*Singer of Tales,* 30–67). He recognized that these formulas were not employed for the benefit of the audience. Rather, they were used as a tool for the "singer in the rapid composition of his tale" (*Singer of Tales,* 30).

[77] Lord, *Singer of Tales,* 65. In a similar fashion, Lohr uses the phrase "short sentences and noun-adjective combinations" to refer to Matthew's use of phrases such as "the Prophets and the Law" (οἱ προφῆται καὶ ὁ νόμος, Matt 11:13), "heirs to the

Likewise, in Mark, the frequent use of καὶ in paratactic construction, while not formulaic in character like those phrases highlighted by Lord, functions as a repetitive device throughout the Markan text.[78] There are many other examples of "microscopic" use of redundancy within the Synoptic Tradition. For but one example, the Gospel writers employ pleonasm (e.g., Mark 1:21–22 — ἐδίδασκεν, τῇ διδαχῇ, διδάσκων; 4:1–2 — διδάσκειν, ἐδίδασκεν, τῇ διδαχῇ) and repetition (e.g., the use of οἱ μαθηταὶ in Mark 2:18) to emphasize their depiction of Jesus as a teacher having disciples.[79] This use of repetition is not confined to Mark alone, but is employed by Matthew and Luke as well (e.g., Matt 22:16//Mark 12:14//Luke 20:21).[80] These stylistic features often take on a mnemonic function, thereby "aiding memory and thus safeguarding information."[81]

On a larger, macroscopic scale, individual phrases, sentences, or sections can bracket larger groupings of traditions both in oral and literary works. Included in this category are most of the oft-cited rhetorical

---

kingdom" (υἱοὶ τῆς βασιλείας, Matt 8:12), "blind guides" (ὁδηγοὶ τυφλοὶ, Matt 15:14, 23:16, 23:24), "brood of snakes" (γεννήματα ἐχιδνῶν, Matt 23:33), etc. Interestingly, Lohr uses these phrases as examples of ones "used repeatedly" by Matthew ("Oral Techniques," 407), although with the exception of "blind guides," the phrases listed here only occur in the listed form *once*. It seems that these Matthean phrases are used in varied fashion, not like the "noun-epithet" phrases discussed by Lord. As noted above (§3.3.4), Lohr assumes that these features are attributable to Matthew's "oral style" of composition and subsequently does not take into consideration the possibility that these could simply be attributable to Matthean redactional tendencies and preferred language. Lohr uses these "oral indicators" uncritically without discretion ("Oral Techniques," 407).

[78] Kloppenborg et al., note that the metrical repetition observed by Parry and Lord "play a much less significant role [in the Gospels] than they do in Homer," see Kloppenborg, Formation, 45. Also, see Notopoulos, "Parataxis," 1–23 for a study on the use of parataxis in the Homeric epics.

[79] See Richard A. Burridge, Four Gospels, One Jesus? A Symbolic Reading [Grand Rapids: Eerdmans, 1994], 39, and Byrskog, Only Teacher, 200–201. Burridge mentions pleonasm as a characteristic of Markan style and narrative technique. It seems however, that this feature of Markan style is more effective if the tradition is heard rather than silently read. Achtemeier uses the term "anaphora" in a similar manner ("Omne Verbum Sonat," 23). For the repetitive use of οἱ μαθηταὶ in Mark 2:18 see Dewey, Public Debate, 90.

[80] For the case of paying tribute to Caesar (Aland §280-Matt 22:16//Mark 12:14//Luke 20:12), the question of the pericope's origin/dependency is not important. Regardless of one's source-critical solution to this pericope's origins, the fact remains that one or more of the Gospel authors have used pleonasm to emphasize Jesus as Teacher.

[81] Abel, "Psychology," 277. Barrett, "Re-examination," 321 also points to Luke 13:25–30 where he believes that the repetition of θύραν in Luke 13:25 is an mnemonic link back to the preceding section (Luke 13:24) where στενῆς θύρας is used, and is possibly an "indication of oral tradition."

characteristics within both oral and written texts. Ring composition, chiasmus, inversion, etc., are all examples of the use of larger groupings of words or phrases in a redundant manner to structure, emphasize, and organize traditions.[82]

What is more significant than the presence of repetition within traditions is the purpose for their inclusion within the Gospel tradition. These features are best understood as fulfilling a need that exists for both the oral performer and the audience. Within written traditions that are intended for a silent, personal reading audience, repetition is unnecessary and perhaps undesired.[83] Within the context of oral performance and aural reception however, repetition is not only appreciated, but is a necessary and welcomed characteristic. Okpewho, among others, has shown that the audience is involved integrally in the "creative process" of the performance event, and that repetition can serve both the aesthetic and functional needs of the performer.[84] Aesthetically, if a performer "drew a favorable response" from a particular statement, then it is likely that the performer would repeat the statement again.

From a functional perspective, the "temporary" character of oral communication means that repetition is necessary in "keeping the speaker and listener on track"[85], and to "keep the listener abreast"[86] of what is

---

[82] Harvey details these structural devices in his part 2 entitled "Oral Patterning in Antiquity" (*Listening*, 61–118). Given Harvey's own observations, this section would be better titled "aural patterning," for although one can be fairly certain of the aural reception of these traditions, letters, and books, we cannot be certain of their *oral origins*. It is better to focus on the reception history of the traditions, and thus, *aural patterning* seems a more appropriate term.

[83] Many scholars have commented on Mark's lack of literary skill (e.g., E. Trocmé, *The Formation of the Gospel According to Mark* [Philadelphia: Westminster Press, 1975], 68–72; Vincent Taylor, *The Gospel According to St. Mark* [London: Macmillan & Co., 1966], 52). The Markan use of parataxis is among the evidence presented for the poor writing skills of its author. Behind such a thesis is the presumption that a written narrative should contain more varied literary devices. Since Mark has a greater frequency of parataxis and asyndeton, it is argued that he is a poorly skilled writer. If the presence of parataxis is related to the Gospel's relationship to oral performance, then it is no longer appropriate to regard Mark as a poor writer. Rather, he should be understood as an effective communicator. If Mark is understood in relation to oral performance then the repetitive devices serve a functional rather than aesthetic role within his Gospel. In this respect, to measure Mark's literary achievement against other more "literary" works would be to evaluate Mark against a standard that he himself did not hope to achieve.

[84] Okpewho, *African Oral Literature*, 15. Okpewho highlights this characteristic of proverbial traditions; their appeal "is achieved through the repetition of sounds in successive words or lines . . ." (*African Oral Literature*, 238).

[85] Ong, *Orality and Literacy*, 39–40.

[86] Achtemeier, "Omne Verbum Sonat," 23.

being said.[87] In orally oriented societies, both modern and ancient, repetition is a "dire necessity" and is required to ensure the preservation of traditions that are central to a community's self-identity.[88] Repetition functions as a signpost used by the performer to direct and guide the listener as necessary. Here, the demands of orality can be contrasted with those of literacy. Axel Olrik in his highly influential "Epic Laws of Folk Narrative" describes the situation (*das Gesetz der Wiederholung*) as follows:

> In literature, there are many means of producing emphasis, means other than repetition. For example, the dimensions and significance of something can be depicted by the degree and detail of the description of that particular object or event. In contrast, folk narrative lacks this full-bodied detail, for the most part, and its spare descriptions are all too brief to serve as an effective means of emphasis . . . there is but one alternative: repetition.[89]

Repetition takes on two forms, the repetition of key phrases or sections within a tradition, and the repetition entailed in the multiple-retellings of stories to facilitate memorization.[90] Gerhardsson highlighted this latter pedagogical method within early Rabbinic Judaism, and both Rainer Riesner and Samuel Byrskog have proceeded down a similar path in their study of possible early Christian pedagogy.[91] For the purposes of this study

---

[87] See Ong, *Orality and Literacy*, 35 for the futility of thinking in "non-mnemonic terms" within a highly oral culture.

[88] Kelber, *Oral and Written Gospel*, 66–67; also see Gray, "Repetition," 289–303. From an oral tradition perspective, the birth narratives in both Matthew and Luke function in a similar fashion. At the surface they detail and narrate Jesus' birth. However, more significantly, they function as community-forming and identifying traditions which are integral to all orally oriented cultures. Veronika Görög-Karady has studied how several African people-groups have appropriated the Biblical creation accounts in Genesis and modified them in order to depict their own social issues and place within society. Here, an origins tradition has taken on a greater significance, for it not only depicts their origins as humans, but also defines their self-identity and establishes boundaries for their community ("Retelling Genesis: The Children of Eve and the Origin of Inequality," in *Genres, Forms, Meanings: Essays in African Oral Literature* [ed. Veronika Görög-Karady; Oxford: Journal of the Anthropological Society of Oxford, 1983]).

[89] Olrik, "Epic Laws," 132–133.

[90] See Ong, *Orality and Literacy*, 33–34, Gerhardsson, *Memory and Manuscript*, 168, and Kelber, *Oral and Written Gospel*, 66–67.

[91] Gerhardsson writes "if transmission takes place in writing, a document must be handed over or copied. If a text is 'handed over' in a purely oral way, it must be done by way of repetition" ("Illuminating the Kingdom: Narrative Meshalim in the Synoptic Gospels," in *Jesus and the Oral Gospel Tradition* [JSNTSup 64; Sheffield: JSOT Press, 1991], 306). Also see Riesner, *Jesus als Lehrer, passim*, and Byrskog, *Only Teacher*, 158–160. Okpewho's work on African oral traditions is illuminating here. He discusses a "formal" type of training whereby tradition transmission is based upon "constant repetition" of a teacher's words. This can result in a "fixed" tradition which remains

however, the former type of repetition is more significant and deserves further attention.

It would be possible to detail the many rhetorical devices that could be included under the collective term "redundancies." The list could be expanded to address rhetorical/structural features such as chiasm, ring composition, inclusio, catch-word composition etc.[92] These features are all examples of repetition that have received much prior attention and therefore need not be elaborated in detail here. Although it is beyond the scope of this present study, it is important to note that these redundant characteristics, while not definitive indicators of a prior oral tradition-history, are important nevertheless. [93] These rhetorical features are integral to all oral speech, and one would be hard pressed to find traditions that have their genesis in oral performance lacking these rhetorical and structural characteristics.

5.4.5 Variability: Flexibility and Stability of Oral Tradition

5.4.5.1 Flexibility

While redundancy is the occurrence of repetition, etc. within a text or tradition, variability is the form in which those redundant features occur. This in fact is Dundes' second major criterion for labelling a tradition "folklore," and it will be helpful to examine how this criterion is made manifest in orally transmitted traditions.

Dundes is not alone in insisting that variation is the key characteristic of folklore (e.g., variation in number, name, and sequence.). Other folklore scholars have reinforced his basic premise, and have clearly demonstrated that this characteristic is typical of folklore. Lord noted that multiple performances of the epic traditions were never repeated verbatim, regardless of the singer or the type of song being performed. In his words,

---

quite stable (*African Oral Literature*, 21–23). This type of transmission resembles that proposed by Gerhardsson in his *Memory and Manuscript* (1961), and subsequently reaffirmed in a more recent (1991) article: "I still believe that there also existed a more programmatic form of transmission: somebody actually 'handed over' a Jesus-text to another who received it in an appropriate way, whether a single text or a collection. This could be one either orally or in writing, or in both ways" ("Illuminating," 306).

[92] For a more detailed catalog of these devices see Harvey, *Listening to the Text*, 97–118 and David E. Aune, *The Westminster Dictionary of New Testament and Early Christian Literature and Rhetoric* (Louisville: Westminster John Knox, 2003), *passim*.

[93] Kloppenborg's comment on "catchword composition" is equally applicable to other forms of redundancy as well: "Catchword composition . . . belongs as much to the literary sphere as it does to the oral, and is employed widely in literary composition, especially of a sapiential variety . . . The mere presence of catchword connectives neither proves nor excludes oral composition and transmission" (*Formation*, 48–49).

"one of the earmarks of an oral traditional narrative is its textual fluidity, which is to say, because it has no fixed original it is constantly being repeated without concern for word-for-word retelling of a set, established text."[94] In this case, Lord's statement reflects the consensus view among experts in folklore. More often than not what is retained is not the *ipsissima verba* of a performance, but rather the basic outline of the story itself.[95] This basic "outline" is what the oral performer attempts to achieve, all the while adapting pre-existing traditions and incorporating new traditions into the highly complex woven fabric of community life.[96] This "verbal variability"[97] is one of the key characteristics of oral tradition and although it is not a definitive criterion capable of distinguishing oral from written tradition, it can be helpful in shifting the probability of a tradition's origins in one direction or another.[98]

The variable character of oral communication is so well documented in the field of folklore that it does not require extensive support here. What is more important for the purposes of this current study is that these

---

[94] Lord, "Gospels," 37. Also, see Okpewho who writes; "[e]ach performance is the product of one specific moment or context and, in a creative tradition of the oral epic, is never exactly repeated. Though there are some fixed structural laws which the narrative will obey by the very nature of its oral medium, the results of any performance depend mainly on the particular audience, mood, and atmosphere" (*Epic in Africa*, 135).

[95] Lord writes that "[o]ne is not concerned with transmission of text, but with transmission a) of the art of composition and b) of the story itself" ("Gospels," 37). Stemberger, *Introduction*, 38–30 also refers to Lord's work, and questions the ability to recover the *ipsissima verba* of the individual rabbis.

[96] The oral performer recognizes the need for traditions to be adaptive in communal life. Harold Scheub, a leading folklorist who has done extensive work with the Xhosa of South Africa, writes the following about a storyteller named Mrs. Zenani: "Stories in the oral tradition were never meant to be memorized, Mrs. Zenani argues, nor were they meant to be frozen in time. The storyteller is constantly in the process of linking the present and the past: it is therefore crucial that the images be flexible, that their union be evanescent" (Scheub, *Xhosa*, 3).

[97] Finnegan, *Oral Literature in Africa*, 8.

[98] Although the majority of scholars in both folklore and New Testament research currently recognize that there are no "clear-cut" boundaries between oral and literary tradition, this was not always the case. Ruth Finnegan wrote in 1970: "one of the striking characteristics of oral as distinct from written literature is its verbal variability . . ." (*Oral Literature in Africa*, 8). It is the confidence with which Finnegan makes the statement that is no longer acceptable. One could argue that Finnegan's "verbal variability" is a *possible* indicator of the "likelihood" that a tradition is derivative from an oral milieu. Once again the aforementioned *via negativa* is helpful here; if redundant forms of a tradition exhibit *no* variability, it would be difficult to argue that in their current form they are direct transcriptions of an oral performance, or in the words of Horsley an "oral-derived text" (*Whoever*, 122).

characteristics, which are deemed vital for folklore and oral communication, are also prevalent within the Synoptic Tradition.

The very existence of three Synoptic Gospels is in itself powerful testimony to the fact that for the early church, the Jesus tradition was at its very core a multiform manifestation of the powerful impact that Jesus had upon his earliest followers.[99] The "problem" of "different" versions of Jesus tradition only becomes such once the tradition has been transformed by its inscription into concrete objects that could subsequently be analyzed in ways not previously possible. As the early church began to compile and collect the traditions that had become the basis for their newly formed communities, the traditions began to acquire a sacred status, and the subsequent inscription of those traditions allowed for the detailed comparison of these multiform expressions of Jesus. Textuality had taken grasp of the tradition and the newly acquired sacred status of the tradition then required interpretative harmonization and explication in order to function in its new role as an authoritative *text*.

This multiform, variable expression of the early Jesus tradition is entirely reflective of its origins within a highly oral milieu. The intensive work undertaken on questions of Synoptic interrelationships over the past century has performed an excellent service by demonstrating the high levels of verbatim agreement within both the double and triple tradition. While highly instructive and important, this highly literary approach to the Synoptic Gospels has overshadowed the fact that despite the significant level of agreement amongst the Gospels, they could contain some material which has not been derived from the redactional use of a shared *textual Vorlage*.

As is the case with any discipline, one can get so immersed in the minutiae of a particular field of research that it becomes difficult to see beyond the immediate context of that discipline and examine the subject afresh from a different perspective. Folklorists give us just such an opportunity to "step back" and examine anew well-entrenched paradigms and theses. In Lord's "fresh" reading of the Synoptic Gospels, he noted extensive similarities between the written Synoptic Tradition and the type of traditions that he recorded and transcribed from the former Yugoslavia. Based upon these similarities, he concluded that the level of verbatim agreement and variability among the Synoptic Gospels was characteristic of their indebtedness to the processes of oral communication. Lord noted that the level of variability in the parallel traditions in the Synoptic

---

[99] This concept of "impact" plays an important role in Dunn's recent work *Jesus Remembered*.

Gospels often corresponded to that which he observed in his fieldwork.[100]
He also documented the occurrence of blocks, or sequences of material
that occurs in different contexts and in different order in each of the
respective Gospels.[101] These observations led Lord to classify the
Synoptics as "oral traditional literature."[102] In conclusion he writes:

> I have seen reason to believe that the Synoptic Gospels exhibit certain characteristics of
> oral traditional literature. *First,* for example, their texts vary from one another to such an
> extent as to rule out the possibility that, as a whole, one could have been copied from
> another. In this respect they have the appearance of three oral traditional variants of the
> same narrative and non-narrative materials. It is true that on occasion the texts are so
> close that one should not rule out manuscript transmission; hence, it may be that oral
> tradition has sometimes had written sources affecting the text, not merely in respect to
> content but also as *text.*[103]

Many scholars have questioned the legitimacy of this designation,
including C. H. Talbert who raised some valid concerns in his written
response to Lord, but while so doing, revealed his misunderstanding of the
question and his "textual bias." Talbert's response to Lord is another
example of the "either/or" problem discussed previously. Lord makes it
quite clear that there are places where one "should not rule out manuscript
transmission."[104] In these cases, Lord is fully aware of the possibility that
the Synoptic Gospels were produced in an environment where the authors
might have had access to written source texts. Unfortunately, Talbert's
response suggests that he is arguing against an "exclusively oral" position
that goes beyond that which Lord himself argues. Talbert argues that the
literary activity of Greco-Roman/Jewish authors such as Josephus indicates
that the characteristics pointed out by Lord are also found in the "literary
tradition of Greco-Roman antiquity."[105] This leads Talbert to the

---

[100] For example, Appendix IV to Lord's *Singer of Tales* includes a comparison of five
different versions of "return songs" sung by four different individuals. The variation in
the performances is strikingly familiar to those familiar with the variation within the
Synoptic Tradition; see Lord, *Singer of Tales,* 260–265.

[101] In another appendix Lord transcribes four versions of a performance entitled
"Marko and Nina" sung by Petar Vidic. The transcription is displayed in a four-column
synopsis format and is quite illustrative of the type of sequencing deemed significant by
Lord; see Lord, *Singer of Tales,* 235–241.

[102] Lord, "Gospels," 90.

[103] Lord, "Gospels," 90.

[104] Lord, "Gospels," 90.

[105] His argument is based upon several observations regarding the ability of ancient
authors to reproduce phenomena similar to that seen in the NT. His evidence is primarily
from Josephus and other highly literate Greco-Roman and early Christian authors. It
would seem inappropriate to compare the Synoptic Gospels as literary works to the more
formal Hellenistic Greek literary works in the way he does. If the Gospels were intended

conclusion that "[t]he Synoptics do not seem readily to fit the category of oral traditional literature."[106] Such a response leads to the polarization of "orality" against "literacy," which, as we have noted above, is a view that is no longer accepted by the majority of New Testament scholarship.

Talbert's line of argumentation suggests that he fundamentally misunderstands what advocates of orality are attempting to demonstrate. Here his line of critique is similar to that offered by Henaut, in that they both construct a false dichotomy between orality and literacy, then argue that evidence of the latter (literary dependency) is evidence that the former (oral tradition) played no part in the composition of the Synoptic Gospels. We must avoid juxtaposing orality against literacy when evaluating the merits of Lord's thesis. His work raises larger issues that have great significance for our understanding of the process of Gospel formation.

While it might be difficult to accept without modification Lord's classification of the Gospels as oral-traditional literature, his recognition of the oral background of the Gospels still has great significance for the current debate. Despite the critique of Talbert and others, several issues raised by Lord remain worthy of discussion today, including that of sequence, verbatim agreement, and pericope order.[107] Although for the most part neglected, Lord's work prompts one to ask whether the Gospels can *only* be understood in their relationship to highly literary works, or whether they can, or perhaps should also be considered from within the context of oral performance.[108] While Lord's primary goal was not to

---

to be works of "literature" analogous to those of Josephus, then why are they not written in a more formal style rather than the more colloquial style in Koine Greek?

[106] Charles H. Talbert, "Oral and Independent or Literary and Interdependent? A Response to Albert B. Lord," in *The Relationships Among the Gospels: An Interdisciplinary Dialogue* (ed. William O. Walker Jr.; San Antonio: Trinity University Press, 1978), 101.

[107] Most critiques of Lord's work center around the question of anachronism and the relevance of his work with respect to the Gospel tradition. It is indeed the case that Lord worked on *sung epics* — a media-transmission model which on the surface is quite different than that proposed by the majority of scholars working on the early Jesus movement. The recognition of this fact need not lead one to dismiss Lord's observations altogether. As suggested above, in this case what is significant is that the phenomena observed by Lord have for the most part been supported by folklore studies from various parts of the world. It is necessary to separate the specific *Sitz im Leben* under which Lord worked from the general observations he made regarding the processes of oral transmission. The "epic" genre extends beyond the former Yugoslavia and exists in other geographical regions such as the sub-Saharan Africa; see Okpewho, *Epic in Africa*. Okpewho is one of many scholars who have shown that many of the characteristics of oral transmission documented by Lord are applicable within an African context.

[108] Thomas P. Haverly, "Oral Traditional Literature and the Composition of Mark" (Ph.D. Thesis, University of Edinburgh, 1983) has argued that the Gospel of Mark

propose a new genre classification for the Synoptic Gospels,[109] his work did make it possible to conceive of the tradition in more fluid terms, and challenged all New Testament scholars to look beyond the quest for "authentic" Jesus material and the *ipsissima verba Jesu.*

5.4.5.2 Stability

While it is clear that flexibility is an integral aspect of the transmission of oral tradition, we must explore the possibility that there are other characteristics of oral communication that can affect the way in which tradition is transmitted. This additional step is important, for if one were to end the discussion at this stage, the logical inference from our previous discussion would be to understand oral tradition as incapable of preserving or maintaining reliable tradition. Such a view, of course, has been adopted in the past, and has negatively impacted our understanding of the early Jesus tradition for the better part of the last century. With this in view, we must press forward and inquire as to whether or not there are other significant characteristics of oral tradition that are maybe overlooked when one focuses solely on its variable nature.

This question naturally leads us to ask if there are stabilizing forces that help maintain and preserve tradition by acting as a counterbalance to its inherent variability. In addressing this possibility, two fundamental questions must be raised. First we must ask whether orally-oriented communities have the *desire* to maintain and stabilize their tradition, and second, whether orally-oriented communities have the *ability* to do so.

---

exhibits oral-formulaic characteristics. Apart from his work, Lord's work on the Gospels ("Gospels") has, for the most part, been largely neglected despite its importance in the discussion. While he has been critiqued on the minutiae of his argument, his greater thesis remains significant and demands our further attention. It is encouraging that several of the key arguments of Lord have begun to rise to the surface within New Testament scholarship. In particular, Lord's concept of "performance sequences" has been taken up recently (e.g., Horsley and Draper, *Whoever*). Also, verbatim agreement and pericope order remain significant entry points into the discussion (see chapter 6 for more on verbatim agreement and variability).

[109] Although Lord's intention was not specifically to propose a new genre classification for the Gospels, he classified the Gospels as "myth," which, for Lord, was a means by which people express "what happened in terms of already existent patterns of story" ("Gospels," 39). Dundes correctly notes that this is not the best term to describe the Gospels, describing it as "a genre mistake almost as misguided as considering them folktales . . . [which], of course, by definition are fiction as opposed to history or truth. The Gospels are clearly legends, not myths, if one accepts the definition of myth as a sacred narrative explaining how the world and humankind came to be in their present form, whereas a legend is a narrative told as true set in the postcreation world" ("Preface to Theory of Oral Composition," 18).

To answer the first question, it is necessary to examine in more detail the function of tradition, and its performers, in what we have labeled *orally-oriented* communities. The community within which the oral performer functions is a *traditional* one, where traditions are not told simply for purposes of entertainment but serve a far more significant purpose. In these so-called traditional communities, a category in which the early Christian communities should be included, orally transmitted tradition functions as the means by which these people-groups establish their self-identity.[110] In this context, tradition is precious, something that would be handled with care, not easily changed, embellished, nor created *de novo*. Boundaries are established (either consciously or unconsciously) which help the community maintain the general stability of a tradition during multiple retellings.[111] The adaptive variability of oral tradition functions within the bounds of a traditional setting, thus ensuring that key elements of a tradition remain intact.

The adaptive variability of oral tradition is also offset by the role of eyewitness testimony. As Taylor and others have pointed out, eyewitness testimony helps to stabilize a tradition.[112] Byrskog's *Story as History* —

---

[110] Gerd Theissen defines community identity as that which "includes all values, norms and traditions which give a group self-awareness and identity. By 'identity' we mean that a positive picture of a group is constructed on the basis of an adequate consensus and is balanced with the picture of other groups which has been arrived at" (*Sociology of Early Palestinian Christianity* [Philadelphia: Fortress Press, 1978], 31). Theissen also discusses the question of continuity between the Jesus tradition and the early church: "If we presuppose that a tradition is genuine, we may assume that those who handed it down shaped their lives in accordance with the tradition. If we assume that it [the Jesus tradition] originated within the Jesus movement in the period after Easter, we can presuppose that those who handed it down shaped the tradition in accordance with their life. In either case the result is the same: there is a correspondence between the social groups which handed down the tradition and the tradition itself" (*Palestinian Christianity*, 3–4).

[111] Here, recent work on social memory theory can be helpful. Alan Kirk and Tom Thatcher, in a forthcoming publication, have suggested that there are eight ways in which recent research on social memory can be applied to early Christianity. Among the eight points of which they suggest warrant further investigation is "normative memory" ("Social Memory and the Study of Early Christianity," [forthcoming]: 1–13). They point out the significance of this theory within the field of social memory which has highlighted the "formative" and "normative" functions of tradition (cf. Jan Assmann, "Collective Memory and Cultural Identity," *New German Critique* 65 [1995]: 125–133). Kirk and Thatcher ask to what extent the normative function of communal memory had an influence upon moral formation. For this and their other seven points, see "Social Memory," 10–12.

[112] Taylor writes, "the presence of eyewitnesses, for at least a generation, would serve as a check on corruptions innocently due to imagination . . ." (*Formation*, 208). Stein also notes that eyewitnesses play a important role in the Lukan prologue: "Luke's own

History as Story emphasizes the importance of *autopsy* in Greco-Roman culture and highlights its significance in the process of early Christian tradition transmission.[113] Within a traditional setting, eyewitnesses are a stabilizing, self-corrective force used to help counterbalance the variable character of oral communication.[114]

If we work under the premise that the early Jesus communities did care about preserving and maintaining their traditions, we must still inquire as to what extent they would have been *successful* in their attempt to stabilize their received traditions. It is clear that we cannot fully address fully specific issues, but it is possible to make some tentative observations. Lord noted on several occasions that despite the variability associated with oral performance, performers (i.e., tradents) could transmit traditions with what could be described as a "fair degree of fixity," particularly if they are "the retellings of a given storyteller or of narrators in a closed group."[115] Genre

---

perception of the oral period is that the process of the transmission of the materials was carried out by eyewitnesses . . . this group cannot be limited to the Twelve, but it must also be pointed out that the term 'eyewitness', although a common term in literary introductions, must be taken quite seriously in the Lukan prologue . . ." (*Gospels and Tradition*, 45). Abel is correct to note on the other hand that the presence of eyewitnesses "does not necessarily insure the accurate preservation of the traditions found in the Gospels" ("Psychology," 274), although it does suggest a reasonable setting whereby it is possible to do so.

[113] See Byrskog, *Story*, 146–175. Although Byrskog's study deals more with "oral history" than the process of tradition transmission with which we are concerned here, it can be viewed as a helpful complement to our current discussion. Also, it is not necessary to draw a sharp distinction between oral history and oral tradition. Scheub describes the difference between oral history and the oral storytelling as such, [t]he one deals in facts, the other gives facts their contexts and so converts them to truth" (*Tongue*, 52).

[114] Assmann uses the phrase "kommunikative Gedächtnis" to describe the influence exerted by eyewitness testimony in the formation of social memory (*Das kulturelle Gedächtnis. Schrift, Erinnerung und politische Identität in frühen Hochkulturen* [München: C. H. Beck, 1992], 50–56). He also suggests that communities reach a critical stage in their development once the eyewitness tradens begin to die (*kulturelle Gedächtnis*, 11), and that they must then turn from communicative memory to more long-lasting forms of memory which he describes as "kulturelle Gedächtnis" (*kulturelle Gedächtnis*, 218–221). See also, Schröter, *Jesus Worte*, 462–463 who draws upon the work of Assmann.

[115] Lord, "Gospels," 38. It would seem that the traditions circulated within early Jesus communities would fit Lord's category of "narrators in a closed group." If the early Jesus movement was characterized by charismatic itinerant preachers as suggested by Theissen (Theissen, *Palestinian Christianity*, 8–16), then we have a situation where individuals visited established communities, "deposited" Jesus tradition, and then moved on. In such a setting it is likely that those traditions were subsequently circulated among the members of local community under the watchful eye of their established elders. Therefore, it should not be surprising that the Jesus tradition plays a relatively minor role

also plays a significant role in the overall stability of a tradition. Generally speaking, the level of attainable *fixity* often varies according to the genre classification of any particular tradition. Both folklorists and New Testament scholars have recognized that proverbs and other "fixed form" genres are generally transmitted with a greater level of fixity than other longer narrative performances.[116] In particular, cultic and ritual contexts tend to stabilize a tradition, as has been demonstrated through the fieldwork of many folklorists.[117]

5.4.5.3 Flexibility and Stability: A Synthesis

It is at this point in the discussion that we return to the previously mentioned work of Bailey to explore in more detail his proposed model. We revisit Bailey's model of *informal controlled oral tradition* and evaluate it from within the context of our current discussion on *flexibility* and *stability*. Bailey suggests that the so-called *informal uncontrolled* model of Bultmann and the *formal controlled* model of Gerhardsson both

---

within the Pauline corpus. Rather than deduce that Paul was not aware of any Jesus material related to these topics, it is far more likely that the local communities were already in possession of these traditions, and that Paul therefore had no need to state them explicitly in his letters (cf. Dunn, *Paul the Apostle*, 650–653). Given the context of our current discussion, Paul's frustration with the local congregations he addresses is likely due to the fact that they are *not* recognizing the authority of the tradition that they have already accepted as formative for their new identity.

[116] Scholarship on folklore tradition has demonstrated that there *are* verbal forms that can be transmitted more or less verbatim. Aphorisms and short sayings material are the primary candidates; P. D. Beuchat, "Riddles in Bantu," in *The Study of Folklore* (ed. Alan Dundes; Englewood Cliffs: Prentice Hall, 1965), 183 has made the distinction between "fixed content" and "fixed wording" (cf. Foley, *Oral Composition*, xi). Beuchat suggests that fixed wording is the type of category under which proverbs fall, while fixed content, or "free-phrase" is that which is most often associated with folklore forms — "[t]he *content is fixed*, but the wording is not [italics mine]" ("Riddles," 183). See also Anderson, "Oral Tradition," 36.

[117] The verbatim transmission of longer, extended performances has been recorded by folklore experts — particularly those performances within a *cultic* context. Joel Sherzer has studied the Cuna of Panama and has, over a span of nine years, observed the verbatim repetition of lengthy "puberty rite" rituals ("The Interplay of Structure and Function in Kuna Narrative, or, How to Grab a Snake in the Darien," in *Georgetown University Round Table on Languages and Linguists* [ed. Deborah Tannen; Washington: Georgetown University Press, 1981]). Also, see Ong, *Orality and Literacy*, 57–66 for several other examples of the verbatim transmission of oral tradition, in particular those which derive from "special linguistic or musical constraints" (*Orality and Literacy*, 63). It is noteworthy that several New Testament traditions exhibit an apparent stability that seems due largely to their function within the context of ritual/sacramental worship. For example, the Lord's Prayer (Matt 6:7–13//Luke 11:1–4), and the Last Supper (Matt 26:26–29//Mark 14:22–25//Luke 22:15–20; cf. 1 Cor 11:23–29).

exist today within the Middle East.[118] The former manifests itself in what Bailey labels "rumor transmission" and for the latter he tells of his personal experience while studying under Shaykh Sayyed, who had the entire Qur'an and the *Alfiyat Ibn Malik* committed to memory and with "total recall" at seventy-five years of age.[119] Bailey then proceeds to suggest that the majority of examples of tradition transmission fall within a different set of parameters, and that this model can help elucidate how the early Jesus tradition was transmitted.

On the basis of his thirty years of personal experience in the Middle East, Bailey suggests that one can discern *three* major levels of flexibility within oral traditional material. They are as follows: 1) *No Flexibility*.[120] Within this category are proverbs and poems, which Bailey argues cannot be recited among a community "with so much as a *word* out of place" or the storyteller will be "corrected by a chorus of voices."[121]   2) *Some Flexibility*. This category is comprised of parables and "recollections of historical people and events important to the identity of the community."[122] Bailey's conclusions on this category of material are profound. Based upon his experience of telling a story to a group of students from Beirut and then discussing what elements of the story were necessary for it to be a "correct" retelling, he concludes:

> ... [h]ere was continuity and flexibility. Not continuity and change. The distinction is important. Continuity and change could mean that the story teller could change say 15% of the story — any 15%. Thus after seven transmissions of the story theoretically *all* of the story could be changed. But *continuity* and *flexibility* mean that the main lines of the story *cannot* be changed at *all*. The story can endure one different transmission through a chain of a hundred and one different people and the inner core of the story remains intact. Within the structure, the storyteller has flexibility within limits to "tell his own way." But the basic story line remains the same. By telling and retelling, the story does not evolve from A to B to C. Rather the original structure of the story remains the same but it can be colored green or red or blue.[123]

---

[118] Bailey, "Informal Controlled," 38.

[119] The *Alfiyat Ibn Malik* is a collection of Arabic couplets each of which defines an aspect of Arabic grammar, see, Bailey, "Informal Controlled," 38.

[120] Bailey, "Informal Controlled," 42.

[121] Bailey, "Informal Controlled," 42. Compare Scheub, *Tongue*, 280, who describes the telling of the tale "The Land was Seized" by Chief Ndumiso Bhotomane. The performance is interrupted by the interjection of someone from the audience: "Well, it was not good. The government attacked. And that is the origin of the war of Ngcayechibi. That is how this land — [*Member of audience: Sharhili was not anxious to fight*] — Sarhili was not at all anxious to fight."

[122] Bailey, "Informal Controlled," 42–43.

[123] Bailey, "Informal Controlled," 44.

3) *Total Flexibility.* This category contains "the telling of jokes, the reporting of the casual news of the day, the reciting of tragedies in nearby villages and (in the case of inter-communal violence) atrocity stories."[124] Within this category, there is no stability or controls placed upon the material, and the material "floats and dies in a state of total instability."[125]

One of the strengths of Bailey's model of *informal controlled* oral tradition is that it presents a process of transmission that coheres with Lord's oral theory and subsequent folklore studies on the process of oral transmission.[126] While Lord ruled out the likelihood of what Bailey terms *informal uncontrolled*, and *formal controlled* transmission, he felt strongly that there were communal bounds and limitations that enabled the tradition to achieve what could be labeled a "fixed" state. According to Lord, the tradition was transmitted within acceptable parameters which were established and empowered by the community itself.[127] Bailey's observations agree with Lord's comments regarding the oral performer's emphasis on the "story itself." Bailey's proposal is helpful for it avoids the extremes that were typical of earlier studies on oral tradition in the New Testament. His awareness of the delicate balance between "fixity" and "flexibility" within the Synoptic Tradition is a welcome change to the "either/or" approaches that we have discussed previously.[128] His work, while clearly anecdotal and not the product of a rigorous methodology, does reflect much of the same insights that have been brought forth

---

[124] Bailey, "Informal Controlled," 45. Abel's "rumor transmission" would be included in this category.

[125] Bailey, "Informal Controlled," 45.

[126] This is an important point, for it suggests that Bailey is observing oral communicative principles that are applicable to a wider context than that which he observed in the Middle East. One might be tempted to dismiss Bailey's research on the grounds of his "anachronistic" use of contemporary Palestinian society for studying the Synoptic Tradition, but as we suggested above, the danger is not with anachronism *per se*, but whether or not the observed phenomena are applicable to a wider context. The model proposed by Bailey coheres with more "universal" principles as described by Lord, Ong, Havelock, *et al.*, and as such, we must be open to the possibility that what we are studying is in reality the continuation of an ongoing oral-traditioning process that can shed light on the transmission of the early Jesus tradition.

[127] Lord, "Gospels," 37.

[128] This observation is supported by the work of Kirk and Thatcher. In their work on social memory, they have suggested that "continuity and change in early Christianity" is a subject that can prove helpful in understanding the interrelationship between the past and present and how it is mediated by communal social memory. They suggest that "[s]olutions have tended to default to the extremes: either total replication of the traditional past in the present, or total re-invention of the past within the present. Social memory theory moves us towards a more plausible, tightly interactional model that correlates the two factors . . ." (Kirk and Thatcher, "Social Memory," 12).

independently by folklorists and those from other related disciplines.[129] Bailey's holistic approach to the process of tradition transmission is welcomed, and he is one of the first scholars to approach the topic of oral tradition and the Synoptic Gospels from a Middle Eastern perspective.

The succinct portrait of communal self-stabilization presented above flows from the many significant insights derived from advances made in folklore studies. The portrait presented by Bailey is congruous with the findings of leading folklorists such Lord, Dundes, and others.[130] These studies lead us to suggest that there is sufficient reason to believe that the early Jesus communities not only desired to preserve and maintain the traditions that served an important function as self-identity markers, but that they were capable of preserving the central elements and themes of these traditions.

5.5 Conclusion

In this chapter we have suggested that the advances in folklore research can help shed light upon the transmission of the early Jesus tradition. This interdisciplinary approach has been adopted in an attempt to examine the process of tradition transmission in a way not possible via an *inferential* textual methodology alone. We examined the question of anachronism, and

---

[129] Although Bailey does not cite directly any contemporary studies on orality (e.g., Lord, Ong, Foley, etc.), his work does share much in common with contemporary oral theory. Bailey emphasizes the importance of the theme, or story in his category of *Some Flexibility*. This is quite similar to Lord's approach of the Synoptic Tradition ("Gospels," 37). Bailey's observations also agree with Lord's in regard to the function or role of the community in keeping a tradition within certain "parameters" (see Lord, "Gospels," 37, and Bailey, "Informal Controlled," 39–40). If Bailey was *not* influenced by contemporary sociological studies on orality (as the evidence would suggest), then his observations are even *more powerful*, for they then provide us with *independent correlation* of the same phenomenon studied by Lord and other folklorists.

[130] Liisa Malkki, in her study of Hutu refugees, details a process of communal stabilization similar to that described by Bailey. She writes, "[a]ccounts of . . . key events very quickly circulated among the refugees, and, often in a matter of days, acquired what can be characterized as "standard versions" in the telling and retelling. These "standard versions" were not simply isolated accounts of particular events, told for the sake of telling and soon to be forgotten. Rather, they were accounts which, while becoming increasing formulaic, also became more didactic . . . In this sense the "standard versions" acted as diagnostic and mnemonic allegories connecting events of everyday life with wider historical processes impinging on the Hutu . . ." (*Purity and Exile: Violence, Memory, and National Cosmology among Hutu Refugees in Tanzania* [Chicago: University of Chicago, 1995], 106; cited from Kirk and Thatcher, "Social Memory," 11–12).

suggested that the existence of anachronism is not in itself reason to dismiss an argument outright. Some theses are hindered by anachronistic arguments, while in other cases the phenomena under examination are not manifestations of a specific culture in a specific time nor specific place and therefore not adversely affected by the charge of anachronism.

The extensive work of folklorists has been helpful in that their work helps establish heuristic categories that enable us to study the Jesus tradition from within its original highly oral context. By adopting the category of "folklore", it is possible to approach the Synoptic Tradition from a perspective not possible otherwise. Once any negative connotations associated with the term "folklore" are removed and the term is severed from any implications regarding the historicity of the tradition, it is then possible to use the insights offered by folklorists to great advantage. They have demonstrated that verbal variability is one of the key characteristics of folklore, and some scholars such as Dundes and Lord have examined the Hebrew Bible and the New Testament from that perspective, highlighting the multiform repetition of traditions and the variability therein. Their subsequent conclusion is that the canonical Biblical texts exhibit the key characteristics of folklore, thereby suggesting that they have close ties to the oral world of antiquity.

In our exploration of the key characteristics of oral communication, we suggested that they could be grouped into two primary categories — *redundancy* and *variability*. We noted that the flexibility and variability inherent within orally transmitted tradition, including that of folklore, is counterbalanced by a thematic fixity; that is, the freedom with which an oral performer adapts and embellishes a tradition is bound by the constraints placed on the performer by the community itself. We concluded by discussing the significance of Bailey's work for understanding the transmission of the early Jesus tradition. His model of *informal controlled oral tradition* coheres with that observed by folklorists, and appears to be derived independently from the research of folklorists and other scholars such as Lord. This independent observation is significant and leads us to ask whether such a model can help elucidate the complex factors surrounding the early transmission of Jesus material.

Chapter 6

Statistical Analysis of Synoptic Gospel Pericopes

6.1 Introduction

It is now necessary to test the hypothesis that was first put forward by
Bailey, and developed in more detail recently by Dunn. Dunn has taken
Bailey's *informal controlled* model of tradition transmission to the next
level by examining a selection of Synoptic pericopes from this "Middle
Eastern" perspective, and he concludes that the variability and fixity
within the some pericopes raises fundamental questions regarding their
origins. He asks whether the traditions/pericopes he examines are only
explicable in strictly literary terms (i.e., redactional changes to a shared
source *text*), or, in following the lead of Bailey, whether they might reflect
an ongoing process of oral tradition-transmission that was a key
component of the early Jesus movement.

Following his summary of Bailey, Dunn himself poses the question
which we will address below: "[t]he key question, of course, is whether we
can find the marks of such "informal controlled oral tradition" in the
Synoptic Tradition itself."[1] Dunn proceeds to study a varied selection of
both double and triple tradition passages and explores some additional
parallels between the Synoptic Gospels, Acts, and Paul. Dunn makes clear
by way of his subsequent analysis that his answer to the question is yes —
there is evidence of an oral traditioning process within the Synoptic
Tradition. His summary is as follows:

Our own examination of the Jesus tradition itself confirmed the relevance of the oral
paradigm and the danger of assuming (consciously or otherwise) the literary paradigm.
The findings did not call into serious question the priority of Mark or the existence of a
document Q. But in each of the examples marshalled the degree of variation between
clearly parallel traditions, and the inconsequential character of so much of the variations,
should hardly have encouraged an explanation in terms of literary dependence . . . the
combination of stability and flexibility positively cried out to be recognized as typically
oral in character. That probably implies in at least some cases that the variation was due
to knowledge and use of the same tradition in oral mode, as part of the community
tradition familiar to Matthew and Luke.[2]

---

[1] Dunn, "Oral Memory 2001," 93.
[2] Dunn, "Oral Memory 2001," 128.

In Dunn's summary we find several key points of contact with our current discussion. We clearly identify ourselves as in agreement with several of his observations, including his warning regarding the "danger" of assuming the literary paradigm.[3] Of additional interest are his statements on the "degree of variation" between the parallel traditions and his description of the "stability and flexibility" within the tradition.

From the perspective of our previous discussion on folklore, there can be no denying that what Dunn observes are clear examples of the *redundancy* and *variability* that we have suggested are the *sine qua non* of folklore and in turn that of oral tradition. What is not clear however, is the extent to which these phenomena are specific to the group of pericopes labeled "oral" by Dunn, and, the extent to which his observations are also applicable to the more "literary" pericopes.

Several questions arise from the model proposed by Bailey and put into full expression by Dunn. First, it is necessary to examine the possibility that the "fixity" and "flexibility" within the Synoptic Tradition extends beyond those pericopes that have been classified as "oral." Second, does the phenomenon of variability and stability within the Synoptic Tradition provide us with some sort of criteria to discern "oral" from "literary" within the tradition? Third, are there distinctive differences in the level of *internal* variability between the two categories of traditions (i.e., "oral" and "literary"')? Fourth, in what way does the variability and fixity observed by Bailey and Dunn correspond with the level of verbatim agreement within individual pericopes? And finally, in what ways, if any, does the internal variability and fixity within pericopes give us additional insight into their possible tradition-history? In essence, we will attempt to develop a method of analysing the selected pericopes, which will, in turn, enable us to examine the folkloristic characteristics of internal variability and stability. In is our intention that the results of this examination will allow us to probe further into the question of oral tradition and the Gospels.

With regard to the intended aims of this chapter, it is necessary to state in clear terms what we will, and will not, be attempting to accomplish. As stated previously throughout the earlier chapters, *we are not in any way suggesting that the Gospel writers did not make use of written sources when composing their accounts.* On the contrary, we feel that it is quite

---

[3] See ch. 2 above. For Dunn's similar critique of the over-reliance upon the literary paradigm see, Dunn, "Default Setting," *passim.* Werner H. Kelber. "The Two-Source Hypothesis: Oral Tradition, the Poetics of Gospel Narrativity, and Memorial Arbitration" (Paper presented at the SNTS Annual Meeting, Durham, UK, 2002), 19, suggests that "Dunn's contribution warrants deep reflection . . ." and that he has "broken the dominantly *literary* paradigm of gospel relationships foisted upon us."

clear that the two-source hypothesis provides the proper framework for examining the Synoptic Problem. Literary sources abounded, and the Gospel writers no doubt utilized these sources, primarily Mark and Q. *We are also not attempting to provide definitive criteria for determining oral from literary material within the tradition.* Rather, we will test the thesis advanced by Dunn and see whether his envisaged model of tradition transmission can be quantified in more concrete terms.

Before engaging a collection of selected double tradition pericopes, it is necessary to address briefly several preliminary matters. We first turn our attention to the potential danger of using statistics in a heavy-handed manner in a field such as Biblical Studies. We shall discuss the difference between a *descriptive* and an *inferential* statistical method, and subsequently adopt a *descriptive* analysis of the data, thereby avoiding the problems often associated with an *inferential* approach to statistical analysis.

We shall then proceed to discuss the process of selection and categorization of the pericopes which will be examined, followed by the presentation of our statistical method. In the subsequent analysis, the full text of each pericope under examination will be presented in synoptic form, followed by a presentation of the data in tabular form. Three charts will be presented for each pericope that will enable the reader to analyze quickly the pericope in question. This will be followed by a brief commentary on the results of the analysis, and tentative conclusions will be offered at the end of the chapter. Now we must move on to discuss some necessary preliminary matters.

6.2   Statistical Methods and Biblical Scholarship

Statistical methods have been appropriated by Biblical scholars for over a century and a half, and have subsequently been applied in many sub-fields of study, including both the Hebrew Bible and the New Testament. Recent advances in computer technology have made it significantly easier for the non-specialist to engage in what was, for a long period of time, a task best left to mathematicians and scientists. Despite the ascendancy of the "electronic revolution," the appeal to statistics is not universally accepted as a valid method by some biblical scholars and theologians who feel that the use of cold, analytical scientific methods are not appropriate in the study of literary compositions — particularly those contained within the Biblical canon. After all, the humanities are often falsely contrasted with the sciences as though they exist in separate, mutually exclusive realms of reality — it is argued that scientists deal with a concrete, black and white, objective reality, while humanities scholars work with less "tangible" evidence that requires more sensitivity to the intricacies of human interaction and the socio-cultural situation in which we live. As a result, humanities scholars feel that it is difficult to express highly complex issues in "black and white" (i.e., binary) terms, and prefer to express complex, nuanced arguments as shades of grey between the extreme cold, harsh digital extremes of zeros and ones. Fortunately, it is not necessary to view the sciences and the humanities in such antithetical terms. We are justified in looking beyond the apparent gap between the two disciplines towards an understanding of the sciences and humanities as complementary systems of thought and logic that can work together in a kind of intellectual-symbiosis in order to mutually inform and strengthen one another. It is from this perspective that we hope to explore the role of statistics in addressing some of the larger questions at hand in this current work.

6.2.1 *Potential Abuse*

It has been mentioned by more than one biblical scholar that statistics appeal to the common desire to obtain objective, definitive, even irrefutable results.[4] The difficulty in having such a high view of statistics is that it can lead to the unvoiced assumption that numerical analysis is inherently objective and the use thereof is beyond reproach.[5] In fact, one does not have to look far to find evidence to the contrary; that is, statistical studies can analyze the same material, and easily arrive at differing, or at times contradictory, conclusions. Forbes' summary of past work is illuminating:

Based on statistical analysis, it has been asserted that the first twenty-three chapters of Genesis do conform to the Documentary Hypothesis (Chenique 1967; Houk 1983), and it likewise has been asserted that they (and indeed the entire book) do not (Radday and Shore 1985). It has been asserted that Isaiah is not from one hand (Radday 1973), and that it is (Adams and Rencher 1973). It has been asserted that Philippians, Colossians, and 1–2 Thessalonians are from one hand (Wake 1948), and that they are from three hands (Morton 1978).[6]

---

[4] For one example, see Carlston and Norlin who note that "exegetes are probably no less prone than anybody else to long for something mathematical, something clearly right or wrong . . ." ("Once More," 59).

[5] Mattila recognizes the danger in such an impetus to use statistics — "It is a well-known adage that statistics can be misleading. Nevertheless, there persists a stubborn tendency to regard numerical representations of data as inherently objective" ("Still Clouded," 313).

[6] A. Dean Forbes, "Statistical Research on the Bible," *The Anchor Bible Dictionary* 6: 185.

From Forbes' summary it is apparent that one must be highly cautious if and when statistical arguments are used to either formulate or support any thesis. They are not "pure" and "unbiased" lights that illumine the path to truth, but can be manipulated to support almost any claim that the researcher desires.[7]

6.2.2   *Statistical Method and Inferential Statistics*

The contradictory conclusions reached by various scholars, despite employing scientific methods of analysis of texts leads one to wonder how and why such discrepancies have resulted from a statistical study of the same problem. The answer to such a question is at the same time both simple and complex. At the most basic level, the answer to the question is three-fold: 1) use of faulty data, 2) use of a faulty statistical method, and 3) faulty interpretation of statistical results.[8] Two more specific, mathematically-oriented reasons for discrepancies and difficulties can be summarized as follows: 1) incorrect assumptions about the characteristics of the data set (i.e., type of distribution), and 2) use of sample size insufficiently large enough to provide a meaningful analysis. These difficulties have negatively affected many statistical studies on the Biblical text, as aptly summarized once again by Forbes.

These problems have led some scholars to abandon the use of inferential statistics when approaching the Biblical text, preferring to work within the more secure area of descriptive statistics. Descriptive statistics use statistical methods to describe the characteristics of a particular data set. Inferential statistics on the other hand, go beyond a straightforward descriptive analysis of the text in an attempt to *infer* or hypothesize certain characteristics about a unknown data set based upon the statistical analysis of a previously studied collection of material. Thus, inferential statistics by their very nature are more subjective and speculative than their descriptive counterpart. Despite this warning, it is quite difficult to draw the line between inferential and descriptive statistics. Both methods interact with one another, and even the researcher who engages in a descriptive approach can unconsciously lapse into the realm of inference. Here, we will attempt to avoid the use of inferential statistics, preferring to simply describe the characteristics of a given data set.

---

[7] I am reminded of a recent conversation I had in passing with Dr. David Nolland, Lecturer in Physics, University of Liverpool, UK, who, while we were discussing statistics, said something like, "they are just numbers, you can [potentially] make them say anything you want." His warning reminds one of the potential dangers inherent with any statistical study done without adequate controls or undertaken using improper methods.

[8] Forbes, "Statistical Research," 185.

6.3   Verbatim Agreement and the Scope of Q

Thomas Bergemann has argued that the criterion of verbatim agreement is the only decisive test for assigning individual pericopes to Q.[9] Thus he has recognized the need to separate the argument for the existence of "Q" from that regarding its scope.[10] He suggests that other commonly used arguments such as the argument from order are not alone sufficient for including a pericope in Q. Bergemann summarizes the work of several scholars in the past who have recognized the fundamental importance of the criterion of verbatim agreement, in particular H. J. Holtzmann, who was the first scholar to formulate clearly this criterion.[11] Bergemann also surveys the work of others who have used the criterion of verbatim agreement to divide the double tradition into various categories. In the late 19th century, Paul Ewald divided the double tradition into three sections based upon a pericope's level of verbatim agreement with its corresponding parallel. He then went on to argue that only the material from the first section, containing the highest level of verbatim agreement, can be attributed to Q.[12] Wilhelm Bussmann posited two separate source documents to account for the disparity in the degree of verbatim agreement across the double tradition,[13] and other scholars such as Barrett, Hawkins, Taylor and Davies & Allison have all recognized that the varying levels of verbatim agreement across the double tradition requires the division of the double tradition into two or more categories.[14]

---

[9] Thomas Bergemann, *Q auf dem Prüfstand: die Zuordnung des Mt/Lk-Stoffes zu Q am Beispiel der Bergpredigt* (Forschungen zur Religion und Literatur des Alten und Neuen Testaments 158; Göttingen: Vandenhoeck & Ruprecht, 1993).

[10] See above, ch. 2.

[11] See Bergemann, *Q auf dem Prüfstand*, 16; H. J. Holtzmann, *Die synoptischen Evangelien* (Leipzig: Wilhelm Engelmann, 1863).

[12] Paul Ewald, *Das Hauptproblem der Evangelienfrage und der Weg zu seiner Lösung: eine akademische Vorlesung nebst Exkursen* (Leipzig: J.C. Hinrichs, 1890).

[13] Wilhelm Bussmann, *Synoptische Studien* (Halle: Buchhandlung des Waisenhauses, 1925). Barrett also called into question "the theory that the material which we have called Q was all derived from one written document . . ." ("Re-examination," 320). Also, see Honoré, "Statistical Study," 135, who following his statistical study concludes that "[t]here is, however, nothing to show that Q was a single document. At best, one might think of a collection of source material arranged in no particular order."

[14] Hawkins divided the double tradition into three categories ("class A," "B," and "C") based upon the "degree of probability that they rest upon, or at the very least show the influence of, a common written tradition" ("Probabilities," 112). It must be noted that Hawkins did not include individual verses which "contain no words at all which are actually identical in the Greek of the two Gospels" ("Probabilities," 110). This process of extracting individual verses out of pericopes parallels the flawed methodology employed by Carlston and Norlin (see above, §2.4.2).

In all of these studies, there has been a universal recognition that verbatim agreement is the primary test for a pericope's inclusion in Q. Bergemann argues that this test is the only objective test, unlike discerning redaction or authorial style, which tend to be quite subjective in practice.[15] All scholars who work with the criterion of verbatim agreement, including Bergemann, Carlston and Norlin, Honoré, and others, must define the term and address the question "what constitutes 'agreement'"? We must also address this same question.

As noted above in §2.4, in their study of the Matthean and Lukan double tradition, Carlston and Norlin arrived at significantly higher levels of verbatim agreement than other scholars such as Honoré. Subsequently, Carlston and Norlin's results have been used to bolster the arguments for a written Q and have led some scholars to include almost all of the double tradition into the reconstructed Q text. However, as we shall see, the strength of this argument is based upon the methodology of "excision" employed by Carlston and Norlin, and their definition of "verbatim agreement." Once one refines the concept of verbatim agreement and questions the usefulness of their method, Carlston and Norlin's argument can no longer be sustained, and the wholesale assignment of the double tradition to a Q text is problematic. Therefore, it is necessary at this stage to examine the fundamental reason behind the disparity between the statistical figures compiled by Honoré and Carlston and Norlin. In addition to the aforementioned excising of portions of various pericopes, the disparity between the two sets of figures is also due to their differing methodology for calculating verbatim agreement. As will become clear, most positions regarding the interrelationship between the Synoptic Gospels are based upon one's understanding of the term "agreement." Answers to questions such as, "what is agreement?," or, "what constitutes 'agreement'?," will, to a great extent, influence both how one approaches the Synoptic Problem, and ultimately affect one's conclusions regarding the issues at hand.

Carlston and Norlin follow the basic method for determining percent agreement, i.e., divide the number of verbatim words shared between Matthew and Luke by the total number of words in each respective parallel version. The final step entails averaging the percent agreement in both

---

[15] Goodacre notes the highly subjective and circular use of redaction to argue for the existence of Q — "We only have any idea of the contents of Q by attempting to reconstruct the document. And the primary means by which Q is reconstructed is *by means of redaction-criticism.* There is thus an unavoidable circularity in using this argument in favour of the existence of Q — a tool that has been used to generate a document is said to corroborate the existence of the document that has been generated" (Goodacre, *Maze,* 143).

Matthew and Luke to arrive at a single average figure for agreement. This procedure is followed by virtually all scholars working with the criterion of verbatim agreement. Where individual scholars differ is in their method for calculating the number of verbatim words in each parallel.

Carlston and Norlin worked with a very loose definition of what constitutes "agreement," and therefore their verbatim word count was significantly higher than that offered by other scholars. They included words as agreements if "they seem on examination to be more or less random synonyms reflecting no substantial difference in meaning."[16] This definition of "agreement" does not allow for an objective comparison of the double tradition. In so doing, Carlston and Norlin have made the *subjective* choice of *assuming* redactional activity when there are words of the same or similar definition. Carlston and Norlin work with the assumption that similar words reflect editorial activity by default, and thus these synonyms are considered to be in verbatim agreement with one another. This rather free definition of "agreement" led Carlston and Norlin to even count ἰάθη (Matt 8:13) as in "agreement" with ὑγιαίνοντα (Luke 7:10) in the pericope of the Centurion's Servant (Aland §85/Huck §86).[17] Mattila and O'Rourke strongly criticized Carlston and Norlin's definition of verbatim agreement, and Carlston and Norlin's definition was, by their own admission in a subsequent article (1999), a mistake which they "would not do if we were to repeat the study today."[18]

---

[16] Carlston and Norlin, "Once More," 63.

[17] Carlston and Norlin specifically list these two words, ἰάθη (to heal) and ὑγιαίνοντα (to be healthy/sound) as "perhaps the most extreme case" ("Once More," 63), although unfortunately they do not provide a detailed breakdown of their statistical study to allow for the confirmation of this statement. For example, if they counted ἰάθη and ὑγιαίνοντα as synonyms, what about παῖς and δοῦλον? It would seem possible that Carlston and Norlin would also count these two words as synonyms, a procedure which would thus seem inappropriate.

[18] For a critique of Carlston and Norlin's "loose" definition of agreement, see Mattila, "Still Clouded," 319–324 and O'Rourke, "Statistical Procedures," 272. Also, Denaux, "Q-Passages," 120 notes that Carlston and Norlin's conclusions should be corrected due to their loose definition of "verbal agreement." For Carlston and Norlin's admission concerning their earlier methodology, see Carlston and Norlin, "Further Observations," 120. Carlston and Norlin realize their loose definition of "agreement" was a shortcoming in their 1971 article. They justify their earlier method due to the fact that they "had already spent a great deal of time in this laborious enterprise before recognizing what was happening" ("Further Observations," 120); thus they imply that they recognized at the time that their methodology was lacking. Carlston and Norlin's 1999 defense of their methodology reveals that they still miss the point — ". . . our original hesitancy about a very rigid definition (exactly the same form of exactly the same word), is still of some force. Some geographical terms can be spelled in different ways . . . [and] many texts use the historical present rather than a simple past tense . . ." (Carlston and Norlin, "Further Observations," 120). This statement reveals the extent to which they underestimate the

Other scholars have used different definitions of verbatim agreement, all of which are more restrictive than that used by Carlston and Norlin. As mentioned earlier, Honoré used a definition of agreement that yielded a far lower level of agreement across the entire double tradition. His definition was the use of "the same grammatical form of the same word."[19] Bergemann also defined agreement as words that agreed in grammatical form, and Morgenthaler used an even more restrictive definition that required not only an agreement in grammatical form, but also an agreement in *sequence* within the pericope in question. In sum, although the four scholars with whom we have interacted have proposed different definitions of verbatim agreement, they can for the most part be divided into two groups. Morgenthaler, Honoré, and Bergemann can be grouped together as having a more restrictive definition of agreement, one with which we find ourselves in agreement, and Carlston and Norlin stand alone in opposition, offering a far more "loose" definition of verbatim agreement.

In concluding the discussion about verbatim agreement and the scope of Q, we are led to the conclusion that previous studies have arrived at rather divergent results when comparing the level of agreement in both the double and triple tradition. Verbatim agreement is paramount in the discussion regarding the documentary nature of Q, and also its unity as a single, written text. Perhaps most significantly, Kloppenborg Verbin relies heavily on the work of Carlston and Norlin to support his thesis of a written, unified Q; and although he admits that "a new study of the problem is desirable," he also suggests that the overall result achieved by Carlston and Norlin would not change.[20] In fact, the divergence between

---

true significance of their methodological shortcomings. Their defense is just the type of situation of which one must be mindful when looking at double tradition parallels. Different spellings of geographical terms does not *a priori* indicate that there is textual redaction taking place. If we are to give serious attention to the role of oral tradition in the development of the Synoptic Tradition, then we must take into account the possibility that different communities (i.e., geographical locales) very possibly could have used different terms to describe the same features (regions, cities, etc.), and thus, the differences do not require the explanation of redaction of a common source text. Despite Carlston and Norlin's response to Mattila and O'Rourke, the fact remains that their *earlier* 1971 work, which utilized elevated levels of verbatim agreement, remains one of the key focal points in the discussion.

[19] Honoré, "Statistical Study," 97. The "same word" indicated a shared lemma, or lexical root.

[20] Kloppenborg, *Excavating Q*, 58. Here, Kloppenborg Verbin surprisingly affirms Carlston and Norlin's findings despite the strong critique of Mattila. He undervalues the strength of Mattila's critique in a rather dismissive fashion, "[u]nfortunately, Mattila's argument is not based on an independent analysis and fails to use the comprehensive statistical tables by Morgenthaler (1971)" (*Excavating Q*, 58). To her defense, Mattila

the previous statistical studies on the double tradition coupled with the reliance upon questionable results by scholars such as Kloppenborg Verbin, requires that we "revisit" the question of verbatim agreement and its significance for understanding the possible role of oral tradition in the formation of the early Jesus tradition.

Of paramount importance in the current context regarding verbatim agreement is the question of how the statistics on verbatim agreement have been employed in the argument for the scope of Q itself. As we shall see below, statistics on verbatim agreement have been used in a rigid manner that does not take serious account of the variability within the tradition itself.

6.4 Variability within the Synoptic Tradition

Following his study of the double tradition, Bergemann shows that the level of verbatim agreement between Matthew and Luke varies from 8% to 100%, and the double tradition pericopes are almost evenly distributed across the entire range of values.[21] This distribution of agreement has correctly led Bergemann to ask how it is that at times Matthew and Luke appear to follow their source text quite faithfully, and at other times appear to completely change their source text. The answer offered by Bergemann is that these double tradition pericopes are not from the same source text. He is willing to attribute to a single Q document various pericopes that exceed a certain level of verbatim agreement, which, according to Bergemann, is indicative of an author copying a source text.[22] Here,

---

does not attempt to present new statistics to counter Carlston and Norlin. Her argument is not at all based on either her use or non-use of Morgenthaler. Her primary thrust is to critique Carlston and Norlin's methodology and subsequently, she does not attempt to substitute any statistics of her own — it seems that Kloppenborg Verbin's critique is unwarranted.

[21] Bergemann, *Q auf dem Prüfstand*, 56. Denaux faults Bergemann for not referring to Robert Morgenthaler's comprehensive statistical study of the Synoptic Gospels ("Q-Passages," 119). Despite this shortcoming, Morgenthaler's statistics demonstrate the same distribution of verbatim agreement. He goes beyond Bergemann in that he tabulates separate word counts and % agreement for the words (narrative) and sayings (*logia*) of each pericope, see Robert Morgenthaler, *Statistische Synopse* (Zurich: Gotthelf-Verlag, 1971), 33–65.

[22] Also, cf. Barrett, "Re-examination," 322: "we may say that the part of the Q material where agreement is closest may be satisfactorily explained as derived from a single common Greek source; but that the remainder cannot be explained without recourse to some parallel version, and that it is simpler to suppose that Matthew and Luke in collecting their material used traditions which were similar but not identical than that they each had identical copies of one source (a supposition sufficiently improbable

pericopes that have an average percent agreement above approximately 70% are attributed to a single written source "Q." Denaux expresses concern regarding this step, asking "what image of Q is thereby derived?"[23] He fears that Bergemann's approach excises much from the hypothetical Q, thereby leaving a smaller collection of material which, upon further inspection, might no longer display the "thematic and formal coherence" that is currently popular among Q scholars today.[24] While Denaux's observation is insightful, it is not relevant for the line of questioning with which Bergemann is engaged. Questions regarding the unity and thematic/theological coherence of Q are relevant, but Bergemann suggests that they should not dictate the investigation into the scope of Q. One must first establish the scope of Q before engaging in a discussion regarding its coherence or unity.

Bergemann is not the only scholar to recognize that the variation among the double tradition is a difficult hurdle to overcome when assigning the pericopes to a source text. Honoré's work preceded that of Bergemann, and he also recognized the importance of this variation. He designed a test to examine just such variation and concluded what one would expect — the level of verbatim agreement across the Synoptic Tradition is highly variable. O'Rourke and Mattila have both questioned how helpful Honoré's "coefficients of variance" truly are, for they demonstrate, in the words of Mattila, "what is already patently obvious — that the pattern of verbatim agreement over the synoptic data is highly variable and erratic."[25] Despite the critique of O'Rourke and Mattila, Honoré's observation remains — the *level of verbatim agreement is not uniform, but highly variable.* Given this fundamental observation, one is led to the following question; if the primary criterion for assigning a double tradition pericope to a hypothetical source document is verbatim agreement, but the level of verbatim agreement is highly variable, then one must take steps to analyze on a pericope-by-pericope basis which portions of the double tradition should be assigned to Q. We also must reflect on the significance of both the variability in agreement among the pericopes of the Synoptic Tradition in a way not previously addressed by the aforementioned scholars.

Previous work has focused on the characteristic variability in agreement *across* the pericopes of the double tradition. Although significant, it does not provide a full picture of the nature of agreement within the tradition.

---

on geographical and historical grounds), which in the case of one of them was contaminated with a parallel version."

[23] Denaux, "Q-Passages," 122.

[24] Kloppenborg, *Excavating Q*, 67. Also, see Kloppenborg Verbin's section on "The Character and Reconstruction of Q" (Kloppenborg, *Excavating Q*, 55–111).

[25] See O'Rourke, "Statistical Procedures," 277 and Mattila, "Still Clouded," 317.

Rosché notes that only a limited percentage of Q has an average verbal correspondence above 54%, and that 68% of what is commonly accepted as "Q" verses show less than the average degree of verbal correspondence.[26] A quick survey of Morgenthaler's *Statistische Synopse* confirms Rosché's conclusions. Morgenthaler's breakdown of the distribution of agreement between the double tradition reveals that the large majority (78.5%) of "Q" is between 20 and 80% agreement, 13.2% of "Q" exists in the upper range of agreement (80%-98%), and 8.2% resides in the lower range of agreement (0–19%).[27] It is clear from both Rosché and Morgenthaler that the extremely high level of agreement in the double tradition exists within only a limited percentage of the material.

This observation cuts in two opposite directions. One can dissect the results offered above and argue that the level of verbatim agreement in the double tradition is not high enough to posit a common written source to account for the *entirety* of the common Matthean and Lukan material not found in Mark. This in fact is the conclusion reached by Rosché, Bergemann, and others, who, although they arrive at different conclusions regarding the nature of the double tradition, all affirm that it is not derivative from the same source.[28] It is also possible to argue that the variation characteristic of the double tradition is also characteristic of the variation between Matthew and Luke in the triple tradition, and therefore Matthew and Luke apparently use both of their sources (i.e., Mark and Q) with the same level of editorial adaptation. Both Denaux and Kloppenborg Verbin are but two examples of those who prefer the merits of this second argument.[29]

In order to understand fully the variable nature of verbatim agreement within the Synoptic Tradition, we must move beyond previous work that has focused strictly on a comparison between individual pericopes within the double tradition. Specifically, it is necessary to look at the variable nature of verbatim agreement *within each pericope itself.* This is a different approach than what has been attempted previously with regard to the double tradition. Previous studies have generally assigned a *single figure* of verbatim agreement to each individual pericope, and in so doing they overlook the possibility that there could be significant variation within *an individual* pericope. As we have examined in the previous

---

[26] Rosché, "Words of Jesus," 217–218.

[27] Morgenthaler, *Statistische Synopse*, 261, cited by Kloppenborg, *Excavating Q*, 63.

[28] Rosché concludes that the common tradition is best explained by an appeal to "independent courses of oral, pregospel transmission" ("Words of Jesus," 220). Bergemann suggests that there was a *Grundrede* that was used by Matthew and Luke in addition to the written "Q" source.

[29] See Denaux, "Q-Passages," 120, and Kloppenborg, *Excavating Q*, 64.

chapter, variability is an integral part of oral communication, and as such, an attempt must be made to discern its presence within the double tradition, and to examine its function within the tradition. This, in turn, will enable us to understand better the process of Synoptic Gospel formation and the role that oral tradition played in that process.

6.5 Methodology

It will be helpful at the outset to state once again the intended goals of this statistical study. This study is *not* an attempt to the question of the existence of a "Q" source text behind the common Matthean and Lukan double tradition, nor is it an attempt to question the overall status of "Q" as a *text*. Rather, *we will operate under the assumption that there is a "Q" source, and that it is a written document to which the Gospel authors had access.* Neither is this an attempt to provide a comprehensive examination of the whole of the double tradition. What is envisaged here is a descriptive analysis of selected double tradition material, whereby we examine the internal variability and stability of selected double tradition pericopes, some of which are most certainly derived from a written "Q" document, and some of which might possibly be derived from shared oral traditions that were in circulation among the early Jesus communities at the time of the inscription of Matthew and Luke.

Our primary goal is to analyze the selected double tradition pericopes from a *folkloristic* perspective and to see if that approach can lend any additional insight into the tradition-history behind the extant double tradition passages. The development and application of our methodology is also, in itself, one of the goals of the examination that follows. It is hoped that our methodology will provide a basis for further research on the Synoptic Tradition, particularly from the perspective of folklore and oral tradition.

Given our desire to remain, as much as possible, within the realm of descriptive statistics, the following analysis of selected double tradition pericopes will take on a more open-ended approach, in contrast with a heavy-handed approach that has weakened several statistical approaches in the past.[30] Interaction with the various statistics will be in the form of narrative description rather than mathematical formula. The over-emphasis

---

[30] Forbes recognizes this as a shortcoming of many statistical studies on the Bible. In summary he states that "Most distressingly, we have repeatedly seen investigations embarked upon with sweeping claims of assent-demanding objectivity only to witness their ultimate invalidation through special pleading and selective attention to results" ("Statistical Research," 204).

on statistical formulae and complicated mathematical argumentation, such as those found in Honoré's work and others, is inaccessible to many who are not well-versed in the so-called "pure" sciences, and as such will be avoided.[31] It is the goal of this present work to present the data in a form accessible to the non-mathematician who might be more interested in the general, overall argument, and to provide the raw analytical data necessary for further, more detailed research by those inclined to do so. We shall also avoid the temptation to draw inference beyond the characteristics of the proposed data set and to apply our findings to the remainder of the double tradition. Additional work will be needed to determine if the insights gathered below are applicable to other pericopes of the double tradition.

6.5.1 Selection of Double Tradition Pericopes

As previously mentioned, this study will not attempt a comprehensive analysis of the entire double and triple tradition, but rather, will focus on a select group of double tradition pericopes and a "control group" which will hopefully lend valuable insight into the role of oral tradition in the formation of the Synoptic Gospel tradition. We will divide the pericopes under examination into three groups (A, B, C).

Group "A" will consist of the pericopes that Dunn has labeled as *possibly oral in origin*,[32] and include the following pericopes: "On Murder and Wrath" (Matt 5:21–26//Luke 12:57–59, Aland §55), "On Retaliation" (Matt 5:38–42//Luke 6:29–30, Aland §58), "The Lord's Prayer" (Matt 6:7–15//Luke 11:1–4, Aland §62), "The Two Ways" (Matt 7:13–14//Luke 13:23–24, Aland §72), "The Centurion of Capernaum" (Matt 8:5–13//Luke 7:1–10, Aland §85), "Divisions within Households" (Matt 10:34–36//Luke 12:51–53, Aland §102), "The Parable of the Great Supper" (Matt 22:1–14//Luke 14:15–24, Aland §279).[33]

---

[31] The great weakness in many statistical studies on the biblical canon is with regard to their over-complexity. Honoré's work exhibits some of these features; among the several complex formulas therein is that of his "coefficient of variance" ("Statistical Study," 127) and "coefficients of variance of variances" ("Statistical Study," 131). His detailed statistical analysis reads quite like a mathematical theorem, and as such is at times difficult to follow — despite this author's previous university degree in the "pure sciences."

[32] The following pericopes have been selected from the three articles that Dunn has recently published in the area of oral tradition ("Oral Memory 2000," "Oral Memory 2001," and "Default Setting"). Although Dunn's goals are somewhat different in the articles, he does suggest that the pericopes we have selected are possibly best explained by an appeal to "oral tradition."

[33] Others have agreed with Dunn's assessment, cp. Barrett, "Re-examination," 321, who suggests that the following passages "cannot be accounted for by editorial activity":

Group "B" will include those pericopes Dunn suggests are *clearly literarily dependent* upon an extra-canonical source text (Q). According to Dunn these are passages "where the wording is so close that a literary dependence is the most obvious explanation."[34] The following pericopes will be included in this group: "On Following Jesus" (Matt 8:19b-22//Luke 9:57b-60a, Aland §89), "Jesus' Witness concerning John" (Matt 11:7–19//Luke 7:24–35, Aland §107), "Jesus' Thanksgiving to the Father" (Matt 11:25–27//Luke 10:21–22, Aland §109), "The Return of the Evil Spirit" (Matt 12:43–45//Luke 11:24–26, Aland §120), "Jesus' Lament over Jerusalem" (Matt 23:37–39//Luke 13:34–35, Aland §285), "The Parable of the Good Servant and the Wicked Servant" (Matt 24:45–51//Luke 12:41–46, Aland §297).[35]

Our final group "C" will serve as a control group against which we will be able to compare the findings derived from groups A and B. Here we will analyze a selection of triple tradition passages which Kloppenborg has called "an obvious control which few . . . have chosen to employ."[36] He suggests that if one compares Matthew with Luke in these triple tradition passages (by removing Mark from the discussion), one notes "as wide a disparity in verbal agreement in the Markan pericopae as there is in "Q" pericopae."[37] This is a necessary step for which Kloppenborg faults Bergemann for not pursuing in his study of the double tradition. Kloppenborg concludes that such disparity is "precisely what one should expect of two authors independently reproducing Mark. This is no reason to believe that Mark was really two or three documents; it only means that Matthew and/or Luke sometimes intervened substantially in their sources and at other times did not. The same applies, mutatis mutandis, to Q."[38] The "control"'passages presented by Kloppenborg include: "If Any Man would Come after Me" (Matt 16:24–28//Mark 8:34–9:1//Luke 9:23–27, Aland §160), "The Time of the Coming: the Parable of the Fig Tree" (Matt 24:32–36//Mark 13:28–32//Luke 21:29–33, Aland §293), "The Parable of

---

Luke 6:29 (Coat-stealing), Luke 11:44 (Pharisees and tombs), Luke 12:6 (The price of sparrows), Luke 16:16 (The Kingdom of God and violence).

[34] Dunn, "Oral Memory 2000," 314.

[35] For the likely literary passages see Dunn, "Oral Memory 2000," 314. The list proposed by Davies and Allison overlaps with that proposed by Dunn (Matt 11:4–11//Luke 7:22–28, Matt 11:25–27//Luke 10:21–22, Matt 23:27–38//Luke 13:34–35, Matt 24:45–51//Luke 12:42b-46), although Davies and Allison's list contains additional passages (Matt 2:7b-10//Luke 2:7b-9, Matt 7:3–5//Luke 6:41–42, Matt 7:7–11//Luke 11:9–13, Matt 11:21–23//Luke 10:13–15). For their list see Davies and Allison, *Matthew*, 116.

[36] Kloppenborg, *Excavating Q*, 64.

[37] Kloppenborg, *Excavating Q*, 64.

[38] Kloppenborg, *Excavating Q*, 64.

the Wicked Husbandmen" (Matt 21:33–46//Mark 12:1–12//Luke 20:9–19, Aland §278), and "The Death of Jesus" (Matt 27:45–54//Mark 15:33–39//Luke 23:44–48, Aland §347).

According to Kloppenborg, these four passages exhibit a wide range of verbatim agreement, ranging from 12% to 80% and contain a high proportion of speech material. Therefore, these pericopes make for a valid comparison to the so-called "Q" material since variable levels of verbatim agreement and a high concentration of speech material are all prominent features of the so-called "Q material." Here Kloppenborg has rightly pointed out the varying levels of agreement between these four pericopes. Although these pericopes vary in terms of their overall levels of verbatim agreement, they have not been examined with a view towards the internal variability within each individual pericope itself. Does an examination of the internal variability within the individual control pericopes lend any insight into the possible tradition-history of some selected double tradition material? When subjected to further examination, do the control pericopes cited by Kloppenborg truly exhibit the same characteristics as the pericopes from groups "A" and "B"?

Towards this end it is necessary to examine these "control" passages with a view towards their internal variability, and to see how they compare to the group "A" and "B" passages. Of the four passages that Kloppenborg cites as helpful control passages, we will examine the two that have the lowest levels of overall verbatim agreement, "The Parable of the Wicked Husbandmen" — Aland §278 (32%) and "The Death of Jesus" — Aland §347 (12%). Of the four passages cited by Kloppenborg, these two are most likely to exhibit characteristics similar to the group "A" pericopes due to their lower levels of overall agreement. Aland §160 and §293 have much higher levels of overall agreement and therefore will not be as helpful a comparison to the group "A" pericopes.

To engage the individual pericopes in order to study the level of variation *within each pericope*, it is first necessary to devise a method of partitioning each pericope into various sections. Then we can perform statistical analysis on each section of both the Matthean and Lukan parallels. Each pericope is analyzed with a view towards its natural "insertion points." These insertion points represent natural breaks in the text which separate the pericope into "units of sense." These divisions represent points whereby an editor might conveniently either insert, or possibly remove material.[39] Not coincidentally, these "insertion points" often

---

[39] Admittedly, the method chosen relies partially on intuition and personal judgment. The partitioning of a pericope is in itself a value judgment, although an attempt has been made to keep such value judgments to a minimum. One is reminded that the production of Gospel Synopses is also dependent upon these "value judgments" (cf. Bernard

fall at verse divisions, although at times they do not. Common arguments for the existence of a written Q include an appeal to the relative sequence of the material common to Matthew and Luke.[40] If we accept the argument that Matthew and Luke scanned Q, picked out *logia* and inserted them into their running narrative, then these "insertion points" would most likely fit the proposed setting for the use of a "Q" text by Matthew and Luke. The issue regarding the origin of the material is important, but need not be decided at this juncture.

Following the division of a pericope into sections based upon these insertion points, the next step is to attempt to match up a section from one pericope with a section from its parallel pericope that contains equivalent *content.* Here it is important to stress the term *content.* When comparing the level of variability within an individual pericope, one can only perform a *meaningful* analysis on two parallel sections of a passage if the two sections have shared *subject content.* It would be a shortcoming to test two obviously divergent sections with one another and compile various figures such as verbatim agreement, etc. For example, in comparing the introductory sections of Aland §62 (The Lord's Prayer, see Table 5, sections 1, 2) these introductions are not useful in determining the level of verbatim agreement between the two parallels. Matthew and Luke have both prefaced the main body of the prayer itself with non-parallel material that describes different subject matter (Matt 6:7–8, Luke 11:1). In this case, one must question the significance of any agreements between the two introductory sections. Matthew and Luke both agree on several words such as αὐτόν, and ἐν, although these agreements occur in introductory passages that do not contain parallel subject matter. What would be the significance of such a comparison? Any verbatim agreement apart from shared thematic content could very well be coincidental. Pure chance would dictate that any two particular authors would employ a certain number of verbatim words with one another, regardless of subject matter. However, such agreements would not indicate in any significant sense that there has been direct literary dependence of one author upon the other, and as we noted earlier in chapter 2, this reduces the usefulness of such an observation.

Orchard, "Are All Gospel Synopses Biassed?," *TZ* 34 [1978]: 149–162, David L. Dungan, "Theory of Synopsis Construction," *Biblica* 61 [1980]: 305–329). Also, positing an "insertion point" does not necessarily imply the possible literary or oral origins of the inserted material, or of the pericope itself.

[40] See Tuckett, *Q*, 8–10, and Vincent Taylor. "The Original Order of Q," in *The Two-Source Hypothesis: A Critical Appraisal.* Edited by Arthur J. Bellinzoni. Macon: Mercer University Press, 1985. Repr. in *New Testament Essays: Studies in Memory of T. W. Manson, 1893–1958.* Edited by A. J. B. Higgins. (Manchester: Manchester University Press, 1959), 295–317.

Therefore, sections in one pericope that do not have parallel *content* in a corresponding section will, by our definition, not share any common words or verbatim words, and will be referred to as "non-parallel sections" (NP). Although these sections, by default, contain 0% verbatim agreement, they nevertheless must be listed as individual sections and count towards the overall statistics for the individual pericope.[41] It is evident that once these sections are removed, the variability within a pericope is greatly reduced, and the level of overall agreement within a pericope is subsequently elevated. For these reasons, the NP sections will be clearly marked and left in the presented text. The following selected pericopes are presented in a way that makes it easy to identify and analyze these parallel and non-parallel (NP) sections.[42]

The following section headings each entail an aspect of the statistical analysis of each double tradition pericope. Among them are some familiar figures (e.g., verbatim agreement), while others are presented in this study

---

[41] Here we can see with clarity the contrast between this proposed method and that embraced by Carlston and Norlin. The NP sections often occur in the introduction or conclusion to a pericope. Therefore, they were excised by Carlston and Norlin *prior* to their analysis and their verbatim agreement calculations. They also removed "material within a Huck-Lietzmann section which is peculiar to either Luke or Matthew" ("Once More," 61). Once again, both of these methods contributed to the overall high levels of verbatim agreement calculated by Carlston and Norlin.

[42] There are also "out-of-context" parallels which occur in a few pericopes (Aland §85, §107, §347). These are additional parallels that are listed in Aland's synopsis, but correspond to material within a Matthean or Lukan NP section. For these cases, we will place a reference to the parallel by inserting the chapter and verse reference in small type across from the NP section. There are benefits in adopting such an approach. While one might be tempted to move this out-of-context material from another location *outside* the pericope under examination to line it up with a section therein, there are legitimate reasons not to do so. First, we are analyzing the pericopes from a folkloristic perspective apart from the assumption that all of the pericopes under examination have been derived from a written Q text. From this perspective, the order of the tradition within Matthew and Luke could very well be traditional and not redactional. That is, each of the Matthean and Lukan parallels might have taken its extant form during its pre-textual existence in the context of oral performance. If this is the case for one or more of the pericopes under examination, then by relocating material from one location to another within a gospel would be upsetting the original performance sequence of the tradition. The situation is slightly different for one of the pericopes underexamination — Aland §347. There are two such parallels in §347. In addition to one parallel which fits the description given above (see p. 266), there exists an "out-of-order" parallel which is contained *within* the boundaries of Aland's pericope division. In this case, the verse in question (Luke 23:45) has been relocated down to parallel Matt 27:51 since Luke 23:45 exists within the bounds of Aland's pericope division. For more on this see the commentary for Aland §347 (p. 270). In addition, parallels noted by Aland which are derived from other gospels (e.g., Mark or John) are not included in the pericope tables for the material under examination is double tradition material.

for the first time. All of these figures can be found in the tables associated with each individual pericope. Unless specifically mentioned, each of the figures below are calculated for *each section* of a pericope and for the pericope as a *whole*.

6.5.2   Words, Matthew; Words, Luke (W)

This figure represents the total word count for each respective Matthean and Lukan double tradition parallel. The text of each selected pericope follows the pericope divisions from Aland's *Synopsis quattuor Evangeliorum*.[43] The words counts are tabulated for both Matthew and Luke, with introductions and conclusions intact, in contrast to the method used by Carlston and Norlin.[44]

6.5.3   Shared Words (SW, %SW)

This is a figure that represents the number of words a pericope *shares* with its corresponding parallel section. It includes the number of words that share a verbal root (lemma) but differ in grammatical form. For example the following word pairs, τῷ ἀντιδίκῳ / τοῦ ἀντιδίκου (Matt 5:25//Luke 12:58) represent two *shared words* in that they are derived from the same verbal roots (*definite article*, ἀντίδικος), but are not verbatim. As is the case with verbatim agreement, the figure for number of shared words is shared by both parallel pericopes (SW). This figure allows the researcher to observe quickly the relationship between the number of words a pericope shares with its corresponding parallel, and likewise, how many of those "shared words" are in verbatim agreement with one another. Thus, the number of shared words must *always* be equal to or greater than the number of verbatim words shared by two parallels (i.e., verbatim words is a subset of SW). The percentage of shared words (%SW) is calculated for all parallel sections in Matthew and Luke and for the pericope as a whole, and represents the percentage of words that are shared between both parallels (number of shared words/number of total words*100).

6.5.4   Agreement in Order (OR, %OR)

For each figure of "shared words" (SW) there is a corresponding figure for the level of "order," or "sequence" of the shared words. Thus, it is possible with the proposed method to discern the relationship between the number of shared words, along with the level of their corresponding agreement in relative order. This calculation is a single figure shared by each parallel

---

[43] Kurt Aland and Eberhard Nestle, *Synopsis quattuor Evangeliorum* (Stuttgart: Württembergische Bibelanstalt, 1964).

[44] See above for Carlston and Norlin's excision of introductions and conclusions.

section in both parallel pericopes (OR), and a figure is also calculated for the pericope as a whole. For example, a section within a Matthean or Lukan pericope could contain 20 "shared words," 18 of which appear in the same order in its corresponding parallel. A figure for % order (%OR) is thereby calculated by means of a simple calculation (words in order/shared words*100). For this example the corresponding % agreement in order would be 18/20*100=90%. Therefore, it is possible to study both the phenomena of shared vocabulary alongside the level of agreement in order without either calculation affecting the other.

6.5.5 *Verbatim Agreement (VB, %VB)*

The above-mentioned discussion on verbatim agreement must inform how the term is understood in this context. Here, we will follow the definition of verbatim agreement presented by Bergemann, that is, identical words in identical form. This will be followed in a consistent manner, and will be more strict than the definition offered by Honoré, who considered pairs of words such as ἐκ / ἐξ, and οὐ / οὐκ as agreement with one another because they are "merely formally, not grammatically different."[45] Admittedly this might seem rather harsh, but is necessary to eliminate as much subjectivity as possible.[46] This figure is shared by both Matthew and Luke in each parallel section and also expressed as a total number of words in agreement for the entire pericope (VB). The percentage of verbatim agreement (%VB) is calculated using the standard formula (number of words in verbatim agreement/total words*100).

6.5.6 *Percentage of Pericope (%Mt, %Lk)*

This figure represents the length of each section of a pericope in terms of its percentage of the total number of words in the pericope. The corresponding %Mt and %Lk is calculated by counting the number of words in each section of a pericope and dividing that sum by the total number of words in its respective parallel (words in section/total words in pericope*100). The %Mt and %Lk allows one to quickly ascertain the relative length of a pericope section. These percentages can then be used in conjunction with the aforementioned %SW and %VB to determine the overall significance of any agreements between Matthean and Lukan

---

[45] Honoré, "Statistical Study," 97.

[46] O'Rourke comments that a more "loose" definition of verbatim agreement is "not necessarily wrong ... rather there is no statistical control from such a judgment" ("Statistical Procedures," 272). In this context, the detailed analysis of each double tradition pericope will be presented for evaluation, thereby enabling subsequent researchers to see quickly which words were counted as "agreements."

double tradition. These figures are only calculated for each individual section, and not for the entire pericope, for the sum of the section percentages always equals 100%.

6.5.7   Presentation of Statistical Data

All of the compiled and calculated statistical data is presented in tabular form along side the Matthean and Lukan text which is formatted as is commonly seen in printed synopses. Accompanying the tabular and textual data are two bar charts and one bubble chart for each pericope. Each of the charts is based upon the tabular data, and does not provide the reader with any additional information beyond what is listed in the table. Rather, they allow the researcher to visually grasp the internal characteristics of each pericope at a glance. There are separate bar charts for the Matthean and Lukan data, and each chart contains three data series: 1) % Agreement (%VB), 2) % of Pericope (%Mt/%Lk), and 3) % Shared Words (%SW). The bubble chart is a graphic representation of the level of verbatim agreement (%VB) represented on the vertical (Y) axis, and the percent of pericope (%Mt/%Lk) represented as the *area* of each corresponding bubble. Therefore, the smaller the bubble, the smaller a percentage of the whole pericope is contained within the section and conversely, the larger the bubble, the greater the percentage of the whole pericope is contained within the section. In addition, a running commentary will be interwoven among the tables and charts, and allow for additional interaction with each pericope. The commentary will function as a means by which the more interesting and perhaps significant features of each pericope are brought to the fore and interacted with. There will be no attempt to provide a comprehensive examination of the pericopes, nor will their be detailed interaction with the extensive secondary literature dealing with the various critical issues associated with each pericope.

There is additional information included in the parallel synoptic presentation of each pericope. The leftmost column contains the section number and can include two additional notations: 1) "NP" — indicates that the section does not contain a parallel in its corresponding parallel version, 2) "CORE" — indicates that a specified section contains elevated levels of verbatim agreement that contrasts to the level of agreement in the remainder of the pericope. Below each section's text there are four figures designated "W," "SW," "OR," "VB." These are the raw figures used for the subsequent calculation of "number of words" in each section, %SW, %OR, and %VB respectively. The value "w" contains two values for each parallel section — that is, one for Matthew, and one for Luke. For example the following value for w — "w=20/15" indicates that the Matthean section contains 20 words and the Lukan section 15.

The parallel synoptic texts are also specially formatted to indicate the various types of agreement therein. The formatting of the text follows the following conventions: 1) A "NP" section is indicated with "NP" in the left-most column, 2) Underlined text indicates a "SW" (shared word), 3) Bold text indicates a "VB" (verbatim word), and 4) italicized text indicates that the shared word or verbatim word does not occur the same relative order within the Matthean and Lukan parallels. These italicized words are used to calculate the agreement in order (%OR) between the two parallels. The total number of shared words in the pericope can therefore be tabulated by adding all underlined and bold words together. These visual indicators along with the summaries located below each section number allow for easy cross-referencing between the Synoptic texts and the corresponding tabular and graphical data.

6.6 Group "A" Pericopes

6.6.1 Aland §55 — On Murder and Wrath

Table 1. Aland §55, Synoptic Text

	Matt 5	Luke 12
1 NP	[21] Ἠκούσατε ὅτι ἐρρέθη τοῖς ἀρχαίοις, Οὐφονεύσεις· ὃς δ᾽ ἂν φονεύσῃ, ἔνοχος ἔσται τῇ κρίσει. [22] ἐγὼ δὲ λέγω ὑμῖν ὅτι πᾶς ὁ ὀργιζόμενος τῷ ἀδελφῷ αὐτοῦ ἔνοχος ἔσται τῇ κρίσει· ὃς δ ἂν εἴπῃ τῷ ἀδελφῷ αὐτοῦ, ῥακά, ἔνοχος ἔσται τῷ συνεδρίῳ· ὃς δ ἂν εἴπῃ, Μωρέ, ἔνοχος ἔσται εἰς τὴν γέενναν τοῦ πυρός. [23] ἐὰν οὖν προσφέρῃς τὸ δῶρόν σου ἐπὶ τὸ θυσιαστήριον κἀκεῖ μνησθῇς ὅτι ὁ ἀδελφός σου ἔχει τι κατὰ σοῦ, [24] ἄφες ἐκεῖ τὸ δῶρόν σου ἔμπροσθεν τοῦ θυσιαστηρίου, καὶ ὕπαγε πρῶτον διαλλάγηθι τῷ ἀδελφῷ σου, καὶ τότε ἐλθὼν πρόσφερε τὸ δῶρόν σου.	
	W=94/0, SW=0, OR=0, VB=0	

2 NP		⁵⁷ Τί δὲ καὶ ἀφ ἑαυτῶν οὐ κρίνετε τὸ δίκαιον
	W=0/9, SW=0, OR=0, VB=0	
3	²⁵ ἴσθι εὐνοῶν τῷ ἀντιδίκῳ σου ταχὺ ἕως ὅτου εἶ μετ αὐτοῦ ἐν τῇ ὁδῷ, μήποτέ σε παραδῷ ὁ ἀντίδικος τῷ κριτῇ, καὶ ὁ κριτὴς τῷ ὑπηρέτῃ, καὶ εἰς φυλακὴν βληθήσῃ	⁵⁸ ὡς γὰρ ὑπάγεις μετὰ τοῦ ἀντιδίκου σου ἐπ ἄρχοντα, ἐν τῇ ὁδῷ δὸς ἐργασίαν ἀπηλλάχθαι ἀπ αὐτοῦ, μήποτε κατασύρῃ σε πρὸς τὸν κριτήν, καὶ ὁ κριτής σε παραδώσει τῷ πράκτορι, καὶ ὁ πράκτωρ σε βαλεῖ εἰς φυλακήν.
	W=30/37, SW=20, OR=16, VB=14	
4 CORE	²⁶ ἀμὴν λέγω σοι, οὐ μὴ ἐξέλθῃς ἐκεῖθεν ἕως ἂν ἀποδῷς τὸν ἔσχατον κοδράντην.	⁵⁹ λέγω σοι, οὐ μὴ ἐξέλθῃς ἐκεῖθεν ἕως καὶ τὸ ἔσχατον λεπτὸν ἀποδῷς.
	W=13/12, SW=10, OR=9, VB=9	

Table 2. Aland §55, Statistical Summary

Sec. #	Wds (Mt)	Wds (Lk)	SW	OR	VB	%SW (Mt)	%SW (Lk)	%OR	%VB (Mt)	%VB (Lk)	%Mt	%Lk
1	94	0	0	0	0	0%	0%	0%	0%	0%	69%	0%
2	0	9	0	0	0	0%	0%	0%	0%	0%	0%	16%
3	30	37	20	16	14	67%	54%	80%	47%	38%	22%	64%
4	13	12	10	9	9	77%	83%	90%	69%	75%	9%	21%
TOT	137	58	30	25	23	22%	52%	83%	17%	40%		

Figure 1. Agreement, Sec. Length, Shared Words (Aland §55, Matt)

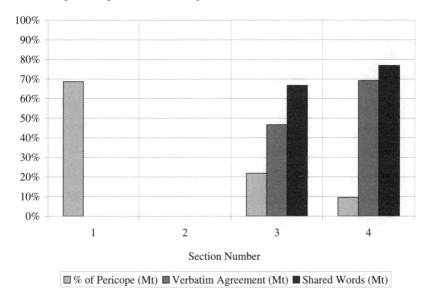

Figure 2. Agreement, Sec. Length, Shared Words (Aland §55, Luke)

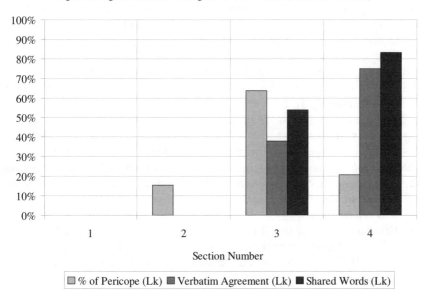

Figure 3. Agreement vs. Pericope Length (Aland §55)

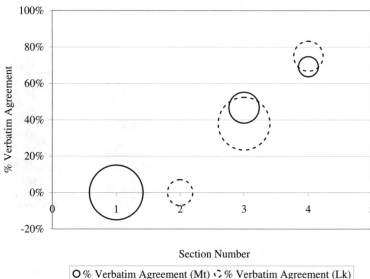

Section Number

O % Verbatim Agreement (Mt) ☽ % Verbatim Agreement (Lk)

1) An initial look at Table 1 indicates that there is a "core" in section 4 that concludes the pericope with the admonition regarding the last "penny" (κοδράντην, Matt) or "copper" (λεπτὸν, Luke). This core exists on a thematic level and its importance is reflected by the high level of verbatim agreement in section 4. Neither term is common in the Synoptics; κοδράντης occurs elsewhere only in Mark 12:42, and λεπτόν only in Mark 12:52 and Luke 21:2. The low frequency of either term in the Synoptic Gospels makes it difficult to appeal to word frequencies to determine redactional tendencies to account for the differing term. The remainder of the core is strikingly similar, although not verbatim as indicated in Table 1, Figure 1, and Figure 2.

2) The level of agreement in section 4 is 69%/75% (Matt/Luke), and is significantly higher than the average percent agreement of 17%/40%. Therefore, in this pericope, the overall %VB does not accurately reflect the character of the agreement within the story. A look at Figure 3 supports this assessment. Section 3 of both Matthew and Luke contains a significant percentage of the overall length of the pericope (22%/64%), although the %VB is relatively low (47%, 38%). On the other hand, section 4 contains a smaller percentage of the story (9%, 21%) but has a much higher %VB (69%,75%). This indicates that for both Matthew and Luke, the overall low 24% overall %VB does not take seriously that section 4 contains a large concentration of verbatim words.

3) In addition, sections 1 and 2 comprise a significant percentage of the overall pericope (69%/16%), and are NP sections that do not contain any SW or VB words.

4) Section 3 also contains several SW which are close to verbatim, but differ in case alone. Matthew uses the dative case to describe the "accuser" and the "judge" (τῷ ἀντιδίκῳ σου / τῷ κριτῇ), while Luke does so with the genitive and accusative cases (τοῦ ἀντιδίκου σου / τὸν κριτήν). The last line of section 3 contains and interesting inversion of sequence between the object (εἰς φυλακὴ) and their respective verbs (βληθήσῃ, Matt; βαλει, Luke).

5) Overall, this pericope is highly variable, with the agreement concentrated in the thematic "core" of section 4, apart from which there is little extended agreement. The overall percent of agreement does not accurately reflect the variable character of this pericope. It is clear that both the Matthean and Lukan parallels are variations of the same tradition. Here there is variation in the telling of the story, particularly in section 3 where there is a common retelling of the story, although with varying points of detail such as "guard" (τῷ ὑπηρέτῃ) in Matt 5:25 in contrast with "officer" (τῷ πράκτορι) in Luke 12:58.

6.6.2   Aland §58 — On Retaliation

Table 3. Aland §58, Synoptic Text

	Matt 5	Luke 6
1 NP	[38] Ἠκούσατε ὅτι ἐρρέθη, Ὀφθαλμὸν ἀντὶ ὀφθαλμοῦ καὶ ὀδόντα ἀντὶ ὀδόντος. [39] ἐγὼ δὲ λέγω ὑμῖν μὴ ἀντιστῆναι τῷ πονηρῷ·	
	W=18/0, SW=0, OR=0, VB=0	
2	ἀλλ᾽ ὅστις **σε** ῥαπίζει εἰς **τὴν** δεξιὰν **σιαγόνα** [σου], στρέψον αὐτῷ **καὶ τὴν ἄλλην·**	[29] τῷ τύπτοντί **σε** ἐπὶ **τὴν σιαγόνα** πάρεχε **καὶ τὴν ἄλλην,**
	W=13/10, SW=6, OR=6, VB=6	
3	[40] **καὶ τῷ** θέλοντί <u>σοι</u> κριθῆναι **καὶ τὸν χιτῶνά** σου λαβεῖν, ἄφες αὐτῷ **καὶ τὸ ἱμάτιον·**	**καὶ** ἀπὸ τοῦ αἴροντός <u>σου</u> **τὸ ἱμάτιον** **καὶ τὸν χιτῶνα** μὴ κωλύσῃς.
	W=15/12, SW=7, OR=5, VB=6	

	Matt 5	Luke 6
4 NP	[41] καὶ ὅστις σε ἀγγαρεύσει μίλιον ἕν, ὕπαγε μετ᾽ αὐτοῦ δύο	
	W=10/0, SW=0, OR=0, VB=0	
5	[42] τῷ **αἰτοῦντί σε** <u>δός</u>, **καὶ** τὸν θέλοντα **ἀπὸ** σοῦ δανίσασθαι **μὴ** ἀποστραφῇς.	[30] παντὶ **αἰτοῦντί σε** <u>δίδου</u>, **καὶ** **ἀπὸ** τοῦ αἴροντος τὰ <u>σὰ</u> **μὴ** ἀπαίτει.
	W=12/12, SW=7, OR=7, VB=5	

Table 4. Aland §58, Statistical Summary

Sec. #	Wds (Mt)	Wds (Lk)	SW	OR	VB	%SW (Mt)	%SW (Lk)	%OR	%VB (Mt)	%VB (Lk)	%Mt	%Lk
1	18	0	0	0	0	0%	0%	0%	0%	0%	26%	0%
2	13	10	6	6	6	46%	60%	100%	46%	60%	19%	29%
3	15	12	7	5	6	47%	58%	71%	40%	50%	22%	35%
4	10	0	0	0	0	0%	0%	0%	0%	0%	15%	0%
5	12	12	7	7	5	58%	58%	100%	42%	42%	18%	35%
TOT	68	34	20	18	17	29%	59%	90%	25%	50%		

Figure 4. Agreement, Sec. Length, Shared Words (Aland §58, Matt)

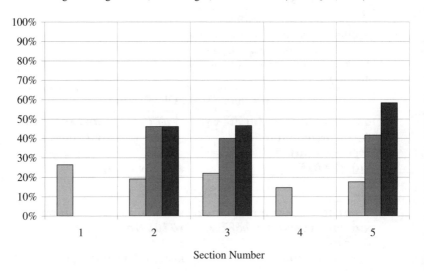

Section Number

□ % of Pericope (Mt)　■ Verbatim Agreement (Mt)　■ Shared Words (Mt)

Figure 5. Agreement, Sec. Length, Shared Words (Aland §58, Luke)

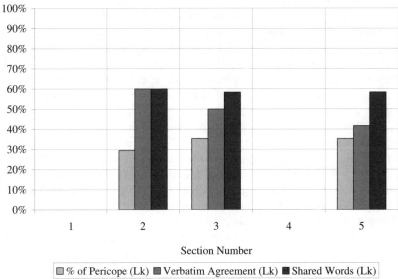

Figure 6. Agreement vs. Pericope Length (Aland §58)

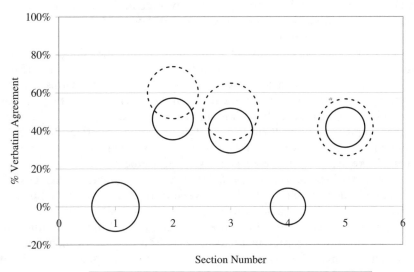

1) Unlike Aland §55 (On Murder and Wrath), there is no apparent "core" that contains the major crux of the story. Here, sections 2–5 are of equal thematic significance within the overall narrative itself. There are two non-parallel sections in the pericope (sections 1 and 4). The level of agreement in sections 2 and 3 are roughly the same for both Matthew (46%/40%) and Luke (60%/50%). Figure 6 clearly illustrates this phenomenon; the Lukan sections 2 and 3 are both higher than their Matthean parallels, and Matthew contains additional NP sections (1, 4) that are absent from Luke.

2) NP section 4 occurs in the main body of the pericope, unlike Aland §55 (On Murder and Wrath), where the NP section in Matthew occurs at the beginning of the pericope. The second NP section (sec. 4; Matt 5:41) contains a fuller version of the Lukan admonitions. Matt 5:39b–40 contains two examples (turn cheek, coat/cloak) that are paralleled in Luke, although Matthew's NP section serves to develop further the story by adding a third example of this ethic — καὶ ὅστις σε ἀγγαρεύσει μίλιον ἕν, ὕπαγε μετ' αὐτοῦ δύο (Matt 5:41). The existence of the Matthean version of the pericope fits well the ancient use of "threes" in oral storytelling settings.[47]

3) Of interest is the relative uniformity of sections 2, 3, and 5, and their similar level of agreement with respect to their relative section lengths. In this pericope, the average percent agreement for Luke (50%) is in accord with the levels observed in sections that have a parallel with Matthew (i.e., sections 2 (60%), 3 (50%), and 5 (42%)), although the %VB in sections 2 and 3 is higher than the overall pericope average of 33%. Matthew on the other hand, exhibits a somewhat lower overall level of %VB in relation to the overall pericope average of 33%.

4) It is necessary to examine in more detail the similarities and differences between the Matthean and Lukan parallels. In section 3 (Matt 5:40//Luke 6:29b), both Matthew and Luke use the same terms for the clothing (τὸν χιτῶνά, τὸ ἱμάτιον) although the order in which they appear is inverted. Other than those VB agreements, Matthew and Luke vary rather significantly in their use of this common tradition. Matt 5:42 contains an antithesis between beg (αἰτοῦντί) and borrow (δανίσασθαι), while Luke uses beg and "take away" (τοῦ αἴροντος).

Matthew's use of δανίσασθαι (Matt 5:42) is unique in his gospel, although it does occur in the Lukan version of Aland §59 (On Love of One's Enemies; Luke 6:34) which immediately follows in sequence after this pericope (Aland §58). Luke uses δανίζουσιν in Luke 6:34, although he does not do so earlier in Luke 6:30. It is necessary to inquire as to whether, in this case, Matthew and/or Luke have consciously deviated

---

[47] See Olrik, "Epic Laws," 133 for the classic exposition of the "law of threes."

from a written "Q" source. From a redaction-critical perspective, if Matt 5:42 is the reading closer to his written source in his use of "borrow," then Luke has intentionally replaced δανίσασθαι with τοῦ αἴροντος although Luke is comfortable using "lend" and "borrow" language only a few verses later in Luke 6:34–35. Likewise, if Luke in using the antithesis beg/take away (Luke 6:30) represents a reading that more closely reflects his possible written source text then we are in a similar situation in trying to explain Matthew's editorial activity. In this case, Matthew would have replaced the "Q" saying with the beg/borrow saying, although he does not utilize the same language in verses 46–47.

We are therefore left with no less than three possible solutions to account for the extant form of this tradition. The first possibility is that Matthew and Luke had access to a different source text; second, that they freely edited a shared source text (i.e., "Q"); or third, that the eccentricities in the parallel texts are reflective of the possibility that the two traditions represent varying oral versions of a similar tradition sequence to which both Matthew and Luke had access. While it must be recognized that all three options are possible, without any additional external evidence, the variation in language, the overall low level of VB within the pericope, and the thematic stability exhibited within the pericope can be explained by an appeal to an existence of varying forms of the tradition within different Christian communities.

6.6.3 Aland §62 — The Lord's Prayer

Table 5. Aland §62, Synoptic Text

	Matt 6	Luke 11
1 NP	⁷ Προσευχόμενοι δὲ μὴ βατταλογήσητε ὥσπερ οἱ ἐθνικοί, δοκοῦσιν γὰρ ὅτι ἐν τῇ πολυλογίᾳ αὐτῶν εἰσακουσθήσονται. ⁸ μὴ οὖν ὁμοιωθῆτε αὐτοῖς, οἶδεν γὰρ ὁ πατὴρ ὑμῶν ὧν χρείαν ἔχετε πρὸ τοῦ ὑμᾶς αἰτῆσαι αὐτόν.	
	W=32/0, SW=0, OR=0, VB=0	
2 NP		¹ καὶ ἐγένετο ἐν τῷ εἶναι αὐτὸν ἐν τόπῳ τινὶ προσευχόμενον, ὡς ἐπαύσατο, εἶπέν τις τῶν μαθητῶν αὐτοῦ πρὸς αὐτόν, Κύριε, δίδαξον ἡμᾶς προσεύχεσθαι, καθὼς

	Matt 6	Luke 11
		καὶ ᾽Ιωάννης ἐδίδαξεν τοὺς μαθητὰς αὐτοῦ.
	W=0/30, SW=0, OR=0, VB=0	
3	⁹ οὕτως οὖν προσεύχεσθε ὑμεῖς·	² εἶπεν δὲ αὐτοῖς, "Οταν προσεύχησθε, λέγετε,
	W=4/6, SW=1, OR=1, VB=0	
4	**Πάτερ** ἡμῶν ὁ ἐν τοῖς οὐρανοῖς, **ἁγιασθήτω τὸ ὄνομά σου,** ¹⁰ **ἐλθέτω ἡ βασιλεία σου,**	**Πάτερ,** **ἁγιασθήτω τὸ ὄνομά σου·** **ἐλθέτω ἡ βασιλεία σου**
	W=14/9, SW=9, OR=9, VB=9	
5 NP	γενηθήτω τὸ θέλημά σου, ὡς ἐν οὐρανῷ καὶ ἐπὶ γῆς.	
	W=10/0, SW=0, OR=0, VB=0	
6	¹¹ **Τὸν ἄρτον ἡμῶν τὸν ἐπιούσιον** δὸς ἡμῖν σήμερον·	³ **τὸν ἄρτον ἡμῶν τὸν ἐπιούσιον** δίδου ἡμῖν τὸ καθ ἡμέραν·
	W=8/10, SW=7, OR=7, VB=6	
7	¹² **καὶ ἄφες ἡμῖν τὰ** ὀφειλήματα **ἡμῶν,**	⁴ **καὶ ἄφες ἡμῖν τὰς** ἁμαρτίας **ἡμῶν,**
	W=6/6, SW=5, OR=5, VB=4	
8	ὡς **καὶ** ἡμεῖς ἀφήκαμεν τοῖς ὀφειλέταις ἡμῶν·	**καὶ** γὰρ αὐτοὶ ἀφίομεν παντὶ ὀφείλοντι ἡμῖν·
	W=7/7, SW=4, OR=4, VB=1	
9	¹³ **καὶ μὴ εἰσενέγκῃς ἡμᾶς εἰς πειρασμόν,** ἀλλὰ ῥῦσαι ἡμᾶς ἀπὸ τοῦ πονηροῦ.	**καὶ μὴ εἰσενέγκῃς ἡμᾶς εἰς πειρασμόν.**
	W=12/6, SW=6, OR=6, VB=6	
10 NP	¹⁴ ᾽Εὰν γὰρ ἀφῆτε τοῖς ἀνθρώποις τὰ παραπτώματα αὐτῶν, ἀφήσει καὶ ὑμῖν ὁ πατὴρ ὑμῶν ὁ οὐράνιος· ¹⁵ ἐὰν δὲ μὴ ἀφῆτε τοῖς ἀνθρώποις, οὐδὲ ὁ πατὴρ ὑμῶν ἀφήσει τὰ παραπτώματα ὑμῶν.	

	Matt 6	Luke 11
	W=30/0, SW=0, OR=0, VB=0	

Table 6. Aland §62, Statistical Summary

Sec. #	Wds (Mt)	Wds (Lk)	SW	OR	VB	%SW (Mt)	%SW (Lk)	%OR	%VB (Mt)	%VB (Lk)	%Mt	%Lk
1	32	0	0	0	0	0%	0%	0%	0%	0%	26%	0%
2	0	30	0	0	0	0%	0%	0%	0%	0%	0%	41%
3	4	6	1	1	0	25%	17%	100%	0%	0%	3%	8%
4	14	9	9	9	9	64%	100%	100%	64%	100%	11%	12%
5	10	0	0	0	0	0%	0%	0%	0%	0%	8%	0%
6	8	10	7	7	6	88%	70%	100%	75%	60%	7%	14%
7	6	6	5	5	4	83%	83%	100%	67%	67%	5%	8%
8	7	7	4	4	1	57%	57%	100%	14%	14%	6%	9%
9	12	6	6	6	6	50%	100%	100%	50%	100%	10%	8%
10	30	0	0	0	0	0%	0%	0%	0%	0%	24%	0%
TOT	123	74	32	32	26	26%	43%	100%	21%	35%		

Figure 7. Agreement, Sec. Length, Shared Words (Aland §62, Matt)

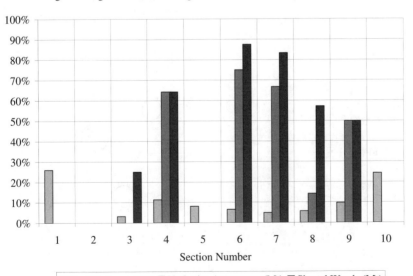

Figure 8. Agreement, Sec. Length, Shared Words (Aland §62, Luke)

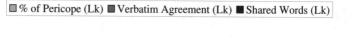

Figure 9. Agreement vs. Pericope Length (Aland §62)

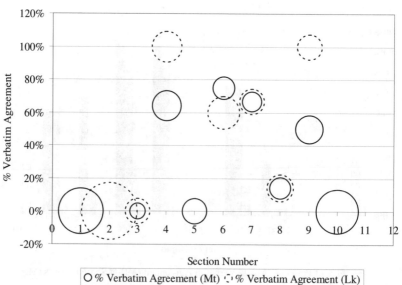

The text of the Lord's Prayer has been divided into ten sections; each parallel section (apart from the NP sections — 1, 2, 5, 10) contains relatively few words. The distribution of the length of the main sections is approximately equal. The area of the bubbles in Figure 9 is quite uniform, and the ease with which the pericope can be divided into almost equal sections reflects the rhythmic character apparent in the text. This metrical regularity seems to support the notion that this text served a liturgical and/or instructional function in the early Jesus communities.[48]

1) There are noticeably high levels of agreement within several of the sections of the main body (sections 4, 6–9). Although these passages have levels of agreement significantly higher than the average for the entire pericope (26%), these sections appear to be of equal thematic significance to the other sections containing lower levels of agreement (i.e., sections 3, 8). These centrally located sections, therefore, do not seem to function as a "core" in the same way as the "core" functioned in Aland §55 (above).

2) A quick glance at Figure 9 reveals the striking variability within the pericope. Although the length of the main sections is relatively uniform, the %VB within those sections varies considerably, from 100% (Luke, sections 4, 9) to low levels of agreement in Luke, sections 3 and 8 (0%, 14%). Section 8 deserves particular mention for it is significantly different in character than the other parallel sections of the pericope. Figure 7 clearly illustrates how this section varies from its surrounding context. There is a high %SW (57%), but a very low %VB (14%).

3) The NP section of Matthew (Matt 6:10b) occurs in the middle of the prayer's main body (sec. 5), and the other NP sections occur in both the introduction (secs. 1, 2) and the closing (sec. 10) of the parallels.

4) The overall level of agreement in the pericope is 26% for the pericope as listed in Table 5. If a "purified" double tradition is examined however (sec. 1, 2, 5, 10),[49] then the %VB increases to 55%. The contrast between our 26% VB and the 55% for a "purified" tradition illustrates how the method employed by Carlston and Norlin can artificially raise the overall level of verbatim agreement within an individual pericope. In either case, these levels of verbatim agreement are in sharp contrast to the level

---

[48] In particular see Joachim Jeremias, *New Testament Theology: The Proclamation of Jesus* (New York: Scribner, 1971), 194–195 — "Matthew gives us a Jewish-Christian and Luke a Gentile-Christian catechism." The short length of each section would facilitate the easy recollection or recitation of the various phrases of the prayer. See also Sandt & Flusser's discussion of the Lord's Prayer in the *Didache* 8:2–3 for a similar conclusion (Sandt and Flusser, *Didache*, 293–296). Also, cf. Betz, *Sermon on the Mount*, 371.

[49] The use of a "purified" double tradition would be in line with the previously mentioned method of Carlston and Norlin, and is significantly higher than the level of VB with the NP sections included.

of VB in the pericope's individual sections. Despite the liturgical character of this tradition, there is significant internal variability between the parallel accounts.

6.6.4 Aland §85 — The Centurion of Capernaum

Table 7. Aland §85, Synoptic Text

	Matt 8	Luke 7
1	⁵ <u>εἰσελθόντος</u> δὲ αὐτοῦ **εἰς Καφαρναοὺμ**	¹ Ἐπειδὴ ἐπλήρωσεν πάντα τὰ ῥήματα αὐτοῦ εἰς τὰς ἀκοὰς τοῦ λαοῦ, <u>εἰσῆλθεν</u> **εἰς Καφαρναούμ.**
	W=5/14, SW=3, OR=3, VB=2	
2	προσῆλθεν αὐτῷ <u>ἑκατόνταρχος</u> παρακαλῶν αὐτὸν ⁶ καὶ λέγων, κύριε, ὁ παῖς μου βέβληται ἐν τῇ οἰκίᾳ παραλυτικός, δεινῶς βασανιζόμενος.	² Ἑκατοντάρχου δέ τινος δοῦλος κακῶς ἔχων ἤμελλεν τελευτᾶν, ὃς ἦν αὐτῷ ἔντιμος. ³ ἀκούσας δὲ περὶ τοῦ Ἰησοῦ ἀπέστειλεν πρὸς αὐτὸν πρεσβυτέρους τῶν Ἰουδαίων, ἐρωτῶν αὐτὸν ὅπως ἐλθὼν διασώσῃ τὸν δοῦλον αὐτοῦ.
	W=18/31, SW=1, OR=1, VB=0	
3 NP	⁷ καὶ λέγει αὐτῷ · ἐγὼ ἐλθὼν θεραπεύσω αὐτόν. ⁸ καὶ ἀποκριθεὶς ὁ ἑκατόνταρχος ἔφη,	
	W=12/0, SW=0, OR=0, VB=0	
4 NP		⁴ οἱ δὲ παραγενόμενοι πρὸς τὸν Ἰησοῦν παρεκάλουν αὐτὸν σπουδαίως, λέγοντες ὅτι ἄξιός ἐστιν ᾧ παρέξῃ τοῦτο, ⁵ ἀγαπᾷ γὰρ τὸ ἔθνος ἡμῶν καὶ τὴν συναγωγὴν αὐτὸς ᾠκοδόμησεν ἡμῖν. ⁶ ὁ δὲ Ἰησοῦς ἐπορεύετο σὺν αὐτοῖς. ἤδη δὲ αὐτοῦ οὐ μακρὰν ἀπέχοντος ἀπὸ τῆς οἰκίας ἔπεμψεν φίλους ὁ ἑκατοντάρχης λέγων αὐτῷ,
	W=0/48, SW=0, OR=0, VB=0	

	Matt 8	Luke 7
5 CORE	κύριε, οὐκ εἰμὶ ἱκανὸς ἵνα μου ὑπὸ τὴν στέγην εἰσέλθῃς· ἀλλὰ μόνον εἰπὲ λόγῳ, καὶ ἰαθήσεται ὁ παῖς μου.	κύριε, μὴ σκύλλου, οὐ γὰρ ἱκανός εἰμι ἵνα ὑπὸ τὴν στέγην μου εἰσέλθῃς· ⁷ διὸ οὐδὲ ἐμαυτὸν ἠξίωσα πρὸς σὲ ἐλθεῖν· ἀλλὰ εἰπὲ λόγῳ, καὶ ἰαθήτω ὁ παῖς μου.
	W=19/28, SW=18, OR=16, VB=16	
6 CORE	⁹ καὶ γὰρ ἐγὼ ἄνθρωπός εἰμι ὑπὸ ἐξουσίαν, ἔχων ὑπ᾽ ἐμαυτὸν στρατιώτας, καὶ λέγω τούτῳ, πορεύθητι, καὶ πορεύεται, καὶ ἄλλῳ, ἔρχου, καὶ ἔρχεται, καὶ τῷ δούλῳ μου, ποίησον τοῦτο, καὶ ποιεῖ.	⁸ καὶ γὰρ ἐγὼ ἄνθρωπός εἰμι ὑπὸ ἐξουσίαν τασσόμενος, ἔχων ὑπ᾽ ἐμαυτὸν στρατιώτας, καὶ λέγω τούτῳ, πορεύθητι, καὶ πορεύεται, καὶ ἄλλῳ, ἔρχου, καὶ ἔρχεται, καὶ τῷ δούλῳ μου, ποίησον τοῦτο, καὶ ποιεῖ.
	W=30/31, SW=30, OR=30, VB=30	
7 CORE	¹⁰ ἀκούσας δὲ ὁ ᾽Ιησοῦς ἐθαύμασεν καὶ εἶπεν τοῖς ἀκολουθοῦσιν, ἀμὴν λέγω ὑμῖν, παρ᾽ οὐδενὶ τοσαύτην πίστιν ἐν τῷ ᾽Ισραὴλ εὗρον.	⁹ ἀκούσας δὲ ταῦτα ὁ ᾽Ιησοῦς ἐθαύμασεν αὐτόν, καὶ στραφεὶς τῷ ἀκολουθοῦντι αὐτῷ ὄχλῳ εἶπεν, λέγω ὑμῖν, οὐδὲ ἐν τῷ ᾽Ισραὴλ τοσαύτην πίστιν εὗρον.
	W=20/23, SW=18, OR=15, VB=15	
8 NP	¹¹ λέγω δὲ ὑμῖν ὅτι πολλοὶ ἀπὸ ἀνατολῶν καὶ δυσμῶν ἥξουσιν καὶ ἀνακλιθήσονται μετὰ Αβραὰμ καὶ ᾽Ισαὰκ καὶ ᾽Ιακὼβ ἐν τῇ βασιλείᾳ τῶν οὐρανῶν· ¹² οἱ δὲ υἱοὶ τῆς βασιλείας ἐκβληθήσονται εἰς τὸ σκότος τὸ ἐξώτερον· ἐκεῖ ἔσται ὁ κλαυθμὸς καὶ ὁ βρυγμὸς τῶν ὀδόντων.	cp. 13:28–29
	W=43/0, SW=0, OR=0, VB=0	

	Matt 8	Luke 7
9	[13] καὶ εἶπεν ὁ ' Ιησοῦς τῷ ἑκατοντάρχῃ, ὕπαγε, ὡς ἐπίστευσας γενηθήτω σοι. **καὶ ἰάθη** ὁ παῖς [αὐτοῦ] ἐν τῇ ὥρᾳ ἐκείνῃ.	[10] **καὶ** ὑποστρέψαντες εἰς τὸν οἶκον οἱ πεμφθέντες εὗρον <u>τὸν</u> δοῦλον ὑγιαίνοντα.
	W=19/11, SW=2, OR=2, VB=1	

Table 8. Aland §85, Statistical Summary

Sec. #	Wds (Mt)	Wds (Lk)	SW	OR	VB	%SW (Mt)	%SW (Lk)	%OR	%VB (Mt)	%VB (Lk)	%Mt	%Lk
1	5	14	3	3	2	60%	21%	100%	40%	14%	3%	8%
2	18	31	1	1	0	6%	3%	100%	0%	0%	11%	17%
3	12	0	0	0	0	0%	0%	0%	0%	0%	7%	0%
4	0	48	0	0	0	0%	0%	0%	0%	0%	0%	26%
5	19	28	18	16	16	95%	64%	89%	84%	57%	11%	15%
6	30	31	30	30	30	100%	97%	100%	100%	97%	18%	17%
7	20	23	18	15	15	90%	78%	83%	75%	65%	12%	12%
8	43	0	0	0	0	0%	0%	0%	0%	0%	26%	0%
9	19	11	2	2	1	11%	18%	100%	5%	9%	11%	6%
TOT	*166*	*186*	*72*	*67*	*64*	*43%*	*39%*	*93%*	*39%*	*34%*		

Figure 10. Agreement, Sec. Length, Shared Words (Aland §85, Matt)

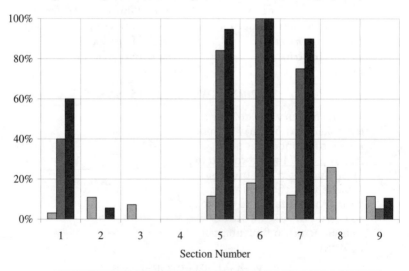

□ % of Pericope (Mt) ■ Verbatim Agreement (Mt) ■ Shared Words (Mt)

Figure 11. Agreement, Sec. Length, Shared Words (Aland §85, Luke)

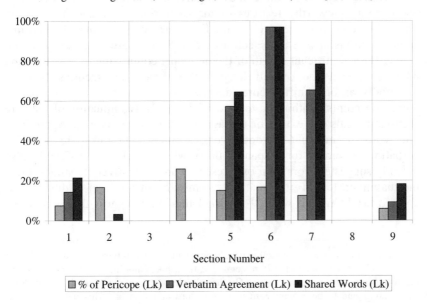

Figure 12. Agreement vs. Pericope Length (Aland §85)

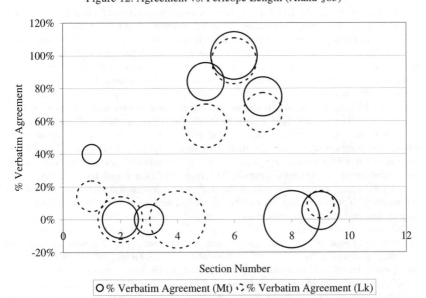

1) A brief scan of all three above figures and tables indicates that there are several noteworthy features of the Centurion's Servant. The text in Table 7 reveals that there are, for the first time, what appear to be multiple "core" sections. These core sections (secs. 5, 6, 7) are all connected, and extend for a significant length of the pericope, comprising 41% (Matt) and 44% (Luke) of the overall length. The three core sections function essentially as one unified core, despite the existence of two theoretical "insertion points" within the text (secs. 5/6, 6/7). Examination of the core sections reveals the extent of the agreement in sections 5–7. Apart from one word in section 6 (τασσόμενος), Matthew and Luke are in 100% verbatim agreement for a span of thirty words. McIver and Carroll have recently suggested from their own research on their university students that the maximum length of verbatim transmission of an "oral tradition" was approximately fifteen words.[50] Beyond that they suggest that a tradition

---

[50] Based on their experimental psychological study of 43 university students, McIver and Carroll suggest that "what is remembered from jokes and historical accounts is the macro-meaning, not the exact words. On the other hand, some genres, such as aphorisms and poetry, tend to be remembered word for word or not at all. This means that it is possible to transmit longer sequences of words accurately using aphorisms, poetry, and words set to music. These observations led to the formulation of a criterion to establish the presence of copying: unless found in poetry, words set to music, or aphorisms, 16 or more words that are exactly the same in two or more documents indicate that a process of copying has taken place" (Robert K. McIver and Marie Carroll, "Experiments to Develop Criteria for Determing the Existence of Written Sources, and Their Potential Implications for the Synoptic Problem," *Journal of Biblical Literature* 121:4 [2002]: 687). While their study is fascinating, several questions arise from their methodology. First, one must question their choice of subjects. It is necessary to ask whether results derived from highly literate college/university students who have "grown-up" in the hyper-literate 20th and 21st centuries would be comparable to those derived from more highly-oral peoples. Also, the experiment that McIver and Carroll suggest was "perhaps most instructive" was conducted by asking students to choose six out of eight stories with which they were familiar, and then testing their ability to recall the stories in three different ways: 1) recall with no source before them, 2) recall after looking at a source, 3) recall while having the written source in front of them. Not surprisingly, the level of recall for #1 was quite minimal. Unfortunately, this experiment does not resemble the process which led to the formation of the Synoptic Gospels. The Jesus tradition would have entered into a community which would have valued the tradition as foundational for their communal self-identity. It would have been repeatedly recited and performed, all the while being shaped and molded by the process of communal self-stabilization (see above, ch. 5). McIver and Carroll's experiment is not capable of duplicating these conditions. Also, the tradition presented to illustrate their findings contained only 2 words of "sayings material," and was a "news report" on the sinking of the Titanic ("Experiments," 670). The Titanic tradition contained no mnemonic aids to facilitate memorization (unlike a significant portion of the Jesus tradition), and was a thoroughly modern depiction of a historical account. These among other issues suggest that further study is necessary to

must have been derivative of a text, and therefore the product of redaction of an original source text. While there are significant difficulties with McIver and Carroll's methodology, their general conclusions tend to be in line with those observed by other folklorists, and do support the possibility that this pericope might be related to a source text in some manner.

2) The significant majority of the agreement occurs within the central section of the story. The only other section with any noteworthy agreement is section 1, where the Centurion is entering Capernaum εἰσελθόντος/εἰσελθὼν εἰς Καφαρναοὺμ (Matt 8:5//Luke 7:1), although the length of the section (3%/8%) is relatively small in comparison to the larger core sections (secs. 5, 6, 7).

3) The three NP sections (secs. 3, 4, 8) all occur within the main body of the pericope, and do not function as introductions or conclusions to their respective parallel (cf. Aland §58, §62, §102, §279). NP sections 4 and 8 are quite long and occupy a large percentage of the overall length of their parallels: section 4 is 26% of the overall length of Luke, and section 8 comprises 26% of the Matthean parallel.

4) Attention should also be drawn to the agreement in relative order (%OR) in the core sections. Sections 5 and 7 in particular each contain more variation in sequence than previously observed in the other pericopes. Section 5 contains a sequential inversion of the words εἰμι ἱκανός (Matt 8:8) with ἱκανός εἰμι (Luke 7:6) and the word μου exists out of sequence within the ἵνα . . . εἰσέλθῃς clause (Matt 8:8//Luke 7:6). Section 7 also contains several different words out of sequence with their corresponding parallel. The verb εἶπεν (in the clause beginning with καὶ εἶπεν in Matt 8:10) is reserved for the end of the clause in Luke 7:9 (καὶ . . . εἶπεν). Later in the same section, Matthew and Luke both contain the same verbatim words, but they juxtapose the phrase ἐν τῷ Ἰσραὴλ with τοσαύτην πίστιν, therefore, both authors have agreed to a large extent on the precise *wording* of this section, but not on the placement of the words therein.

6.6.5 Aland §102 — Divisions within Households

Table 9. Aland §102, Synoptic Text

	Matt 10	Luke 12
1	[34] Μὴ νομίσητε ὅτι ἦλθον βαλεῖν **εἰρήνην**	[51] δοκεῖτε ὅτι **εἰρήνην** παρεγενόμην δοῦναι

---

determine if McIver and Carroll's work can help one understand better the Jesus tradition as "oral tradition."

	Matt 10	Luke 12
	ἐπὶ τὴν γῆν· οὐκ ἦλθον βαλεῖν εἰρήνην ἀλλὰ μάχαιραν.	ἐν τῇ γῇ οὐχί, λέγω ὑμῖν, ἀλλ᾽ ἢ διαμερισμόν.
	W=15/14, SW=6, OR=6, VB=2	
2 NP		52 ἔσονται γὰρ ἀπὸ τοῦ νῦν πέντε ἐν ἑνὶ οἴκῳ διαμεμερισμένοι, τρεῖς ἐπὶ δυσὶν καὶ δύο ἐπὶ τρισίν,
	W=0/17, SW=0, OR=0, VB=0	
3	35 ἦλθον γὰρ διχάσαι ἄνθρωπον κατὰ τοῦ πατρὸς αὐτοῦ καὶ θυγατέρα κατὰ τῆς μητρὸς αὐτῆς καὶ νύμφην κατὰ τῆς πενθερᾶς αὐτῆς,	53 διαμερισθήσονται πατὴρ ἐπὶ υἱῷ καὶ υἱὸς ἐπὶ πατρί, μήτηρ ἐπὶ τὴν θυγατέρα καὶ θυγάτηρ ἐπὶ τὴν μητέρα, πενθερὰ ἐπὶ τὴν νύμφην αὐτῆς καὶ νύμφη ἐπὶ τὴν πενθεράν.
	W=20/27, SW=9, OR=9, VB=2	
4 NP	36 καὶ ἐχθροὶ τοῦ ἀνθρώπου οἱ οἰκιακοὶ αὐτοῦ.	
	W=7/0, SW=0, OR=0, VB=0	

Table 10. Aland §102, Statistical Summary

Sec. #	Wds (Mt)	Wds (Lk)	SW	OR	VB	%SW (Mt)	%SW (Lk)	%OR	%VB (Mt)	%VB (Lk)	%Mt	%Lk
1	15	14	7	7	2	47%	50%	100%	13%	14%	36%	24%
2	0	17	0	0	0	0%	0%	0%	0%	0%	0%	29%
3	20	27	9	9	2	45%	33%	100%	10%	7%	48%	47%
4	7	0	0	0	0	0%	0%	0%	0%	0%	17%	0%
TOT	42	58	16	16	4	38%	28%	100%	10%	7%		

Figure 13. Agreement, Sec. Length, Shared Words (Aland §102, Matt)

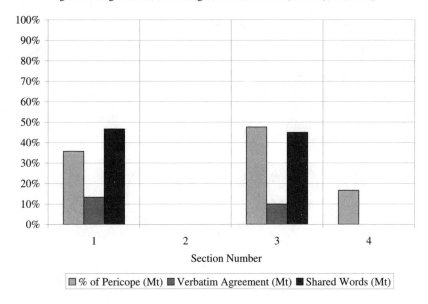

Figure 14. Agreement, Sec. Length, Shared Words (Aland §102, Luke)

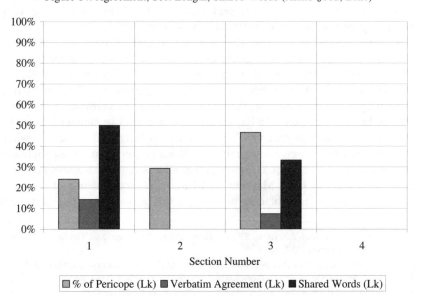

Figure 15. Agreement vs. Pericope Length (Aland §102)

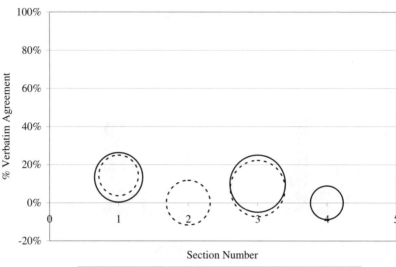

O % Verbatim Agreement (Mt) ᴖ % Verbatim Agreement (Lk)

The pericope has a very low overall level of verbatim agreement (Matt, 10%; Luke, 7%), and the length of the pericope itself is rather short, therefore it is difficult to estimate the significance of the few agreements that exist. Strictly adhering to our notion of verbatim agreement, the only agreements are the words ὅτι and εἰρήνην which appears at the very beginning of the pericope itself (sec. 1 — Matt 10:34, Luke 12:51), and καὶ which serves an additive function in two clauses near the end of the pericope (sec. 3).[51] The only other words that are almost in agreement are ἀλλὰ / ἀλλ᾽, although they do not fit our criterion for verbatim agreement.[52] It is clear in this instance that the attribution of this story to a written Q is *not* primarily on the basis of its level of verbatim agreement. This is another example of what we referred to earlier in chapter two as the "working assumption that Q=q" (see above, p.44, n.100). That is, when passages that have such a low level of verbatim agreement are attributed to Q, there exists an implicit assumption that all passages with *shared content* have been derived from Matthew and Luke's redactional use of a shared written source. Such is the case here where this pericope has been assigned

---

[51] Ong, *Orality and Literacy*, 37; cf. Henderson, "Didache and Orality," 294 and Dewey, "Oral Methods," 37.

[52] It is recognized that this decision regarding the distinction between ἀλλὰ and ἀλλ᾽ is tenuous, but to maintain methodological consistency it has been decided to refrain from designating them as being in verbatim agreement with one another.

to a written Q because of the *shared content* between Matthew and Luke, *not* because of its level of verbatim agreement.[53]

1) The level of shared words (%SW) in sections 1 and 3 is much higher than the levels of %VB in the corresponding sections, due to both authors' use of similar terminology with which they tell their respective stories. Five of the shared words in section 3 that are not in verbatim agreement are based upon shared lexical roots, but that is not sufficient to meet our criterion for verbal agreement. It is difficult to make any definitive statement about the level of variability in this particular pericope due to the quite low number of overall words, and the even lower number of VB words. The sample size of these numbers is too low to justify their use in any definitive manner. Rather, in this case we can look at other factors in conjunction with the compiled statistics in our analysis of this pericope.

2) The variability within the pericope deserves further attention. In this case, we have an instance of variability around a series of fixed words and themes (peace, turmoil) followed by the expansion of the nature of the turmoil. It is noteworthy that the manner of the expansion is quite variable — man against father // father against son, daughter against mother // mother against daughter, daughter-in-law against mother-in-law // mother-in-law against daughter-in-law. For argument's sake, if we were to approach this tradition from the perspective of the two-source hypothesis and assume that Matthew and Luke had derived their accounts from a written Q source, then one of the authors (i.e., Matthew or Luke) has deliberately rearranged his source material. That is, the source material probably contained either daughter/mother followed by daughter-in-law/mother-in-law (the order represented by Matt), or the reverse, mother/daughter followed by mother-in-law/daughter-in-law. It would therefore be possible to explain the phenomena by means of a conscious editorial decision. However, we must ask whether the occurrence of this verbal variability around a stable thematic core can *only* be understood from a literary-critical perspective.

The first couplet in Matt 10:35 is man/father, while Luke employs father/son in his parallel tradition. Matthew's version contains an obvious parallel to Mic 7:6, although he uses the term ἄνθρωπον rather than the more logical "son" (בֵּן/ υἰὸς) which is found in the MT, LXX, *Gos. Thom.* 16:3b, and in Luke's parallel account (Luke 12:53). In this case, Luke's tradition fits more closely the stated analogy (father/son — mother/daughter — mother-in-law/daughter-in-law).

---

[53] The argument from order does not help in this case either. Matt 10:34–36//Luke 12:51–53 does not appear in the same relative order in Matthew and Luke's gospel, unlike the Centurion's Servant (Aland §85, see above), which appears in the same relative order in both Matthew and Luke.

Here we can see that the "oral hypothesis" is capable of providing an explanation of the present character of the tradition. From a *folkloristic* perspective, it is clear that these two traditions can be accounted for by the existence of this tradition in multiple forms (performances) that co-existed within the living communal traditions of the earliest Christian communities. We have here a fine example of the oral processes at work in this passage. It is apparent that the key term which forms the pivotal point for the antithetical language is εἰρήνην. This term has been used as the starting point for the pericope, and both authors have responded with a similar point, although expressing it in their own unique manner. In this case both Matthew and Luke use acceptable opposites to their shared use of the term εἰρήνην. Matthew's "sword" (μάχαιραν) and Luke's "division" (διαμερισμόν) are quite different opposites to "peace," but each term is appropriate to their respective author's account.

As for the three couplets in the body of the pericope, they can be explained by the desire for the storyteller to retain the traditional grouping of threes. In this case, the desire to express the tension among family members goes beyond the desire to transmit the tradition verbatim when retelling the story. Such is the way in which the ancient storyteller operated. From an oral tradition perspective, it would seem that the process of oral transmission had successfully retained what would be recognized by the hearer as vital — both stories would be viewed as synomymous with one another. As the hearer heard this story performed, he or she would have heard the antithesis between the ideal of peace and sword/division, and the natural expression of the division in three parts would conform to traditional expectations. In addition, Luke also employs the term division in three instances (Luke 12:51 — διαμερισμόν; 12:52 — διαμεμερισμένοι, 12:53 — διαμερισθήσονται). In conclusion, one must ask whether a redactional explanation is the only adequate means to describe the process that led to the tradition's extant form. The Matthean and Lukan versions of this pericope resemble the characteristic variability and stability that one would expect from an orally transmitted tradition.

4) As for the level of verbatim agreement, in this case, the overall level of agreement does correlate well with the level of internal variability within the pericope. The two sections containing parallel material (sections 1, 3) range in %VB from 10%/7% in section 3 (Matt/Luke), to 13%/14% in section 1 for both Matthew and Luke respectively.

6.6.6 Aland §279 — The Parable of the Great Supper

Table 11. Aland §279, Synoptic Text

	Matt 22	Luke 14
1 NP		[15] Ἀκούσας δέ τις τῶν συνανακειμένων ταῦτα εἶπεν αὐτῷ, Μακάριος ὅστις φάγεται ἄρτον ἐν τῇ βασιλείᾳ τοῦ θεοῦ.
	W=0/16, SW=0, OR=0, VB=0	
2	[1] καὶ ἀποκριθεὶς ὁ Ἰησοῦς πάλιν **εἶπεν** ἐν παραβολαῖς <u>αὐτοῖς</u> λέγων, [2] ὡμοιώθη ἡ βασιλεία τῶν οὐρανῶν <u>ἀνθρώπῳ</u> βασιλεῖ, ὅστις <u>ἐποίησεν</u> γάμους τῷ υἱῷ αὐτοῦ.	[16] ὁ δὲ **εἶπεν** <u>αὐτῷ</u>, <u>ἄνθρωπός</u> τις <u>ἐποίει</u> δεῖπνον μέγα, καὶ ἐκάλεσεν πολλούς,
	W=23/12, SW=5, OR=5, VB=2	
3	[3] **καὶ ἀπέστειλεν** <u>τοὺς δούλους</u> **αὐτοῦ** καλέσαι <u>τοὺς κεκλημένους</u> εἰς τοὺς γάμους, καὶ οὐκ ἤθελον ἐλθεῖν.	[17] **καὶ ἀπέστειλεν** <u>τὸν δοῦλον</u> **αὐτοῦ** τῇ ὥρᾳ τοῦ δείπνου εἰπεῖν <u>τοῖς κεκλημένοις</u>, ἔρχεσθε, ὅτι ἤδη ἕτοιμά ἐστιν. [18] καὶ ἤρξαντο ἀπὸ μιᾶς πάντες παραιτεῖσθαι.
	W=15/22, SW=7, OR=7, VB=3	
4 NP	[4] πάλιν ἀπέστειλεν ἄλλους δούλους λέγων, εἴπατε τοῖς κεκλημένοις, Ἰδοὺ τὸ ἄριστόν μου ἡτοίμακα, οἱ ταῦροί μου καὶ τὰ σιτιστὰ τεθυμένα, καὶ πάντα ἕτοιμα· δεῦτε εἰς τοὺς γάμους.	
	W=27/0, SW=0, OR=0, VB=0	
5	[5] οἱ δὲ ἀμελήσαντες ἀπῆλθον, ὃς μὲν εἰς τὸν ἴδιον **ἀγρόν**, ὃς δὲ ἐπὶ τὴν ἐμπορίαν αὐτοῦ· [6] οἱ δὲ λοιποὶ κρατήσαντες τοὺς δούλους	ὁ πρῶτος εἶπεν αὐτῷ, **ἀγρὸν** ἠγόρασα καὶ ἔχω ἀνάγκην ἐξελθὼν ἰδεῖν αὐτόν· ἐρωτῶ σε, ἔχε με παρῃτημένον. [19] καὶ ἕτερος εἶπεν, ζεύγη βοῶν ἠγόρασα πέντε καὶ

	Matt 22	Luke 14
	αὐτοῦ ὕβρισαν καὶ ἀπέκτειναν.	πορεύομαι δοκιμάσαι αὐτά· ἐρωτῶ σε, ἔχε με παρῃτημένον. [20] καὶ ἕτερος εἶπεν, Γυναῖκα ἔγημα καὶ διὰ τοῦτο οὐ δύναμαι ἐλθεῖν.
	W=26/42, SW=1, OR=1, VB=1	
6 NP		[21] καὶ παραγενόμενος ὁ δοῦλος ἀπήγγειλεν τῷ κυρίῳ αὐτοῦ ταῦτα.
	W=0/9, SW=0, OR=0, VB=0	
7	[7] ὁ δὲ βασιλεὺς ὠργίσθη, καὶ πέμψας τὰ στρατεύματα αὐτοῦ ἀπώλεσεν τοὺς φονεῖς ἐκείνους καὶ τὴν πόλιν αὐτῶν ἐνέπρησεν. [8] τότε λέγει <u>τοῖς δούλοις</u> **αὐτοῦ**, ὁ μὲν γάμος ἕτοιμός ἐστιν, οἱ δὲ κεκλημένοι οὐκ ἦσαν ἄξιοι·	τότε <u>ὀργισθεὶς</u> ὁ οἰκοδεσπότης εἶπεν <u>τῷ δούλῳ</u> **αὐτοῦ**,
	W=34/8, SW=4, OR=4, VB=1	
8	[9] πορεύεσθε οὖν ἐπὶ τὰς διεξόδους τῶν ὁδῶν, καὶ ὅσους ἐὰν εὕρητε καλέσατε εἰς τοὺς γάμους. [10] καὶ <u>ἐξελθόντες</u> οἱ δοῦλοι ἐκεῖνοι **εἰς τὰς ὁδοὺς** συνήγαγον πάντας οὓς εὗρον, πονηρούς τε καὶ ἀγαθούς· καὶ ἐπλήσθη ὁ γάμος ἀνακειμένων.	ἔξελθε ταχέως εἰς τὰς πλατείας καὶ ῥύμας τῆς πόλεως, καὶ τοὺς πτωχοὺς καὶ ἀναπείρους καὶ τυφλοὺς καὶ χωλοὺς εἰσάγαγε ὧδε. [22] καὶ εἶπεν ὁ δοῦλος, κύριε, γέγονεν ὃ ἐπέταξας, καὶ ἔτι τόπος ἐστίν. [23] καὶ εἶπεν ὁ κύριος πρὸς τὸν δοῦλον, <u>ἔξελθε</u> **εἰς τὰς ὁδοὺς** καὶ φραγμοὺς καὶ ἀνάγκασον εἰσελθεῖν, ἵνα γεμισθῇ μου ὁ οἶκος·
	W=36/53, SW=4, OR=4, VB=3	
9 NP	[11] εἰσελθὼν δὲ ὁ βασιλεὺς θεάσασθαι τοὺς ἀνακειμένους εἶδεν ἐκεῖ ἄνθρωπον οὐκ ἐνδεδυμένον ἔνδυμα γάμου· [12]	

Matt 22	Luke 14
καὶ λέγει αὐτῷ, ἑταῖρε, πῶς εἰσῆλθες ὧδε μὴ ἔχων ἔνδυμα γάμου· ὁ δὲ ἐφιμώθη. ¹³ τότε ὁ βασιλεὺς εἶπεν τοῖς διακόνοις, Δήσαντες αὐτοῦ πόδας καὶ χεῖρας ἐκβάλετε αὐτὸν εἰς τὸ σκότος τὸ ἐξώτερον· ἐκεῖ ἔσται ὁ κλαυθμὸς καὶ ὁ βρυγμὸς τῶν ὀδόντων.	
W=55/0, SW=0, OR=0, VB=0	

10	¹⁴ πολλοὶ **γάρ** εἰσιν κλητοὶ ὀλίγοι δὲ <u>ἐκλεκτοί.</u>	²⁴ λέγω **γὰρ** ὑμῖν ὅτι οὐδεὶς τῶν ἀνδρῶν ἐκείνων τῶν <u>κεκλημένων</u> γεύσεταί μου τοῦ δείπνου.
	W=7/14, SW=2, OR=2, VB=1	

Table 12. Aland §279, Statistical Summary

Sec. #	Wds (Mt)	Wds (Lk)	SW	OR	VB	%SW (Mt)	%SW (Lk)	%OR	%VB (Mt)	%VB (Lk)	%Mt	%Lk
1	0	16	0	0	0	0%	0%	0%	0%	0%	0%	9%
2	23	12	5	5	2	22%	42%	100%	9%	17%	10%	7%
3	15	22	7	7	3	47%	32%	100%	20%	14%	7%	13%
4	27	0	0	0	0	0%	0%	0%	0%	0%	12%	0%
5	26	42	1	1	1	4%	2%	100%	4%	2%	12%	24%
6	0	9	0	0	0	0%	0%	0%	0%	0%	0%	5%
7	34	8	4	4	1	12%	50%	100%	3%	13%	15%	5%
8	36	53	4	4	3	11%	8%	100%	8%	6%	16%	30%
9	55	0	0	0	0	0%	0%	0%	0%	0%	25%	0%
10	7	14	2	2	1	29%	14%	100%	14%	7%	3%	8%
TOT	223	176	23	23	11	10%	13%	100%	5%	6%		

Figure 16. Agreement, Sec. Length, Shared Words (Aland §279, Matt)

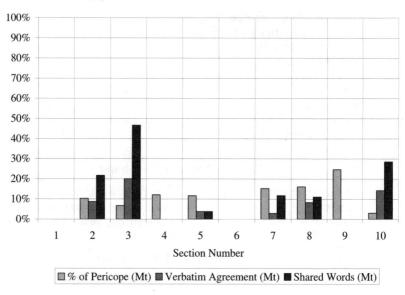

Figure 17. Agreement, Sec. Length, Shared Words (Aland §279, Luke)

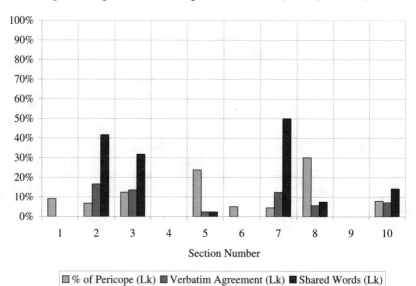

Figure 18. Agreement vs. Pericope Length (Aland §279)

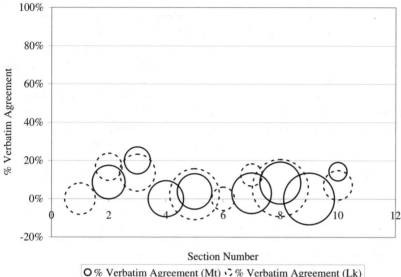

Section Number

O % Verbatim Agreement (Mt) ᴖ % Verbatim Agreement (Lk)

1) The overall level of agreement in this pericope is quite low, varying from 4%/2% in section 5 to 20%/14% in section 3. Figure 16 and Figure 17 illustrate the high %SW in sections 2, 3 (Matt and Luke) and section 7 of Luke. In all of these sections the %VB words is no greater than 50% of the overall %SW. Thus these sections have a level of shared content that is greater than the level of verbatim agreement alone might suggest. Figure 18 illustrates the relatively even distribution of words in the Matthean parallel, with the shortest sections 3 and 10 exhibiting the highest levels of verbatim agreement. The Lukan parallel exhibits a greater variation of section length, with the longest section (sec. 8) exhibiting a level of %VB almost equivalent to the Lukan average.

2) The NP sections (secs. 1, 4, 6, 9) are located primarily within the main body of the narrative, with the exception of section 1, which serves as the Lukan introduction to the parable. Both Matthew and Luke include two NP sections; the Matthean sections contain 37% of the overall Matthean parallel while the Lukan NP sections contain 14% of the overall Lukan length.

3) While both stories have striking similarities, the very low level of verbatim agreement makes the attribution of this pericope to a common source text (i.e., Q) less than certain. Even if both Matthew and Luke highly redacted a common source document, it would seem likely that they would share more vocabulary than that exhibited in the parallel texts. In

fact, Kloppenborg Verbin uses just such an argument in a section from *Excavating Q* entitled 'The Character and Reconstruction of Q." In evaluating previous statistical work by Bergemann, Kloppenborg Verbin suggests that "[a]ssuming that Matthew and Luke were independent in their use of a common source, random probability would predict that the two evangelists would agree on only 25 percent of the words of Q, since either Matthew or Luke could choose to retain the wording of the source or to vary it."[54] Even if Matthew and Luke "randomly" chose either to agree or disagree with a written source text, they would probably agree with their choice of language more often than they do in this pericope. Despite the low levels of agreement in this pericope, sections of it are still included in IQP's *Critical Edition of Q*.[55] Selected sections of Matthew and Luke are included in the reconstructed text. The English of the reconstructed text is as follows:

A certain person prepared a [[large]] dinner, [[and invited many]]. And he sent his slave [[at the time of the dinner]] to say to the invited: Come, for it is now ready. <<One declined because of his>> farm. <<Another declined because of his business>>. <<And the slave went away. He said <> these things to his master.>> Then the householder, enraged, said to his slave go out on the roads, and whomever you find, invite, so that my house may be filled.

---

[54] Kloppenborg, *Excavating Q*, 62–63. Kloppenborg Verbin uses this argument in his critique of Bergemann's work. In particular, Kloppenborg takes issue with Bergemann's rigid use of verbatim agreement as the only significant criterion to either assign or reject a pericope from "Q." Here Kloppenborg uses the "25 percent" argument to suggest that two authors could independently use a common source text and still exhibit a low percentage of agreement. Therefore, verbatim agreement should not be used as the primary criterion for determining the scope of Q. We fail to recognize the significance of such an observation. As Kloppenborg himself makes clear, Matthew and Luke did not "randomly" choose words from their source text. Therefore, one should expect *higher* levels of verbatim agreement in the double tradition than the 25% level that "random choice" would dictate. In the course of the same argument, Kloppenborg states that "[t]he fact that some pericopae display lower agreement does not mean that they are automatically to be excluded from Q; it only means that, as expected, sometimes either Matthew or Luke (or both) chose to vary the wording of their sources" (*Excavating Q*, 64). It seems that, in this instance, the argument changes shape to suit whatever twists and turns are encountered along the road. If 25% "random probability" is what we should expect (which we should not), then what are we to do with a pericope such as the one currently under discussion (Aland §279) since the overall agreement is *below* 5%? If this level of verbatim agreement is not low enough to discount it from inclusion into Q, what is? It is clear that other considerations are more important in determining the scope of Q than verbatim agreement.

[55] The *Critical Edition of Q* includes portions of this pericope in Q. For those familiar with the sigla of the synopsis, it is summarized as Q 14:~~15~~, 16–18, ?19–20?, 21, ~~22~~, 23, ~~24~~. In sum, the introduction to Luke's parallel (Luke 14:15) is not included, nor are any of the more interesting details from either Matthew or Luke.

Text enclosed within double brackets "[[ ]]" indicates that this is included in the reconstructed text, although it is "rated" a {C} in following with the UBS[4] ratings system of {A}-{D}. Text enclosed within the double arrows "<< >>" is considered "pre-critical" in that it exists in only one Gospel, and represents the use of the Q "text" by only one Gospel author. If the questionable sections of the reconstructed text are removed, the text loses even more of the detail that it has in its reconstructed form. What remains then is "A certain person prepared a dinner. And he sent his slave to say to the invited: come, for it is now ready. One declined because of his farm. Another declined because of his business. And the slave went away. He said these things to his master. Then the householder, enraged, said to his slave go out on the roads, and whomever you find, invite, so that my house may be filled." Even this shortened version of the Q pericope contains uncertainty, for the two excuse clauses (<<One declined because of his>>, <<Another declined because of his business>>) although considered "pre-critical" are vital for the overall coherence of the story itself. Apart from these pre-critical clauses the story would not make any sense. It is understandable that there is hesitancy over the confident attribution of these verses to "Q," but, in this case, if Q is to be useful as a *coherent story,* something must be assigned to the Q text itself.

One must ask of the likelihood that the story as it is reconstructed by the *IQP* is closer to the original performance than either the Matthean or Lukan parallels. In a communal setting where oral performers and storytellers are highly valued, the reconstructed Q pericope would not have been as memorable for those in the listening audience as either the Matthean or Lukan versions of the tradition. The very details that would have made for an exciting story have been excised from the text — the oxen (Matt 22:4, Luke 14:19), the fatted calves (Matt 22:4), an enraged king with soldiers (Matt 22:7), and other details. All these details would have made for an exciting storytelling experience and the tradition as such would be adopted by a performer seeking approval from his/her audience.[56] Under the two-source hypothesis, these details would be understood as the product of Matthew and Luke's redactional or authorial

---

[56] Isidore Okpewho highlights the desire for a performer to appeal to his/her audience: "Herein, then, lie two of the principal factors motivating the delivery of the text of oral literature: one, the performers are anxious to say things that will please the ears of their audiences, that will be 'good music' to their ears, so to speak . . ." (Okpewho, *African Oral Literature*, 70). Dunn also notes the importance of this dimension of storytelling. He cites Funk and Hoover, *Five Gospels*, 300 — "[s]ince the words ascribed to Jesus vary, and since there is nothing distinctive about them, we must assume they were created by storytellers," and then rightly proceeds to ask, "[why] would story-tellers create such unmemorable words, and why then would they be held constant in other retellings?" (*Remembered*, 214).

activity. However, from an oral performance perspective, it seems unlikely that the Q version of this tradition would have been written in the first place, particularly if the tradition is older than the canonical Gospels and therefore closer to the oral milieu of the first century.

A quick glance at *Gos. Thom.* 64 is helpful for it suggests that even a "sayings source" would be concerned to present a parable in a form that would appeal to an audience. The *Gos. Thom.* account includes a reasonably complete version of this tradition, much fuller than the reconstructed Q 14:16–18, ?19–20?, 21, 23. The Q pericope contains a total of 62 words (including the pre-critical excuse clauses) while the *Thomas* version retells the same account with 146 words. *Thomas* includes the excuse clauses as does Luke,[57] and both Luke and Thomas have presented these excuses in a traditional triadic form that is fully compatible with that of an oral performance.[58] If the *Gos. Thom.* contains vivid imagery that would appeal to an early Christian audience, it forces us to ask whether "Q," in contrast to *Thomas,* would contain such an underwhelming narrative.

4) In summary, the little verbatim agreement between the Matthean and Lukan versions is once again overshadowed by the extreme diversity of their language. While both parallels are clearly depicting the same story, it seems in this case that oral performance can provide sufficient explanatory power to account for the great diversity that exists between the two extant versions of this pericope. Both parallels are clearly depicting the same event, and the great diversity between the two traditions can be explicated by an appeal to its multiform existence as a performance unit within the context of early Christian community.

6.7   Group "B" Pericopes

6.7.1   Aland §89 — On Following Jesus

Table 13. Aland §89, Synoptic Text

	Matt 8	Luke 9
1 NP	[18] Ἰδὼν δὲ ὁ Ἰησοῦς ὄχλον περὶ αὐτὸν ἐκέλευσεν ἀπελθεῖν εἰς τὸ πέραν.	

---

[57] Thomas' three excuse clauses are: 1) "I have bought a house," 2) "my friend is to be married," and 3) "I have bought an estate and I am going to collect the rent" (*Gos. Thom.* 64).

[58] Cf. Aland §102, above, where Luke also employs a traditional grouping of threes.

	Matt 8	Luke 9
	W=12/0, SW=0, OR=0, VB=0	
2 CORE	[19] **καὶ προσελθὼν εἷς γραμματεὺς εἶπεν** <u>αὐτῷ</u>, **διδάσκαλε, ἀκολουθήσω σοι ὅπου ἐὰν ἀπέρχῃ.** [20] **καὶ** <u>λέγει</u> **αὐτῷ ὁ᾽Ιησοῦς, αἱ ἀλώπεκες φωλεοὺς ἔχουσιν καὶ τὰ πετεινὰ τοῦ οὐρανοῦ κατασκηνώσεις, ὁ δὲ υἱὸς τοῦ ἀνθρώπου οὐκ ἔχει ποῦ τὴν κεφαλὴν κλίνῃ.**	[57] **καὶ πορευομένων αὐτῶν ἐν τῇ ὁδῷ εἶπέν τις πρὸς** <u>αὐτόν</u>, **ἀκολουθήσω σοι ὅπου ἐὰν ἀπέρχῃ.** [58] **καὶ** <u>εἶπεν</u> **αὐτῷ ὁ᾽Ιησοῦς, αἱ ἀλώπεκες φωλεοὺς ἔχουσιν καὶ τὰ πετεινὰ τοῦ οὐρανοῦ κατασκηνώσεις, ὁ δὲ υἱὸς τοῦ ἀνθρώπου οὐκ ἔχει ποῦ τὴν κεφαλὴν κλίνῃ.**
	W=38/41, SW=34, OR=34, VB=32	
3	[21] <u>ἕτερος</u> **δὲ τῶν μαθητῶν [αὐτοῦ] εἶπεν αὐτῷ, κύριε, ἐπίτρεψόν μοι πρῶτον** <u>ἀπελθεῖν</u> **καὶ θάψαι τὸν πατέρα μου.**	[59] εἶπεν δὲ πρὸς <u>ἕτερον</u>, ἀκολούθει μοι. ὁ δὲ **εἶπεν,** [κύριε,] **ἐπίτρεψόν μοι** <u>ἀπελθόντι</u> **πρῶτον θάψαι τὸν πατέρα μου.**
	W=16/17, SW=11, OR=10, VB=9	
4	[22] **ὁ δὲ᾽Ιησοῦς** <u>λέγει</u> **αὐτῷ, ἀκολούθει μοι, καὶ ἄφες τοὺς νεκροὺς θάψαι τοὺς ἑαυτῶν νεκρούς.**	[60] <u>εἶπεν</u> **δὲ** <u>αὐτῷ</u>, **ἄφες τοὺς νεκροὺς θάψαι τοὺς ἑαυτῶν νεκρούς,** σὺ δὲ ἀπελθὼν διάγγελλε τὴν βασιλείαν τοῦ θεοῦ.
	W=15/18, SW=10, OR=9, VB=9	
5 NP		[61] εἶπεν δὲ καὶ ἕτερος, ἀκολουθήσω σοι, κύριε· πρῶτον δὲ ἐπίτρεψόν μοι ἀποτάξασθαι τοῖς εἰς τὸν οἶκόν μου. [62] εἶπεν δὲ ὁ Ιησοῦς, οὐδεὶς ἐπιβαλὼν τὴν χεῖρα ἐπ᾽ ἄροτρον καὶ βλέπων εἰς τὰ ὀπίσω εὔθετός ἐστιν τῇ βασιλείᾳ τοῦ θεοῦ.
	W=0/38, SW=0, OR=0, VB=0	

Table 14. Aland §89, Statistical Summary

Sec. #	Wds (Mt)	Wds (Lk)	SW	OR	VB	%SW (Mt)	%SW (Lk)	%OR	%VB (Mt)	%VB (Lk)	%Mt	%Lk
1	12	0	0	0	0	0%	0%	0%	0%	0%	15%	0%
2	38	41	34	34	32	89%	83%	100%	84%	78%	47%	36%
3	16	17	11	10	9	69%	65%	91%	56%	53%	20%	15%
4	15	18	10	9	9	67%	56%	90%	60%	50%	19%	16%
5	0	38	0	0	0	0%	0%	0%	0%	0%	0%	33%
TOT	*81*	*114*	*55*	*53*	*50*	*68%*	*48%*	*96%*	*62%*	*44%*		

Figure 19. Agreement, Sec. Length, Shared Words (Aland §89, Matt)

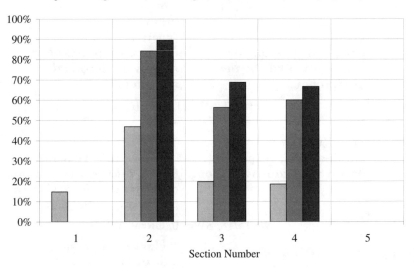

Figure 20. Agreement, Sec. Length, Shared Words (Aland §89, Luke)

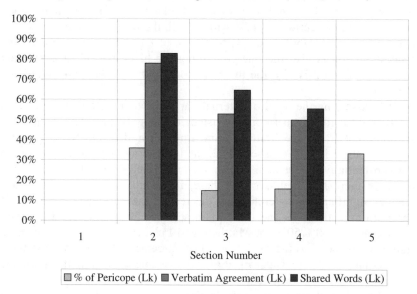

Figure 21. Agreement vs. Pericope Length (Aland §89)

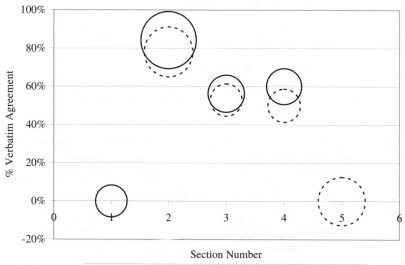

1) In this pericope, the NP sections occur in the introduction (sec. 1; Matt 8:18) and the conclusion (sec. 5; Luke 9:61–62). The main body consists of three sections (sec. 2–4) in which the level of agreement varies from a low of 60%/50% (sec. 4) to a high of 84%/78% in section 2. The longest section is also the one containing the highest level of agreement (sec. 2). Section 2 is also the thematic core, and extends for 47%/36% of the pericope.

2) In assessing the level of internal variability, we note that the overall %VB is 48% for the pericope as listed in Table 13 and without the NP sections that frame the Matthean and Lukan parallels the %VB is 69%. Although there is a core in section 2, the level of agreement in that core is not substantially higher than that in sections 3 and 4, which suggests that although there is a thematic core here, it has not been transmitted in a manner significantly different than the rest of the pericope. The level of verbatim agreement for the three main sections 2, 3, and 4 is 84%/78%, 56%/53%, and 60%/50% for Matthew and Luke respectively. All of these figures correspond to the overall level of agreement. In this case the level of internal variability suggests that the agreements within the pericope occur in a relatively consistent manner.

3) The NP sections occur at the beginning of the Matthean parallel, and at the end of the Lukan text, serving as the introduction and conclusion to the pericope.

6.7.2 Aland §107 — Jesus concerning John

Table 15. Aland §107, Synoptic Text

	Matt 11	Luke 7
1	⁷ τούτων δὲ πορευομένων ἤρξατο ὁ Ιησοῦς λέγειν τοῖς ὄχλοις περὶ ᾽Ιωάννου,	²⁴ ᾽Απελθόντων δὲ τῶν ἀγγέλων ᾽Ιωάννου ἤρξατο λέγειν πρὸς τοὺς ὄχλους περὶ ᾽Ιωάννου,
	W=11/12, SW=7, OR=7, VB=5	
2	τί ἐξήλθατε εἰς τὴν ἔρημον θεάσασθαὶ κάλαμον ὑπὸ ἀνέμου σαλευόμενὸν	τί ἐξήλθατε εἰς τὴν ἔρημον θεάσασθαὶ κάλαμον ὑπὸ ἀνέμου σαλευόμενὸν
	W=10/10, SW=10, OR=10, VB=10	
3	⁸ ἀλλὰ τί ἐξήλθατε ἰδεῖν ἄνθρωπον ἐν μαλακοῖς ἠμφιεσμένὸν ἰδοὺ οἱ τὰ μαλακὰ φοροῦντες	²⁵ ἀλλὰ τί ἐξήλθατε ἰδεῖν ἄνθρωπον ἐν μαλακοῖς ἱματίοις ἠμφιεσμένὸν ἰδοὺ οἱ ἐν ἱματισμῷ ἐνδόξῳ

	Matt 11	Luke 7
	ἐν τοῖς οἴκοις τῶν βασιλέων εἰσίν.	καὶ τρυφῇ ὑπάρχοντες ἐν τοῖς βασιλείοις εἰσίν.
	W=19/21, SW=14, OR=14, VB=13	
4	⁹ ἀλλὰ τί ἐξήλθατε ἰδεῖν προφήτην ναί, λέγω ὑμῖν, καὶ περισσότερον προφήτου.	²⁶ ἀλλὰ τί ἐξήλθατε ἰδεῖν προφήτην ναί, λέγω ὑμῖν, καὶ περισσότερον προφήτου.
	W=11/11, SW=11, OR=11, VB=11	
5	¹⁰ οὗτός ἐστιν περὶ οὗ γέγραπται, Ἰδοὺ ἐγὼ ἀποστέλλω τὸν ἄγγελόν μου πρὸ προσώπου σου, ὃς κατασκευάσει τὴν ὁδόν σου ἔμπροσθέν σου.	²⁷ οὗτός ἐστιν περὶ οὗ γέγραπται, Ἰδοὺ ἀποστέλλω τὸν ἄγγελόν μου πρὸ προσώπου σου, ὃς κατασκευάσει τὴν ὁδόν σου ἔμπροσθέν σου.
	W=21/20, SW=20, OR=20, VB=20	
6	¹¹ Ἀμὴν λέγω ὑμῖν, οὐκ ἐγήγερται ἐν γεννητοῖς γυναικῶν μείζων Ἰωάννου τοῦ βαπτιστοῦ·	²⁸ λέγω ὑμῖν, μείζων ἐν γεννητοῖς γυναικῶν Ἰωάννου οὐδείς ἐστιν·
	W=12/9, SW=7, OR=6, VB=7	
7	ὁ δὲ μικρότερος ἐν τῇ βασιλείᾳ τῶν οὐρανῶν μείζων αὐτοῦ ἐστιν.	ὁ δὲ μικρότερος ἐν τῇ βασιλείᾳ τοῦ θεοῦ μείζων αὐτοῦ ἐστιν.
	W=11/11, SW=10, OR=10, VB=9	
8 NP	¹² ἀπὸ δὲ τῶν ἡμερῶν Ἰωάννου τοῦ βαπτιστοῦ ἕως ἄρτι ἡ βασιλεία τῶν οὐρανῶν βιάζεται, καὶ βιασταὶ ἁρπάζουσιν αὐτήν. ¹³ πάντες γὰρ οἱ προφῆται καὶ ὁ νόμος ἕως Ἰωάννου ἐπροφήτευσαν· ¹⁴ καὶ εἰ θέλετε δέξασθαι, αὐτός ἐστιν Ἡλίας ὁ μέλλων ἔρχεσθαι. ¹⁵ ὁ ἔχων ὦτα ἀκουέτω.	cp. 16.16a
	W=42/0, SW=0, OR=0, VB=0	

	Matt 11	Luke 7
9 NP	cp. 21.31b-32	(^{29} καὶ πᾶς ὁ λαὸς ἀκούσας καὶ οἱ τελῶναι ἐδικαίωσαν τὸν θεόν, βαπτισθέντες τὸ βάπτισμα Ἰωάννου· ^{30} οἱ δὲ Φαρισαῖοι καὶ οἱ νομικοὶ τὴν βουλὴν τοῦ θεοῦ ἠθέτησαν εἰς ἑαυτούς, μὴ βαπτισθέντες ὑπ αὐτοῦ.)
	W=0/32, SW=0, OR=0, VB=0	
10	^{16} τίνι δὲ ὁμοιώσω τὴν γενεὰν ταύτην ὁμοία ἐστὶν **παιδίοις καθημένοις** ἐν ταῖς ἀγοραῖς ἃ προσφωνοῦντα τοῖς ἑτέροις	^{31} τίνι οὖν ὁμοιώσω τοὺς ἀνθρώπους τῆς γενεᾶς ταύτης, καὶ τίνι εἰσὶν ὅμοιοί ^{32} ὅμοιοί εἰσιν **παιδίοις** τοῖς ἐν ἀγορᾷ **καθημένοις** καὶ προσφωνοῦσιν ἀλλήλοις,
	W=17/22, SW=14, OR=12, VB=6	
11	^{17} **λέγουσιν, ηὐλήσαμεν ὑμῖν καὶ οὐκ ὠρχήσασθε· ἐθρηνήσαμεν καὶ οὐκ** ἐκόψασθε.	ἃ λέγει, **ηὐλήσαμεν ὑμῖν καὶ οὐκ ὠρχήσασθε· ἐθρηνήσαμεν καὶ οὐκ** ἐκλαύσατε.
	W=10/11, SW=10, OR=10, VB=9	
12	18 ἦλθεν γὰρ Ἰωάννης **μήτε ἐσθίων μήτε πίνων, καὶ** λέγουσιν, **δαιμόνιον ἔχει·**	33 ἐλήλυθεν γὰρ Ἰωάννης ὁ βαπτιστὴς μὴ **ἐσθίων** ἄρτον **μήτε πίνων** οἶνον, **καὶ** λέγετε, **δαιμόνιον ἔχει·**
	W=11/15, SW=11, OR=11, VB=8	
13	19 ἦλθεν ὁ **υἱὸς τοῦ ἀνθρώπου ἐσθίων καὶ πίνων, καὶ** λέγουσιν, **Ἰδοὺ ἄνθρωπος φάγος καὶ οἰνοπότης,** τελωνῶν **φίλος καὶ ἁμαρτωλῶν.**	34 ἐλήλυθεν ὁ **υἱὸς τοῦ ἀνθρώπου ἐσθίων καὶ πίνων, καὶ** λέγετε, **Ἰδοὺ ἄνθρωπος φάγος καὶ οἰνοπότης, φίλος** τελωνῶν **καὶ ἁμαρτωλῶν.**
	W=19/19, SW=17, OR=15, VB=15	
14	**καὶ ἐδικαιώθη ἡ σοφία ἀπὸ** τῶν ἔργων **αὐτῆς.**	35 **καὶ ἐδικαιώθη ἡ σοφία ἀπὸ** πάντων τῶν τέκνων **αὐτῆς.**
	W=8/9, SW=7, OR=7, VB=7	

Table 16. Aland §107, Statistical Summary

Sec. #	Wds (Mt)	Wds (Lk)	SW	OR	VB	%SW (Mt)	%SW (Lk)	%OR	%VB (Mt)	%VB (Lk)	%Mt	%Lk
1	11	12	7	7	5	64%	58%	100%	45%	42%	5%	6%
2	10	10	10	10	10	100%	100%	100%	100%	100%	5%	5%
3	19	21	14	14	13	74%	67%	100%	68%	62%	9%	10%
4	11	11	11	11	11	100%	100%	100%	100%	100%	5%	5%
5	21	20	20	20	20	95%	100%	100%	95%	100%	10%	10%
6	12	9	7	6	7	58%	78%	86%	58%	78%	6%	4%
7	11	11	10	10	9	91%	91%	100%	82%	82%	5%	5%
8	42	0	0	0	0	0%	0%	0%	0%	0%	21%	0%
9	0	32	0	0	0	0%	0%	0%	0%	0%	0%	16%
10	17	22	14	12	6	82%	64%	86%	35%	27%	8%	11%
11	10	11	10	10	9	100%	91%	100%	90%	82%	5%	5%
12	11	15	11	11	8	100%	73%	100%	73%	53%	5%	7%
13	19	19	17	15	15	89%	89%	88%	79%	79%	9%	9%
14	8	9	7	7	7	88%	78%	100%	88%	78%	4%	4%
TOT	202	202	138	133	120	68%	68%	96%	59%	59%		

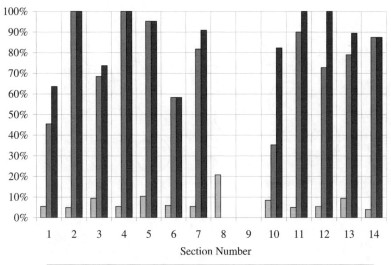

Figure 22. Agreement, Sec. Length, Shared Words (Aland §107, Matt)

□ % of Pericope (Mt)   ■ Verbatim Agreement (Mt)   ■ Shared Words (Mt)

Figure 23. Agreement, Sec. Length, Shared Words (Aland §107, Luke)

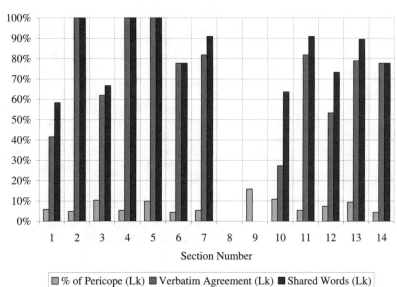

Section Number

☐ % of Pericope (Lk)   ▣ Verbatim Agreement (Lk)   ■ Shared Words (Lk)

Figure 24. Agreement vs. Pericope Length (Aland §107)

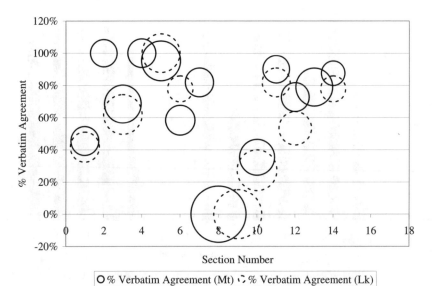

Section Number

O % Verbatim Agreement (Mt)   ʘ % Verbatim Agreement (Lk)

1) Apart from the introductory section 1, the first half of the pericope (sections 2–7) exhibits an overall high level of agreement, ranging from 68%/62% (sec. 3) to 100%/100% (secs. 2, 4). The high level of agreement resumes following section 10 and continues through the remainder of the pericope.

2) Section 10 immediately follows ὁ ἔχων ὦτα ἀκουέτω which concludes the previous section. The NP sections (secs. 8, 9) occur within the main body of the pericope and serve as a transition between two halves of the pericope. There is a marked difference in the character of the agreement following section 10. Beginning in section 10, there is a clear increase in the number of SW in relation to the %VB. Section 10 contains only 6 VB words, but 14 shared words. This trend continues for sections 11–13. Therefore, it appears that Matt 11:16//Luke 7:31 marks the beginning of the second half of the pericope, in which either Matthew or Luke (or both) have edited their source material in a manner different than they did in the first half of the story. The high level of overall agreement seems to be the clear work of editorial activity, most likely the result of the direct appropriation of material derived from a common source text.

3) The overall level of verbatim agreement in the pericope as listed in Table 15 is 59%, and if one examines the tradition apart from sections 8 and 9 then the overall level of agreement rises to 73%. If one considers that this pericope might have been two separate traditions that have been linked together by the NP sections (as suggested by the significantly different character of sections 1–7 and 10–14), then the higher level of agreement (72%) accurately reflects the level of agreement in each of the individual sections of the pericope.

6.7.3 Aland §109 — Jesus' Thanksgiving to the Father

Table 17. Aland §109, Synoptic Text

	Matt 11	Luke 10
1	^{25} Ἐν ἐκείνῳ τῷ καιρῷ ἀποκριθεὶς ὁ Ἰησοῦς εἶπεν, ἐξομολογοῦμαί σοι, πάτερ, κύριε τοῦ οὐρανοῦ καὶ τῆς γῆς, ὅτι ἔκρυψας ταῦτα ἀπὸ σοφῶν καὶ συνετῶν καὶ ἀπεκάλυψας αὐτὰ νηπίοις· ^{26} ναί, ὁ πατήρ, ὅτι οὕτως εὐδοκία ἐγένετο ἔμπροσθέν σου.	^{21} Ἐν αὐτῇ τῇ ὥρᾳ ἠγαλλιάσατο ἐν τῷ πνεύματι τῷ ἁγίῳ καὶ εἶπεν, ἐξομολογοῦμαί σοι, πάτερ, κύριε τοῦ οὐρανοῦ καὶ τῆς γῆς, ὅτι ἀπέκρυψας ταῦτα ἀπὸ σοφῶν καὶ συνετῶν, καὶ ἀπεκάλυψας αὐτὰ νηπίοις· ναί, ὁ πατήρ, ὅτι οὕτως εὐδοκία ἐγένετο ἔμπροσθέν σου.

	Matt 11	Luke 10
	W=37/41, SW=30, OR=30, VB=30	
2	[27] **Πάντα μοι παρεδόθη ὑπὸ τοῦ πατρός μου, καὶ οὐδεὶς** ἐπιγινώσκει <u>τὸν υἱὸν</u> **εἰ μὴ ὁ πατήρ,** οὐδὲ <u>τὸν πατέρα</u> τις ἐπιγινώσκει **εἰ μὴ ὁ υἱὸς καὶ ᾧ ἐὰν βούληται ὁ υἱὸς ἀποκαλύψαι.**	[22] **Πάντα μοι παρεδόθη ὑπὸ τοῦ πατρός μου, καὶ οὐδεὶς** γινώσκει τίς ἐστιν <u>ὁ υἱὸς</u> **εἰ μὴ ὁ πατήρ,** καὶ τίς ἐστιν <u>ὁ πατὴρ</u> **εἰ μὴ ὁ υἱὸς καὶ ᾧ ἐὰν βούληται ὁ υἱὸς ἀποκαλύψαι.**
	W=32/34, SW=29, OR=29, VB=24	

Table 18. Aland §109, Statistical Summary

Sec. #	Wds (Mt)	Wds (Lk)	SW	OR	VB	%SW (Mt)	%SW (Lk)	%OR	%VB (Mt)	%VB (Lk)	%Mt	%Lk
1	37	41	30	30	30	81%	73%	100%	81%	73%	54%	55%
2	32	34	29	29	24	91%	85%	100%	75%	71%	46%	45%
TOT	69	75	59	59	54	86%	79%	100%	78%	72%		

Figure 25. Agreement, Sec. Length, Shared Words (Aland §109, Matt)

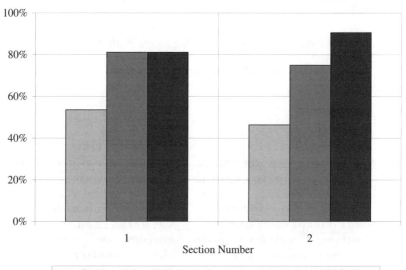

Figure 26. Agreement, Sec. Length, Shared Words (Aland §109, Luke)

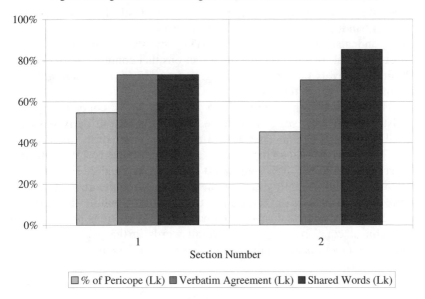

Section Number

☐ % of Pericope (Lk) ■ Verbatim Agreement (Lk) ■ Shared Words (Lk)

Figure 27. Agreement vs. Pericope Length (Aland §109)

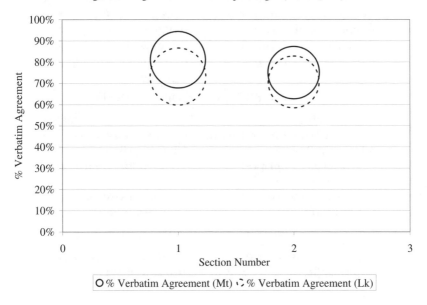

Section Number

O % Verbatim Agreement (Mt) ↻ % Verbatim Agreement (Lk)

1) This pericope displays a high level of internal consistency. Figure 27 reveals that Matthew and Luke are almost identical. The corresponding Matthean and Lukan bubbles for each section almost share the same center, and also are similar in area. This reveals that the parallels are almost identical. In addition, the three sections that contain parallel content exhibit high levels of agreement, ranging from 75%/71% (section 2) to a high of 81%/73% (section 1).

2) In summary, the overall high level of %VB coupled with the consistent %Mt/%Lk suggests that this story was indeed derived from a shared written source that extended for the entire length of the pericope.

3) The overall level of agreement for the pericope is 75%, which is almost identical to the individual %VB for sections 1 and 2. This indicates that the internal variability within the pericope is quite low. A look at Figure 27 confirms this observation — the area of the bubbles in sections 1 and 2 are almost identical, which indicates that the sections are comprised of an almost equal percentage of overall words in the pericope, and the level of agreement is also quite similar in both Matthew and Luke in those same sections.

6.7.4   Aland §120 — The Return of the Evil Spirit

Table 19. Aland §120, Synoptic Text

	Matt 12	Luke 11
1	[43]"Οταν δὲ τὸ ἀκάθαρτον πνεῦμα ἐξέλθῃ ἀπὸ τοῦ ἀνθρώπου, διέρχεται δῑ ἀνύδρων τόπων ζητοῦν ἀνάπαυσιν, καὶ <u>οὐχ</u> εὑρίσκει.	[24]"Οταν τὸ ἀκάθαρτον πνεῦμα ἐξέλθῃ ἀπὸ τοῦ ἀνθρώπου, διέρχεται δῑ ἀνύδρων τόπων ζητοῦν ἀνάπαυσιν, καὶ <u>μὴ</u> εὑρίσκον
	W=18/17, SW=17, OR=17, VB=15	
2	[44] τότε λέγει, εἰς τὸν οἶκόν μου ἐπιστρέψω ὅθεν ἐξῆλθον καὶ ἐλθὸν εὑρίσκει σχολάζοντα σεσαρωμένον καὶ κεκοσμημένον.	λέγει, ὑποστρέψω εἰς τὸν οἶκόν μου ὅθεν ἐξῆλθον [25] καὶ ἐλθὸν εὑρίσκει σεσαρωμένον καὶ κεκοσμημένον.
	W=16/14, SW=13, OR=13, VB=13	
3	[45] τότε πορεύεται καὶ παραλαμβάνει μεθ᾽ ἑαυτοῦ	[26] τότε πορεύεται καὶ παραλαμβάνει

Matt 12	Luke 11
ἑπτὰ ἕτερα πνεύματα πονηρότερα ἑαυτοῦ, καὶ εἰσελθόντα κατοικεῖ ἐκεῖ·	ἕτερα πνεύματα πονηρότερα ἑαυτοῦ ἑπτά, καὶ εἰσελθόντα κατοικεῖ ἐκεῖ,
W=15/13, SW=13, OR=12, VB=13	
4 καὶ γίνεται τὰ ἔσχατα τοῦ ἀνθρώπου ἐκείνου χείρονα τῶν πρώτων.	καὶ γίνεται τὰ ἔσχατα τοῦ ἀνθρώπου ἐκείνου χείρονα τῶν πρώτων.
W=10/10, SW=10, OR=10, VB=10	
5 οὕτως ἔσται καὶ τῇ γενεᾷ NP ταύτῃ τῇ πονηρᾷ.	
W=8/0, SW=0, OR=0, VB=0	

Table 20. Aland §120, Statistical Summary

Sec. #	Wds (Mt)	Wds (Lk)	SW	OR	VB	%SW (Mt)	%SW (Lk)	%OR	%VB (Mt)	%VB (Lk)	%Mt	%Lk
1	18	17	17	17	15	94%	100%	100%	83%	88%	27%	31%
2	16	14	13	13	13	81%	93%	100%	81%	93%	24%	26%
3	15	13	13	12	13	87%	100%	92%	87%	100%	22%	24%
4	10	10	10	10	10	100%	100%	100%	100%	100%	15%	19%
5	8	0	0	0	0	0%	0%	0%	0%	0%	12%	0%
TOT	67	54	53	52	51	79%	98%	98%	76%	94%		

Figure 28. Agreement, Sec. Length, Shared Words (Aland §120, Matt)

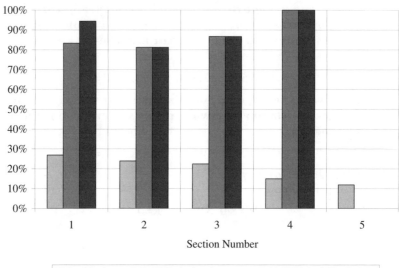

Figure 29. Agreement, Sec. Length, Shared Words (Aland §120, Luke)

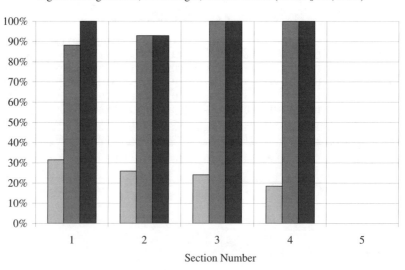

Figure 30. Agreement vs. Pericope Length (Aland §120)

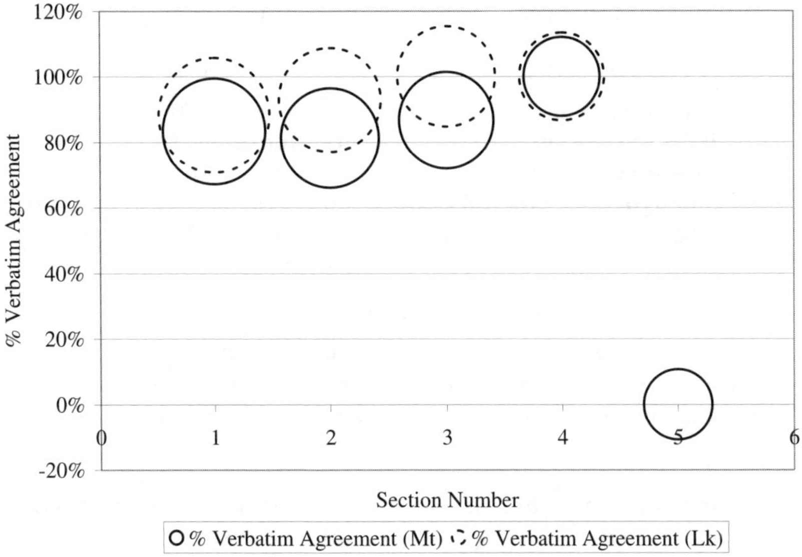

O % Verbatim Agreement (Mt) ⊃ % Verbatim Agreement (Lk)

1) This pericope is quite similar to Aland §109 in that the overall level of agreement in the parallel sections is extremely high, ranging from 81% (section 2, Matt) to 100% (section 4). In addition, the length of each of the parallel sections is almost the same, with Luke and Matthew each containing a few additional, non-parallel words in sections 1–3. Almost all of the words in common between Matthew and Luke in sections 1–4 are verbatim, and there are only two words which are SW that are not also verbatim.

2) Once again, the NP section 5 is included at the end of the Matthean parallel, and functions as a conclusion to the pericope. The high level of VB in the whole of the pericope coupled with its absence in Luke raises the possibility that section 5 might be a Matthean editorial addition to the end of his source material. In this pericope, the distribution of the VB words is relatively uniform in sections 1–4.

3) Here the overall level of agreement (84%) is quite similar to that exhibited in sections 1–4 of the pericope, and as such, accurately reflects the level of internal variability in the story. That is, there is very little variation in the tradition, and given the long sections of practically verbatim agreement, we can see clearly the strength that the literary paradigm has in accounting for the extant form of this tradition.

6.7.5   Aland §285 — Jesus' Lament over Jerusalem

Table 21. Aland §285, Synoptic Text

	Matt 23	Luke 13
1	[37] Ἰερουσαλὴμ Ἰερουσαλήμ, ἡ ἀποκτείνουσα τοὺς προφήτας καὶ λιθοβολοῦσα τοὺς ἀπεσταλμένους πρὸς αὐτήν,	[34] Ἰερουσαλὴμ Ἰερουσαλήμ, ἡ ἀποκτείνουσα τοὺς προφήτας καὶ λιθοβολοῦσα τοὺς ἀπεσταλμένους πρὸς αὐτήν,
	W=12/12, SW=12, OR=12, VB=12	
2	ποσάκις ἠθέλησα ἐπισυναγαγεῖν τὰ τέκνα σου, ὃν τρόπον ὄρνις ἐπισυνάγει τὰ νοσσία αὐτῆς ὑπὸ τὰς πτέρυγας, καὶ οὐκ ἠθελήσατε.	ποσάκις ἠθέλησα ἐπισυνάξαι τὰ τέκνα σου ὃν τρόπον ὄρνις τὴν ἑαυτῆς νοσσιὰν ὑπὸ τὰς πτέρυγας, καὶ οὐκ ἠθελήσατε.
	W=19/18, SW=16, OR=16, VB=14	
3	[38] ἰδοὺ ἀφίεται ὑμῖν ὁ οἶκος ὑμῶν ἔρημος. [39] λέγω γὰρ ὑμῖν, οὐ μή με ἴδητε ἀπ᾽ ἄρτι ἕως ἂν εἴπητε, εὐλογημένος ὁ ἐρχόμενος ἐν ὀνόματι κυρίου.	[35] ἰδοὺ ἀφίεται ὑμῖν ὁ οἶκος ὑμῶν. λέγω [δὲ] ὑμῖν, οὐ μὴ ἴδητέ με ἕως [ἥξει ὅτε] εἴπητε, εὐλογημένος ὁ ἐρχόμενος ἐν ὀνόματι κυρίου.
	W=25/20, SW=20, OR=19, VB=20	

Table 22. Aland §285, Statistical Summary

Sec. #	Wds (Mt)	Wds (Lk)	SW	OR	VB	%SW (Mt)	%SW (Lk)	%OR	%VB (Mt)	%VB (Lk)	%Mt	%Lk
1	12	12	12	12	12	100%	100%	100%	100%	100%	21%	24%
2	19	18	16	16	14	84%	89%	100%	74%	78%	34%	36%
3	25	20	20	19	20	80%	100%	95%	80%	100%	45%	40%
TOT	56	50	48	47	46	86%	96%	98%	82%	92%		

Figure 31. Agreement, Sec. Length, Shared Words (Aland §285, Matt)

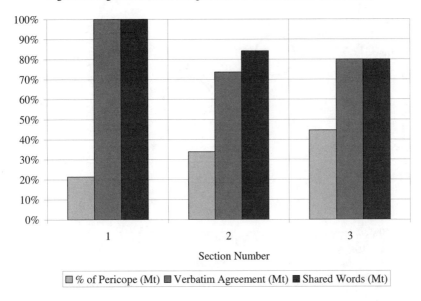

Figure 32. Agreement, Sec. Length, Shared Words (Aland §285, Luke)

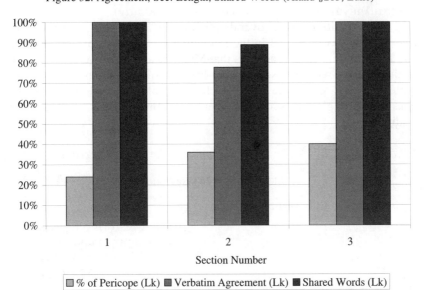

Figure 33. Agreement vs. Pericope Length (Aland §285)

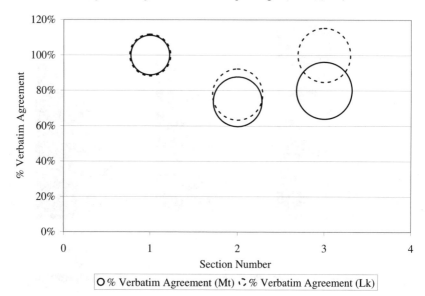

O % Verbatim Agreement (Mt)   ⊃ % Verbatim Agreement (Lk)

1) This pericope is marked by a high level of verbatim agreement and internal consistency. The level of agreement in section 2 is slightly lower than it is in the section both before and after, and is attributable to the existence of two shared word pairs which are not in verbatim agreement (ἀπεσταλμένους / ἐπισυνάξαι and νοσσία / νοσσιάν).

2) This tradition has an overall %VB of 84%, and this is very much in line with the levels of VB in the individual sections 1–3 of both Matthew and Luke. In this case, it appears that Matthew and Luke were very regular in their use of whatever source they had for this particular tradition. It is quite unlikely, given the flexible character of oral tradition, that such consistently high levels of agreement are attributable to a shared oral tradition.

6.7.6   Aland §297 — The Good Servant and the Wicked Servant

Table 23. Aland §297, Synoptic Text

	Matt 24	Luke 12
1 NP		[41] Εἶπεν δὲ ὁ Πέτρος, Κύριε, πρὸς ἡμᾶς τὴν παραβολὴν ταύτην λέγεις ἢ καὶ πρὸς πάντας [42] καὶ εἶπεν ὁ κύριος,

	Matt 24	Luke 12
	W=0/19, SW=0, OR=0, VB=0	
2	⁴⁵ **Τίς ἄρα ἐστὶν ὁ πιστὸς δοῦλος καὶ φρόνιμος ὃν κατέστησεν ὁ κύριος ἐπὶ τῆς** οἰκετείας **αὐτοῦ τοῦ** <u>δοῦναι</u> αὐτοῖς τὴν τροφὴν **ἐν καιρῷ** ⁴⁶ **μακάριος ὁ δοῦλος ἐκεῖνος ὃν ἐλθὼν ὁ κύριος αὐτοῦ εὑρήσει** *οὕτως ποιοῦντα·*	**Τίς ἄρα ἐστὶν ὁ πιστὸς** οἰκονόμος **ὁ φρόνιμος, ὃν καταστήσει ὁ κύριος ἐπὶ τῆς** θεραπείας **αὐτοῦ τοῦ** <u>διδόναι</u> **ἐν καιρῷ** [τὸ] σιτομέτριον; ⁴³ **μακάριος ὁ δοῦλος ἐκεῖνος, ὃν ἐλθὼν ὁ κύριος αὐτοῦ εὑρήσει Ποιοῦντα** *οὕτως·*
	W=35/34, SW=29, OR=28, VB=28	
3	⁴⁷ <u>ἀμὴν</u> **λέγω ὑμῖν ὅτι ἐπὶ πᾶσιν τοῖς ὑπάρχουσιν αὐτοῦ καταστήσει αὐτόν.**	⁴⁴ <u>ἀληθῶς</u> **λέγω ὑμῖν ὅτι ἐπὶ πᾶσιν τοῖς ὑπάρχουσιν αὐτοῦ καταστήσει αὐτόν.**
	W=11/11, SW=11, OR=11, VB=10	
4	⁴⁸ *ἐὰν δὲ εἴπῃ ὁ* κακὸς **δοῦλος ἐκεῖνος ἐν τῇ καρδίᾳ αὐτοῦ, Χρονίζει** *μου* **ὁ κύριος,** ⁴⁹ **καὶ ἄρξηται τύπτειν τοὺς** συνδούλους αὐτοῦ, <u>ἐσθίῃ</u> δὲ **καὶ** <u>πίνῃ</u> μετὰ τῶν <u>μεθυόντων,</u> ⁵⁰ **ἥξει ὁ κύριος τοῦ δούλου ἐκείνου ἐν ἡμέρᾳ ᾗ οὐ προσδοκᾷ καὶ ἐν ὥρᾳ ᾗ οὐ γινώσκει,** ⁵¹ **καὶ διχοτομήσει αὐτὸν καὶ τὸ μέρος αὐτοῦ μετὰ τῶν** ὑποκριτῶν **θήσει·**	⁴⁵ *ἐὰν δὲ εἴπῃ ὁ* **δοῦλος ἐκεῖνος ἐν τῇ καρδίᾳ αὐτοῦ, Χρονίζει ὁ κύριός** *μου* ἔρχεσθαι, **καὶ ἄρξηται τύπτειν τοὺς** παῖδας καὶ τὰς παιδίσκας, <u>ἐσθίειν</u> τε **καὶ** <u>πίνειν</u> καὶ <u>μεθύσκεσθαι,</u> ⁴⁶ **ἥξει ὁ κύριος τοῦ δούλου ἐκείνου ἐν ἡμέρᾳ ᾗ οὐ προσδοκᾷ καὶ ἐν ὥρᾳ ᾗ οὐ γινώσκει, καὶ διχοτομήσει αὐτὸν καὶ τὸ μέρος αὐτοῦ μετὰ τῶν** ἀπίστων **θήσει.**
	W=55/57, SW=48, OR=44, VB=45	
5 NP	ἐκεῖ ἔσται ὁ κλαυθμὸς καὶ ὁ βρυγμὸς τῶν ὀδόντων.	
	W=9/0, SW=0, OR=0, VB=0	

Table 24. Aland §297, Statistical Summary

Sec. #	Wds (Mt)	Wds (Lk)	SW	OR	VB	%SW (Mt)	%SW (Lk)	%OR	%VB (Mt)	%VB (Lk)	%Mt	%Lk
1	0	19	0	0	0	0%	0%	0%	0%	0%	0%	16%
2	35	34	29	28	28	83%	85%	97%	80%	82%	32%	28%
3	11	11	11	11	10	100%	100%	100%	91%	91%	10%	9%
4	55	57	48	44	45	87%	84%	92%	82%	79%	50%	47%
5	9	0	0	0	0	0%	0%	0%	0%	0%	8%	0%
TOT	110	121	88	83	83	80%	73%	94%	75%	69%		

Figure 34. Agreement, Sec. Length, Shared Words (Aland §297, Matt)

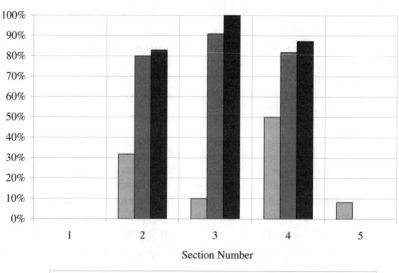

Figure 35. Agreement, Sec. Length, Shared Words (Aland §297, Luke)

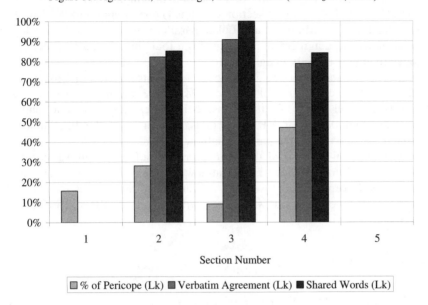

Figure 36. Agreement vs. Pericope Length (Aland §297)

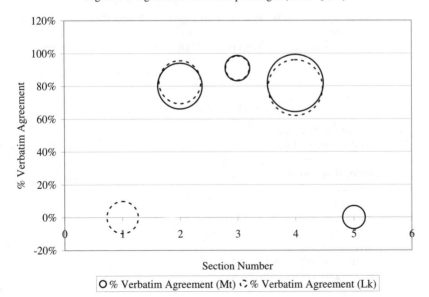

1) The main body of this pericope contains high levels of verbatim agreement, with the longest section (section 4) comprising 50%/47% of the total length of the Matthean and Lukan parallels. Sections 2–4 have a high level of verbatim agreement and apart from four shared words in section 4 they are almost entirely in agreement.

2) The NP sections once again occur at the introduction of Luke (Luke 12:41) and the conclusion of Matthew (Matt 24:51b), and as was the case in several other group "B" traditions, their "bracketing" function coupled with the high levels of VB in sections 2–4 suggests the likelihood of redactional activity on the part of Matthew and Luke.

3) Individual sections of the pericope reflect a highly uniform use of a common tradition to which both Matthew and Luke had access. The high levels of agreement and low level of variability throughout the parallel sections does correspond with the overall level of VB (72%) in the pericope as a whole.

6.8 Group "C" Pericopes

6.8.1 Aland §347 — The Death of Jesus

Table 25. Aland §347, Synoptic Text

	Matt 27	Luke 23
1	⁴⁵ Ἀπὸ δὲ _ἕκτης ὥρας_ **σκότος ἐγένετο** ἐπὶ πᾶσαν τὴν γῆν ἕως ὥρας ἐνάτης.	⁴⁴ Καὶ ἦν ἤδη ὡσεὶ _ὥρα ἕκτη_ καὶ **σκότος ἐγένετο** ἐφ᾽ ὅλην τὴν γῆν ἕως ὥρας ἐνάτης _(v. 45 relocated below to sec. 3)_
	W=13/16, SW=9, OR=8, VB=7	
2 NP	⁴⁶ περὶ δὲ τὴν ἐνάτην ὥραν ἀνεβόησεν ὁ Ἰησοῦς φωνῇ μεγάλῃ λέγων· ἠλι ἠλι λεμα σαβαχθανι τοῦτ᾽ ἔστιν· θεέ μου θεέ μου, ἱνατί με ἐγκατέλιπες ⁴⁷ τινὲς δὲ τῶν ἐκεῖ ἑστηκότων ἀκούσαντες ἔλεγον ὅτι Ἡλίαν φωνεῖ οὗτος. ⁴⁸ καὶ εὐθέως δραμὼν εἷς ἐξ αὐτῶν καὶ λαβὼν σπόγγον	cp v.36

	Matt 27	Luke 23
	πλήσας τε ὄξους καὶ περιθεὶς καλάμῳ ἐπότιζεν αὐτόν.	
	W=52/0, SW=0, OR=0, VB=0	
3	⁴⁹ οἱ δὲ λοιποὶ ἔλεγον· ἄφες ἴδωμεν εἰ ἔρχεται Ἠλίας σώσων αὐτόν. ⁵⁰ **ὁ δὲ Ἰησοῦς** πάλιν κράξας **φωνῇ μεγάλῃ** ἀφῆκεν **τὸ πνεῦμα.**	⁴⁶ καὶ φωνήσας **φωνῇ μεγάλῃ ὁ Ἰησοῦς** εἶπεν· πάτερ, εἰς χεῖράς σου παρατίθεμαι **τὸ πνεῦμά** μου. τοῦτο δὲ εἰπὼν ἐξέπνευσεν.
	W=21/19, SW=6, OR=4, VB=6	
4	⁵¹ Καὶ ἰδοὺ **τὸ καταπέτασμα τοῦ ναοῦ ἐσχίσθη** ἀπ᾽ ἄνωθεν ἕως κάτω εἰς δύο	⁴⁵ τοῦ ἡλίου ἐκλιπόντος, **ἐσχίσθη** δὲ **τὸ καταπέτασμα τοῦ ναοῦ** μέσον.
	W=13/10, SW=5, OR=4, VB=5	
5 NP	καὶ ἡ γῆ ἐσείσθη καὶ αἱ πέτραι ἐσχίσθησαν, ⁵² καὶ τὰ μνημεῖα ἀνεῴχθησαν καὶ πολλὰ σώματα τῶν κεκοιμημένων ἁγίων ἠγέρθησαν, ⁵³ καὶ ἐξελθόντες ἐκ τῶν μνημείων μετὰ τὴν ἔγερσιν αὐτοῦ εἰσῆλθον εἰς τὴν ἁγίαν πόλιν καὶ ἐνεφανίσθησαν πολλοῖς.	
	W=36/0, SW=0, OR=0, VB=0	
6	⁵⁴ <u>Ὁ δὲ ἑκατόνταρχος</u> καὶ οἱ μετ᾽ αὐτοῦ τηροῦντες τὸν Ἰησοῦν <u>ἰδόντες</u> τὸν σεισμὸν καὶ <u>τὰ γενόμενα</u> ἐφοβήθησαν σφόδρα, <u>λέγοντες·</u> ἀληθῶς θεοῦ υἱὸς **ἦν οὗτος.**	⁴⁷ <u>Ἰδὼν</u> **δὲ** <u>ὁ ἑκατοντάρχης</u> <u>τὸ γενόμενον</u> ἐδόξαζεν τὸν θεὸν <u>λέγων·</u> ὄντως ὁ ἄνθρωπος **οὗτος** δίκαιος **ἦν.**
	W=24/16, SW=9, OR=6, VB=4	

	Matt 27	Luke 23
7 NP		⁴⁸ καὶ πάντες οἱ συμπαραγενόμενοι ὄχλοι ἐπὶ τὴν θεωρίαν ταύτην, θεωρήσαντες τὰ γενόμενα, τύπτοντες τὰ στήθη ὑπέστρεφον.
		W=0/16, SW=0, OR=0, VB=0

Table 26. Aland §347, Statistical Summary

Sec. #	Wds (Mt)	Wds (Lk)	SW	OR	VB	%SW (Mt)	%SW (Lk)	%OR	%VB (Mt)	%VB (Lk)	%Mt	%Lk
1	13	16	9	8	7	69%	56%	89%	54%	44%	8%	21%
2	52	0	0	0	0	0%	0%	0%	0%	0%	33%	0%
3	21	19	6	4	6	29%	32%	67%	29%	32%	13%	25%
4	13	10	5	4	5	38%	50%	80%	38%	50%	8%	13%
5	36	0	0	0	0	0%	0%	0%	0%	0%	23%	0%
6	24	16	9	6	4	38%	56%	67%	17%	25%	15%	21%
7	0	16	0	0	0	0%	0%	0%	0%	0%	0%	21%
TOT	159	77	29	22	22	18%	38%	76%	14%	29%		

Figure 37. Agreement, Sec. Length, Shared Words (Aland §347, Matt)

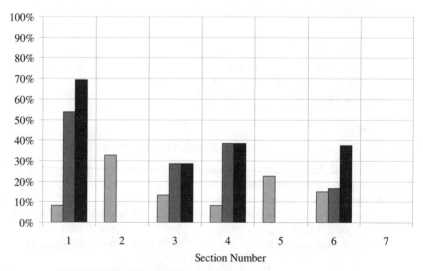

% of Pericope (Mt) ■ Verbatim Agreement (Mt) ■ Shared Words (Mt)

Figure 38. Agreement, Sec. Length, Shared Words (Aland §347, Luke)

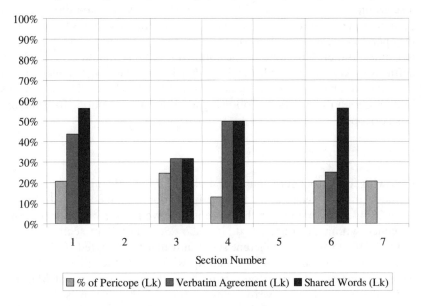

Figure 39. Agreement vs. Pericope Length (Aland §347)

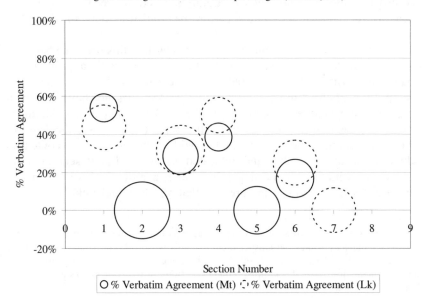

There are several preliminary matters to address at the outset of this discussion. First, we will discuss the difficulty in dividing up this particular pericope into sections. There are several possible ways in which the pericope can be divided. All of these divisions involve value judgements, therefore none of the following options should be considered definitive. Also, as we will detail further below, the conclusions derived from the following analysis are not affected by the choice that one makes in dividing up the parallels. Following are the various options for studying this pericope:

Division of Pericope Sections

Following our procedure thus far, Luke 23:45 would most naturally be included in the "sense unit" located in section 1 immediately following Luke 23:44. The first option therefore is to leave Luke 23:45 in its original sequence within the Lukan text. If Luke 23:45 is left in section 1, then Luke 23:44–45 forms a coherent sense unit that is disrupted if one moves verse 45 down to section 4 to match up with its Matthean parallel. If one were to approach this pericope *apart* from the assumption that Matthew and Luke were editing a written source (i.e., Mark), then it is difficult to justify disjointing Luke 23:45 from its original order within the Lukan sequence. In this case, without having access to a physical source text, there are no clear grounds for assuming that the out-of-order parallel is due to Matthew and Luke's editorial activity. Without access to a source *text*, the order of the material *could* be traditional and not redactional. In this scenario, the sense units could therefore be studied as they stand in their existing position within Matthew and Luke respectively.[59]

However, as we recall from the above discussion, this pericope has been used as an analogy to compare how Matthew and Luke edit, appropriate, or adapt their written Markan source. In this scenario, Luke's description of the splitting of the temple curtain (Luke 23:45) does not have a context parallel within Matthew's section 1. Rather, Luke 23:45 parallels Matthean material in section 4 (Matt 27:51). Therefore, in this case, the "out-of-order" parallel material in Luke 23:45 could be moved from the context in which it occurs in Luke, and relocated below in Luke, section 4, to correspond with its Matthean parallel. Such a move is justified in this instance, for, if one grants the premise that Matthew and Luke are *editing*

---

[59] Here, Lord in his work on the Gospels suggests that one must "respect" the extant tradition sequences within the Gospel texts. For this reason, Lord avoids using printed synopses, rather, "the texts which one is working must themselves make known their inner segmentation . . . oral traditional composers think in terms of blocks and series of blocks of tradition" ("Gospels," 59).

Mark, then it is reasonable to approach the pericope from this perspective (i.e., that Matthew and Luke have chosen to relocate their source material to another location during the editing of their respective accounts). This is the option which we will adopt and therefore we will relocate Luke 23:45 down to section 4 to match up with its Matthean parallel (cf. Table 25, sec. 5). The dotted lines and arrows on Table 25 indicate the movement of this material.

It is another similar situation with regards to the material in Luke 23:46 (sec. 4). Once again there is a level of ambiguity and arbitrariness that cannot be avoided. Luke's φωνῇ μεγάλῃ ὁ Ἰησοῦς εἶπεν· πάτερ, εἰς χεῖράς σου παρατίθεμαι τὸ πνεῦμά μου can be listed as paralleling Matthew in one of two locations. First, it can be located in section 2 alongside Matthew 27:46. The justification for this is based upon the similar use of the φωνῇ μεγάλῃ in Matt 27:46. However, it is necessary to examine further the context of the phrase in both gospels in order to determine the proper location of Luke 23:46 within the pericope sections.

Matt 27:46 depicts the last words of Jesus (ἠλι ἠλι λεμα σαβαχθανι), and φωνῇ μεγάλῃ is used to introduce those words. In this section (Matt 27:46–48), the emphasis is on the utterance of the last words themselves. However, Matthew also uses φωνῇ μεγάλῃ later on in section 3 (Matt 27:50). In this latter context, Matthew uses the phrase to describe the *death* of Jesus. Jesus is depicted as crying out in a loud voice and then yielding up his spirit (ἀφῆκεν τὸ πνεῦμα). Here the emphasis is clearly on the death of Jesus, which is the same context within which the phrase φωνῇ μεγάλῃ is used by Luke. The emphasis in Luke is clearly on the death of Jesus, not on his last words. While Luke's use of φωνῇ μεγάλῃ could be paralleled with Matt 27:46, it seems appropriate to locate it within section 3 where both Matthew and Luke narrate the actual *death* of Jesus (cf. the parallel-alignment offered by Aland §347). In addition, both Matthew and Luke use τὸ πνεῦμα within the same context of the narration of Jesus' death. Matthew uses ἀφῆκεν and Luke παρατίθεμαι to indicate yielding/committing of Jesus' πνεῦμα. Within the context of Jesus' death, the common use of πνεῦμα by Matthew and Luke seems sufficiently similar in its application to consider them parallel with one another.

Analysis of Pericope

Moving beyond these preliminary matters, this pericope is the first of our two "control" pericopes, and has several features worth examining in more detail. For this pericope we will focus our attention on the character of the NP sections, the existence of "out-of-order" parallels, and the distribution of agreement in the sections which do parallel one another. The possible significance of these features will then be addressed in conclusion.

a) The first point of interest is regarding the NP sections within the pericope. Aland §347 contains several NP sections that occur within its main body (secs. 2, 5). Each of these NP sections is significantly longer than any of the other Matthean sections. Sections 2 and 5 extend for a total of 52 and 36 words respectively, and these sections together comprise a large percentage of the overall length of Matthew (56%). Long, extended NP sections do not occur in the majority of the group "A" pericopes. Aland §58 (On Retaliation), §62 (The Lord's Prayer), and §102 (Divisions Within Households) all contain NP sections within the body of the pericope itself. However, in each instance the length of the NP section typically is shorter than that observed here in Aland §347. The NP section in Aland §58 (sec. 4) is 10 words in length; the NP section in Aland §62 (sec. 5), 10 words; and the NP section in Aland §102 (sec. 2) is 17 words in length.

The longer length of the NP sections in §347 does resemble the length of NP sections within one group "B" passage. Aland §107, sections 8 and 9 are NP sections which are 42 and 32 words long respectively. One group "A" passage in particular (Aland §85 — Centurion's Servant) does contain NP sections with lengths comparable to those observed here in Aland §347. Aland §85, section 4 is 48 words in length, and section 8 is 43 words in length. These NP sections are located immediately preceeding and following sections containing high levels of verbatim agreement. The only other group "A" pericope which has NP sections of such length is Aland §279, although this is not surprising given the very low overall levels of agreement within that pericope.

Further, if the Luke 23:45 were *not* relocated from section 1 to section 4, then section 4 would be combined with section 5, and then the length of the current NP section 5 would be 49 words instead of the current length of 36 words. As such, the argument regarding the length of the NP sections here would be *strengthed* if Luke 23:45 was not moved.

b) The second point of interest is with regard to the "out-of-order" parallels which occur within the pericope. As discussed in the introductory section above, the occurrence of these parallels makes it difficult to make any definitive judgements regarding the division of this pericope. Despite this difficulty, we can note that these "out-of-order" parallels occur in other places within the pericopes selected for this study. In particular, group "B" pericope Aland §107 contains two such possible parallels to the NP sections therein (sections 8, 9), and the only group "A" pericope to contain such a parallel is once again Aland §85 (Centurion's Servant). Given our previous analysis of Aland §85 we are led to ask whether it may be significant that such non-context parallels appear in both "literary" groups "C" and "B," but only occur within the group "A" pericope that has long, extended sections of verbatim agreement (i.e., Aland §85).

c) The third matter needing further discussion is the character of the agreement within the sections that are parallel with one another.

In assessing the significance of this pericope for our overall thesis, we must return to the reason for including this parallel in our study. As we recall, Kloppenborg suggested that this *triple tradition* pericope illustrated the disparity with which Matthew and Luke used both Mark and Q. Therefore, according to Kloppenborg, there is no need to postulate multiple source documents, or oral tradition, to account for double tradition pericopes with such differing levels of VB. However, as we observed in the previous analysis of the group "A" pericopes, the overall, single figure of verbatim agreement does not always provide a clear picture of the character of the agreement within the Matthean and Lukan parallels.

If we examine the sections that are parallel with one another (i.e., secs. 1, 3, 4, 6), there appears to be a level of consistency that was not very common in several of the group "A" passages. Figure 38 illustrates this phenomenon. The parallel sections exhibit characteristics similar to several group "B" (i.e., "literary") pericopes (e.g., Aland § 120 — The Return of the Evil Spirit, § 285 — Jesus' Lament Over Jerusalem). There are no sections that contain high levels of agreement such as the "core" sections in some of the group "A" (i.e., "oral") pericopes. The character of agreement within this pericope is more consistent, and the parallel sections do not appear to exhibit the same characteristic variability that we observed in most of the so-called "oral" passages (group "A"). Once again the conclusion drawn from such an observation can not be more than tentative, but it does suggest that Kloppenborg's use of this pericope as an analogy to indicate that Matthew and Luke have edited Mark in the same manner as they have edited Q must be subjected to further scrutiny.

6.8.2 Aland §278 — The Parable of the Wicked Husbandmen

Table 27. Aland §278, Synoptic Text

	Matt 21	Luke 20
1	[33] Ἄλλην παραβολὴν ἀκούσατε. ἄνθρωπος ἦν οἰκοδεσπότης ὅστις ἐφύτευσεν ἀμπελῶνα καὶ φραγμὸν αὐτῷ περιέθηκεν καὶ ὤρυξεν ἐν αὐτῷ ληνὸν καὶ	[9] Ἤρξατο δὲ πρὸς τὸν λαὸν λέγειν τὴν παραβολὴν ταύτην· ἄνθρωπός [τις] ἐφύτευσεν ἀμπελῶνα

Matt 21	Luke 20
ᾠκοδόμησεν πύργον **καὶ ἐξέδετο αὐτὸν γεωργοῖς** **καὶ ἀπεδήμησεν.** ³⁴ ὅτε δὲ ἤγγισεν ὁ <u>καιρὸς</u> τῶν καρπῶν, **ἀπέστειλεν** τοὺς <u>δούλους</u> αὐτοῦ **πρὸς τοὺς γεωργοὺς** λαβεῖν <u>τοὺς καρποὺς</u> αὐτοῦ. ³⁵ **καὶ λαβόντες** **οἱ γεωργοὶ** τοὺς δούλους αὐτοῦ ὃν μὲν <u>ἔδειραν</u>, ὃν δὲ ἀπέκτειναν, ὃν δὲ ἐλιθοβόλησαν.	**καὶ ἐξέδετο αὐτὸν γεωργοῖς** **καὶ ἀπεδήμησεν** χρόνους ἱκανούς· ¹⁰ **καὶ** <u>καιρῷ</u> **ἀπέστειλεν** **πρὸς τοὺς γεωργοὺς** <u>δοῦλον</u> ἵνα ἀπὸ <u>τοῦ καρποῦ</u> τοῦ ἀμπελῶνος δώσουσιν αὐτῷ· **οἱ** δὲ **γεωργοὶ** ἐξαπέστειλαν αὐτὸν <u>δείραντες</u> κενόν.

W=61/42, SW=21, OR=20, VB=16

2	³⁶ πάλιν **ἀπέστειλεν** ἄλλους <u>δούλους</u> πλείονας τῶν πρώτων, καὶ ἐποίησαν αὐτοῖς ὡσαύτως.	¹¹ **καὶ** προσέθετο ἕτερον πέμψαι <u>δοῦλον</u>· οἱ δὲ κἀκεῖνον δείραντες καὶ ἀτιμάσαντες ἐξαπέστειλαν κενόν. ¹² **καὶ** προσέθετο τρίτον πέμψαι· οἱ δὲ καὶ τοῦτον τραυματίσαντες ἐξέβαλον.

W=11/23, SW=1, OR=1, VB=0

3	³⁷ ὕστερον **δὲ** ἀπέστειλεν πρὸς αὐτοὺς τὸν υἱὸν αὐτοῦ *λέγων·* *ἐντραπήσονται* **τὸν υἱόν μου.** ³⁸ **οἱ δὲ γεωργοὶ** *ἰδόντες* τὸν υἱὸν εἶπον ἐν ἑαυτοῖς· **οὗτός ἐστιν ὁ κληρονόμος·** δεῦτε **ἀποκτείνωμεν αὐτὸν** καὶ σχῶμεν <u>τὴν κληρονομίαν</u> αὐτοῦ, ³⁹ **καὶ λαβόντες αὐτὸν** *ἐξέβαλον* ἔξω τοῦ **ἀμπελῶνος** καὶ **ἀπέκτειναν.** ⁴⁰ ὅταν οὖν ἔλθῃ **ὁ κύριος τοῦ ἀμπελῶνος,** τί	¹³ *εἶπεν* **δὲ** ὁ κύριος τοῦ ἀμπελῶνος· τί ποιήσω• πέμψω **τὸν υἱόν μου** τὸν ἀγαπητόν· ἴσως τοῦτον *ἐντραπήσονται.* ¹⁴ *ἰδόντες* δὲ αὐτὸν **οἱ γεωργοὶ** διελογίζοντο πρὸς ἀλλήλους λέγοντες· **οὗτός ἐστιν ὁ κληρονόμος·** **ἀποκτείνωμεν αὐτόν,** ἵνα ἡμῶν γένηται <u>ἡ κληρονομία.</u> ¹⁵ **καὶ** <u>ἐκβαλόντες</u> **αὐτὸν** ἔξω τοῦ **ἀμπελῶνος** **ἀπέκτειναν.** τί οὖν *ποιήσει* αὐτοῖς **ὁ κύριος τοῦ ἀμπελῶνος**

Matt 21	Luke 20
ποιήσει τοῖς γεωργοῖς ἐκείνοις	
W=55/52, SW=31, OR=25, VB=27	

	Matt 21	Luke 20
4	[41] λέγουσιν αὐτῷ· κακοὺς κακῶς **ἀπολέσει** αὐτοὺς **καὶ** τὸν **ἀμπελῶνα** ἐκδώσεται **ἄλλοις** *γεωργοῖς,* οἵτινες ἀποδώσουσιν αὐτῷ τοὺς καρποὺς ἐν τοῖς καιροῖς αὐτῶν.	[16] ἐλεύσεται καὶ **ἀπολέσει** τοὺς *γεωργοὺς* τούτους **καὶ** δώσει τὸν **ἀμπελῶνα** **ἄλλοις.**
	W=21/11, SW=6, OR=5, VB=5	
5	[42] *λέγει* **αὐτοῖς** ὁ Ἰησοῦς· οὐδέποτε ἀνέγνωτε ἐν ταῖς γραφαῖς· **λίθον ὃν ἀπεδοκίμασαν οἱ οἰκοδομοῦντες, οὗτος ἐγενήθη εἰς κεφαλὴν γωνίας** παρὰ κυρίου ἐγένετο αὕτη καὶ ἔστιν θαυμαστὴ ἐν ὀφθαλμοῖς ἡμῶν	ἀκούσαντες δὲ εἶπαν· μὴ γένοιτο. [17] ὁ δὲ ἐμβλέψας **αὐτοῖς** *εἶπεν·* τί οὖν ἐστιν τὸ γεγραμμένον τοῦτο· **λίθον ὃν ἀπεδοκίμασαν οἱ οἰκοδομοῦντες, οὗτος ἐγενήθη εἰς κεφαλὴν γωνίας**
	W=29/26, SW=12, OR=11, VB=11	
6 NP	[43] διὰ τοῦτο λέγω ὑμῖν ὅτι ἀρθήσεται ἀφ᾽ ὑμῶν ἡ βασιλεία τοῦ θεοῦ καὶ δοθήσεται ἔθνει ποιοῦντι τοὺς καρποὺς αὐτῆς.	
	W=19/0, SW=0, OR=0, VB=0	
7 NP	[44] [καὶ ὁ πεσὼν ἐπὶ τὸν λίθον τοῦτον συνθλασθήσεται· ἐφ᾽ ὃν δ᾽ ἂν πέσῃ λικμήσει αὐτόν.]	[18] πᾶς ὁ πεσὼν ἐπ᾽ ἐκεῖνον τὸν λίθον συνθλασθήσεται· ἐφ᾽ ὃν δ᾽ ἂν πέσῃ, λικμήσει αὐτόν.
	W=0/15, SW=0, OR=0, VB=0	
8	[45] Καὶ ἀκούσαντες **οἱ ἀρχιερεῖς** καὶ οἱ Φαρισαῖοι *τὰς*	[19] Καὶ ἐζήτησαν οἱ γραμματεῖς καὶ **οἱ ἀρχιερεῖς** ἐπιβαλεῖν ἐπ᾽ αὐτὸν τὰς χεῖρας ἐν αὐτῇ

Matt 21	Luke 20
παραβολὰς αὐτοῦ **ἔγνωσαν** ὅτι περὶ <u>αὐτῶν</u> λέγει· ⁴⁶ καὶ ζητοῦντες αὐτὸν κρατῆσαι **ἐφοβήθησαν** <u>τοὺς</u> ὄχλους, ἐπεὶ εἰς προφήτην αὐτὸν εἶχον.	τῇ ὥρᾳ, καὶ **ἐφοβήθησαν** <u>τὸν</u> λαόν, **ἔγνωσαν** γὰρ ὅτι πρὸς <u>αὐτοὺς</u> <u>εἶπεν τὴν παραβολὴν</u> ταύτην.
W=27/29, SW=10, OR=6, VB=5	

Table 28. Aland §278, Statistical Summary

Sec. #	Wds (Mt)	Wds (Lk)	SW	OR	VB	%SW (Mt)	%SW (Lk)	%OR	%VB (Mt)	%VB (Lk)	%Mt	%Lk
1	61	42	21	20	16	34%	50%	95%	26%	38%	27%	21%
2	11	23	1	1	0	9%	4%	100%	0%	0%	5%	12%
3	55	52	31	25	24	56%	60%	81%	44%	46%	25%	26%
4	21	11	7	5	5	33%	64%	71%	24%	45%	9%	6%
5	29	26	12	11	11	41%	46%	92%	38%	42%	13%	13%
6	19	0	0	0	0	0%	0%	0%	0%	0%	9%	9%
7	0	15	0	0	0	0%	0%	0%	0%	0%	0%	8%
8	27	29	10	6	5	37%	34%	60%	19%	17%	12%	15%
TOT	223	198	82	68	61	37%	41%	83%	27%	31%		

Figure 40. Agreement, Sec. Length, Shared Words (Aland §278, Matt)

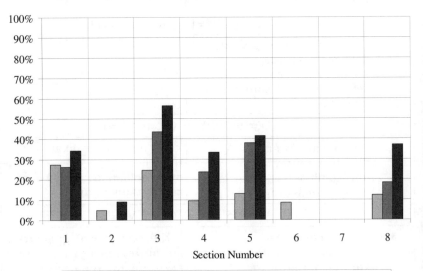

Figure 41. Agreement, Sec. Length, Shared Words (Aland §278, Luke)

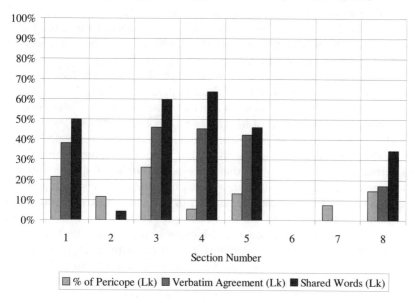

Figure 42. Agreement vs. Pericope Length (Aland §278)

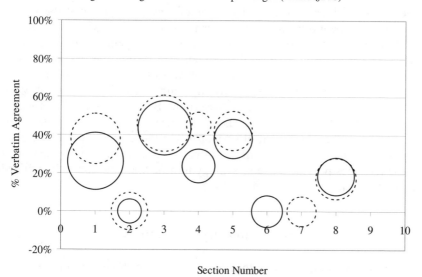

This pericope is the second of our two "control" pericopes, and has several features worth examining in more detail. For this pericope we will focus our attention on the distribution of verbatim agreement in the various sections of the pericope. The possible significance of these features will then be addressed in conclusion.

The pericope contains two NP sections (6, 7), which are located within the main body of Matthean and Lukan parallels. The NP sections are relatively short in comparison to most of other sections of the pericope, and comprise only 9%/8% of Matthew and Luke respectively.

The overall level of verbatim agreement in the pericope is 29% (122/421*100), and each of the individual parallel sections contain levels of verbatim agreement (%VB) that correspond roughly to this overall level of agreement. Figure 42 illustrates how Luke and Matthew both edit their Markan source with a certain regularity. In particular, Lukan sections 1, 3–5 exhibit quite similar levels of agreement (38%, 46%, 45%, 42%; see Figure 41). Although Luke and Matthew's use of Mark is relatively consistent, neither parallel contains a section with exceptionally high levels of agreement as was the case with several other so-called "oral" pericopes such as Aland §55 (On Murder and Wrath), §62 (The Lord's Prayer), §85 (The Centurion of Capernaum). However, the pattern of relatively consistent levels of verbatim agreement does correspond with the distribution of agreement within some group "B" pericopes, in particular Aland §120, and §285.

As was the case with Aland §347, we must evaluate the significance of these observations against the backdrop of how these pericopes have been used by Kloppenborg. Once again, this pericope was specifically employed by him as an illustration by way of analogy that Matthew and Luke edited Mark in the same manner as they edited "Q." While the overall level of agreement in §278 is comparable to several of the group "A" passages, there is a certain level of regularity in Matthew and Luke's use of Mark which resembles that observed in the group "B" (i.e., "literary") passages. As was the case with §347, the differences between the patterns of agreement within these control pericopes and those in group "A" are once again sufficient enough to warrant further investigation into the claim that these passages provide a useful analogy to how Matthew and Luke utilized both Mark and Q.

6.9   Summary of Findings

It is now necessary to draw together some of the threads from the above analysis of the three groups of pericopes and to answer some of the question proposed above. Although the above selection of pericopes was necessarily limited, there are several observations that deserve mention. A folkloristic examination of groups "A-oral," "B-literary," and "C-control" with a view towards their internal variability has helped bring to the fore some of the complex issues involved in determining the possible role of oral tradition in the formation of the selected double tradition passages. Following are a list of several conclusions presented by way of summary:

1) First and perhaps most significantly, the above examination on the phenomenon of internal variability can help us understand better the character of the tradition. We have noted in several instances above how the overall percentage of verbatim agreement in a pericope is not always a very helpful indicator of the level of internal variability within the double tradition.

One of the foundational arguments for a cohesive Q text (unified, coherent theology, etc.) is that Matthew and Luke edited their Markan source in the same manner as they edited the hypothetical "Q" document. Scholars such as Kloppenborg Verbin have come to this conclusion based upon their observation that the overall levels of verbatim agreement *across* the double *and* triple tradition is highly variable. However, once one examines the level of internal variability within each individual pericope and the distribution of verbatim agreement therein, it becomes clear that assigning a *single figure* of verbatim agreement to an individual pericope tends to gloss over the dynamism at work within the tradition itself. An examination of the control group "C" supports this observation. Although the %VB is similar between group "C" and several of the "oral" (group A) pericopes, the character of the distribution of verbatim agreement is different between the pericopes of both groups.

Despite the similar levels of verbatim agreement between the selected double tradition passages in group "A" and the triple tradition control passages (group "C"), there is a discernable difference in how the agreements and disagreements manifest themselves in both groups.

The presence of the large non-parallel (NP) sections in control passages such as Aland §347 (The Death of Jesus) has dramatically lowered the overall level of verbatim agreement (VB) in the pericope. Subsequently, Kloppenborg Verbin cites Aland §347 as containing 12% verbatim agreement, and suggests that this indicates that Matthew and Luke edited Mark in the same way that they edited Q. However, one must look beyond the single 12% level of verbatim agreement within the pericope. The length of the extended NP sections within the pericope resembles more closely the use of NP sections within the so-called literary (group "B") passages.

The second control group (C) pericope (Aland §278 — The Parable of the Wicked Husbandmen) is also helpful in highlighting the differences between the three groups of traditions currently under examination. Although the overall level of verbatim agreement in Aland §278 is only 32%, there is generally less internal variability within the pericope than those in group "A." A look at Figure 41 lends support to such an observation. In the chart, it is clear that the agreement is distributed relatively evenly throughout the pericope. Sections 1 and 3–5 each have levels of verbatim agreement of approximately 40%, which strongly correlates with the overall %VB for the entire pericope (32%). Once again, this suggests that Matthew and Luke utilized Mark with a consistency not typically observed in the so-called "oral" (group A) passages. Despite the overall low level of verbatim agreement, this pericope does exhibit characteristics different enough from those pericopes in our "oral" group "A" to warrant further investigation into the claim that they serve as a helpful analogy to how Matthew and Luke edited Q.

The data presented above also suggests that the group "A" (oral) pericopes exhibit a greater overall level of internal variability than those in both group "B" (literary) and control group "C." Several of the group "A" pericopes contain significant levels of internal variability, in particular Aland §55 (On Murder and Wrath) and §62 (The Lord's Prayer), although some admittedly do not (Aland §58 — On Retaliation). For those group "A" (oral) pericopes that do not exhibit a high level of internal variability (i.e., Aland §102), this seems to some extent due to the small number of sections within a pericope itself. In the case of Aland §279 (Parable of the Great Supper), there is substantial variation in the level of internal variability, and although the very low overall level of VB throughout the pericope makes it difficult to definitively determine the significance of the distribution of agreement, the other features within the parallel can be explained by the characteristic variability and stability inherent in community-based oral performance.

2) A more detailed examination of the Non-Parallel (NP) sections also reveals significant insight into the development of the double tradition.

Further examination of the function of the NP sections suggests that they serve a different function in groups "A" (oral) and "B" (literary). The following tables illustrate the physical location of the NP sections in both groups of tradition:

Table 29. Pericopes with NP Sections in Body of Pericope

Aland Section	Grp.	NP Sec.	Fig.	Critical Ed. of Q
§58 – On Retaliation	A	1,4	4–6	Q 6:29–30
§62 – Lord's Prayer	A	1,2,5,10	7–9	Q 11:2b-4

§85 – Centurion's Servant	A	3,4,8	10–12	Q 7:1, 3, 6b-9, ?10?
§102 – Divisions Within Households	A	2,4	13–15	Q 12:[49], 51, 53
§279 – Parable of Great Supper	A	1,4,6,9	16–18	Q 14:16–18, ?19–20?, 21, 23
§107 – Jesus Concerning John	B	8,9	22–24	Q 7:24–28 / Q 7:[29–30] / Q 7:31–35
§347 – The Death of Jesus	C	2,3,6,8	37–39	
§278 – The Parable of the Wicked Hus.	C	6,7	40–42	

Table 30. Pericopes with NP Sections at Start and Finish of Pericope

Aland Section	Grp.	NP Sec.	Fig.	Critical Ed. of Q
§89 – On Following Jesus	B	1,5	19–21	Q 9:57–60
§109 – Jesus' Thanksgiving to the Father	B	-	25–27	Q 10:21 / Q 10:22
§120 – The Return of the Evil Spirit	B	5	28–30	Q 11:24–26
§285 – Jesus' Lament over Jerusalem	B	-	31–33	Q 13:34–35
§297 – Good & Wicked Servant	B	1,5	34–36	Q 12:42–46
§55 – On Murder & Wrath	A	1,2	1–3	Q 12:58–59

Table 29 illustrates how the NP sections within the so-called oral pericopes (group A) are generally located within the main body of the pericope and tend to be relatively short in length. In all of the group "A" passages except for Aland §55 (On Murder and Wrath), NP sections were interspersed within the parallel and tended to be short and explanatory in nature. Here, the explanatory power of oral performance and performance variations comes to the fore. In the group "A" pericopes the NP material tends to resemble the type of changes and characteristic variability that one would expect in the multiple retellings of traditions which were orally derived, or, those which would characterize the retelling of a source tradition in what Dunn has described as Matthew or Luke working in "oral mode."[60]

In comparison to the function of the NP sections within group "A" pericopes, the NP sections listed in Table 29 occur at the beginning and/or end of pericopes and serve as introductions and/or conclusions to their respective parallel. In the case of the so-called "literary" pericopes (group "B") with high levels of verbatim agreement, the NP sections are generally used to introduce or conclude a pericope while the main body of the

---

[60] See p.98 for Dunn's description of "oral mode."

pericope itself remains untouched. One possible explanation for this phenomena is that when Matthew or Luke were working closely with a written source tradition and they remained close to the wording of that source (e.g., most group "B" pericopes), they tended to avoid inserting additional material into their narrative, preferring instead to remain faithful to both the wording and the content of their source.

An analysis of the function of the NP sections also lends additional insight into the so-called "control" pericopes (group "C"). In Aland §347 (The Death of Jesus) the NP sections occur in several locations within the pericope, and comprise a large percentage of its overall length. Sections 2 and 4 of the pericope contain 40% and 31% of the Matthean parallel. A total of 71% of the pericope consists of the NP sections, and despite this large percentage of NP material, sections 1 and 3 depict a relatively *uniform* distribution of verbatim agreement (cf. Figure 37, Figure 38). This suggests that Matthew and Luke seem to be inserting new, different blocks of material into their own narrative. One can envision that Matthew or Luke had access to a written source text, and at times inserted, or left out large sections, to meet their own redactional concerns. As noted above, the long length of these NP sections is unlike the character of the NP sections within group "A" pericopes. The only group "A" pericope which has NP sections as long as those within Aland §347 is Aland §85 (Centurion's Servant), and we subsequently asked whether this might be significant given our earlier discussion on Aland §85.

3) The level of internal variability is greater overall in group "A" than it is in group "B," but it is not clear given the scope of this study whether this variability can be used as an indicator of oral tradition behind the extant texts. It must be recognized that the level of internal variability does tend to be inversely proportional to the overall level of verbatim agreement, particularly in the "literary" (group "B") pericopes. That is, as the overall level of agreement within a tradition increases, the level of internal variability must also decrease to some extent since a tradition in 100% agreement with another parallel tradition would be entirely consistent and lacking any variation. Once again, we are faced with the likelihood that the existence of traditions in multiple versions, coupled with internal variability, is not *in itself* a definitive indicator of an oral pre-history of a tradition. This is not to suggest, as does Henaut, that one cannot discern the existence of oral tradition within the Synoptic Gospels, but rather one must make such an assessment by examining the overall characteristics in a tradition, not just the internal variability therein.

4) The internal stability (i.e., the "core") is also an important factor in examining the differences between the three different groups. Here once again, the differences between the groups cannot be adequately grasped by

examining the overall level of verbatim agreement between the pericopes within both groups. A comparison of pericopes in groups A, B, and C, reveals that those in group "A" (oral) exhibit several "core" sections that are very high in agreement (Aland §55, sec. 4; Aland §85, sec. 5–7). Group "B" pericopes also exhibit "core" sections in which the elements that are thematically significant exhibit high levels of verbatim agreement (Aland §89, sec. 2). However, these group "B" "core" passages do not stand out from their surroundings as do the core passages of group "A." This leads us to suggest that among the pericopes chosen for this study, the existence of a thematic core is significant only in pericopes that have a low overall level of verbatim agreement. When the level of verbatim agreement within thematically significant sections becomes indistinguishable from that in other sections within the pericope, it is no longer a useful key to understanding the possible tradition-history of a parallel passage. As for the two pericopes in group "C," both lack any core sections in which the level of verbatim agreement is significantly higher than its surrounding sections.

5) The above examination of the internal variability within our selected pericopes has helped us evaluate the claim put forth by scholars such as Dunn that these traditions can be explained by an appeal to "oral tradition."[61] Our examination of these group "A" pericopes yields mixed results.

In certain cases, the character of the distribution of verbatim agreement within the pericope appeared to reflect the variable character of oral tradition (Aland §55 — On Murder and Wrath, §62 — The Lord's Prayer). For other group "A" pericopes such as Aland §102 and §279, the overall level of verbatim agreement within the pericope was so low that it made the significance of the variation within questionable.

We approached Aland §279 (Parable of the Great Supper, Table 11) from an oral tradition perspective informed by contemporary folklore studies and noted how our knowledge of the oral substratum behind the Synoptic Gospels might serve as a corrective to over-confident attempts at reconstructing an original Q tradition. In comparing the Matthean and Lukan parallels to the theoretical reconstructed "Q" text, we were forced to question the viability of such a reconstruction. Matthew and Luke in their extant form fit well with their original function as an orally performed tradition. In this case, approaching the tradition from a strictly literary perspective, while adopting early form-critical assumptions such as linearity and evolutionary tradition development, led to a situation where the tradition was reconstructed apart from its historical context, and

---

[61] See p.98 and §6.1 for more on Dunn's recent work with what we have designated as group "A" passages.

subsequently lacked several features which would have been appreciated by the earliest recipients of the Jesus tradition.

Aland §102 (Divisions Within Households) also contains such low levels of agreement that it becomes difficult to estimate the significance of the internal variability. However, once again, other factors must be taken into account when evaluating the possible tradition history of the extant tradition. Despite the low levels of agreement, both parallels clearly depict the same story, and the variation within is explicable via an appeal to oral tradition. Both Matthew and Luke have retold their received tradition by employing a traditional grouping of threes that describes in more detail the antithesis between εἰρήνην and μάχαιραν (Matt) and διαμερισμόν (Luke). The tradition was transmitted with a combination of both variability and stability which is characteristic of folklore and in turn oral tradition.

The explanatory power of oral tradition is not equally strong for all of the pericopes examined in the so-called "oral" group (A). Our examination of Aland §85 (The Centurion's Servant) highlighted the difficulty in attributing the current form of the pericope to the influence of oral tradition. In this case, the distribution of the agreement was discernibly different than in the other "oral" pericopes. The pericope contains very long and extended "core" sections (secs. 5–7, Figure 12) which are almost 100% in verbatim agreement. This is distinct from the other pericopes such as Aland §55, in which the core section is substantially shorter in length. Although the long, extended core in Aland §85 (secs. 5–7) contains predominantly sayings material, which lends itself towards memorization, one must question whether or not such an extended section with such high levels of agreement can be attributed to an oral process of tradition transmission/formation. Long NP sections both precede and follow the "core" sections 5–7, and it seems reasonable to suggest that in this instance the existence of these extended NP sections could be due to the editorial insertions of material into a common source text to which Matt and Luke had access.

6) Other Observations:

On the Reconstruction of Q

As noted above, Kloppenborg suggests that an examination of Matthew and Luke's use of Mark in the triple tradition material is helpful, for it provides us with an analogy to how they edit or appropriate the Q material into their double tradition passages. If one were to grant Kloppenborg's argument, and subsequently accept that Matthew and Luke used Mark in the same manner as they used a Q text, then our analysis of Aland §347 (The Death of Jesus) suggests that the ongoing attempt to reconstruct a comprehensive critical text of Q runs into several difficulties. That is, if we examine Matthew and Luke in the triple tradition *apart* from Mark, and then attempt to reconstruct the original Markan text (as we would reconstruct "Q"), we would notice that the reconstructed text can be significantly different from the extant text.

The primary cause of this difficulty is the manner by which the Q text is reconstructed from the Matthean and Lukan parallels. In practice, the reconstructed Q text is the product of a minimalist approach to the tradition, which works under the assumption that the form-critical assumptions of growth, expansion, and linearity are operative in the process of tradition transmission from a written Q text to the form which we now have in the Synoptic Tradition.[62] This can be illustrated by our examination of Aland §347 (The Death of Jesus).

In the case of Aland §347 (The Death of Jesus, Matt 27//Mark 15//Luke 23), the Markan text more closely resembles the longer Matthean parallel. If one were to examine subsequently the Matthean and Lukan parallels *without* the benefit of having the Markan text (i.e., Mark 15:33-15:39), one could understandably assume that the shorter parallel (in this case Luke) is closer to the original, and therefore may be tempted to excise the additional Matthean material and reconstruct a text that looks more like the shorter Lukan parallel. However, if one were to reconstruct the Markan text under this assumption, significant sections of the extant Markan text would be omitted. Of the sections that would be left out of the reconstructed text are Mark 15:34–35 (the cry of dereliction), Mark 15:36 (offering a sponge of vinegar, Elijah coming to save/take him down). In sum, if Matthew and Luke's use of Mark is any indication of how they would have used Q, then the reconstruction of a "critical edition of Q" will forever be at best an approximation of one possible form of the source text, but by no means a definitive one.

VB, SW, and OR

The levels of verbatim agreement (VB) in general are quite close to the corresponding level of shared words (SW) within individual sections of parallels. This suggests that when Matthew and Luke choose to use the same lexical root of a particular word from their source (either oral or literary), they tend to reproduce their source verbatim. On most occasions, the morphology of the incorporated source word(s) remains intact. There

---

[62] See above, chs. 2, 3 for more on the difficulty in assuming that the Synoptic Tradition developed in linear, evolutionary manner.

are exceptions to this, in particular Aland §107 (Jesus Concerning John), where sections 10–14 contain an unusually low level of verbatim words in comparison to the level of shared words. In this case, a look at the internal variability within the pericope helps us distinguish the front half of the pericope (sec. 1–7) from the second half.

However, this observation does not lend any insight into how often or to what extent Matthew and Luke chose to use a synonym of a word contained in their source. While this is possible in a study of triple tradition passages that are clearly derivative of Mark, to do so in the double tradition passages is highly speculative without access to an original, non-reconstructed source text.

Among the more surprising findings is in regard to the agreement in word order (%OR) within the pericopes. From our limited examination, there appears to be no significant difference in the level of agreement in word order between the "oral" (A), "literary" (B), or "control" (C) groups.[63] The agreement in word order within individual pericopes overall is very high and this again suggests that when a a tradition is utilized, either oral or literary, Matthew and Luke tend to replicate the original word order of the passage as well. This is somewhat surprising given the relative flexibility of word order in Koine Greek. Our study was not able to consider whether this replication of word order is due to the word order within the tradition to which Matthew and Luke had access, or whether there are other factors which may have led Matthew and Luke to reproduce the internal word order within their double tradition passages.

---

[63] For the majority of the pericopes studied above, most sections are have %OR figures of 100%. The three pericopes with the greatest level of variation in %OR are Aland §85 (group "A"), Aland §107 (group "B"), and Aland §278 (group "C").

Chapter 7

Conclusion

We began our journey in chapter 2 by examining the extent to which the study of the Synoptic Gospels has been marked by an excessive bias towards an exclusively literary paradigm. We focused on two categories of scholarship; "alternative theories" of the Synoptic problem and the two-source hypothesis. For our examination of the alternative theories, we paid particular attention to the work of Farmer and Sanders, and used them to illustrate the extent to which the textual paradigm has influenced our understanding of the question of Synoptic interrelationships. In our subsequent examination of the two-source hypothesis, we noted that the same bias towards texts was present, despite the early recognition that one must account for the possible influence of oral tradition on the formation of the Gospel tradition.

We then turned our attention towards more recent work on "Q" and examined several of the key arguments that have led many scholars (rightly) to conclude that there is a textual source behind the common Matthean and Lukan double tradition. Unfortunately, the strength of the argument for the *existence* of a common source has resulted in the over-confident attribution of much, if not all, of the shared double tradition to the now posited written source text (i.e., Q). We suggested that this was in part due to the methodological difficulties of previous studies, and their highly literary approach to the double tradition. It was deemed necessary to revisit the question of verbatim agreement and the possible role that it might have in determining, not only the scope of a Q text, but also the possibility that some double tradition passages are not the result of the textual redaction of a common source text.

Given the way in which previous scholarship has dealt with the question of oral tradition and the Gospels, it was necessary to take time to examine in greater detail the history of scholarship that has led to the situation described above, and to seek a way forward in the debate on oral tradition and its proper role in discussion of Christian origins.

Our goals in chapter 3 were two-fold. First, it was necessary to understand better why the modern study of the Synoptic Gospels has become so "text-centered." To that end, we examined the historical roots behind the study of the Synoptic Gospels, with particular interest in the early form-critical view of oral tradition and the process of tradition transmission. Our survey of the NT form-critics Bultmann, Dibelius, and Gerhardsson gave us valuable insight into the way in which scholarship has developed in this respect. Despite arriving at quite different conclusions, all three scholars recognized that the study of oral tradition was important; however, they misunderstood how oral tradition functioned, due in large part to their approach to oral tradition as simply a variant of textual transmission. For these form-critics, both oral and written tradition developed in a linear fashion and the extant tradition could be studied without regard for the medium of transmission. Our survey of the early form-critics enabled us to see more clearly why the strict literary paradigm has become so firmly entrenched in Synoptic Gospel research.

Second, we turned our attention toward more recent attempts to overcome an overly literary approach to the Synoptic Tradition. We began by illustrating how NT scholarship was transformed by the influence of the pioneering work of Lord. His work represented the beginning of a new chapter in New Testament research, one which, for the first time, would begin to grapple seriously with the implications derived from the work of twentieth century sociology, anthropology, and folklore studies. Subsequent NT scholarship was then evaluated through the lens of the formative studies of Lord, Ong, and others who have studied in detail orally-based cultures. There was a clear development of thought within NT circles and, with the exception of Henaut, we noted that most work on oral tradition improved on that which preceded it, although there were additional areas which remained unexplored and demanded further attention.

Although progress had been made toward counteracting a strictly literary approach to the Gospel tradition, our survey exposed the need for a much more careful analysis of the relationship between orality and literacy. Henaut's work questioned the very premise that one should assume an oral prehistory behind the Synoptic Tradition, and as we noted in chapters 1 and 2, a highly literary approach remains at the center of Gospel studies to this day. Given this observation and the nature of this present work, it was necessary to work out in more detail the relationship between oral communication and written texts and to examine further the historical setting in which the Jesus tradition was initially performed and subsequently transmitted.

Therefore, in chapter 4 we examined the complex relationship in antiquity between oral communication and written texts. We interacted with a wide range of primary source material through a primarily diachronic approach, in an attempt to formulate a composite picture of how oral tradition was viewed in antiquity. Our focus was on the following three areas: the oral origins of traditions and texts, oral sources for texts, and the relationship between oral performance and written texts. Our survey of the primary source material illustrated the extent to which oral tradition was integrated into all aspects of life in antiquity. We illustrated that texts were often heard rather than read silently, composition was typically by means of dictation, and oral performance was an integral part of the process of writing a text. Oral tradition served both as a source for texts, and often served as the impetus for the initial inscription of the text itself.

In addition, we noted that despite the proliferation of texts during the time of Gospel production, they were not intended to supplant oral communication, but at times were viewed as less valuable than tradition which could be acquired through the oral/aural interaction with other eyewitnesses (αὐτόπται). Texts themselves were also perceived as "holy objects" worthy of veneration, and this attitude towards them reflected the ancient perception of texts.

Our model compelled us to question the adequacy of the strictly literary approach to the tradition which had occupied us to this stage. Given the resultant portrayal of the relationship between oral communication and written texts in chapter 4, we suggested that solutions which do not take into serious account the influence of oral tradition must be deemed historically unlikely and therefore less-than-adequate models for understanding the question of Synoptic Gospel formation and interrelationships.

Having established the likelihood that oral tradition played a vital role in the development of the Gospel tradition, it was then necessary to inquire as to *how* oral communication functioned, and to develop a more thoroughly thought-through theory of oral communication. We began chapter 5 with an examination of several important issues related to the characteristics of oral communication. It was suggested that the two primary approaches to studying the Jesus tradition are by means of either an *inferential media model* or an *interdisciplinary model*. The limitations of an inferential model were detailed and subsequent attention was directed towards the development and application of an interdisciplinary media model with a view towards examining the development and transmission of the early Jesus tradition. The question of the applicability of twentieth century studies for understanding the Jesus tradition was also addressed, and the potential danger of anachronism was discussed.

Following the discussion of preliminary matters, we examined briefly the question of Gospel genre and suggested that the genre of *folklore*, while not replacing the more literary genre categories, can help us to understand better the processes behind the development of the Synoptic Tradition. Once the negative connotations often associated with the term were removed from the discussion, it was proposed that folklore could be a helpful heuristic tool for analyzing the Synoptic Tradition. We inquired whether it was possible to use the resources provided us by way of recent folklore scholarship to clarify further the way in which tradition transmission functioned, and concluded that they could provide us with additional insight into the transmission of the early Jesus tradition and the development of the Synoptic Tradition.

We then proceeded to examine recent folklore studies by leading folklorists and New Testament scholars alike, and drew attention to any points of similarity in the hope that they present a way forward in the ongoing debate regarding Synoptic Gospel formation. Subsequent attention was given to leading folklorists such as Dundes, who has examined the Biblical canon from his unique, exterior perspective, free from the internal debates and issues that typically occupy Gospel scholars. Following our examination of the findings of folklorists, we suggested that *redundancy* and *variability* are the two major characteristics of orally transmitted tradition. Further examination led us to propose that that the variable character of oral communication is counterbalanced by a *thematic fixity* whereby communal boundaries are established which help maintain the general stability of a tradition during multiple retellings. Several scholars have suggested recently that the Synoptic Tradition exhibits these characteristics of "fixity" and "flexibility," and that this helps clarify on several occasions the relationship between Matthean and Lukan double tradition pericopes.

In the final chapter of this study, our primary goals were two-fold. Our first goal was to develop a methodology which could be used to study the presence of variability and stability in the Synoptic Tradition. This in turn would allow us to test the hypothesis that was put forward by the scholars mentioned in the previous chapter, in particular that offered by Bailey and Dunn. We would then be able see to what extent this methodology can help us to examine the double tradition from a folkloristic perspective. Other observations we also made along the way, the results of which were detailed throughout the discussion.

We returned once again to the phenomenon of verbatim agreement, which we initially discussed in chapter 2, this time in reference to the prominent characteristic of Synoptic variability and stability. We surveyed previous studies of the phenomenon of verbatim agreement, and suggested that another method is needed to examine the tradition from a folkloristic perspective as earlier detailed in chapter 5.

While previous statistical studies of verbatim agreement in the double tradition have done a sufficient job in illustrating the wide range of verbatim agreement *across* the double tradition as a whole, we suggested that they have not placed enough emphasis on the *internal variability* within individual pericopes, and have not given adequate attention to the possibility that this phenomenon might, to some extent, illuminate the process of tradition transmission which preceded the tradition's inscription into a Gospel text. Given the extent to which variability is a key characteristic of folklore, it was necessary to question whether a single figure of verbatim agreement for a pericope accurately reflected the distribution of agreement within the pericope itself.

After covering some preliminary matters regarding the use of statistics in a field such as Biblical studies, we developed and detailed a method whereby it was possible to examine effectively both the internal variability and fixity within individual pericopes. To begin our analysis we chose a selection of double tradition pericopes that have been labeled as "oral" (group "A") and "literary" (group "B") by Dunn, and also included two triple tradition passages to serve as a "control" (group "C") against which we could compare the results from groups "A" and "B." We proceeded to ask several questions which we hoped to address with our methodology, and then engaged the tradition itself. Following our study, we were then in a position to see how the phenomena of variability and stability might help us to address some questions regarding the process of tradition transmission that led to the formation of the pericopes under examination.

We suggested that an examination of the phenomenon of internal variability can help us better understand the character of the tradition. We noted that the overall level of variability within those passages labeled "oral" by Dunn was greater than those labeled "literary," but equally significant, the level of variability in the "oral" pericopes was also greater than the level of variability within the "control" passages (group "C") as well. While not providing us with any clear criteria for discerning the presence of oral tradition behind the extant Synoptic Tradition, our study highlighted the explanatory power offered by a folkloristic approach to the tradition whereby the variability and stability within the tradition could be accounted for by an appeal to a "living" tradition which was repeatedly performed by members of the early Christian communities. Although it is clear that it is not possible to state *definitively* that Dunn's "oral" passages (group "A") are indeed derivative of oral performance or even have an oral prehistory, there is at least a sufficient convergence of evidence to suggest that such a thesis is plausible for at least several of his selected pericopes.

We found ourselves in agreement with Dunn's assessment in several places. By focusing on internal variability we were able to appreciate how the character of the tradition reflected its possible relationship to oral performance. That is, in several instances the Synoptic parallels clearly were multiform variations of the same traditions, which probably stemmed from the same originating source, but were characteristically remembered and transmitted in varying performances.

However, the evidence was not entirely supportive of all of Dunn's pericopes. Our examination of internal variability also highlighted the difficulty in attributing a pericope to the possible influence of oral tradition. Our analysis of the "Centurion's Servant" pericope (Aland §85, see above, §6.6.4) illustrated this difficulty. While at first the variability within the pericope suggests that it might have come to Matthew and Luke via oral tradition, the lengthy sections of verbatim agreement therein were unique among the group "A" pericopes we studied, and as such, forced us to ask whether this pericope might be attributable to Matthean and Lukan editorial activity.

We also suggested that the concept of a "core" is an important factor in determining the possible tradition-history of a parallel pericope. The folkloristic characteristic of stability (i.e., "core") which has been emphasized by Dunn and Bailey only occurred in group "A" pericopes. However, we also noted that the existence of a "core" within a tradition is only significant in pericopes that have a low overall level of verbatim agreement. When the level of verbatim agreement within thematically significant sections becomes indistinguishable from that in the other sections within the pericope, the usefulness of a "core" is diminished. This leads us to ask whether the presence of "core" sections within group "A" pericopes, coupled with the absence of such sections within the group "B" and group "C" pericopes could be significant. While such a question needs to be asked, it is beyond the scope of this current project to do so.

We can now take a step back and provide a tentative evaluation of the thesis put forth by Bailey and Dunn with regard to the presence of variability and stability within the Synoptic Tradition. From our folkloristic perspective, the thesis of Bailey and Dunn does correspond to a certain extent with the observed variability and stability within at least portions of the double tradition. Our methodology has proven to be helpful in illustrating the extent to which recent claims regarding Gospel "orality" have corresponded with the characteristics deemed significant by folklorists and NT scholars alike. While none of our findings above constitute *definitive* evidence for the oral origins of selected double tradition pericopes, we must, at the very least, be willing to recognize the significant explanatory power of an oral performance model of early Christian tradition transmission. This, in turn, can help refocus our attention on the "living" tradition that was in circulation during the time when Matthew and Luke wrote their respective Gospels.

Given the extent to which oral communication dominated ancient society, we must look beyond the rigid, highly — and often exclusively literary models of Synoptic Gospel interrelationships that dominate the current academic landscape. Despite the understandable desire to reconstruct an elegant model of Gospel interrelationships, which a strictly literary paradigm enables one to do, we must begin a shift away from an exclusively literary model of Synoptic interrelationships towards an understanding of the Jesus tradition that is able to take account of the highly oral milieu that existed during the time of Gospel composition. This, of course, might require a significant revision of the historical-critical method that has driven NT scholarship for more than one hundred years. The model that results from such a process might not prove as straightforward or as elegant as one would desire, but arguably it will be more faithful to the character of the Jesus tradition and to the historical context within which it was initially performed and subsequently transmitted.

Bibliography

Abel, Ernest L. "The Psychology of Memory and Rumor Transmission and Their Bearing on Theories of Oral Transmission in Early Christianity." *Journal of Religion* 51 (1971): 270–281.

Achtemeier, Paul J. "Omne Verbum Sonat: The New Testament and the Oral Environment of Late Western Antiquity." *Journal of Biblical Literature* 109:1 (1990): 3–27.

Aland, B., K. Aland, J. Karvidopoulos, C. M. Martini, and B. M. Metzger, eds. *The Greek New Testament*. 4th ed. Stuttgart: Deutsche Bibelgesellschaft, 1994.

Aland, B., K. Aland, J. Karvidopoulos, C. M. Martini, and B. M. Metzger, eds. *Novum Testamentum Graece*. 27th ed. Stuttgart: Deutsche Bibelgesellschaft, 1993.

Aland, Kurt and Eberhard Nestle. *Synopsis quattuor Evangeliorum*. Stuttgart: Württembergische Bibelanstalt, 1964.

Alexander, Loveday C. A. "Ancient Book Production and the Circulation of the Gospels." Pages 71–105 in *The Gospels for All Christians*. Edited by Richard Bauckham. Edinburgh: T&T Clark, 1998.

Alexander, Loveday C. A. "Luke's Preface in the Pattern of Greek Preface Writing." *Novum Testamentum* 28 (1986): 48–74.

Alexander, Loveday C. A. "The Living Voice: Scepticism towards the Written Word in Early Christianity and in Graeco-Roman Texts." Pages 221–247 in *The Bible in Three Dimensions: Essays in Celebration of Forty Years of Biblical Studies in the University of Sheffield*. Edited by D. J. A. Clines, S. E. Fowl, and S. E. Porter. JSOTSup 87. Sheffield: Sheffield Academic Press, 1990.

Alexander, Loveday C. A. *The Preface to Luke's Gospel: Literary Convention and Social Context in Luke 1:1–4 and Acts 1:1*. SNTSMS 78. Cambridge: Cambridge University Press, 1993.

Allen, W. C. "Did St. Matthew and St. Luke Use the Logia?" *Expository Times* 11 (1899): 424–426.

Anderson, Øivind. "Oral Tradition." Pages 17–58 in *Jesus and the Oral Gospel Tradition*. Edited by Henry Wansbrough. JSNTSup 64. Sheffield: JSOT Press, 1991.

Assmann, Jan. "Collective Memory and Cultural Identity." *New German Critique* 65 (1995): 125–133.

Assmann, Jan. *Das kulturelle Gedächtnis. Schrift, Erinnerung und politische Identität in frühen Hochkulturen*. Munich: C. H. Beck, 1992.

Audet, Jean-Paul. *La Didachè: Instructions des apôtres*. Paris: Gabalda, 1958.

Aune, David E. "Oral Tradition and the Aphorisms of Jesus." Pages 211–265 in *Jesus and the Oral Gospel Tradition*. Edited by Henry Wansbrough. JSNTSup 64. Sheffield: JSOT Press, 1991.

Aune, David E. "Prolegomena to the Study of Oral Tradition in the Hellenistic World." Pages 59–106 in *Jesus and the Oral Gospel Tradition*. Edited by Henry Wansbrough. JSNTSup 64. Sheffield: JSOT Press, 1991.

Aune, David E. *The Westminster Dictionary of New Testament and Early Christian Literature and Rhetoric*. Louisville: Westminster/ John Knox, 2003.

Bailey, Kenneth E. "Informal Controlled Oral Tradition and the Synoptic Gospels." *Asia Journal of Theology* 5:1 (1991): 34–54.

Bar-Ilan, Meir. "Illiteracy in the Land of Israel in the First Centuries C.E.." Pages 46–61 in *Essays in the Social Scientific Study of Judaism and Jewish Society*. Edited by Simcha Fishbane, Stuart Schoenfeld, and A. Goldschlaeger. New York: KTAV, 1992.

Barrett, C. K. "Q: A Re-examination." *Expository Times* 54 (1943): 320–323.

Barrett, C. K. *A Critical and Exegetical Commentary of the Acts of the Apostles*. 2 vols. International Critical Commentary. Edinburgh: T & T Clark, 1994.

Barton, Stephen C. "Can We Identify the Gospel Audiences?" Pages 173–194 in *The Gospels for All Christians*. Edited by Richard Bauckham. Grand Rapids: Eerdmans, 1998.

Bascom, William R. "Verbal Art." *Journal of American Folklore* 68 (1955): 245–252.

Ben-Amos, Dan. "Folklore in the Ancient Near East." Pages 818–828 in vol. 2 of *Anchor Bible Dictionary*. 6 Volumes. Edited by David Noel Freedman. New York: Doubleday, 1991.

Bergemann, Thomas. *Q auf dem Prüfstand: die Zuordnung des Mt/Lk-Stoffes zu Q am Beispiel der Bergpredigt*. Forschungen zur Religion und Literatur des Alten und Neuen Testaments 158. Göttingen: Vandenhoeck & Ruprecht, 1993.

Berkowitz, L., K. A. Squitier, eds. *Thesaurus linguae: Canon of Greek Authors and Works*. New York: OUP, 1990.

Bernard, J. H. *The Gospel According to St. John*. 2 vols. Edinburgh: T&T Clark, 1928.

Betz, Hans Dieter. *The Sermon on the Mount. A Commentary on the Sermon on the Mount, including the Sermon on the Plain*. Hermeneia. Minneapolis: Fortress Press, 1995.

Beuchat, P. D. "Riddles in Bantu." Pages 182–207 in *The Study of Folklore*. Edited by Alan Dundes. Englewood Cliffs: Prentice Hall, 1965.

Bligh, John. *Galatians in Greek: A Structural Analysis of Paul's Epistle to the Galatians*. Detroit: University Press, 1966.

Blomberg, Craig L. *Jesus and the Gospels: an Introduction and Survey*. Nashville: Broadman & Holman, 1997.

Boomershine, Thomas E. "Biblical Megatrends: Towards a Paradigm for the Interpretation of the Bible in Electronic Media." Pages 144–157 Society of Biblical Literature Seminar Papers: Society of Biblical Literature, 1987.

Boomershine, Thomas E. "Peter's Denial as Polemic or Confession: The Implications of Media Criticism for Biblical Hermeneutics." *Semeia* 39 (1987): 47–68.

Borgen, P., Kåre Fuglseth, Roald Skarsten, *The Philo Index, A Complete Greek Word Index to the Writings of Philo of Alexandria*. Grand Rapids: Eerdmans, 2000.

Boring, M. Eugene. *Sayings of the Risen Jesus: Christian Prophecy in the Synoptic Tradition*. Cambridge: Cambridge University Press, 1982.

Botha, Pieter J. J. "Greco-Roman Literacy as Setting for New Testament Writings." *Neotestamentica* 26 (1992): 195–215.

Botha, Pieter J. J. "Mark's Story of Jesus and the Search for Virtue." Pages 156–184 in *The Rhetorical Analysis of Scripture*. Edited by Stanley E. Porter and Thomas H. Olbricht. JSNTSup 146. Sheffield: Sheffield Academic Press, 1997.

Briggs, Katharine M. and Ruth L. Tongue, eds. *Folktales of England*. London: Routledge, 1965.

Brown, Raymond E. *The Gospel According to John*. 2 vols. Garden City: Doubleday, 1966.

Bultmann, Rudolf K. *Die Geschichte der synoptischen Tradition*. Göttingen: Vandenhoeck & Ruprecht, 1931.

Bultmann, Rudolf K. *Die Geschichte der synoptischen Tradition*. Göttingen: Vandenhoeck & Ruprecht, 1957.

Bultmann, Rudolf K. *The History of the Synoptic Tradition*. Translated by John Marsh. New York: Harper and Row, 1963.

Burridge, Richard A. *Four Gospels, One Jesus? A Symbolic Reading*. Grand Rapids: Eerdmans, 1994.

Burridge, Richard A. *What are the Gospels?: a Comparison with Graeco-Roman Biography*. Cambridge: Cambridge University Press, 1992.

Bussmann, Wilhelm. *Synoptische studien*. Halle: Buchhandlung des Waisenhauses, 1925.

Butler, B. C. *The Originality of St. Matthew: A Critique of the Two-Document Hypothesis*. Cambridge: Cambridge University Press, 1951.

Byrskog, Samuel. *Jesus the Only Teacher: Didactic Authority and Transmission in Ancient Israel, Ancient Judaism and the Matthean Community*. Coniectanea Biblica: New Testament Series 24. Stockholm: Almqvist & Wiksell International, 1994.

Byrskog, Samuel. *Story as History — History as Story: The Gospel Tradition in the Context of Ancient Oral History*. WUNT 123. Tübingen: Mohr Siebeck, 2000.

Carlston, Charles E. and Dennis Norlin. "Once More- Statistics and Q." *Harvard Theological Review* 64 (1971): 59–78.

Carlston, Charles E. and Dennis Norlin. "Statistics and Q- Some Further Observations." *Novum Testamentum* 41 (1999): 108–123.

Charles, R. H., *The Apocrypha and Pseudepigrapha of the Old Testament*. 2 vols. Oxford: OUP, 1963.

Charlesworth, J. H., ed. *The Old Testament Pseudepigrapha*. 2 vols. Garden City: Doubleday, 1985.

Conrad, Edgar. "Heard But Not Seen: The Representation of 'Books' in the Old Testament." *JSOT* 54 (1992): 45–59.

Conzelmann, Hans. *The Theology of St. Luke*. Translated by G. Buswell. New York: Harper & Row, 1960.

Crossan, John Dominic. *Four Other Gospels: Shadows on the Contours of Canon*. Minneapolis: Winston, 1985.

Crossan, John Dominic. *The Historical Jesus: The Life of a Mediterranean Jewish Peasant*. San Francisco: HarperSanFrancisco, 1991.

Culley, Robert C. "An Approach to the Problem of Oral Tradition." *Vetus Testamentum* 13 (1963): 112–125.

Culley, Robert C. "Oral Tradition and Biblical Studies." *Oral Tradition* 1 (1986): 30–65.

Danby, H., *The Mishnah, Translated from the Hebrew with Introduction and Brief Explanatory Notes*. Oxford: OUP, 1933.

Daniels, Peter D. and William Bright, eds. *The World's Writing Systems*. New York: Oxford University, 1996.

Davies, Philip R. *Scribes and Schools: The Canonization of the Hebrew Scriptures*. Library of Ancient Israel. Louisville: Westminster John Knox, 1998.

Davies, W. D. and Dale C. Allison. *A Critical and Exegetical Commentary on the Gospel According to St. Matthew*. 3 vols. International Critical Commentary on the Holy Scriptures. Edinburgh: T & T Clark, 1988.

Davis, Casey Wayne. *Oral Biblical Criticism: The Influence of the Principles of Orality on the Literary Structure of Paul's Epistle to the Philippians*. JSNTSUP 172. Sheffield: Sheffield Academic Press, 1999.

Denaux, Adelbert. "Criteria For Identifying Q-Passages: A Critical Review of a Recent Work by T. Bergemann." *Novum Testamentum* 37:2 (1995): 105–129.

Derrenbacker, Robert A. "Greco-Roman Writing Practices and Luke's Gospel." Pages 61–83 in *The Gospels According to Michael Goulder: a North American Response*. Edited by Christopher A. Rollston. Harrisburg: Trinity Press International, 2002.

Dewey, Joanna. "From Oral Stories to Written Texts." Pages 20–28 in *Women's Sacred Scriptures*. Edited by Pui-Lan Kwok and Elisabeth Schüssler Fiorenza. Maryknoll: Orbis, 1998.

Dewey, Joanna. "Mark as Aural Narrative: Structures as Clues to Understanding." *Sewanee Theological Review* 36 (1992): 45–56.

Dewey, Joanna. "Oral Methods of Structuring Narrative in Mark." *Interpretation* 43 (1989): 32–44.

Dewey, Joanna. *Markan Public Debate : Literary Technique, Concentric Structure, and Theology in Mark 2:1–3:6*. Chico: Scholars Press, 1980.

Dibelius, Martin. *Die Formgeschichte des Evangeliums*. Tübingen: J.C.B. Mohr, 1919.

Dibelius, Martin. *Die Formgeschichte des Evangeliums*. Tübingen: J.C.B. Mohr, 1933.

Dibelius, Martin. *From Tradition to Gospel*. Translated by Bertram Lee Woolf. Cambridge: James Clarke, 1971.

Downing, F. G. "A Paradigm Perplex: Luke, Matthew and Mark." *New Testament Studies* 38 (1992): 15–36.

Downing, F. G. "Word-Processing in the Ancient World: The Social Production and Performance of Q [evidence for Oral Composition of Gospel Tradition]." *Journal for the Study of the New Testament* 64 (1996): 29–48.

Draper, Jonathan A. "The Sermon on the Plain (Luke 6:12–7:17) as Oral Performance: Pointers to "Q" as Multiple Oral Performance." Unpublished, private correspondence. Originally presented at the SBL Annual Meeting, Nashville, November 2000.

Duff, Paul Brooks. "Processions." Pages 469–473 in vol. 5 of *The Anchor Bible Dictionary*. 6 Volumes. Edited by David Noel Freedman. New York: Doubleday, 1996.

Dundes, Alan. *Holy Writ as Oral Lit: The Bible as Folklore*. Lanham: Rowman & Littlefield, 1999.

Dundes, Alan. "The Hero Pattern and the Life of Jesus." Pages 223-261 in *In Quest of the Hero*. Otto Rank, Lord Raglan, and Alan Dundes. Princeton: Princeton University Press, 1990.

Dundes, Alan. *The Morphology of North American Indian Folktales*. Helsinki: Academia Scientiarum Fennica, 1964.

Dundes, Alan. *The Study of Folklore*. Englewood Cliffs: Prentice-Hall, 1965.

Dundes, Alan. Preface to *The Theory of Oral Composition*, edited by John Miles Foley. Bloomington: Indiana University Press, 1988.

Dungan, David L. "Theory of Synopsis Construction." *Biblica* 61 (1980): 305–329.

Dungan, David L. *The History of the Synoptic Problem*. ABRL. New York: Doubleday, 1999.

Dunn, James D. G. "Altering the Default Setting: Re-envisaging the Early Transmission of the Jesus Tradition." *NTS* 49 (2003): 139–175.

Dunn, James D. G. "Jesus in Oral Memory: The Initial Stages of the Jesus Tradition." Pages 287–326 in *SBL 2000 Seminar Papers*. SBLSP 39. Atlanta: Society of Biblical Literature, 2000.

Dunn, James D. G. "Jesus in Oral Memory: The Initial Stages of the Jesus Tradition." Pages 84–145 in *Jesus: A Colloquium in the Holy Land*. Edited by Doris Donnelly. New York: Continuum, 2001.

Dunn, James D. G. *Jesus Remembered*. Grand Rapids: Eerdmans, 2003.

Dunn, James D. G. *The Theology of Paul the Apostle*. Edinburgh: T&T Clark, 1998.

Eberhard, Wolfram, ed. *Folktales of China*. New York: Washington Square Press, 1973.

Ehrman, Bart D. *The New Testament and Other Early Christian Writings*. New York: Oxford University Press, 1998.

Ehrman, Bart D. *The New Testament: A Historical Introduction to the Early Christian.* New York: Oxford, 1997.

Ehrman, Bart D. *The Orthodox Corruption of Scripture : The Effect of Early Christological Controversies on the Text of the New Testament.* New York: Oxford University Press, 1993.

Elliger, K. and W. Rudolph, eds. *Biblia Hebraica Stuttgartensia.* Stuttgart: Deutsche Bibelgesellschaft, 1990.

Epp, E. J. "The Multivalence of the Term "Original Text" in New Testament Textual Criticism." *HTR* 92 (1999): 245–281.

Ewald, Paul. *Das Hauptproblem der Evangelienfrage und der Weg zu seiner Lösung: eine akademische Vorlesung nebst Exkursen.* Leipzig: J.C. Hinrichs, 1890.

Farmer, William R. "A Fresh Approach to Q." in *Christianity, Judaism and Other Greco-Roman Cults: Studies for Morton Smith at Sixty.* Edited by Jacob Neusner. Studies in Judaism in Late Antiquity. Leiden: E. J. Brill, 1975.

Farmer, William R. *The Synoptic Problem.* New York: Macmillan, 1964.

Farrer, Austin M. "On Dispensing With Q." Pages 55–88 in *Studies in the Gospels: Essays in Memory of R. H. Lightfoot.* Edited by D. E. Nineham. Oxford: Blackwell, 1955.

Finnegan, Ruth. "How Oral is Oral Literature?" *BSOAS* 37 (1974): 52–64.

Finnegan, Ruth. *Oral Literature in Africa.* Oxford: Oxford University Press, 1970.

Finnegan, Ruth. *Oral Poetry: Its Nature, Significance, and Social Context.* Cambridge: Cambridge University Press, 1977.

Fitzmyer, Joseph A. *Acts of the Apostles.* The Anchor Bible 31. New York: Doubleday, 1998.

Foley, John Miles. *How to Read an Oral Poem.* Chicago: University of Illinois, 2002.

Foley, John Miles. *Immanent Art: From Structure to Meaning in Traditional Oral Epic.* Bloomington: Indiana University Press, 1991.

Foley, John Miles. *The Theory of Oral Composition: History and Methodology.* Bloomington: Indiana University Press, 1988.

Forbes, A. Dean. "Statistical Research on the Bible." Pages 185–206 in vol. 6 of *The Anchor Bible Dictionary.* Edited by David Noel Freedman. New York: Doubleday, 1992.

Frazer, James G. "The Fall of Man." Pages 72–97 in *Sacred Narrative.* Edited by Alan Dundes. Berkeley: University of California Press, 1984. Repr. pages 45–77 from *Folklore in the Old Testament.* London: 1918.

Frazer, James G. *Folklore in the Old Testament: Studies in Comparative Religion, Legend and Law.* 3 vols. London: Macmillan, 1918.

Freyne, Seán. *Galilee, Jesus and the Gospels.* Philadelphia: Fortress Press, 1988.

Funk, Robert W. and Roy W. Hoover. *The Five Gospels: the Search for the Authentic Words of Jesus. New Translation and Commentary.* New York: Macmillan, 1993.

Gamble, Harry Y. *Books and Readers in the Early Church: A History of Early Christian Texts.* New Haven: Yale University Press, 1995.

Gaster, Moses. "Folk-Lore in the Old Testament." *Folk-Lore* 30 (1919): 71–76.

Gerhardsson, Birger. "Illuminating the Kingdom: Narrative Meshalim in the Synoptic Gospels." Pages 266–309 in *Jesus and the Oral Gospel Tradition.* JSNTSup 64. Sheffield: JSOT Press, 1991.

Gerhardsson, Birger. *Memory and Manuscript: Oral Tradition and Written Transmission in Rabbinic Judaism and Early Christianity.* Translated by Eric J. Sharpe. Uppsala: C. W. K. Gleerup, 1961.

Gilliard, Frank D. "More Silent Reading in Antiquity: Non Omne Verbum Sonabat." *Journal of Biblical Literature* 112 (1993): 689–694.

Glover, Richard. "The Didache's Quotations and the Synoptic Gospels." *New Testament Studies* 5 (1958): 12–29.

Goodacre, Mark. "A Monopoly on Marcan Priority? Fallacies at the Heart of Q." Pages 583–622 in *SBL 2000 Seminar Papers*. SBLSP 39. Atlanta: Society of Biblical Literature, 2000.

Goodacre, Mark. *The Case Against Q: Studies in Markan Priority and the Synoptic Problem*. Harrisburg: Trinity Press International, 2002.

Goodacre, Mark. *The Synoptic Problem: A Way Through the Maze*. London: Sheffield Academic Press, 2001.

Goody, Jack and Ian Watt. "The Consequences of Literacy." Pages 27–68 in *Literacy in Traditional Societies*. Edited by Jack Goody. Cambridge: Cambridge University Press, 1968.

Goody, Jack. *The Domestication of the Savage Mind*. Cambridge: Cambridge University Press, 1977.

Görög-Karady, Veronika. "Retelling Genesis: The Children of Eve and the Origin of Inequality." Pages 31–44 in *Genres, Forms, Meanings: Essays in African Oral Literature*. Edited by Veronika Görög-Karady. Oxford: Journal of the Anthropological Society of Oxford, 1983.

Goulder, Michael D. "Is Q a Juggernaut?" *JBL* 115 (1996): 667–681.

Goulder, Michael D. "Luke's Compositional Origins." *NTS* 39 (1993): 150–152.

Goulder, Michael D. "On the Order of a Crank." Pages 111–130 in *Synoptic Studies*. Edited by Christopher M. Tuckett. JSNTSup 7. Sheffield: Sheffield Academic Press, 1984.

Goulder, Michael D. *Luke: A New Paradigm*. 2 vols. JSNTSup 20. Sheffield: JSOT, 1989.

Gray, Bennison. "Repetition in Oral Literature." *Journal of American Folklore* 84 (1971): 289–303.

Guijarro, Santiago. "The Family in First-Century Galilee." Pages 42-65 in *Constructing Early Christian Families: Family as Social Reality and Metaphor*. Edited by Halvor Moxnes. New York: Routledge, 1997.

Gunkel, Hermann. *Genesis*. Translated by Mark E. Biddle. Macon: Mercer, 1997.

Gunkel, Hermann. *The Folktale in the Old Testament*. Translated by Michael D. Rutter. Sheffield: Almond Press, 1987.

Gunkel, Hermann. *The Legends of Genesis*. New York: Schocken Books, 1964.

Güttgemanns, Erhardt. *Offene Fragen zur Formgeschichte des Evangeliums: Eine Methodologische Skizze der Grundlagenproblematik der Form-und Redaktionsgeschichte*. 54. München: C. Kaiser, 1970.

Hagner, Donald A. Preface to *The Reliability of the Gospel Tradition*, by Birger Gerhardsson. Peabody: Hendrickson, 2001.

Hahn, Johann Georg von. *Sagwissenschaftliche Studien*. Jena: F. Mauke, 1876.

Haines-Eitzen, Kim. *Guardians of Letters: Literacy, Power, and the Transmitters of Early Christian Literature*. Oxford: Oxford University Press, 2000.

Halliday, M. A. K. *Language as Social Semiotic: The Social Interpretation of Language and Meaning*. Baltimore: University Park Press, 1978.

Harnack, Adolf von. *Geschichte der altchristlichen Litteratur bis Eusebius. Zweiter Theil: Die Chronologie*. 2 vols. Leipzig: J. C. Hinrichs, 1897.

Harris, William V. *Ancient Literacy*. Cambridge: Harvard University Press, 1989.

Harvey, John D. "Orality and Its Implications for Biblical Studies: Recapturing an Ancient Paradigm." *Journal of the Evangelical Theological Society* 45:1 (2002): 99–110.

Harvey, John D. *Listening to the Text: Oral Patterning in Paul's Letters.* Grand Rapids: Baker Books, 1998.

Hatch, E. and H. A. Redpath. *A Concordance to the Septuagint and the Other Greek Versions of the Old Testament.* 3 vols. Oxford: Clarendon, 1897–1906.

Havelock, Eric A. *The Literate Revolution in Greece and Its Cultural Consequences.* Princeton: Princeton University Press, 1982.

Havelock, Eric A. *The Muse Learns to Write: Reflections on Orality and Literacy from Antiquity to the Present.* New Haven: Yale University Press, 1986.

Haverly, Thomas P. "Oral Traditional Literature and the Composition of Mark." Ph.D. Thesis, University of Edinburgh, 1983.

Hawkins, John C. "Probabilities as to the So-Called Double Tradition of St. Matthew and St. Luke." Pages 95–138 in *Oxford Studies in the Synoptic Problem.* Edited by W. Sanday. Oxford: Clarendon Press, 1911.

Head, Peter M. and P. J. Williams. "Q Review." *TynBul* 54:1 (2003): 119–144.

Henaut, Barry W. *Oral Tradition and the Gospels: the Problem of Mark 4.* JSNTSup 82. Sheffield: JSOT Press, 1993.

Henderson, Ian. "Didache and Orality in Synoptic Comparison." *JBL* 111 (1992): 283–306.

Hengel, Martin. *Die johanneische Frage. Ein Lösungsversuch.* WUNT 67. Tübingen: Mohr Siebeck, 1993.

Hengel, Martin. *The 'Hellenization' of Judaea in the First Century After Christ.* Translated by John Bowden. London: SCM Press, 1989.

Hengel, Martin. *The Four Gospels and the One Gospel of Jesus Christ.* Translated by John Bowden. London: SCM Press, 2000.

Herder, Johann Gottfried. "Vom Erlöser der Menschen. Nach unsern ersten drei Evangelien (1796)." Pages 137–252 in Herders Sämmtliche Werke XIX. Edited by B. Suphan. Berlin: Weidmannsche Buchhandlung, 1880.

Herder, Johann Gottfried. "Von Gottes Sohn, der Welt Heiland. Nach Johannes Evangelium. Nebst einer Regel der Zusammenstimmung unserer Evangelien aus ihrer Entstehung und Ordnung (1797)." Pages 253–424 in Herders Sämmtliche Werke XIX. Edited by B. Suphan. Berlin: Weidmannsche Buchhandlung, 1880.

Hezser, Catherine. *Jewish Literacy in Roman Palestine.* TSAJ 81. Tübingen: Mohr Siebeck, 2001.

Holtzmann, H. J. *Die synoptischen Evangelien.* Leipzig: Wilhelm Engelmann, 1863.

Honoré, Anthony M. "A Statistical Study of the Synoptic Problem." *Novum Testamentum* 10 (1968): 95–147.

Horsley, Richard A. and Jonathan A. Draper. *Whoever Hears You Hears Me: Prophets, Performance, and Tradition in Q.* Harrisburg: Trinity Press International, 1999.

Horsley, Richard A. *Bandits, Prophets, and Messiahs.* San Francisco: HarperSanFrancisco, 1988.

Horsley, Richard A. *Hearing the Whole Story: The Politics of Plot in Mark's Gospel.* Louisville: Westminster John Knox, 2001.

Hurtado, Larry W. "The Gospel of Mark: Evolutionary or Revolutionary Document?" Pages 196–211 in *The Synoptic Gospels: A Sheffield Reader.* Edited by Craig A. Evans and Stanley E. Porter. Sheffield: Sheffield Academic Press, 1995.

Jacobson, A.D. "The Literary Unity of Q." *JBL* 101 (1982): 365–389.

Jaffee, Martin S. "Figuring Early Rabbinic Literary Culture: Thoughts Occasioned by Boomershine and J. Dewey." *Semeia* 65 (1994): 67–74.

Jaffee, Martin S. "Writing and Rabbinic Oral Tradition: On Mishnaic Narrative Lists and Mnemonics." *Journal of Jewish Thought and Philosophy* 4 (1994): 123–146.

Jeremias, Joachim. *New Testament Theology: The Proclamation of Jesus*. 2 vols. New York: Scribner, 1971.

Johnson, Luke Timothy. *The Acts of the Apostles*. Sacra Pagina 5. Collegeville, Minn.: Liturgical Press, 1992.

Johnson, Luke Timothy. *The Real Jesus: The Misguided Quest for the Historical Jesus and the Truth of the Traditional Gospels*. San Francisco: HarperSanFrancisco, 1996.

Johnson, Sherman E. *The Griesbach Hypothesis and Redaction Criticism*. SBLMS. Atlanta: Society of Biblical Literature, 1990.

Josephus. Translated by H. St. J. Thackeray et al. 10 vols. Loeb Classical Library. Cambridge: Harvard University Press, 1926–1965.

Keck, Leander E. "Oral Traditional Literature and the Gospels: The Seminar." Pages 103–122 in *The Relationships Among the Gospels: An Interdisciplinary Dialogue*. Edited by William O. Walker Jr. San Antonio: Trinity University Press, 1978.

Kelber, Werner H. "From Aphorism to Sayings Gospel and from Parable to Narrative Gospel." *Foundations & Facets Forum* 1 (1985): 23–30.

Kelber, Werner H. "Mark and Oral Tradition." *Semeia* 16 (1980): 7–55.

Kelber, Werner H. "The Two-Source Hypothesis: Oral Tradition, the Poetics of Gospel Narrativity, and Memorial Arbitration." Paper presented at the SNTS Annual Meeting, Durham, 2002.

Kelber, Werner H. *The Oral and the Written Gospel: The Hermeneutics of Speaking and Writing in the Synoptic Tradition, Mark, Paul, and Q*. Philadelphia: Fortress Press, 1983.

Kennedy, George A. *New Testament Interpretation Through Rhetorical Criticism*. Chapel Hill: University of North Carolina Press, 1984.

Kloppenborg Verbin, John S. "Goulder and the New Paradigm: A Critical Appreciation of Michael Goulder on the Synoptic Problem." Pages 29–60 in *The Gospels According to Michael Goulder: A North American Response*. Harrisburg: Trinity Press International, 2002.

Kloppenborg Verbin, John S. *Excavating Q*. Minneapolis: Fortress Press, 2000.

Kloppenborg, John S. *The Formation of Q*. Philadelphia: Fortress Press, 1987.

Koester, Helmut. *Ancient Christian Gospels*. Philadelphia: Trinity University Press, 1990.

Koester, Helmut. *Synoptische Überlieferung bei den apostolischen Vätern*. Texte und Untersuchungen zur Geschichte der altchristlichen Literatur 65. Berlin: Akademie-Verlag, 1957.

Köhler, Wolf-Dietrich. *Die Rezeption des Matthäusevangeliums in der Zeit vor Irenäus*. WUNT II 24. Tübingen: Mohr, 1987.

Körtner, Ulrich H. J. and Martin Leutzsch. *Papiasfragmente. Hirt des Hermas*. Schriften des Urchristentums 3. Darmstadt: Wissenschaftliche Buchgesellschaft, 1998.

Kraus, Thomas J. "'Uneducated', 'Ignorant', or Even 'Illiterate?' Aspects and Background for an Understanding of ΑΓΡΑΜΜΑΤΟΙ (and ΙΔΙΩΤΑΙ) in Acts 4.13." *NTS* 45 (1999): 434–449.

Kümmel, Werner G. "In Support of Q." Pages 227–243 in *The Two Source Hypothesis: A Critical Appraisal*. Edited by Arthur J. Bellinzoni. Macon: Mercer University Press, 1973.

Kümmel, Werner G. *Introduction to the New Testament*. The New Testament Library. London: SCM Press, 1966.

Kümmel, Werner G. *The New Testament: The History of the Investigation of its Problems*. Translated by S. McClean Gilmour and Howard C. Kee. London: SCM Press, 1973.

Leakey, Richard E. and Roger Lewin. *Origins: What New Discoveries Reveal About the Evolution of Our Species and Its Possible Future*. London: MacDonald & Jane, 1979.

Liddell, H. G., R. Scott, and H. S. Jones. *A Greek-English Lexicon*. 9th ed. Oxford: Oxford University Press, 1968.

Linnemann, Eta. *Is There a Synoptic Problem? : Rethinking the Literary Dependence of the First Three Gospels*. Translated by Robert W. Yarbrough. Grand Rapids: Baker Book House, 1992.

Lohr, Charles H. "Oral Techniques in the Gospel of Matthew." *Catholic Biblical Quarterly* 23 (1961): 403–435.

Lord, Albert B. "Memory, Fixity, and Genre in Oral Traditional Poetries." Pages 451–461 in *Oral Traditional Literature: A Festschrift for Albert Bates Lord*. Edited by John Miles Foley. Ohio: Slavica Publishers, 1980.

Lord, Albert B. "The Gospels as Oral Traditional Literature." Pages 33–91 in *The Relationships Among the Gospels: An Interdisciplinary Dialogue*. Edited by William O. Walker Jr. San Antonio: Trinity University Press, 1978.

Lord, Albert B. *The Singer of Tales*. Cambridge: Harvard University Press, 1960.

Louw, J. P. and E. A. Nida, eds. *Greek-English Lexicon of the New Testament Based on Semantic Domains*. 2 vols. New York: UBS, 1989.

MacDonald, Dennis Ronald. "From Audita to Legenda: Oral and Written Miracle Stories." *Forum* 2:4 (1986): 15–26.

MacDonald, Dennis Ronald. "Thekla, Acts of.." Pages 443–444 in vol. 6 of *The Anchor Bible Dictionary*. Edited by David Noel Freedman. New York: Doubleday, 1996.

MacDonald, Dennis Ronald. *The Legend and the Apostle: The Battle for Paul in Story and Canon*. Philadelphia: Westminster Press, 1983.

Mack, Burton L. *A Myth of Innocence: Mark and Christian Origins*. Philadelphia: Fortress Press, 1988.

Malkki, Liisa H. *Purity and Exile: Violence, Memory, and National Cosmology among Hutu Refugees in Tanzania*. Chicago: University of Chicago, 1995.

Maricola, John. Introduction to Herodotus to *Herodotus: The Histories*, London: Penguin, 1996.

Mattila, Sharon L. "A Problem Still Clouded: Yet Again-Statistics and 'Q'." *Novum Testamentum* 37:4 (1994): 313–329.

McGuire, M. R. P. "Letters and Letter Carriers in Ancient Antiquity." *Classical World* 53 (1960): 148–153, 184–185, 199–200.

McIver, Robert K. and Marie Carroll. "Experiments to Develop Criteria for Determing the Existence of Written Sources, and Their Potential Implications for the Synoptic Problem." *Journal of Biblical Literature* 121:4 (2002): 667–687.

McLuhan, Marshall. *The Gutenberg Galaxy: The Making of Typographic Man*. Toronto: University of Toronto Press, 1962.

Meier, John P. *A Marginal Jew*. 3 vols. New York: Doubleday, 1991.

Meier, Samuel A. "Hammurapi." Pages 39–42 in vol. 3 of *The Anchor Bible Dictionary*. 6 Volumes. Edited by David Noel Freedman. New York: Doubleday, 1996.

Metzger, Bruce M. *A Textual Commentary on the Greek New Testament*. Stuttgart: Deutsche Bibelgesellschaft, 1994.

Meynet, Roland. *Rhetorical Analysis: An Introduction to Biblical Rhetoric*. JSOTSup 256. Sheffield: Sheffield Academic Press, 1998.

Millard, Alan R. "Oral Proclamation and Written Record: Spreading and Preserving Information in Ancient Israel." Pages 237–241 in *Michael*. Edited by Yitzhak Avishur and Robert Deutsch. Tel Aviv: Archaeological Center Publications, 1999.

Millard, Alan R. *Reading and Writing in the Time of Jesus*. Sheffield: Sheffield Academic Press, 2000.

Moberly, Walter. *At the Mountain of God*. JSOTSup. Sheffield: JSOT Press, 1983.

Morgenthaler, Robert. *Statistische Synopse*. Zurich: Gotthelf-Verlag, 1971.

Moulton, W. F. & A. S. Geden. *A Concordance of the Greek Testament*. Edinburgh: T&T Clark, 1978.

Mournet, Terence C. "A Critique of the Presuppositions, Sources, and Methodology of Contemporary Historical Jesus Research." M.T.S. Thesis, Eastern Baptist Theological Seminary, 1999.

Neirynck, Frans. *Duality in Mark: Contributions to the Study of the Markan Redaction*. Louvain: Louvain University Press, 1972.

Neusner, Jacob. Preface to *Memory and Manuscript: Oral Tradition and Written Transmission in Rabbinic Judaism and Early Christianity; with Tradition and Transmission in Early Christianity*, by Birger Gerhardsson. Grand Rapids: Eerdmans, 1998.

Neusner, Jacob. *The Mishnah: A New Translation*. New Haven: Yale University Press, 1991.

Neusner, Jacob. *The Oral Torah*. San Francisco: Harper & Row, 1986.

Neville, David. *Arguments From Order in Synoptic Source Criticism: A History and Critique*. New Gospel Studies 7. Leuven: Peeters, 1994.

Neville, David. *Mark's Gospel — Prior or Posterior?: A Reappraisal of the Phenomenon of Order*. JSNTSup 222. Sheffield: Sheffield Academic Press, 2002.

Niditch, Susan. *Oral World and Written Word: Ancient Israelite Literature*. Library of Ancient Israel. Louisville: Westminister John Knox Press, 1996.

Niederwimmer, Kurt. *Die Didache*. Kommentar zu den Apostolischen Vätern 1. Göttingen: Vandenhoeck & Ruprecht, 1989.

Notopoulos, James A. "Parataxis in Homer: A New Approach to Homeric Literary Criticism." *Transactions of the American Philological Association* 80 (1949): 1–23.

O'Rourke, John. "Some Observations on the Synoptic Problem and the Use of Statistical Procedures." *Novum Testamentum* 16 (1974): 272–277.

Okpewho, Isidore. *African Oral Literature*. Indianapolis: Indiana University Press, 1992.

Okpewho, Isidore. *The Epic in Africa: Toward a Poetics of the Oral Performance*. New York: Columbia University Press, 1979.

Olrik, Axel. "Epic Laws of Folk Narrative." Pages 129–141 in *The Study of Folklore*. Edited by Alan Dundes. Englewood Cliffs: Prentice-Hall, 1965.

Ong, Walter J. *Orality and Literacy: The Technologizing of the Word*. New York: Methuen, 1982.

Orchard, Bernard. "Are All Gospel Synopses Biassed?" *TZ* 34 (1978): 149–162.

Overbeck, Franz. "Über die Anfänge der patristischen Literatur" 48 (1882): 417–472.

Parker, David C. *The Living Text of the Gospels*. Cambridge: Cambridge University Press, 1997.

Parry, Milman. "Whole Formulaic Verses in Greek and Southslavic Heroic Song." *Transactions of the American Philological Association* 64 (1933): 179–197.

Person, Raymond F. "A Rolling Corpus and Oral Tradition: a Not-so-literate Solution to a Highly Literate Problem." Pages 263–271 in *Troubling Jeremiah*. Edited by A. R.

Pete Diamond, Kathleen M. O'Connor, and Louis Stulman. JSOTSup 260. Sheffield: Sheffield Academic Press, 1999.

Philo: Complete Works. Translated by F. H. Colson and G. H. Whittaker. 10 vols. Loeb Classical Library. Cambridge: Harvard University Press, 1929–1935.

Popper, Karl. *The Logic of Scientific Discovery*. London: Hutchinson, 1959.

Propp, Vladimir. *Morphology of the Folktale*. Austin: University of Texas Press, 1968.

Rahlfs, A., ed. *Septuaginta: Id est Vetus Testamentum graece iuxta LXX interpretes*. 2 vols. Stuttgart: Deutsche Bibelgesellschaft, 1935.

Raglan, Lord. *The Hero*. London: Methuen, 1936.

Raglan, Lord. "The Hero of Tradition." *Folk-Lore* 45 (1934): 212-231.

Rank, Otto. *The Myth of the Birth of the Hero*. Translated by F. Robbins and Smith Ely Jelliffe. Nervous and Mental Disease Monograph Series 18. New York: Journal of Nervous and Mental Disease Publishing, 1909.

Reicke, Bo. *The Roots of the Synoptic Gospels*. Philadelphia: Fortress Press, 1986.

Rhoads, David M., Joanna Dewey, and Donald Michie. *Mark as Story: An Interpretation to the Narrative of a Gospel*. Minneapolis: Fortress Press, 1999.

Ricoeur, Paul. *Interpretation Theory: Discourse and the Surplus of Meaning*. Fort Worth: Texas Christian University Press, 1976.

Riesenfeld, Harald. *The Gospel Tradition*. Philadelphia: Fortress Press, 1970.

Riesner, Rainer. "Jesus as Teacher and Preacher." Pages 185–210 in *Jesus and the Oral Gospel Tradition*. JSNTSup 64. Sheffield: Sheffield Academic Press, 1991.

Riesner, Rainer. *Jesus als Lehrer: eine Untersuchung zum Ursprung der Evangelien-Uberlieferung*. WUNT II 7. Tübingen: Mohr Siebeck, 1984.

Rist, John M. *On the Independence of Matthew and Mark*. SNTSMS 32. Cambridge: Cambridge University Press, 1978.

Robinson, James M., Paul Hoffmann, and John S. Kloppenborg. *The Critical Edition of Q*. Hermeneia. Philadelphia: Fortress Press, 2000.

Rordorf, Willy. "Does the Didache Contain Jesus Tradition Independently of the Synoptic Gospels?" Pages 394–423 in *Jesus and the Oral Gospel Tradition*. Edited by Henry Wansbrough. JSNTSup 64. Sheffield: JSOT Press, 1991.

Rosché, Theodore. "The Words of Jesus and the Future of the 'Q' Hypothesis." *JBL* 79 (1960): 210–220.

Sanday, W. "A Plea for the Logia." *ExpT* 11 (1899): 471–473.

Sanders, E. P. "The Overlaps of Mark and Q and the Synoptic Problem." *New Testament Studies* 19 (1973): 453–465.

Sanders, E. P. and Margaret Davies. *Studying the Synoptic Gospels*. Philadelphia: Trinity University Press, 1989.

Sanders, E. P. *Jesus and Judaism*. Philadelphia: Fortress Press, 1985.

Sanders, E. P. *Paul and Palestinian Judaism*. Philadelphia: Fortress Press, 1977.

Sanders, E. P. *The Historical Figure of Jesus*. London: Penguin Books, 1993.

Sanders, E. P. *The Tendencies of the Synoptic Tradition*. SNTSMS 9. Cambridge: Cambridge University Press, 1969.

Sandt, Huub van de and David Flusser. *The Didache: Its Jewish Sources and its Place in Early Judaism and Christianity*. CRINT 5. Assen: Royal Van Gorcum, 2002.

Scheub, Harold. *African Oral Narratives, Proverbs, Riddles, Poetry and Song*. Boston: G. K. Hall, 1977.

Scheub, Harold. *The Tongue is Fire*. Madison: University of Wisconsin Press, 1996.

Scheub, Harold. *The World and the Word : Tales and Observations From the Xhosa Oral Tradition*. Madison: University of Wisconsin Press, 1992.

Schmithals, W. "Vom Ursprung der synoptischen Tradition." *ZTK* 94 (1997): 288–216.

Schmithals, Walter. *Einleitung in die synoptischen Evangelien.* Berlin: de Gruyter, 1985.

Schnelle, Udo. *Einleitung in das Neue Testament.* UTB für Wissenschaft. Göttingen: Vandenhoeck & Ruprecht, 1994.

Schröter, Jens. "The Historical Jesus and the Sayings Tradition: Comments on Current Research." *Neotestamentica* 30 (1996): 151–168.

Schröter, Jens. *Erinnerung an Jesu Worte. Studien zur Rezeption der Logienüberlieferung in Markus Q und Thomas.* WMANT 76. Neukirchen-Vluyn: Neukirchener Verlag, 1997.

Scott, James C. *Domination and the Arts of Resistance: Hidden Transcripts.* New Haven: Yale University Press, 1990.

Scott, James C. *Moral Economy of the Peasant.* New Haven: Yale University Press, 1977.

Sherzer, Joel. "The Interplay of Structure and Function in Kuna Narrative, or, How to Grab a Snake in the Darien." Pages 306–322 in *Georgetown University Round Table on Languages and Linguists.* Edited by Deborah Tannen. Washington: Georgetown University Press, 1981.

Slusser, Michael. "Reading Silently in Antiquity." *JBL* 111 (1992): 499.

Smith, D. Moody. "The Pauline Literature." Pages 245–264 in *It is Written: Scripture Citing Scripture.* Edited by D. A. Carson and H. G. M. Williamson. Cambridge: Cambridge University Press, 1988.

Smith, Morton. Review of Birger Gerhardsson, *Memory and Manuscript. JBL* 82 (1963): 169–176.

Sparks, H. F. D. *The Formation of the New Testament.* London: SCM Press, 1952.

Stager, L. E. "The Archaeology of the Family in Ancient Israel." *BASOR* 260 (1985): 1-35.

Stein, Robert H. *Gospels and Tradition: Studies on Redaction Criticism of the Synoptic Gospels.* Grand Rapids: Baker Book House, 1991.

Stein, Robert H. *The Synoptic Problem: an Introduction.* Grand Rapids: Baker Book House, 1987.

Steiner, George. *Language and Silence: Essays on Language, Literature, and the Inhuman.* New York: Athenaeum, 1967.

Stemberger, Günter. *Introduction to the Talmud and Midrash.* Translated by Markus Bockmuehl. Edinburgh: T&T Clark, 1996.

Streeter, B. H. "On the Original Order of Q." Pages 141–164 in *Oxford Studies in the Synoptic Problem.* Edited by W. Sanday. Oxford: Clarendon Press, 1911.

Streeter, B. H. "The Literary Evolution of the Gospels." Pages 209–228 in *Studies in the Synoptic Problem.* Edited by W. Sanday. Oxford: Clarendon Press, 1911.

Streeter, B. H. *The Four Gospels: A Study of Origins.* London: Macmillan, 1924.

Talbert, Charles H. "Oral and Independent or Literary and Interdependent? A Response to Albert B. Lord." Pages 93–102 in *The Relationships Among the Gospels: An Interdisciplinary Dialogue.* Edited by William O. Walker Jr. San Antonio: Trinity University Press, 1978.

Talmon, Shemaryahu. "Oral Tradition and Written Transmission, or the Heard and the Seen Word in Judaism of the Second Temple Period." Pages 121–158 in *Jesus and the Oral Gospel Tradition.* Edited by Henry Wansbrough. JSNTSup 64. Sheffield: JSOT Press, 1991.

Taylor, Vincent. "The Original Order of Q." Pages 295–317 in *The Two-Source Hypothesis: A Critical Appraisal.* Edited by Arthur J. Bellinzoni. Macon: Mercer University Press, 1985. Repr. from *New Testament Essays: Studies in Memory of T. W. Manson, 1893–1958.* Edited by A. J. B. Higgins. Manchester: Manchester University Press, 1959.

Taylor, Vincent. *The Formation of the Gospel Tradition*. London: Macmillan & Co., 1933.
Taylor, Vincent. *The Gospel According to St. Mark*. London: Macmillan & Co., 1966.
Theissen, Gerd. *Sociology of Early Palestinian Christianity*. Translated by John Bowden. Philadelphia: Fortress Press, 1978.
Thomas, Rosalind. *Literacy and Orality in Ancient Greece*. Cambridge: Cambridge University Press, 1992.
Thoms, William J. "Folklore." Pages 4–6 in *The Study of Folklore*. Edited by Alan Dundes. Englewood Cliffs: Prentice-Hall, 1965. Repr. from *The Athenaeum* 982: 862–63.
Trocmé, E. *The Formation of the Gospel According to Mark*. Philadelphia: Westminster Press, 1975.
Tuckett, Christopher M. "Response to the Two Gospel Hypothesis." Pages 47–62 Edited by David L. Dungan. BETL 95. Leuven: Leuven University Press, 1990.
Tuckett, Christopher M. "The Existence of Q." in *The Gospel Behind the Gospels: Current Studies on Q*. Edited by Ronald A. Piper. SNTSSup 75. Leiden: Brill, 1995.
Tuckett, Christopher M. *Q and the History of Early Christianity: Studies on Q*. Edinburgh: T&T Clark, 1996.
Tuckett, Christopher M. *The Revival of the Griesbach Hypothesis: An Analysis and Appraisal*. Cambridge: Cambridge University Press, 1993.

Unaipon, David. *Legendary Tales of the Australian Aborigines*. Carlton: Melbourne University Press, 2001.

Vansina, Jan. *Oral Tradition as History*. Madison: University of Wisconsin Press, 1985.
Vansina, Jan. *Oral Tradition: A Study in Historical Methodology*. Chicago: Aldine Publishing Company, 1965.

Walls, Andrew F. "Papias and Oral Tradition." *Vigiliae Christianae* 21 (1967): 137–140.
Wansbrough, Henry. Introduction to *Jesus and the Oral Gospel Tradition*, edited by Henry Wansbrough. Sheffield: JSOT Press, 1991.
Wellhausen, Julius. *Prolegomena to the History of Israel*. Translated by J. S. Black and A. Menzies. 2 vols. Gloucester, 1973.
Witherington III, Ben. *The Acts of the Apostles: A Socio-Rhetorical Commentary*. Grand Rapids, Mich.: Eerdmans, 1998.
Woolf, Greg. "Monumental Writing and the Expansion of Roman Society in the Early Empire." *Journal of Roman Studies* 86 (1996): 22–39.

Index of Sources

Hebrew Bible

New Testament

6:7–15	98, 205	22:16	176
6:9–13	126	22:31	140
6:10b	226	23	261
7:3–5	206	23:16	176
7:7–11	206	23:24	176
7:13–14	205	23:27–38	206
7:28	76	23:33	176
8	226, 245	23:37–39	206
8:2–4	21	23–25	148
8:5	232	24	24, 263
8:5–13	205	24:32–36	206
8:7–10	21	24:45–51	206
8:8	232	24:51b	267
8:10	232	26:1	76
8:12	176	26:26–29	187
8:13	199	26:34	172
8:18	249	26:73–75	172
8:19b-22	206	27	267, 286
10	232	27:46	272
10:2–4	172	27:46–48	272
10:34	235	27:50	272
10:34–36	205, 236	27:51	209, 271
10:35	236	28:1	172
11	249, 254		
11:1	76	*Mark*	
11:4–11	206		
11:7–19	206	1–2	87
11:13	175	1:1	87
11:16	254	1:7–8	155
11:21–23	206	1:14	87
11:25–27	206	1:21–22	176
12	257	1:21–28	21
12:5	140	1:40–45	21
12:43–45	206	2:1–12	57
13:13–16	142	2:15–17	57
13:53	76	2:18	176
13–22	148	2:25	140
14:15–22	172	3:1–5	57
15:14	176	3:14	172
15:32–39	20, 172	3:16–19	172
16:24–28	206	4	6, 158
19:1	76	4:1–2	176
19:4	140	4:33–34	94
20:29–34	172	6:35–45	172
21	274	7:1–23	57
21:16	140	7:20–23	61
21:33–46	207	8:1–10	21, 172
21:42	140	8:18	142
22	238	8:34–9:1	206
22:1–14	205	10:2–12	57
22:4	244	10:17–30	57
22:7	244	12:1–12	207

7:1	282	12:42–46	282
7:3	282	12:49	282
7:6b-9	282	12:49–59	97
7:10	282	12:51	282
7:24–28	282	12:53	282
7:29–30	282	12:58–59	282
7:31–35	282	13:34–35	282
9:57–60	282	14:16–18	245, 282
10:21	282	14:19–20	245
10:22	282	14:19–23	282
11:2b-4	281	14:21	245
11:24–26	282	14:23	245

Apostolic and Patristic Fathers

1 Clement

2:8	121
13:1	119

Andrew of Caesarea

On the Apocalypse

12:7–9	117
34:12	117

Augustine

Confessions

4:15:28	143
6:3:3	135, 143

Basilius Caesariensis Theo

Enarratio in prophetam Isaiam

8:212	120

Clement of Alexandria

Stromata

2:6:25	142
2:6:26	142

Epiphanius

Adversus haereses

1:198:13	120

Eusebius

Historia ecclesiastica

3:39	117
3:39:1	117
3:39:15	118, 119
3:39:16	120
3:39:4	119, 144
5:20:7	121
5:8:2–4	121
6:14	144
6:14:5	120
6:14:6	121

Irenaeus

Adversus haereses

5:33:3–4	117

Pliny

Epistulae

2:3	143

Old Testament Pseudepigrapha

4:32	146, 147
5:13	146, 147
6:17	146, 147
6:30–31	147
6:31	146
6:35	147
16:3	147
16:29	147
18:19	147
28:6	147
30:9	147
30:22	147
31:32	147
32:10	147
32:16	147
33:10	147
49:8	147

Letter of Aristeas

| 1 | 124 |
| 1:1 | 124 |

Testament of Dan

| 1:1 | 131 |
| 1:2 | 131 |

Testament of Issac

| 1:4 | 131 |

Testament of Issachar

| 1:1 | 131 |

Testament of Job

| 1:4 | 131 |
| 51:1–4 | 131, 132 |

Testament of Judah

| 1:1 | 131 |
| 1:2 | 131 |

Testament of Levi

| 1:1 | 131 |
| 1:2 | 131 |

Testament of Moses

| 1:17 | 147 |

Testament of Naphtali

1:1	131
1:2	131
1:5	131, 132

Testament of Reuben

1:1	131
2:5	142
2:6	142
2:8–9	142

Testament of Simeon

| 1:1 | 131 |

Testament of Zebulun

| 1:1 | 131 |

Rabbinic Sources

b. Eruvin

| 54b | 123 |

m. Avot

| 1:1 | 123 |

m. Eduyyot

| 8:7 | 123 |

Index of Modern Authors

Index of Subjects and Key Terms

- orally performed 135
- read aloud 135
Homeric poetry 68
- hexameter 135

inclusio 153
International Q Project 9, 44, 45, 243,
    244
Critical Edition of Q, the 43, 45, 243
inversion 177
ipsissima verba 64, 70, 80, 180, 184
Irenaeus 121
Isaiah 147, 195
Isocrates 136

James 119
Jeremiah 132, 133, 137
Jerusalem 38, 64
Jesus communities 40, 162
Jesus tradition 11, 26, 77
- access to 44
- approach to 13
- authenticity 80
- circulation within communities 34,
    52, 65, 72, 85, 91, 94, 98, 101, 122,
    204, 221, 237, 245
- community controls 91, 95, 98, 186,
    188, 189, 190, 291
- cultural setting 30, 95, 160, 181, 191,
    244
- development of 52, 57
- earliest stages of 6, 36, 57, 86, 100,
    159, 164, 191, 285
- fixity and flexibility 98, 192
- historical setting of 12
- inscribed form 13, 94, 100, 292
- oral 3, 44, 52, 98
- origin of 56, 173
- performance of 12, 292
- preservation of 91
- pre-textual 13, 46, 56, 72, 82, 151,
    159, 173
- shaped prior to inscription 95
- transmission of 12, 52, 57, 63, 64, 90,
    91, 99, 158, 159, 164, 188, 291, 293
John 119
Jubilees 110, 146
Judea 113

Kleinliteratur 166

La Chanson de Roland 68

Laodicea 140
Latin 103
laws
- inscription 145
- oral 106
- unwritten 107
- written 106, 107
Laws of Eshunna 105, 129
Letter of Aristeas 124
letters
- Akkadian 130
- ancient 138
- as transcription of oral performance
    130
- dictation 138, 290
- read aloud 138, 153
- relationship to oral performance 130
- Sumerian 130
Levi 131
Linear-B 103
literacy 2, 15, 74, 80
- allows visual organization 76, 152,
    181
- ancient rates of 113, 145, 147, 160
- early Christian 137
- enables chronological framework 87
- human intelligence 103
- in antiquity 113, 144
- Israel, ancient 9
- psychology of 73, 83, 165
- relationship to orality 11, 87, 169
- Roman Palestine 114
literary dependency 3, 8, 11, 31, 33, 92,
    173, 183, 192, 206, 208
literary hypothesis 26
- exclusive dependence upon 26, 93
literary independence 91
literary paradigm 11, 18, 19, 37, 45, 52,
    62, 86, 95, 149, 192, 193, 260, 288,
    289
literary tradition 6
literate culture 112
logia collections 24
Lukan priority 35
Luke, author 124
Luke, Gospel of
- sources behind 24
Lycurgus 136
Lysias 107

manuscript tradition 113
Mari letters 130

Wissenschaftliche Untersuchungen zum Neuen Testament

Alphabetical Index of the First and Second Series

Bolyki, János: Jesu Tischgemeinschaften. 1997. *Volume II/96.*

Bosman, Philip: Conscience in Philo and Paul. 2003. *Volume II/166.*

Bovon, François: Studies in Early Christianity. 2003. *Volume 161.*

Brocke, Christoph vom: Thessaloniki – Stadt des Kassander und Gemeinde des Paulus. 2001. *Volume II/125.*

Brunson, Andrew: Psalm 118 in the Gospel of John. 2003. *Volume II/158.*

Büchli, Jörg: Der Poimandres – ein paganisiertes Evangelium. 1987. *Volume II/27.*

Bühner, Jan A.: Der Gesandte und sein Weg im 4. Evangelium. 1977. *Volume II/2.*

Burchard, Christoph: Untersuchungen zu Joseph und Aseneth. 1965. *Volume 8.*

– Studien zur Theologie, Sprache und Umwelt des Neuen Testaments. Ed. von D. Sänger. 1998. *Volume 107.*

Burnett, Richard: Karl Barth's Theological Exegesis. 2001. *Volume II/145.*

Byron, John: Slavery Metaphors in Early Judaism and Pauline Christianity. 2003. *Volume II/162.*

Byrskog, Samuel: Story as History – History as Story. 2000. *Volume 123.*

Cancik, Hubert (Ed.): Markus-Philologie. 1984. *Volume 33.*

Capes, David B.: Old Testament Yaweh Texts in Paul's Christology. 1992. *Volume II/47.*

Caragounis, Chrys C.: The Development of Greek and the New Testament. 2004. *Volume 167.*

– The Son of Man. 1986. *Volume 38.*

– see *Fridrichsen, Anton.*

Carleton Paget, James: The Epistle of Barnabas. 1994. *Volume II/64.*

Carson, D.A., O'Brien, Peter T. and *Mark Seifrid* (Ed.): Justification and Variegated Nomism. Volume 1: The Complexities of Second Temple Judaism. 2001. *Volume II/140.* Volume 2: The Paradoxes of Paul. 2004. *Volume II/181.*

Ciampa, Roy E.: The Presence and Function of Scripture in Galatians 1 and 2. 1998. *Volume II/102.*

Classen, Carl Joachim: Rhetorical Criticsm of the New Testament. 2000. *Volume 128.*

Colpe, Carsten: Iranier – Aramäer – Hebräer – Hellenen. 2003. *Volume 154.*

Crump, David: Jesus the Intercessor. 1992. *Volume II/49.*

Dahl, Nils Alstrup: Studies in Ephesians. 2000. *Volume 131.*

Deines, Roland: Die Gerechtigkeit der Tora im Reich des Messias. 2004. *Volume 177.*

– Jüdische Steingefäße und pharisäische Frömmigkeit. 1993. *Volume II/52.*

– Die Pharisäer. 1997. *Volume 101.*

– and *Karl-Wilhelm Niebuhr (Ed.):* Philo und das Neue Testament. 2004. *Volume 172.*

Dettwiler, Andreas and *Jean Zumstein (Ed.):* Kreuzestheologie im Neuen Testament. 2002. *Volume 151.*

Dickson, John P.: Mission-Commitment in Ancient Judaism and in the Pauline Communities. 2003. *Volume II/159.*

Dietzfelbinger, Christian: Der Abschied des Kommenden. 1997. *Volume 95.*

Dimitrov, Ivan Z., James D.G. Dunn, Ulrich Luz and *Karl-Wilhelm Niebuhr* (Ed.): Das Alte Testament als christliche Bibel in orthodoxer und westlicher Sicht. 2004. *Volume 174.*

Dobbeler, Axel von: Glaube als Teilhabe. 1987. *Volume II/22.*

Du Toit, David S.: Theios Anthropos. 1997. *Volume II/91.*

Dübbers, Michael: Christologie und Existenz im Kolosserbrief. 2005. *Volume II/191.*

Dunn, James D.G. (Ed.): Jews and Christians. 1992. *Volume 66.*

– Paul and the Mosaic Law. 1996. *Volume 89.*

– see *Dimitrov, Ivan Z.*

Dunn, James D.G., Hans Klein, Ulrich Luz and *Vasile Mihoc* (Ed.): Auslegung der Bibel in orthodoxer und westlicher Perspektive. 2000. *Volume 130.*

Ebel, Eva: Die Attraktivität früher christlicher Gemeinden. 2004. *Volume II/178.*

Ebertz, Michael N.: Das Charisma des Gekreuzigten. 1987. *Volume 45.*

Eckstein, Hans-Joachim: Der Begriff Syneidesis bei Paulus. 1983. *Volume II/10.*

– Verheißung und Gesetz. 1996. *Volume 86.*

Ego, Beate: Im Himmel wie auf Erden. 1989. *Volume II/34.*

Ego, Beate, Armin Lange and *Peter Pilhofer (Ed.):* Gemeinde ohne Tempel – Community without Temple. 1999. *Volume 118.*

Eisen, Ute E.: see *Paulsen, Henning.*

Ellis, E. Earle: Prophecy and Hermeneutic in Early Christianity. 1978. *Volume 18.*

– The Old Testament in Early Christianity. 1991. *Volume 54.*

Endo, Masanobu: Creation and Christology. 2002. *Volume 149.*

Ennulat, Andreas: Die 'Minor Agreements'. 1994. *Volume II/62.*

Ensor, Peter W.: Jesus and His 'Works'. 1996. *Volume II/85.*

Eskola, Timo: Messiah and the Throne. 2001. *Volume II/142.*
- Theodicy and Predestination in Pauline Soteriology. 1998. *Volume II/100.*
Fatehi, Mehrdad: The Spirit's Relation to the Risen Lord in Paul. 2000. *Volume II/128.*
Feldmeier, Reinhard: Die Krisis des Gottessohnes. 1987. *Volume II/21.*
- Die Christen als Fremde. 1992. *Volume 64.*
Feldmeier, Reinhard and *Ulrich Heckel* (Ed.): Die Heiden. 1994. *Volume 70.*
Fletcher-Louis, Crispin H.T.: Luke-Acts: Angels, Christology and Soteriology. 1997. *Volume II/94.*
Förster, Niclas: Marcus Magus. 1999. *Volume 114.*
Forbes, Christopher Brian: Prophecy and Inspired Speech in Early Christianity and its Hellenistic Environment. 1995. *Volume II/75.*
Fornberg, Tord: see *Fridrichsen, Anton.*
Fossum, Jarl E.: The Name of God and the Angel of the Lord. 1985. *Volume 36.*
Foster, Paul: Community, Law and Mission in Matthew's Gospel. *Volume II/177.*
Fotopoulos, John: Food Offered to Idols in Roman Corinth. 2003. *Volume II/151.*
Frenschkowski, Marco: Offenbarung und Epiphanie. Volume 1 1995. *Volume II/79* – Volume 2 1997. *Volume II/80.*
Frey, Jörg: Eugen Drewermann und die biblische Exegese. 1995. *Volume II/71.*
- Die johanneische Eschatologie. Volume I. 1997. *Volume 96.* – Volume II. 1998. *Volume 110.*
- Volume III. 2000. *Volume 117.*
Frey, Jörg and *Udo Schnelle (Ed.):* Kontexte des Johannesevangeliums. 2004. *Volume 175.*
Freyne, Sean: Galilee and Gospel. 2000. *Volume 125.*
Fridrichsen, Anton: Exegetical Writings. Edited by C.C. Caragounis and T. Fornberg. 1994. *Volume 76.*
Garlington, Don B.: 'The Obedience of Faith'. 1991. *Volume II/38.*
- Faith, Obedience, and Perseverance. 1994. *Volume 79.*
Garnet, Paul: Salvation and Atonement in the Qumran Scrolls. 1977. *Volume II/3.*
Gemünden, Petra von (Ed.): see *Weissenrieder, Annette.*
Gese, Michael: Das Vermächtnis des Apostels. 1997. *Volume II/99.*
Gheorghita, Radu: The Role of the Septuagint in Hebrews. 2003. *Volume II/160.*

Gräbe, Petrus J.: The Power of God in Paul's Letters. 2000. *Volume II/123.*
Gräßer, Erich: Der Alte Bund im Neuen. 1985. *Volume 35.*
- Forschungen zur Apostelgeschichte. 2001. *Volume 137.*
Green, Joel B.: The Death of Jesus. 1988. *Volume II/33.*
Gregory, Andrew: The Reception of Luke and Acts in the Period before Irenaeus. 2003. *Volume II/169.*
Gundry, Robert H.: The Old is Better. 2005. *Volume 178.*
Gundry Volf, Judith M.: Paul and Perseverance. 1990. *Volume II/37.*
Hafemann, Scott J.: Suffering and the Spirit. 1986. *Volume II/19.*
- Paul, Moses, and the History of Israel. 1995. *Volume 81.*
Hahn, Johannes (Ed.): Zerstörungen des Jerusalemer Tempels. 2002. *Volume 147.*
Hannah, Darrel D.: Michael and Christ. 1999. *Volume II/109.*
Hamid-Khani, Saeed: Relevation and Concealment of Christ. 2000. *Volume II/120.*
Harrison, James R.: Paul's Language of Grace in Its Graeco-Roman Context. 2003. *Volume II/172.*
Hartman, Lars: Text-Centered New Testament Studies. Ed. von D. Hellholm. 1997. *Volume 102.*
Hartog, Paul: Polycarp and the New Testament. 2001. *Volume II/134.*
Heckel, Theo K.: Der Innere Mensch. 1993. *Volume II/53.*
- Vom Evangelium des Markus zum viergestaltigen Evangelium. 1999. *Volume 120.*
Heckel, Ulrich: Kraft in Schwachheit. 1993. *Volume II/56.*
- Der Segen im Neuen Testament. 2002. *Volume 150.*
- see *Feldmeier, Reinhard.*
- see *Hengel, Martin.*
Heiligenthal, Roman: Werke als Zeichen. 1983. *Volume II/9.*
Hellholm, D.: see *Hartman, Lars.*
Hemer, Colin J.: The Book of Acts in the Setting of Hellenistic History. 1989. *Volume 49.*
Hengel, Martin: Judentum und Hellenismus. 1969, [3]1988. *Volume 10.*
- Die johanneische Frage. 1993. *Volume 67.*
- Judaica et Hellenistica. Kleine Schriften I. 1996. *Volume 90.*
- Judaica, Hellenistica et Christiana. Kleine Schriften II. 1999. *Volume 109.*

– Paulus und Jakobus.
  Kleine Schriften III. 2002. *Volume 141.*
Hengel, Martin and *Ulrich Heckel* (Ed.): Paulus
  und das antike Judentum. 1991. *Volume 58.*
Hengel, Martin and *Hermut Löhr* (Ed.):
  Schriftauslegung im antiken Judentum und
  im Urchristentum. 1994. *Volume 73.*
Hengel, Martin and *Anna Maria Schwemer:*
  Paulus zwischen Damaskus und Antiochien.
  1998. *Volume 108.*
– Der messianische Anspruch Jesu und die
  Anfänge der Christologie. 2001. *Volume 138.*
Hengel, Martin and *Anna Maria Schwemer*
  (Ed.): Königsherrschaft Gottes und himm-
  lischer Kult. 1991. *Volume 55.*
– Die Septuaginta. 1994. *Volume 72.*
Hengel, Martin; *Siegfried Mittmann* and *Anna
  Maria Schwemer* (Ed.): La Cité de Dieu /
  Die Stadt Gottes. 2000. *Volume 129.*
Herrenbrück, Fritz: Jesus und die Zöllner. 1990.
  Volume II/41.
Herzer, Jens: Paulus oder Petrus? 1998.
  Volume 103.
Hoegen-Rohls, Christina: Der nachösterliche
  Johannes. 1996. *Volume II/84.*
Hofius, Otfried: Katapausis. 1970. *Volume 11.*
– Der Vorhang vor dem Thron Gottes. 1972.
  Volume 14.
– Der Christushymnus Philipper 2,6-11. 1976,
  ²1991. *Volume 17.*
– Paulusstudien. 1989, ²1994. *Volume 51.*
– Neutestamentliche Studien. 2000. *Volume 132.*
– Paulusstudien II. 2002. *Volume 143.*
Hofius, Otfried and *Hans-Christian Kammler:*
  Johannesstudien. 1996. *Volume 88.*
Holtz, Traugott: Geschichte und Theologie des
  Urchristentums. 1991. *Volume 57.*
Hommel, Hildebrecht: Sebasmata. Volume 1 1983.
  Volume 31 – Volume 2 1984. *Volume 32.*
Hvalvik, Reidar: The Struggle for Scripture and
  Covenant. 1996. *Volume II/82.*
Johns, Loren L.: The Lamb Christology of the
  Apocalypse of John. 2003. *Volume II/167.*
Joubert, Stephan: Paul as Benefactor. 2000.
  Volume II/124.
Jungbauer, Harry: „Ehre Vater und Mutter".
  2002. *Volume II/146.*
Kähler, Christoph: Jesu Gleichnisse als Poesie
  und Therapie. 1995. *Volume 78.*
Kamlah, Ehrhard: Die Form der katalogischen
  Paränese im Neuen Testament. 1964. *Volume 7.*
Kammler, Hans-Christian: Christologie und
  Eschatologie. 2000. *Volume 126.*
– Kreuz und Weisheit. 2003. *Volume 159.*
– see *Hofius, Otfried.*

Kelhoffer, James A.: The Diet of John the
  Baptist. 2005. *Volume 176.*
– Miracle and Mission. 1999. *Volume II/112.*
Kieffer, René and *Jan Bergman (Ed.):* La Main de
  Dieu / Die Hand Gottes. 1997. *Volume 94.*
Kim, Seyoon: The Origin of Paul's Gospel.
  1981, ²1984. *Volume II/4.*
– Paul and the New Perspective. 2002.
  Volume 140.
– "The 'Son of Man'" as the Son of God.
  1983. *Volume 30.*
Klauck, Hans-Josef: Religion und Gesellschaft
  im frühen Christentum. 2003. *Volume 152.*
Klein, Hans: see *Dunn, James D.G.*.
Kleinknecht, Karl Th.: Der leidende Gerechtfer-
  tigte. 1984, ²1988. *Volume II/13.*
Klinghardt, Matthias: Gesetz und Volk Gottes.
  1988. *Volume II/32.*
Koch, Michael: Drachenkampf und Sonnenfrau.
  2004. *Volume II/184.*
Koch, Stefan: Rechtliche Regelung von
  Konflikten im frühen Christentum. 2004.
  Volume II/174.
Köhler, Wolf-Dietrich: Rezeption des Matthäus-
  evangeliums in der Zeit vor Irenäus. 1987.
  Volume II/24.
Köhn, Andreas: Der Neutestamentler Ernst
  Lohmeyer. 2004. *Volume II/180.*
Kooten, George H. van: Cosmic Christology in
  Paul and the Pauline School. 2003.
  Volume II/171.
Korn, Manfred: Die Geschichte Jesu in
  veränderter Zeit. 1993. *Volume II/51.*
Koskenniemi, Erkki: Apollonios von Tyana in
  der neutestamentlichen Exegese. 1994.
  Volume II/61.
Kraus, Thomas J.: Sprache, Stil und historischer
  Ort des zweiten Petrusbriefes. 2001.
  Volume II/136.
Kraus, Wolfgang: Das Volk Gottes. 1996.
  Volume 85.
– and *Karl-Wilhelm Niebuhr* (Ed.): Früh-
  judentum und Neues Testament im Horizont
  Biblischer Theologie. 2003. *Volume 162.*
– see *Walter, Nikolaus.*
Kreplin, Matthias: Das Selbstverständnis Jesu.
  2001. *Volume II/141.*
Kuhn, Karl G.: Achtzehngebet und Vaterunser
  und der Reim. 1950. *Volume 1.*
Kvalbein, Hans: see *Ådna, Jostein.*
Kwon, Yon-Gyong: Eschatology in Galatians.
  2004. *Volume II/183.*
Laansma, Jon: I Will Give You Rest. 1997.
  Volume II/98.
Labahn, Michael: Offenbarung in Zeichen und
  Wort. 2000. *Volume II/117.*
Lambers-Petry, Doris: see *Tomson, Peter J.*

Lange, Armin: see *Ego, Beate.*

Lampe, Peter: Die stadtrömischen Christen in den ersten beiden Jahrhunderten. 1987, ²1989. *Volume II/18.*

Landmesser, Christof: Wahrheit als Grundbegriff neutestamentlicher Wissenschaft. 1999. *Volume 113.*

– Jüngerberufung und Zuwendung zu Gott. 2000. *Volume 133.*

Lau, Andrew: Manifest in Flesh. 1996. *Volume II/86.*

Lawrence, Louise: An Ethnography of the Gospel of Matthew. 2003. *Volume II/165.*

Lee, Aquila H.I.: From Messiah to Preexistent Son. 2005. *Volume II/192.*

Lee, Pilchan: The New Jerusalem in the Book of Relevation. 2000. *Volume II/129.*

Lichtenberger, Hermann: see *Avemarie, Friedrich.*

Lichtenberger, Hermann: Das Ich Adams und das Ich der Menschheit. 2004. *Volume 164.*

Lierman, John: The New Testament Moses. 2004. *Volume II/173.*

Lieu, Samuel N.C.: Manichaeism in the Later Roman Empire and Medieval China. ²1992. *Volume 63.*

Lindgård, Fredrik: Paul's Line of Thought in 2 Corinthians 4:16-5:10. 2004. *Volume II/189.*

Loader, William R.G.: Jesus' Attitude Towards the Law. 1997. *Volume II/97.*

Löhr, Gebhard: Verherrlichung Gottes durch Philosophie. 1997. *Volume 97.*

Löhr, Hermut: Studien zum frühchristlichen und frühjüdischen Gebet. 2003. *Volume160.*

– *:* see *Hengel, Martin.*

Löhr, Winrich Alfried: Basilides und seine Schule. 1995. *Volume 83.*

Luomanen, Petri: Entering the Kingdom of Heaven. 1998. *Volume II/101.*

Luz, Ulrich: see *Dunn, James D.G.*

Mackay, Ian D.: John's Raltionship with Mark. 2004. *Volume II/182.*

Maier, Gerhard: Mensch und freier Wille. 1971. *Volume 12.*

– Die Johannesoffenbarung und die Kirche. 1981. *Volume 25.*

Markschies, Christoph: Valentinus Gnosticus? 1992. *Volume 65.*

Marshall, Peter: Enmity in Corinth: Social Conventions in Paul's Relations with the Corinthians. 1987. *Volume II/23.*

Mayer, Annemarie: Sprache der Einheit im Epheserbrief und in der Ökumene. 2002. *Volume II/150.*

McDonough, Sean M.: YHWH at Patmos: Rev. 1:4 in its Hellenistic and Early Jewish Setting. 1999. *Volume II/107.*

McGlynn, Moyna: Divine Judgement and Divine Benevolence in the Book of Wisdom. 2001. *Volume II/139.*

Meade, David G.: Pseudonymity and Canon. 1986. *Volume 39.*

Meadors, Edward P.: Jesus the Messianic Herald of Salvation. 1995. *Volume II/72.*

Meißner, Stefan: Die Heimholung des Ketzers. 1996. *Volume II/87.*

Mell, Ulrich: Die „anderen" Winzer. 1994. *Volume 77.*

Mengel, Berthold: Studien zum Philipperbrief. 1982. *Volume II/8.*

Merkel, Helmut: Die Widersprüche zwischen den Evangelien. 1971. *Volume 13.*

Merklein, Helmut: Studien zu Jesus und Paulus. Volume 1 1987. *Volume 43.* – Volume 2 1998. *Volume 105.*

Metzdorf, Christina: Die Tempelaktion Jesu. 2003. *Volume II/168.*

Metzler, Karin: Der griechische Begriff des Verzeihens. 1991. *Volume II/44.*

Metzner, Rainer: Die Rezeption des Matthäusevangeliums im 1. Petrusbrief. 1995. *Volume II/74.*

– Das Verständnis der Sünde im Johannesevangelium. 2000. *Volume 122.*

Mihoc, Vasile: see *Dunn, James D.G..*

Mineshige, Kiyoshi: Besitzverzicht und Almosen bei Lukas. 2003. *Volume II/163.*

Mittmann, Siegfried: see *Hengel, Martin.*

Mittmann-Richert, Ulrike: Magnifikat und Benediktus. *1996. Volume II/90.*

Mournet, Terence C.: Oral Tradition and Literary Dependency. 2005. *Volume II/195.*

Mußner, Franz: Jesus von Nazareth im Umfeld Israels und der Urkirche. Ed. von M. Theobald. 1998. *Volume 111.*

Niebuhr, Karl-Wilhelm: Gesetz und Paränese. 1987. *Volume II/28.*

– Heidenapostel aus Israel. 1992. *Volume 62.*

– see *Deines, Roland*

– see *Dimitrov, Ivan Z.*

– see *Kraus, Wolfgang*

Nielsen, Anders E.: "Until it is Fullfilled". 2000. *Volume II/126.*

Nissen, Andreas: Gott und der Nächste im antiken Judentum. 1974. *Volume 15.*

Noack, Christian: Gottesbewußtsein. 2000. *Volume II/116.*

Noormann, Rolf: Irenäus als Paulusinterpret. 1994. *Volume II/66.*

Novakovic, Lidija: Messiah, the Healer of the Sick. 2003. *Volume II/170.*

Obermann, Andreas: Die christologische Erfüllung der Schrift im Johannesevangelium. 1996. *Volume II/83.*

Öhler, Markus: Barnabas. 2003. *Volume 156.*

Okure, Teresa: The Johannine Approach to Mission. 1988. *Volume II/31.*

Onuki, Takashi: Heil und Erlösung. 2004. *Volume 165.*

Oropeza, B. J.: Paul and Apostasy. 2000. *Volume II/115.*

Ostmeyer, Karl-Heinrich: Taufe und Typos. 2000. *Volume II/118.*

Paulsen, Henning: Studien zur Literatur und Geschichte des frühen Christentums. Ed. von Ute E. Eisen. 1997. *Volume 99.*

Pao, David W.: Acts and the Isaianic New Exodus. 2000. *Volume II/130.*

Park, Eung Chun: The Mission Discourse in Matthew's Interpretation. 1995. *Volume II/81.*

Park, Joseph S.: Conceptions of Afterlife in Jewish Insriptions. 2000. *Volume II/121.*

Pate, C. Marvin: The Reverse of the Curse. 2000. *Volume II/114.*

Peres, Imre: Griechische Grabinschriften und neutestamentliche Eschatologie. 2003. *Volume 157.*

Philonenko, Marc (Ed.): Le Trône de Dieu. 1993. *Volume 69.*

Pilhofer, Peter: Presbyteron Kreitton. 1990. *Volume II/39.*

– Philippi. Volume 1 1995. *Volume 87.* – Volume 2 2000. *Volume 119.*

– Die frühen Christen und ihre Welt. 2002. *Volume 145.*

– see *Ego, Beate.*

Plümacher, Eckhard: Geschichte und Geschichten. Aufsätze zur Apostelgeschichte und zu den Johannesakten. Herausgegeben von Jens Schröter und Ralph Brucker. 2004. *Volume 170.*

Pöhlmann, Wolfgang: Der Verlorene Sohn und das Haus. 1993. *Volume 68.*

Pokorný, Petr and *Josef B. Souček:* Bibelauslegung als Theologie. 1997. *Volume 100.*

Pokorný, Petr and *Jan Roskovec* (Ed.): Philosophical Hermeneutics and Biblical Exegesis. 2002. *Volume 153.*

Porter, Stanley E.: The Paul of Acts. 1999. *Volume 115.*

Prieur, Alexander: Die Verkündigung der Gottesherrschaft. 1996. *Volume II/89.*

Probst, Hermann: Paulus und der Brief. 1991. *Volume II/45.*

Räisänen, Heikki: Paul and the Law. 1983, ²1987. *Volume 29.*

Rehkopf, Friedrich: Die lukanische Sonderquelle. 1959. *Volume 5.*

Rein, Matthias: Die Heilung des Blindgeborenen (Joh 9). 1995. *Volume II/73.*

Reinmuth, Eckart: Pseudo-Philo und Lukas. 1994. *Volume 74.*

Reiser, Marius: Syntax und Stil des Markusevangeliums. 1984. *Volume II/11.*

Rhodes, James N.: The Epistle of Barnabas and the Deuteronomic Tradition. 2004. *Volume II/188.*

Richards, E. Randolph: The Secretary in the Letters of Paul. 1991. *Volume II/42.*

Riesner, Rainer: Jesus als Lehrer. 1981, ³1988. *Volume II/7.*

– Die Frühzeit des Apostels Paulus. 1994. *Volume 71.*

Rissi, Mathias: Die Theologie des Hebräerbriefs. 1987. *Volume 41.*

Roskovec, Jan: see *Pokorný, Petr.*

Röhser, Günter: Metaphorik und Personifikation der Sünde. 1987. *Volume II/25.*

Rose, Christian: Die Wolke der Zeugen. 1994. *Volume II/60.*

Rothschild, Clare K.: Luke Acts and the Rhetoric of History. 2004. *Volume II/175.*

Rüegger, Hans-Ulrich: Verstehen, was Markus erzählt. 2002. *Volume II/155.*

Rüger, Hans Peter: Die Weisheitsschrift aus der Kairoer Geniza. 1991. *Volume 53.*

Sänger, Dieter: Antikes Judentum und die Mysterien. 1980. *Volume II/5.*

– Die Verkündigung des Gekreuzigten und Israel. 1994. *Volume 75.*

– see *Burchard, Christoph*

Salier, Willis Hedley: The Rhetorical Impact of the Sēmeia in the Gospel of John. 2004. *Volume II/186.*

Salzmann, Jorg Christian: Lehren und Ermahnen. 1994. *Volume II/59.*

Sandnes, Karl Olav: Paul – One of the Prophets? 1991. *Volume II/43.*

Sato, Migaku: Q und Prophetie. 1988. *Volume II/29.*

Schäfer, Ruth: Paulus bis zum Apostelkonzil. 2004. *Volume II/179.*

Schaper, Joachim: Eschatology in the Greek Psalter. 1995. *Volume II/76.*

Schimanowski, Gottfried: Die himmlische Liturgie in der Apokalypse des Johannes. 2002. *Volume II/154.*

– Weisheit und Messias. 1985. *Volume II/17.*

Schlichting, Günter: Ein jüdisches Leben Jesu. 1982. *Volume 24.*

Schnabel, Eckhard J.: Law and Wisdom from Ben Sira to Paul. 1985. *Volume II/16.*

Schnelle, Udo: see *Frey, Jörg.*

Schutter, William L.: Hermeneutic and Composition in I Peter. 1989. *Volume II/30.*

Schwartz, Daniel R.: Studies in the Jewish Background of Christianity. 1992. *Volume 60.*

Schwemer, Anna Maria: see *Hengel, Martin*

Scott, James M.: Adoption as Sons of God. 1992. *Volume II/48.*

– Paul and the Nations. 1995. *Volume 84.*

Shum, Shiu-Lun: Paul's Use of Isaiah in Romans. 2002. *Volume II/156.*

Siegert, Folker: Drei hellenistisch-jüdische Predigten. Teil I 1980. *Volume 20* – Teil II 1992. *Volume 61.*

– Nag-Hammadi-Register. 1982. *Volume 26.*

– Argumentation bei Paulus. 1985. *Volume 34.*

– Philon von Alexandrien. 1988. *Volume 46.*

Simon, Marcel: Le christianisme antique et son contexte religieux I/II. 1981. *Volume 23.*

Snodgrass, Klyne: The Parable of the Wicked Tenants. 1983. *Volume 27.*

Söding, Thomas: Das Wort vom Kreuz. 1997. *Volume 93.*

– see *Thüsing, Wilhelm.*

Sommer, Urs: Die Passionsgeschichte des Markusevangeliums. 1993. *Volume II/58.*

Souček, Josef B.: see *Pokorný, Petr.*

Spangenberg, Volker: Herrlichkeit des Neuen Bundes. 1993. *Volume II/55.*

Spanje, T.E. van: Inconsistency in Paul? 1999. *Volume II/110.*

Speyer, Wolfgang: Frühes Christentum im antiken Strahlungsfeld. Volume I: 1989. *Volume 50.*

– Volume II: 1999. *Volume 116.*

Stadelmann, Helge: Ben Sira als Schriftgelehrter. 1980. *Volume II/6.*

Stenschke, Christoph W.: Luke's Portrait of Gentiles Prior to Their Coming to Faith. *Volume II/108.*

Sterck-Degueldre, Jean-Pierre: Eine Frau namens Lydia. 2004. *Volume II/176.*

Stettler, Christian: Der Kolosserhymnus. 2000. *Volume II/131.*

Stettler, Hanna: Die Christologie der Pastoralbriefe. 1998. *Volume II/105.*

Stökl Ben Ezra, Daniel: The Impact of Yom Kippur on Early Christianity. 2003. *Volume 163.*

Strobel, August: Die Stunde der Wahrheit. 1980. *Volume 21.*

Stroumsa, Guy G.: Barbarian Philosophy. 1999. *Volume 112.*

Stuckenbruck, Loren T.: Angel Veneration and Christology. 1995. *Volume II/70.*

Stuhlmacher, Peter (Ed.): Das Evangelium und die Evangelien. 1983. *Volume 28.*

– Biblische Theologie und Evangelium. 2002. *Volume 146.*

Sung, Chong-Hyon: Vergebung der Sünden. 1993. *Volume II/57.*

Tajra, Harry W.: The Trial of St. Paul. 1989. *Volume II/35.*

– The Martyrdom of St.Paul. 1994. *Volume II/67.*

Theißen, Gerd: Studien zur Soziologie des Urchristentums. 1979, ³1989. *Volume 19.*

Theobald, Michael: Studien zum Römerbrief. 2001. *Volume 136.*

Theobald, Michael: see *Mußner, Franz.*

Thornton, Claus-Jürgen: Der Zeuge des Zeugen. 1991. *Volume 56.*

Thüsing, Wilhelm: Studien zur neutestamentlichen Theologie. Ed. von Thomas Söding. 1995. *Volume 82.*

Thurén, Lauri: Derhethorizing Paul. 2000. *Volume 124.*

Tolmie, D. Francois: Persuading the Galatians. 2005. *Volume II/190.*

Tomson, Peter J. and *Doris Lambers-Petry* (Ed.): The Image of the Judaeo-Christians in Ancient Jewish and Christian Literature. 2003. *Volume 158.*

Trebilco, Paul: The Early Christians in Ephesus from Paul to Ignatius. 2004. *Volume 166.*

Treloar, Geoffrey R.: Lightfoot the Historian. 1998. *Volume II/103.*

Tsuji, Manabu: Glaube zwischen Vollkommenheit und Verweltlichung. 1997. *Volume II/93*

Twelftree, Graham H.: Jesus the Exorcist. 1993. *Volume II/54.*

Urban, Christina: Das Menschenbild nach dem Johannesevangelium. 2001. *Volume II/137.*

Visotzky, Burton L.: Fathers of the World. 1995. *Volume 80.*

Vollenweider, Samuel: Horizonte neutestamentlicher Christologie. 2002. *Volume 144.*

Vos, Johan S.: Die Kunst der Argumentation bei Paulus. 2002. *Volume 149.*

Wagener, Ulrike: Die Ordnung des „Hauses Gottes". 1994. *Volume II/65.*

Wahlen, Clinton: Jesus and the Impurity of Spirits in the Synoptic Gospels. 2004. *Volume II/185.*

Walker, Donald D.: Paul's Offer of Leniency (2 Cor 10:1). 2002. *Volume II/152.*

Walter, Nikolaus: Praeparatio Evangelica. Ed. von Wolfgang Kraus und Florian Wilk. 1997. *Volume 98.*

Wander, Bernd: Gottesfürchtige und Sympathi-
santen. 1998. *Volume 104.*
Watts, Rikki: Isaiah's New Exodus and Mark.
1997. *Volume II/88.*
Wedderburn, A.J.M.: Baptism and Resurrection.
1987. *Volume 44.*
Wegner, Uwe: Der Hauptmann von Kafarnaum.
1985. *Volume II/14.*
Weissenrieder, Annette: Images of Illness in the
Gospel of Luke. 2003. Volume II/164.
–, *Friederike Wendt* and *Petra von Gemünden*
(Ed.): Picturing the New Testament. 2005.
Volume II/193.
Welck, Christian: Erzählte ‚Zeichen'. 1994.
Volume II/69.
Wendt, Friederike (Ed.): see *Weissenrieder,
Annette.*
Wiarda, Timothy: Peter in the Gospels . 2000.
Volume II/127.
Wilk, Florian: see *Walter, Nikolaus.*
Williams, Catrin H.: I am He. 2000.
Volume II/113.

Wilson, Walter T.: Love without Pretense. 1991.
Volume II/46.
Wischmeyer, Oda: Von Ben Sira zu Paulus.
2004. *Volume 173.*
Wisdom, Jeffrey: Blessing for the Nations and
the Curse of the Law. 2001. *Volume II/133.*
Wucherpfennig, Ansgar: Heracleon Philologus.
2002. *Volume 142.*
Yeung, Maureen: Faith in Jesus and Paul. 2002.
Volume II/147.
Zimmermann, Alfred E.: Die urchristlichen
Lehrer. 1984, ²1988. *Volume II/12.*
Zimmermann, Johannes: Messianische Texte
aus Qumran. 1998. *Volume II/104.*
Zimmermann, Ruben: Christologie der Bilder
im Johannesevangelium. 2004. *Volume 171.*
– Geschlechtermetaphorik und Gottes-
verhältnis. 2001. *Volume II/122.*
Zumstein, Jean: see *Dettwiler, Andreas*
Zwiep, Arie W.: Judas and the Choice of
Matthias. 2004. *Volume II/187.*

For a complete catalogue please write to the publisher
Mohr Siebeck • P.O. Box 2030 • D–72010 Tübingen/Germany
Up-to-date information on the internet at www.mohr.de